The Marxism of Manuel Sacristán

Historical Materialism Book Series

VOLUME 76

The titles published in this series are listed at *brill.com/hm*

The Marxism of Manuel Sacristán

From Communism to the New Social Movements

By

Manuel Sacristán

Translated and Edited by

Renzo Llorente

BRILL

LEIDEN | BOSTON

This work has been published with a subsidy from the Directorate General of Books, Archives and Libraries of the Spanish Ministry of Culture.

This publication has been typeset in the multilingual "Brill" typeface. With over 5,100 characters covering Latin, IPA, Greek, and Cyrillic, this typeface is especially suitable for use in the humanities.
For more information, please see brill.com/brill-typeface.

ISSN 1570-1522
ISBN 978-90-04-22355-4 (hardback)
ISBN 978-90-04-28052-6 (e-book)

This book is printed on acid-free paper.

Printed by Printforce, the Netherlands

Contents

Acknowledgements

Anyone who takes a serious interest in Manuel Sacristán's work today owes an enormous debt to Salvador López Arnal, whose prodigious scholarship has been critical in disseminating Sacristán's thought and in recovering his intellectual legacy. Indeed, if Sacristán's thought continues to attract interest beyond a relatively small group of disciples and admirers, it is in large part thanks to Salvador's tireless efforts. In addition to bringing out new editions of some of Sacristán's most important writings and interviews, Salvador has rescued many of Sacristán's unpublished pieces (including numerous lectures, which he has transcribed himself), edited several collections of essays on the philosopher's life and thought, and played a key role in the creation of *Integral Sacristán*, an exhaustive, 13-hour documentary about Sacristán. Were it not for Salvador's endeavours, I myself might never have taken much notice of Sacristán: it was precisely one of Salvador's books (the invaluable *Acerca de Manuel Sacristán*, co-edited with Pere de la Fuente), which I discovered by chance in the 1990s, that first convinced me that Sacristán was a Marxist thinker well worth studying. For all of these reasons, and on account of his readiness to respond to each and every one of my queries regarding *Sacristaniana*, my first and most fundamental debt is to Salvador.

There are a number of other debts that I would also like to record here. Yaiza Hernández Velázquez encouraged me to undertake this translation and, even more importantly, took responsibility, on very short notice, for many of the bureaucratic tasks necessary to secure financial support for the project. Vera Sacristán, Manuel Sacristán's daughter, granted permission to reprint most of the material that appears in this anthology and, along with Marti Huetink at Brill, assisted me with various questions regarding translation rights. Ruth MacKay kindly offered to review her translation, first published more than two decades ago, of the essay reprinted here as Chapter 9. I thank all of these people for helping to make this book possible.

In addition to the assistance that I have received from individuals, I have benefited from institutional support, which I would also like to acknowledge here. Saint Louis University, Madrid Campus granted me a sabbatical leave during the Autumn 2012 semester, which enabled me to complete part of the work on the present volume. I also received a translation grant from Spain's Ministry of Culture (which has since become the Ministry of Education, Culture and Sports). I am grateful to both institutions for their support of this project.

Finally, I thank family and friends for their forbearance.

Introduction

A Life of Commitment

Manuel Sacristán Luzón[1] was born in Madrid, on 5 September 1925,[2] the first of three children in a middle-class family. In November 1936, a few months after the outbreak of the Spanish Civil War, the family moved to Valencia, where it remained until February 1937. This was followed by a stay of similar duration in the Italian town of Rivatrigoso, before the family settled in Nice, where it would remain until August 1939 (the Civil War having ended just a few months earlier, with the victory of Franco's quasi-fascist forces). From Nice, the Sacristán family returned to Spain and settled in Barcelona, which would remain Manuel Sacristán's permanent home for the rest of his life.

After completing his secondary schooling in Barcelona, Sacristán began studying law at the University of Barcelona in 1944. In his third year at university, however, he switched to philosophy, though he would later complete his law degree as well. While a student at the university, Sacristán left the Spanish Falange's youth organisation, which he had joined in 1940.[3] (His father had for a time served as the administrator for the youth organisation). His rupture with the Falange, an organisation originally established as a fascist movement, was apparently prompted in large part by the Falangists' proclivity for violence and, in particular, their brutal treatment of *catalanista* students (those students who defended the Catalan cultural identity).[4] In 1949, renal tuberculosis required Sacristán to undergo a nephrectomy, after which he

1 In Spain and other Spanish-speaking countries, one's full name includes the first surname of both of one's parents (each of whom likewise has two last names), with the father's surname usually appearing first. However, in most contexts one only uses the first surname, although both last names are sometimes used when the first surname is unusually common. Hence, the author of the texts translated in the present volume is generally referred to as Manuel Sacristán, and this is how I shall be referring to him hereafter.

2 In preparing this biographical sketch – and some parts of the rest of the introduction as well – I have drawn extensively on Capella 2004, Sempere 1987, Fernández Buey 1995, Fernández Buey 2003, and Fernández Buey and López Arnal 2004. Unless otherwise indicated, all translations from the Spanish are my own.

3 Sempere and Capella both date Sacristán's break with Falangism to 1945–6; Sempere 1987, p. 6; Capella 2004, p. 29, n. 16; yet Fernández Buey contends that it may have occurred as late as 1947; Fernández Buey 2003, p. 31.

4 Fernández Buey 2003, p. 31.

 DOI 10.1163/9789004280526_002

would live with only one kidney.[5] That same year Sacristán was instrumental in the creation of *Laye*, a cultural journal that attracted some of Barcelona's best writers, and one to which Sacristán would himself contribute numerous articles and book reviews before it ceased publication five years later.

In 1954, Sacristán won a merit-based scholarship to undertake post-graduate study in formal logic at the Institut für mathematische Logik und Grundlagenforschung in Münster. The nearly two years that Sacristán spent in Germany proved decisive for his future intellectual and political development. To begin with, Sacristán's stay in Germany enabled him to master the German language – from which he would later translate many works into Spanish – and deepen his familiarity with German culture, for which he felt a strong affinity.[6] In addition, Sacristán's training in Münster would make him one of the very few Spanish philosophers competent in symbolic logic, a branch of philosophy hardly studied in Spain at the time. (The training in the philosophy of science that he received at the Institut also set him apart from most other Spanish philosophers in the late 1950s). Finally, and most importantly, it was during his time in Germany that Sacristán first familiarised himself with the works of Marx and Engels, and came into contact with German communist workers and, through them, the Spanish Communist Party, whose leadership kept its headquarters in Paris at that time. In short, it was in Germany that Sacristán embraced Marxism[7] and first established contact with the organised labour movement, to which he would remain committed for the rest of his life.

Despite being offered a position at the Institut in Münster upon completing his programme of study, Sacristán chose to return to Spain, where, in 1956, he immediately began teaching classes in philosophy and logic as a non-permanent faculty member at the University of Barcelona. By this time (late 1956) Sacristán was a member of the Spanish Communist Party (PCE). He also belonged to the Central Committee of the Unified Socialist Party of Catalonia (PSUC), a national-regional Communist party formed independently of the Spanish Communist Party but closely affiliated with it. This rapid ascent within Spain's main Communist organisations – both of them illegal

5 Fernández Buey and Capella, Sacristán's two most prominent disciples, both stress that this experience would have a profound impact on Sacristán's attitude toward existence; Fernández Buey 2003, p. 32; Capella 2004, p. 33.

6 See Sacristán 2004c, pp. 99–100, for Sacristán's own description of his Germanophilia in regard to literature, philosophy, music, and culture generally.

7 One of the people Sacristán met in Münster was Ulrike Meinhof, some of whose work he would translate and analyse two decades later, after Meinhof's death; see Sacristán 1985b.

and underground at the time – provides striking testimony to the extremely favourable impression that Sacristán made on Party leaders. Sacristán's main responsibility within the PSUC consisted in establishing the first Communist organisations of students and professors within the University of Barcelona and, more generally, in organisational work among the Catalan intelligentsia. (He also occasionally devoted himself to relations with other anti-Francoist opposition parties). Thus began a period in Sacristán's life – nearly a decade – during which he had to distribute his time and energy among several highly demanding commitments. As Sacristán did not hold a full-time position at the university, he found it necessary to do translations and editorial work with different presses in order to supplement his income. He thus combined his teaching duties and academic research with translation and editorial collaborations, on the one hand, and extensive responsibilities as a communist militant (on account of his status within one of Spain's most important Communist organisations), on the other. It was also during this period that Sacristán married, in August 1957, Giulia Adinolfi, an Italian Hispanist – and communist militant – whom he met in Barcelona.

In 1959, Sacristán published his doctoral dissertation, *Las ideas gnoseológicas de Heidegger* (*Heidegger's Epistemological Ideas*), still regarded, more than half a century later, as one of the finest studies of Heidegger's thought written in Spanish. At about the same time, Sacristán began to introduce (and reintroduce) Marxist thought to Spain, helping thereby to initiate the revival of interest in Marx within Spain during the 1960s. Sacristán's discussion of Gramsci in a text written in 1958, for example, was the first mention of the Italian Marxist in Spain,[8] while his 1959 translation and edition of Marx and Engels's writings on nineteenth-century Spanish politics contained the first texts by the founders of Marxism to be legally published in Francoist Spain.[9] At the same time, Sacristán also helped to introduce both analytical philosophy and symbolic logic into Spanish academic philosophy. As for the former, Sacristán translated and wrote the introductions to several works by the American philosopher W.V. Quine, and as regards the latter, it was Sacristán who, in 1964, published the first comprehensive manual on symbolic logic to appear in Spain since the end of the Spanish Civil War (1936–9).[10]

---

8 Sacristán 1984a. Sacristán brought out an anthology of Gramsci's writings, which he had translated, in Mexico in 1970; Gramsci 1970. The lengthy text originally intended as an introduction to this anthology was first published nearly three decades later; Sacristán 1998.

9 Marx and Engels 1959.

10 For Sacristán's contribution to the study of formal logic in Spain, see Vega 2005.

By the mid-1960s, Sacristán had in effect become, as Francisco Fernández Buey puts it, Barcelona's 'public communist';[11] not surprisingly, from an early stage his political and intellectual activities began to attract the attention of the Spanish authorities. Indeed, Sacristán's house was searched no fewer than five times between 1957 and 1972, and he was subject to regular surveillance: in the 1960s, there were police reports on his classes and lectures, and a policeman from the Brigada Político-Social (Francoism's brutal political police) was often posted in front of Sacristán's apartment building.[12] The first major professional ramification of this growing political notoriety occurred in 1962, when Sacristán sought to obtain a newly created Chair in Logic at the University of Valencia. The most competent logician in Spain at the time, Sacristán was plainly superior to the other candidates who participated in the *oposiciones* (public competitive examination) held in Madrid, yet he was nonetheless denied the post by a committee whose members knew little about logic but thought it imperative to reject Sacristán on political and ideological grounds.[13] Three years later, in 1965, Sacristán would be excluded from the university altogether, when his yearly contract was not renewed, likewise for political reasons;[14] the university administration would not rehire him for any significant period of time until more than a decade later, after the death of Franco. The revocation of Sacristán's passport in the early 1960s merely compounded these limitations on his intellectual and professional development, as travelling to conferences and congresses abroad became impossible for many years. (Sacristán only recovered his passport after Franco's death).

Following his exclusion from the university, Sacristán was forced to earn his living by undertaking translation and editorial work for publishing houses (such as writing reports on manuscripts and assuming the editorship of book series). An unusually gifted and highly versatile translator, Sacristán translated texts from German, Italian, English, French, Catalan and classical Greek into his native Spanish. Sacristán's translations constitute an important part of his legacy, not only on account of their calibre and quantity – he published around 100 book-length translations[15] – but also because his position as translator and

11 Fernández Buey 1995, pp. 147–8.

12 Fernández Buey 1995, p. 148; Capella 2004, p. 49, n. 54; pp. 85–7.

13 For a detailed account of this episode, see Martín Rubio 2005.

14 A police report on Sacristán from October 1965, reprinted in Capella 2004, pp. 85–7, offers a vivid illustration of the Francoist authorities' perception of Sacristán.

15 López Arnal, Manchado Alcudia and Sanz González 1999, p. 85. The authors point out that between 1968 and 1971 Sacristán translated no fewer than 26 books, that is, almost seven per year.

editorial influence often enabled him to recommend certain books to be translated, and to thereby turn translating into a form of intellectual and political intervention.[16]

Despite his onerous workload as a translator and his exclusion from the university, Sacristán continued to give public lectures throughout the 1960s and 1970s and, indeed, until the time of his death. Though Sacristán prepared his lectures with great care, he seldom delivered them from a written text. Even so, the quality of Sacristan's lectures, their refinement and coherence, was such that many who attended the lectures surely assumed that they had been written out in advance.[17] Partly on the basis of these public interventions, which proved highly popular and attracted large audiences, Sacristán would become 'by around 1968 ... the most influential communist intellectual in Spain'.[18]

In 1965, the same year as his exclusion from the university, Sacristán became a member of both the PSUC's Executive Committee and the PCE's Central Committee, and in the latter part of the 1960s he served as the editor of the PSUC's theoretical organ, *Nous Horitzons*. While no longer employed as a university instructor, Sacristán remained active as a university organiser. Indeed, he was instrumental in establishing the Sindicato Democrático de Estudiantes (Democratic Student Union), an alternative to Francoism's official student union, at the University of Barcelona in 1966 (Sacristán was in fact the principal author of its founding document). In the spring of 1968, political developments in Czechoslovakia aroused great hope in Sacristán. The subsequent crushing of the 'Prague Spring' by Warsaw Pact soldiers, coupled with the French Communist Party's disheartening response to the May 1968 uprising in Paris, came, Sacristán wrote, as a 'double blow' or 'double shock' [*doble aldabonazo*],[19] and one that occurred at the very moment in which Marxism and communism were finally regaining influence and authority among important sectors of society.[20]

In January 1969, Sacristán resigned from his position in the PSUC's Executive Committee. The PCE (with which the PSUC was affiliated) had condemned the invasion of Czechoslovakia, but the condemnation was, in Sacristán's view, too

16 Folch 2000, p. 38.

17 Cf. Folch 2000, pp. 35, 39, and Sagalés 2002, p. 90. Some of Sacristán's outlines for his lectures have been included by Salvador López Arnal in his editions of Sacristán's texts. See, for example, Sacristán 2005a and 2009b.

18 Fernández Buey and López Arnal 2004, p. 24.

19 Sacristán 1983i, p. 234.

20 Fernández Buey and López Arnal 2004, p. 24. For a detailed account of Sacristán's analysis and interpretation of the Prague Spring and its aftermath, see López Arnal 2010.

mild, and more importantly, it had overlooked the deeper structural problems besetting the project of building socialism in the USSR. Sacristán also took issue with some aspects of the Party's assessment of the political situation in Spain and, more generally, he objected to what he regarded as the unremitting spread of bourgeois values within a party (or parties, since the PCE and the PSUC were officially separate entities) that continued to consist primarily of workers.[21] In any event, Sacristán only informed the Parties' leaders and his friends of his decision – he disdained the spectacle of ritualistic apostasies and deplored their effect on the Left.[22] He remained a rank-and-file militant, as well as a member of the PCE's Central Committee. Sacristán's resignation from his positions of responsibility within the PSUC was accompanied by, and was surely one of the factors contributing to, the first (and apparently most severe) of several serious bouts of depression.[23]

The 'double blow' of 1968 and Sacristán's resignation from a position of leadership within one of Spain's most important Communist organisations marked the end of one period in Sacristán's theoretical-political development (a period that had begun in 1955–6) and the beginning of another. Over the course of the next decade, that is to say, from 1969 through the end of the 1970s, Sacristán would reflect at great length on the failures of the international communist movement and the new challenges facing Marxism, particularly in light of the Communist countries' stagnation and their undeniable likeness, in many fundamental respects, to capitalist countries. It bears noting that Sacristán took for granted that Social Democracy, the other major political tradition deriving from Marxism, had also failed. It was in fact precisely to prevent, as Francisco Fernández Buey puts it, 'a relapse into Stalinism or the gradualist illusion'[24] (i.e. the failed Communist model or the failed Social Democratic project) that

21 In a lecture delivered in Mexico in 1982 or 1983 and addressed to members of the Mexican revolutionary left, Sacristán observed that 'from the sociological point of view', the Spanish Communist Party (PCE) was 'one of the most Marxist parties imaginable', given that 90 percent of its members came from the industrial working class; Sacristán 2005e, p. 112.

22 Colectivo Editor 1987, p. 3.

23 As Xavier Folch emphasises, Sacristán 'viewed his personal project as closely related to political action' (Folch 2000, p. 35). A short series of autobiographical notes from this period, found among Sacristán's papers after his death, help to document Sacristán's state of mind at the time. The notes, whose composition Capella dates between the spring of 1969 and the beginning of 1970, were published by Salvador López Arnal in Sacristán 2003, pp. 57–61.

24 Fernández Buey 2005a, p. 52.

Sacristán insisted on the urgency of rethinking the communist project.[25] As part of this 'rethinking', Sacristán would begin exploring what he called 'post-Leninist' problems, by which he meant those concerns that would ultimately give rise to the 'New Social Movements', and in particular the environmental, feminist and peace movements.

Thanks to the appointment of a new Rector, and added pressure from students and faculty, Sacristán was rehired by the University of Barcelona for the 1972–3 academic year. However, this Rector was soon replaced and the university did not renew Sacristán's yearly contract. In 1973, Sacristán thus found himself excluded from the university for a second time.[26]

During the mid-to-late 1970s, Sacristán seriously considered abandoning political activity altogether, becoming 'depoliticised', in light of the disappointing results of his political work and the fact that his activist commitments left him precious little time to devote to scholarship and research in formal logic and the philosophy of science.[27] Yet although Sacristán would leave the PSUC and PCE altogether in late 1978 or early 1979,[28] he remained politically active and engaged until his death. One remarkable example of the nature and extent of Sacristán's commitment in the 1970s was his volunteer work, from 1973 to 1975, at an alternative centre for adult education in L'Hospitalet de Llobregat, an important industrial suburb of Barcelona.[29] Every week Sacristán would spend a few hours teaching classes in basic literacy and socialist education to

25 According to Francisco Fernández Buey, the overthrow of Allende in Chile in 1973 deeply disturbed Sacristán and reinforced his conviction that it was necessary to start anew; Fernández Buey 2005a, p. 52.

26 Sacristán suffered a new bout of depression after this second expulsion from the university, according to Capella (2004, p. 171, n. 59), who notes that in the spring of 1972 Sacristán had also experienced another, albeit lighter, episode of depression (2004, p. 177, n. 63). Fortunately for Sacristán's family, Sacristán's wife Giulia secured a teaching position at Barcelona's Autonomous University in 1973.

27 Domènech 1987, p. 93, n. 2; Fernández Buey 2005a, p. 53.

28 As Fernández Buey points out, Sacristán left the PSUC and PCE just as the parties were being legalised and going public (with great fanfare), as they emerged from nearly four decades of repression. His departure from the party (or parties) was very discreet, however, and Sacristán, who remained on the radical Left, never had any desire to form a part of the 'ex-communist' marketplace; Fernández Buey 1995, p. 151. For an overview of Sacristán's work within the PSUC, see Pala 2007.

29 Capella writes that Sacristán's work at the school began in 1974 (2004, p. 183), but Jaume Botey, one of the school's founders, states that Sacristán's participation actually began in 1973 and lasted for two and a half years (1997, p. 44).

groups of students made up primarily of working-class men and women who had immigrated to Catalonia from other regions in Spain.

Throughout the late 1970s, Sacristán continued with his public interventions (notably lectures and book presentations), some of which would appear in the left-wing journal *Materiales* [*Materials*], which he founded with some close collaborators in 1977. *Materiales* suffered from financial difficulties and lasted only two years, but in 1979 Sacristán founded, along with Giulia Adinolfi, Francisco Fernández Buey and other friends, a new journal, *mientras tanto* (*in the meantime*), which proved much more successful (it is in fact still in existence today). Like *Materiales*, the new journal represented a broadly Marxist approach to social analysis. Yet unlike its predecessor, *mientras tanto* was expressly conceived as a forum for discussing ecological and feminist issues, as well as socialism, and in time it would concern itself with pacifism and anti-militarism too. This new set of interests reflected the evolution of Sacristán's thought since the end of the 1960s, and his growing preoccupation with, and appreciation of the importance of, 'post-Leninist' problems, the advent of which underscored the need to rethink and reconstruct the socialist programme in new socio-historical circumstances. The title of a volume that compiles many of Sacristán's essays, lectures and interviews from 1979 to 1985, *Pacifismo, ecología y política alternativa* [*Pacifism, Ecology and Alternative Politics*],[30] aptly summarises both Sacristán's main intellectual interests during this period and the political orientation of the journal that he edited.

Franco died in 1975, and within two years Sacristán was rehired by the University of Barcelona. Although he was offered, yet again, work as a fixed-term instructor (at a time when, as Juan-Ramón Capella observes, some of his former students already held permanent academic positions),[31] this re-employment at least marked Sacristán's definitive return to the university.[32]

30 The original Spanish title, altered as a result of an editorial error, was supposed to have been *Pacifismo, ecologismo y política alternativa*, or *Pacifism, Environmentalism* (or *Political Ecology*) *and Alternative Politics*. Sacristán's best-known disciple, Francisco Fernández Buey, actually refers exclusively to the original (unused) title in citing the book; see Fernández Buey 1995, p. 135, p. 142, n. 27, p. 150, n. 36, and p. 152, n. 40; cf. Fernández Buey 2005, p. 11. The recent reprint of this work published by the Spanish newspaper *Público* (Sacristán 2009d) corrected the error in the title. I am indebted to Salvador López Arnal for bringing the title of the *Público* edition to my attention.

31 Capella 2004, p. 204.

32 According to Juan-Ramón Capella, at the beginning of the 1980s Sacristán's classes attracted fewer students than they had in the 1960s: the intellectual climate had changed, as had student tastes (Capella 2004, pp. 244–5). One of the changes that Capella notes in passing is the growth of Catalan nationalism among students. As anyone familiar

Sacristán combined his academic duties with political organising within the university, as he had always done, while also remaining actively involved, throughout these last years of his life, in a number of other causes, including the Comité Antinuclear de Catalunya (the Catalan Anti-Nuclear Committee), the campaign to remove Spain from NATO, and the peace movement.

In February 1980, Giulia Adinolfi, Sacristán's wife, died of cancer. A terrible personal blow for Sacristán, Adinolfi's death was also a severe loss for *mientras tanto*, for she was one of the journal's founders, and in the years immediately preceding her death she had been developing the bases for a distinctive theory of feminism.[33]

Sacristán spent the 1982–3 academic year in Mexico, teaching at the Universidad Nacional Autónoma de México (UNAM). During his period in Mexico, Sacristán married María de los Ángeles Lizón, a Mexican sociologist and the daughter of Spanish exiles. Not long after returning from Mexico, Sacristán underwent open-heart surgery. While the operation was successful, the state of Sacristán's one remaining kidney was such that he would have to begin haemodialysis. In September 1984, Sacristán belatedly received the official academic recognition that he had so long deserved: a beneficiary of a programme intended to recognise and compensate scientists, scholars and researchers who had been professionally marginalised for political reasons under Francoism, Sacristán was made 'special full professor' (*catedrático extraordinario*) at the University of Barcelona. Unfortunately, he would hardly have time to savour this new recognition, for less than a year later, on 27 August 1985, Sacristán died at the end of a dialysis session. He had not yet turned 60.

---

with contemporary Spanish politics will be aware, Catalan nationalism is one of the major political issues in Spain today (along with that of Basque nationalism). Sacristán never wrote at length on nationalism, yet he did defend the right to self-determination and a nation's right to its cultural identity, all the while holding an essentially anti-nationalist position (among other reasons, as Joaquim Sempere points out, because such particularisms constitute an obstacle to the creation of a 'species awareness', which is ever more necessary in an era in which humanity faces monumental ecological challenges; Sempere 1996, pp. 613–14). Francisco Fernández Buey notes that one of Sacristán's main concerns during the last months of his life focused on the attempt to develop a left-wing politics that took into consideration Spain's plurinational, multilingual character and defended a cultural federalism; Fernández Buey 2003, pp. 40–1.

33 For a summary of Adinolfi's views, see Grau Biosca 2006.

Sacristán's Marxism

At the time of his death in 1985, Sacristán was generally regarded as one of Spain's premier post-Civil War philosophers and the country's most important Marxist thinker.[34] While Sacristán made a variety of contributions to philosophy, it seems fair to say, following Francisco Fernández Buey and Salvador López Arnal, that four of his achievements prove especially noteworthy: the (re)introduction of formal logic into Spanish philosophy; the dissemination within Spain, in the late 1950s and early 1960s, of the major currents in post-World War II philosophy; the analysis of Marx and Marxism, at a time when Marxism was prohibited in Spain and Marxology all but unknown; and the development of an innovative approach to the methodology, sociology and politics of science.[35] As the focus of the present anthology is the third contribution listed here, I will focus on Sacristán's work on Marx and Marxism in the remainder of this introduction.

Before turning to the substance of Sacristán's Marxism, however, we should note another of his contributions which, while not reflected in the present anthology, was of critical importance in revitalising Spanish Marxism in the 1960s, 1970s and 1980s: Sacristán's translation of key texts from the Marxist tradition. Indeed, Sacristán translated not only five books by Marx and Engels themselves, but also many essential works by later Marxist writers, including nine books by Lukács and a variety of texts by Gramsci, Marcuse, Heller, Korsch, Labriola, Della Volpe, Adorno, and others.[36] Sacristán produced these translations from the end of the 1950s until the early 1980s, and their role in promoting the development of Marxist theorising in Spain can hardly be overstated, for besides making Marxist texts available in Spanish, Sacristán generally accompanied his book-length translations with excellent prefaces and introductions, and these brief analyses also contributed to and enriched the development of Marxist theorising in Spain. In short, Sacristán deserves a great deal of credit for making a large number of Marxist texts, including many classics, accessible to the Spanish public (and in the case of works not previously translated into Spanish, the Spanish-speaking public more generally).

Let us now turn to the essential characteristics of Sacristán's Marxism.[37] In surveying Sacristán's Marxism, it may be helpful to bear in mind that his

34 For example, see the array of testimony cited in Fernández Buey 1995, pp. 131–2, n. 1.

35 Fernández Buey and López Arnal 2004, pp. 9–10.

36 For a fairly detailed breakdown of Sacristán's translations by subject matter, see López Arnal, Manchado Alcudia and Sanz González 1999, pp. 85–6.

37 A few of the theses developed in this section draw on Llorente 2004.

thinking can be divided into two basic periods, whose contours can perhaps be distilled from the biographical sketch presented above: the period from 1956 to 1968, during which time Sacristán held important responsibilities within the PCE and PSUC; and the period that began, following a few transitional years, in the mid-1970s and lasted until Sacristán's death in 1985.[38] Yet while Sacristán's thought undeniably underwent a notable evolution from the earlier to the later period, the main change in his outlook consists in a broadening of his earlier revolutionary perspective (resulting from his engagement with the 'New Social Movements') and not in a renunciation of any of its core components. Accordingly, although the account presented here refers to the thought of the later Sacristán, it should be borne in mind that there is no outright incompatibility between the early and late Sacristán.

In discussing the contours of Sacristán's Marxism, it seems reasonable to start with his general view of the nature or 'essence' of Marxism. At the most general level, Sacristán tends to refer to Marxism in two distinct yet complementary ways. On the one hand, he describes Marxism, in a more or less conventional fashion, as 'an attempt to rationally structure [*vertebrar*] an emancipatory movement, with the greatest possible amount of knowledge and scientific analysis'.[39] On the other hand, Sacristán often insists that Marx, along with Engels,[40] was above all the originator of a determinate *tradition*, or *culture*, within the modern labour movement: 'I think that what Marx did was more the founding act in the creation of a culture than of the creation of a scientific system'.[41] Whereas the first understanding of Marxism stresses

38 Here I essentially follow Capella's periodisation (Capella 2004, p. 14). Fernández Buey's periodisation of Sacristán's adult intellectual development differs from Capella's inasmuch as it regards the period that extends from 1969–79 as a discrete phase in the evolution of the philosopher's thought (Fernández Buey 2003, p. 31). For a detailed study of Sacristán's intellectual evolution, see, in addition to Capella's biography, Manzanera 1993. *Integral Sacristán* (2006), a collection of four DVDs containing countless interviews with Sacristán's friends, students, colleagues, disciples and family members, likewise sheds considerable light on the philosopher's intellectual development, while also providing a comprehensive and engaging overview of Sacristán's life, work and significance.

39 Sacristán 2004c, p. 109; cf. Sacristán 1996a, pp. 180–1.

40 It is worth noting that Sacristán does not subscribe to the anti-Engelsism found among many Marxist academics and Marx scholars. For example, see Sacristán 2004d, p. 312.

41 Sacristán 2005f, p. 41; cf. Sacristán 2004c, p. 107. In this connection, the following observation from Sacristán's notes is also of interest: 'In general, the fact that there is an obvious Marxist pluralism allows for only two interpretations: either Marxism reduces to the few common theories, or it is a culture and not a theory, a collective consciousness, etc. My thesis' (Sacristán 2003, p. 224).

the scientific-theoretical dimension of Marxist thought, the second points to Marxism's status as a living tradition, which lends itself to different possibilities of development but is invariably characterised by, among other things, a commitment to a communist political programme.[42] Sacristán integrates these two notions in the course of delineating the 'communist worldview' in 'Engels's Task in *Anti-Dühring*', his first major essay (and one of his best) on either Marx or Engels: 'Marxism is ... the attempt to consciously formulate the implications, assumptions and consequences of the effort to create a communist society and culture'.[43] However, while Sacristán certainly endorses the Marxist aim of using knowledge and science to ground the emancipatory project as rigorously as possible, what is of most interest in examining Sacristán's Marxism is his particular interpretation and development of the Marxist tradition, and accordingly this is what I will focus on primarily.

One salient aspect of the Marxist tradition, for Sacristán, is its moral character, that is to say, the fact that it centrally rests on certain normative commitments. In other words, Sacristán's Marxism stresses the moral dimension of the Marxist outlook. As Fernández Buey, perhaps Sacristán's most distinguished disciple, puts it, 'Sacristán thought that the moral inspiration was the main thing in Marx and in all of the important Marxists (Rosa Luxemburg, Lenin, Trotsky, Gramsci, Mariátegui, Guevara)'.[44] Already evident in his first major essay on Marx, Sacristán's belief in the centrality of moral considerations in Marx and Marxism becomes even more explicit in his later writings. For example, in a 1982 lecture, he refers to 'the fundamental idea that has inspired communists [*la gente comunista*] for many years: the idea of a new society, a new morality, a new culture'.[45] In light of this consistent emphasis on the moral foundations of Marxism, it becomes clear that the late Sacristán's defence of a thoroughgoing *moral transformation* (discussed below), which he regarded as a condition of revolutionary change, is in no way at odds with the conception of Marxism that he held even in his earliest writings on Marx and Engels. In any event, partly owing to this moral interpretation of the Marxist tradition, Sacristán maintains a very critical attitude toward scientistic strains within Marxism. Indeed, in an interview from the late 1970s, Sacristán goes so far as

42 Sacristán 2005f, pp. 40–1; Chapter 7 in this collection.

43 See page 138–9 below.

44 Fernández Buey 1996, p. 477; cf. López Arnal 1997, p. 209.

45 Sacristán 1987c, p. 86. Needless to say, in citing this passage I am assuming that Sacristán includes Marxists within the label 'communists'. (As I note below, Sacristán himself preferred to use the label 'communist', rather than 'Marxist', in referring to his own position or outlook).

to claim that it is 'much less false to say that Marxism is a religion than that Marxism is a science'.[46]

Besides its decidedly and explicitly moral orientation, Sacristán's Marxism is also characterised by its *revolutionary* pretensions. That is, Sacristán, himself a revolutionary activist[47] (both during and after his membership in parties that advocated political revolution), assumes that the goal of establishing communism by means of a revolutionary transformation of society is an integral part of Marxism.[48] As he observes in his short essay entitled 'On the Centenary of Karl Marx's Death', 'critically revising [Marx's] work means attempting to maintain or reconstitute its effectiveness as a communist programme', for 'to engage with Marx's work while separating it from its author's communist intentions makes no Marxist sense'.[49] Likewise, when in the editorial written for the inaugural issue of *mientras tanto* Sacristán emphasises that the journal's perspective is one of *social revolution*, he is simply taking for granted that this is the authentic Marxist perspective.[50] For Sacristán, the liberated society – the Marxian communist ideal – represents 'radical otherness with respect to this [our] society',[51] and the attainment of this radically different social order will require revolutionary action.[52]

Another feature that defines Sacristán's Marxism is the rejection of dogmatism, a feature that Fernández Buey seems to have in mind in claiming that the most salient characteristic of Sacristán's Marxism is the 'accentuation of the anti-ideological nature of the revolutionary thought which had its beginning in Marx'.[53] Sacristán's rejection of dogmatism is perhaps most evident in his insistence on the need to rethink many elements of the Marxist tradition in light of the momentous events of 1968 (mentioned above) and, more generally, the dispiriting results in countries in which Marxists had taken power,[54] the

46 Sacristán 2004c, p. 107; cf. Sacristán 1996a, p. 180. (One natural way of defending Sacristán's claim would be to adopt the well-known interpretation of religious belief proposed in Braithwaite 1994).

47 A point rightly stressed by Víctor Rios; see Rios 2007.

48 This point will seem obvious only if one overlooks the fact that some social democrats have also considered themselves 'Marxists'.

49 Seee p. 169 below.

50 Sacristán 1987a, p. 38.

51 See p. 218 below.

52 It is worth noting here that Sacristán was quite scathing in his assessment of contemporary Social Democracy. See, for example, Sacristán 1987a, p. 40 and p. 286 below.

53 Fernández Buey 1995, pp. 143–4.

54 See, for example, Sacristán 2005f, p. 42.

deficiencies besetting the international communist movement, and the challenges posed by the appearance of the 'New Social Movements'. (Sacristán's lecture on the nature of Stalinism, included here, provides one example of his commitment to rethinking the history, evolution and contemporary state of the Marxist tradition). Indeed, Sacristán does not hesitate to propose a refoundation of the entire emancipatory project, urging in the early 1980s – long before the collapse of the 'Communist' states of the Soviet Bloc – that radicals begin anew, as if it were the year 1847, prior to the endless fragmentation into different movements, schools and currents, and 'as if we were all socialists, communists and anarchists, without prejudices among ourselves'.[55]

One final, general feature of Sacristán's Marxism worth noting here is its kinship with analytical Marxism. As has often been pointed out, Sacristán was in many ways something of an analytical Marxist *avant la lettre*,[56] as his work anticipates the clarity and precision that constitute the hallmark of analytical Marxism.[57] This kinship is hardly surprising given Sacristán's training in formal logic and the philosophy of science, and his experience as a lecturer on the methodology of the social sciences in the University of Barcelona's Economics Department. It is evident, for example, in Sacristán's dissatisfaction with 'literary Marxism'[58] and in his insistence that contemporary Marxism must respond to and assimilate the recent findings and discoveries within the social and natural sciences.[59] It is likewise evident in his lack of enthusiasm for Hegelian varieties of Marxism (the different strains of Hegelianised Marxism). Sacristán even anticipates the ethical turn in analytical Marxism – the major analytical Marxists' focus, in their later works, on the normative justification for socialism – and, in particular, some of the conclusions proposed in the later thought of G.A. Cohen.[60] At the same time, Sacristán eschews the relatively apolitical approach to Marx found in some analytical Marxist writing, and

55 Sacristán 2005g, p. 44. Sacristán's readiness to rethink and reconstruct Marxism undoubtedly derives in part from his view that Marx is 'a classic of the social sciences, which means an author who, on the one hand, cannot be relinquished [*un autor ... irrenunciable*] and, on the other, is not up-to-date in every detail' (Sacristán 1996a, p. 180); cf. 2004b, p. 195, and compare the characterisation of Gramsci as a classic theorist on p. 257 below.

56 See, for example, López Arnal 2004a, p. 28.

57 For example, this is evident in Sacristán's efforts to make sense of the dialectic in Chapter 5 below.

58 Compare, for example, Sacristán's comments in Sacristán 2005a, p. 166.

59 Fernández Buey 1995, p. 145.

60 Some examples are given below.

unlike many of the analytical Marxists, he never abandoned Marxism, nor did he ever repudiate left-wing politics.

To be sure, the features of Sacristán's Marxism enumerated thus far – its insistence on the moral underpinnings of the Marxist outlook, its revolutionary orientation, its non-dogmatic character, and its affinities with analytical Marxism – tell us relatively little about the concrete or substantive elements that distinguish Sacristán's variety of Marxism. So what are some of the most distinctive elements of Sacristán's Marxism?

To begin with, Sacristán, who consistently underscores the ambivalent status of the forces of production under capitalism, that is, the fact that they also develop and operate as forces of *destruction*, embraced environmentalism from a relatively early stage of his thinking, and in the later period of his work he sought to develop an ecological Marxism. In fact, Sacristán was among the first European Marxists to appreciate the urgency and magnitude of the global environmental crisis and, accordingly, the need for Marxism to incorporate an ecological perspective into its vision of human emancipation.[61] Indeed, when Sacristán first began promoting an ecologically oriented Marxism in the late 1970s, much of the revolutionary and radical Left was still hostile to this endeavour or, at the very least, appeared uncomprehending. Sacristán himself realised, in any event, that in assuming ecological commitments the radical Left would be forced to modify, perhaps quite significantly in some instances, a few of its basic assumptions. Thus, in presenting the Spanish edition of Wolfgang Harich's *Kommunismus ohne Wachstum?* [*Communism without Growth?*], Sacristán observes that 'every communist who sees in the ecological problem the basic fact concerning the problem of revolution today ... is obliged to revise the notion of communism',[62] and goes on to endorse Harich's rejection of unlimited growth, owing to its effects on the environment and the human species. The necessary revision of the notion of communism, according to Sacristán, involves a shift from the emphasis on libertarianism, in the sense of the freedom and ability to satisfy all of one's possible needs, to an insistence on egalitarianism, in the sense of an equal distribution for all within an insurmountable scarcity.[63] As one means of promoting the requisite

61 Tello 2007 suggests that it would not be incorrect to regard Sacristán as 'the first post-Stalinist ecological Marxist'.

62 Sacristán 1985c, p. 227.

63 Sacristán 1985c, p. 224; cf. 2005d, p. 92. See Ovejero Lucas 2007, pp. 97–8 for a useful brief discussion of Sacristán's thinking in this regard. Sacristán's views on an ecologically-motivated and ecologically-oriented reconceptualisation of 'abundance' anticipates the

ecological consciousness, Sacristán advocates the practice of *austerity*,[64] which will enable us to live fulfilling lives in a world that will always lack the material abundance that according to conventional Marxist assumptions was a necessary condition for the elimination of social conflict. On a more immediate, practical level, Sacristán defends small-scale production and the creation of smaller communities – indeed, he goes so far as to claim that 'the destruction of the capitalist state today necessarily implies the development of small communities'.[65] In this connection, Sacristán does not neglect the challenge posed by the prevalence of capitalist values among workers in the industrialised countries, where even the labour movement has assimilated and tends to identify with such values and the model of 'predatory economic growth'[66] that they sustain. For a man who was both an activist deeply committed to (and long involved with) the labour movement and a thinker who advocated a social-*ecological* revolution, workers' adherence to bourgeois progressivism could hardly be deemed a negligible problem.[67]

In addition to his efforts to unite Marxism and the contemporary environmental movement, Sacristán also sought to reconcile Marxism with contemporary feminism and pacifism. (It is worth noting that *mientras tanto*, the journal co-founded by Sacristán in 1979, continues to characterise itself as red, green, violet, and white, colours that reflect its – and Sacristán's – commitment to working-class emancipation, environmentalism, anti-sexism and the defence of non-violence).[68] In connection with feminism, Sacristán defends, over and above the feminists' rejection of sexism, a *feminisation of the revolutionary subject*, a notion inspired by both his reading of Wolfgang Harich and his exposure to the feminist theory then being developed by Giula Adinolfi (Sacristán's wife and a co-founder of *mientras tanto*).[69] As he writes in a 1979 paper, the agents and proponents of radical social transformation should assume 'the values of positivity, of nourishing continuity, of measure and equilibrium – "compassion" –

theses that G.A. Cohen would begin to defend in the 1990s; for example, see Cohen 1995, pp. 10–11, pp. 128–9.

64 Sacristán 2005d, p. 92; 2005j, p. 155. As Fernández Buey points out, Sacristán conceives of austerity in essentially Stoic or Epicurean terms (Fernández Buey 2005, p. 19).

65 Sacristán 2005c, p. 69.

66 See p. 192 below.

67 See, for example, Sacristán 1987a, pp. 38–40 for some brief discussion of this concern.

68 The journal's website can be found at http://www.mientrastanto.org/. As I note below, Sacristán's own commitment to anti-militarism/pacifism does not entail a categorical rejection of politically-motivated violence.

69 For a brief overview of Adinolfi's ideas in this regard, see Capella 2004, pp. 231–2.

[which] are mainly feminine within our cultural tradition'.[70] (The fact that the adoption of these values also favours the development and consolidation of an ecological outlook merely heightens their appeal in Sacristán's eyes).[71] On the other hand, in the editorial in *mientras tanto*'s inaugural issue, among other places, Sacristán calls on feminism to fuse its revolutionary potential with that of other forces fighting for social freedom.[72]

A third commitment that makes Sacristán's Marxism distinctive is his espousal of pacifism, which, in his case, also entailed a re-evaluation of traditional socialist ideas on the role of violence in history. Sacristán's engagement with pacifism was motivated in large part by the debate over the installation of missiles in Europe in the early 1980s,[73] and more generally by the threat of war in the nuclear age. The pacifism propounded by Sacristán consists, at bottom, of a kind of thoroughgoing anti-militarism. For example, he does not condemn the use of violence by the oppressed in the course of their struggle for emancipation, although he does warn that even these struggles may engender the very dynamic of violence and militaristic mindset denounced by pacifists and anti-militarists.[74] As is the case with his espousal of feminism, Sacristán links the advocacy of pacificism to his concern with ecological questions, underscoring, for example, that nuclear war would threaten the very survival of the species (while even non-nuclear wars, of course, can cause severe environmental devastation). Unfortunately, Sacristán's untimely death prevented him from further developing his ideas on Marxism and pacifism, a topic that remains as important today as it was three decades ago.

One of the things that make the late Sacristán's efforts at Marxist regeneration, and the reconstruction of radical left-wing theory in general, so promising and attractive is that he combines his theoretical proposals with a wholly non-sectarian approach to practical communist politics (an approach facilitated by the fact that he no longer belonged to any political party after 1978 or 1979). One reflection of this approach or disposition appears in a talk given by Sacristán in 1981, in which he urges all of the parties comprising the 'extraparliamentary social left' to merge into a single organisation, and even to fuse with

70 See p. 193 below.

71 Capella, for one, underscores the importance for Sacristán of this aspect of the feminisation of the revolutionary subject (Capella 2004, p. 239). It is worth noting that Sacristán's thinking on this topic bears a certain affinity to some ideas defended by Herbert Marcuse; see, for example, Marcuse 1972, p. 75, pp. 77–8.

72 Sacristán 1987a, p. 40.

73 Sempere 2006, pp. 123–4.

74 See Sacristán 1987d, p. 92.

anarchist groups.[75] This expression of open-mindedness toward anarchism is actually quite typical of Sacristán: in an interview two years later, he suggests that Marxist communists should seek to reunite with the anarchists,[76] and elsewhere he does not hesitate to include anarchism within the 'communist tradition'.[77] The freedom from sectarianism shown by Sacristán in such statements and gestures serves to make his rejection of sectarianism at the level of theory all the more convincing.

In fashioning a version of Marxism that incorporates the chief contributions and concerns of environmentalists, feminists, and pacifists (along with the concrete practices which they entail, including those mentioned above), Sacristán proposes not only a radically different social arrangement, but also a moral radicalisation of the Marxist project, for the changes he advocates amount to nothing less than a profound *moral transformation* of men and women. As Sacristán himself puts it a late 1983 lecture:

> A subject who is neither an oppressor of women, nor culturally violent, nor a destroyer of nature is – let us not deceive ourselves – an individual who must have undergone an important change. If you like ... it has to be an individual who has experienced what in religious traditions was called *a conversion*.[78]

Sacristán's Legacy

Despite the widespread praise for Sacristán's accomplishments at the time of his death in 1985, Sacristán's work has received relatively little attention over the past three decades. Admittedly, the neglect of Sacristán's work outside Spain is not especially surprising. For one thing, Spanish intellectual life under Francoism remained somewhat isolated from international cultural developments and, in any case, trends in Spanish philosophy and political thought have never aroused the same degree of international interest as those

75 Sacristán 2005g, p. 44.

76 Sacristán 2004b, p. 197; cf. 1996b, p. 233, where besides advocating the same idea, Sacristán speaks of the need to promote a 'libertarian socialism'.

77 Sacristán 2005f, p. 41.

78 See p. 250 below (emphasis in the original). Significantly, the philosopher G.A. Cohen, who for many years wrote from a broadly Marxist perspective and remained a socialist egalitarian until the end of his life, eventually reached a rather similar conclusion (Cohen 2000, p. 120).

occurring in, say, Germany, Italy or France. For another, Sacristán's output was relatively modest (for reasons outlined above, namely, severe professional limitations). Not least importantly, Sacristán's orientation and evolution were at odds with most of the influential currents within Marxism during the 1970s and 1980s, such as Althusserianism and Eurocommunism.[79] The relative neglect of Sacristán's work within Spain itself is somewhat more puzzling, if hardly inexplicable: many of the intellectual trends that would discourage interest in Sacristán's project on an international level also proved highly influential in Spain. What is more, Sacristán eschewed self-promotion, and that attitude coupled with his distaste for the media's cultural spectacles also facilitated his posthumous marginalisation and oblivion.[80]

Still, however deplorable the reasons for the neglect of Sacristán's work, it is still fair to ask whether, or rather *why*, his writings merit our attention today. To be sure, Sacristán's texts are of considerable historical interest, comprising as they do one of the most important chapters in the history of Marxist thought in Spain, while also being an important contribution to the development of twentieth-century Spanish social theory in general.[81] Yet what might they offer readers who do not share these interests but who do care about Marx, Marxism or emancipatory social theory? Will they find it worthwhile to read Sacristán today, when Sacristán himself acknowledged on several occasions that he had lacked the time, resources and calm (owing to his political activity and work as a translator and professor) required to produce truly substantial intellectual work?[82]

Despite Sacristán's own scepticism, we can indeed still profit from reading his works today, even if we have little interest in the status of his texts as

---

79 Fernández Buey 1995, pp. 132–3.

80 Colectivo Editor 1987, p. 3. Capella contends that the neglect of Sacristán in Catalonia, to whose cultural and political life he had made such a signal contribution, derives from the fact that he was, on the one hand, a 'red' and, on the other, not a nationalist but an internationalist (Capella 2007, pp. 38–9).

81 Sacristán himself tended to see their value in these terms, remarking in the prefatory note to the texts collected in the first volume of his papers (*Sobre Marx y marxismo. Panfletos y materiales I*) that anyone who chose to read them would be motivated, at least in part, by a 'historical or documentary' interest (Sacristán 1983l, p. 8). Similarly, he states in the prefatory note to the third collection of his papers (*Intervenciones políticas. Panfletos y materiales III*) that the writings contained therein are merely 'documents concerning a period of political and ideological struggles' (Sacristán 1985d, p. 9). Compare Sacristán's rather dismissive assessment of the first two volumes of his papers in his letter to Eloy Fernández Clemente (Sacristán 2005i, p. 51).

82 Sempere 2006, pp. 121–2.

historical documents. In fact, Sacristán's analyses and insights can teach us a great deal about the evolution of the Marxist tradition, the major debates in and challenges to twentieth-century Marxist theory and, not of least importance, Marx's own thought, for Sacristán was among other things an extraordinarily erudite and sophisticated Marx scholar or 'Marxologist'. In connection with the Marxist tradition, one could mention Sacristán's analyses of Eurocommunism and Stalinism, or his reflections on the work of the late Lukács, or his many lucid introductions to key Marxist texts.[83] As for Marxist theory, it has already been noted, for example, that Sacristán sought to integrate other emancipatory projects (the environmental movement, feminism, and pacifism) into a Marxist framework. In doing so, he provided some valuable resources for other theorists who address the same challenges or set themselves similar goals. With regard to Sacristán's contribution to the understanding and interpretation of Marx, it is worth mentioning two topics that figure prominently in some of the selections included in the present anthology. Consider, first of all, Sacristán's novel thesis, discussed at great length in Chapter 1, which holds that Hegel was a major influence on the *late* Marx too. Marx, argues Sacristán, 'rediscovered' Hegel in 1857, and this rediscovery produced an intensification of Hegel's influence during the writing of the *Grundrisse*. Most significantly, Sacristán contends that, paradoxically, it was the rediscovery of Hegel (and Marx's 'reconciliation' with abstraction and a totalising perspective) that allowed Marx to become a true social scientist, so that the most anti-scientific element in Marx's background – namely, his Hegelianism – was precisely what made him a social scientist and inspired the most social-scientific component of his oeuvre.[84]

The second example of Sacristán's contribution to Marx scholarship worth mentioning here is his effort to produce a plausible and satisfactory account of Marx's conception of *dialectic*. Sacristán denies that the dialectic – 'dialectical' reasoning or analysis – constitutes a distinct 'method',[85] as many Marxists are given to claiming. Indeed, Sacristán actually maintains that a dialectical

83 References for writings alluded to here (and not included in the present volume) can be found in 'Further Reading'.

84 Sacristán 2004d, pp. 318–19, 321. One should not conclude from this that Sacristán regards Hegel's influence on Marx as altogether positive. On the contrary, Sacristán holds that Marx's debt to Hegel is, on the whole, a liability. 'Any useful continuation of the Marxist tradition must start by abandoning the Hegelian dialectical scheme regarding the philosophy of history' (see p. 188 below). Indeed, 'the meaning of Marxism is ... anti-Hegelian. The fact that Marx used the language of Hegel is merely a historical anecdote, fortunate in 1840 ..., most unfortunate today' (Sacristán 2003, p. 179).

85 See, for example, Sacristán 2004d, pp. 308–9.

presentation of material is methodologically redundant.[86] But if the dialectic is not a method, then what is it? As Sacristán observes, we can distinguish at least three distinct senses of 'dialectic' in Marx's work; that is, Marx uses the concept to refer to at least three different modes or types of analysis. First, Marx uses 'dialectic' to refer to a form of 'totalising thought' that synthesises and integrates the partial findings produced by the various positive sciences (including the social sciences), with the aim of reconstructing the unity of the object of study. Yet Marx also uses 'dialectic' to refer to a style of thinking that views social phenomena as processual, historical, and, accordingly, continually changing. Finally, Marx sometimes uses 'dialectic' as a term designating a certain kind of endogenous explanation, namely, an explanation that not only derives exclusively from internal factors, but also in some sense reproduces the internal development of the object of study.[87] While Sacristán never adequately systematised any of these three conceptions of dialectic, his observations and preliminary proposals offer valuable resources for future research on this subject.

There is a great deal more that one can learn about Marx and many other topics in reading Sacristán, but rather than enumerating more of Sacristán's insights and theses I would like to conclude this introduction by noting a few things that one might learn from his personal example as a communist intellectual. (When it came to self-definition, Sacristán preferred the label 'communist' to 'Marxist',[88] though he by no means eschewed the latter). Two points in particular bear mentioning in this regard.

First of all, Sacristán combined his intellectual (scholarly, scientific) rigour with an extraordinary degree of moral commitment.[89] Indeed, Sacristán's life

86 See pp. 42–3 below. It is instructive to compare Sacristán's view with both C. Wright Mills's remarks on the dialectic (1962, pp. 129–30, n. 6) and those of Wright, Levine and Sober (1992, p. 6, n. 5).

87 Sacristán analyses Marx's notions of the dialectic and dialectical thought in several of the texts contained in the present volume, including a few essays in the first section ('On Marx and Engels') and the second interview (Chapter 18). For some discussion of Sacristán's interpretation of Marx on the dialectic, see López Arnal and Benach 1999; López Arnal 1997, pp. 214–19; and Ovejero Lucas 2007, pp. 99–100. The brief synthesis of Sacristán's views presented here is indebted to these texts.

88 Fernández Buey 2005a, p. 53. Cf. Sacristán 2009c, p. 263: 'One should not *be* a Marxist (Marx). The only thing of any interest is to decide whether or not one moves within a tradition that tries to advance atop the crest, between the valleys of desire and reality, in search of a sea in which the two converge', original emphasis.

89 Manuel Monereo in particular has underscored this aspect of Sacristán's life and legacy (Monereo 2007, p. 223; compare his remarks in 'Sacristán the Marxist', included in the

and work are marked by a moral radicalism that distinguishes him from many, if not most, leftist intellectuals. To the extent that a large measure of moral radicalism – in the sense of both a principled commitment to a thoroughgoing ethical transformation of society and a prioritisation of this commitment in one's actual political practice – is necessary for effecting revolutionary social change, Sacristán's life and work prove exemplary.

Secondly, Sacristán was a revolutionary philosopher and intellectual who truly managed to unite theory and practice. In the last several years of his life, for example, Sacristán was not only the guiding force behind a non-academic journal, *mientras tanto*, devoted to the analysis of contemporary social questions from a Marxist-feminist-ecological perspective, but also a political activist, both within the (post-Franco) university – his immediate professional milieu and sphere of most direct influence – and in Catalan and Spanish society more generally. As Sacristán disapproved of intellectuals who would enjoy considerable privileges and opportunities for self-cultivation without acknowledging any attendant social responsibility (deriving from their role as the bearers of society's accumulated knowledge),[90] he could hardly have had a high opinion of intellectuals who, while explicitly professing adherence to an emancipatory political doctrine, in reality remain effectively 'apolitical'. It will come as no surprise, then, that Sacristán had no use for a purely academic Marxism.[91] As he writes in an early text, 'a Marxist philosopher can only be a communist militant because there is no Marxism of mere erudition'.[92] This conviction seems as sensible and important today as it was more than half a century ago, when Sacristán first stated it. It is, moreover, another element of Sacristán's legacy, and one that we would do well to embrace today.

second DVD of *Integral Sacristán*). Monereo's identification of Sacristán with a '*radicalidad moral*' or 'moral radicality' inspired my choice of the phrase 'moral radicalism' in the following sentences (Ibid.).

90 Sempere 1996, p. 613; cf. Fernández Buey 1997, p. 37, for a brief account of how Sacristán saw his own role and responsibilities as an 'intellectual worker'.

91 Fernández Buey 2005a, p. 53.

92 Sacristán 2009a, p. 55.

A Note on This Edition

While Manuel Sacristán's works range from studies of symbolic logic to essays in literary criticism, this anthology chiefly focuses on his contributions to the understanding of Marx and Marxism, and on his interventions in debates bearing on political ecology, communist politics, and the 'New Social Movements'. However, the texts assembled here represent a relatively modest sample of Sacristán's output, even on these topics. Information on other important works by Sacristán that address the topics covered in the present anthology is included at the end of the volume.[1]

Only one of the texts included in the anthology (Chapter 9) has been previously published in English, in a translation by Ruth MacKay. The remaining selections are translated into English for the first time. A few of the writings collected here were first delivered as lectures and were only published long after Sacristán's death and without the benefit of his revisions. In the case of these selections, readers will note that I have chosen to preserve the relatively informal, unpolished quality of the texts, rather than venturing to edit Sacristán's talks.

Nearly all numbered footnotes are Sacristán's own. Any footnotes added by the Editor are indicated as such with '[Ed.]'. Editorial interpolations in Sacristán's footnotes appear within brackets. All footnotes that follow an asterisk have been added by the Editor.

The sources for the essays, lectures, and interviews included here are listed below. Selections are reprinted courtesy of Vera Sacristán, unless otherwise noted.

1 It will not be possible to provide a definitive list of Sacristán's works on any topic or question until we have the benefit of Salvador López Arnal's complete, authoritative bibliography (currently in preparation). For the most comprehensive existing bibliography of Sacristán's works, which was compiled before the appearance of most of his posthumously published texts and does not register many unpublished materials, see Capella 1987, as well as the addenda listed in Capella 1995. A list of Sacristán's interventions within and as a leader of the then underground Spanish Communist Party and the Unified Socialist Party of Catalonia can be found in Manzanera Salavert 1995.

 | DOI 10.1163/9789004280526_003

Original Sources[2]

'Marx's Scientific Work and His Notion of Science'
1983 [1980], 'El trabajo científico de Marx y su noción de ciencia', in *Sobre Marx y marxismo. Panfletos y materiales I*, edited by Juan-Ramón Capella, Barcelona: Icaria Editorial, S.A.

'Karl Marx as a Sociologist of Science'
2007 [1983], 'Karl Marx como sociólogo de la ciencia', in *Lecturas de filosofía moderna y contemporánea*, edited by Albert Domingo Curto, Madrid: Editorial Trotta. Reprinted by permission of the publisher.

'Engels's Task in *Anti-Dühring*'
1983 [1964], 'La tarea de Engels en el *Anti-Dühring*', in *Sobre Marx y marxismo. Panfletos y materiales I*, edited by Juan-Ramón Capella, Barcelona: Icaria Editorial, S.A.

'Marx on Spain'
2007 [1983], 'Marx sobre España', in *Lecturas de filosofía moderna y contemporánea*, edited by Albert Domingo Curto, Madrid: Editorial Trotta. Reprinted by permission of the publisher.

'What is Dialectic?'
2009 [1985–5], '¿Qué es la dialéctica?', in *Sobre dialéctica*, edited by Salvador López Arnal, Barcelona: Ediciones de Intervención Cultural/El Viejo Topo.

'One Hundred Years On: To What "Literary Genre" Does Marx's *Capital* Belong?'
2007 [1968], 'Cien años después. ¿A qué "género literario" pertenece *El capital* de Marx?', in *Lecturas de filosofía moderna y contemporánea*, edited by Albert Domingo Curto, Madrid: Editorial Trotta. Reprinted by permission of the publisher.

'On the Centenary of Karl Marx's Death'
2004 [1983], 'En el primer centenario del fallecimiento de K. Marx', in *Escritos sobre EL CAPITAL (y textos afines)*, edited by Salvador López Arnal, Barcelona: Fundación de Investigaciones Marxistas/Ediciones de Intervención Cultural/El Viejo Topo.

---

2 Dates in square brackets indicate original date of composition/production.

'Which Marx Will Be Read in the Twenty-First Century?'
1987 [1983], '¿Qué Marx se leerá en el siglo XXI?', in *Pacifismo, ecología y política alternativa*, edited by Juan-Ramón Capella, Barcelona: Icaria Editorial, S.A.

'Political Ecological Considerations in Marx'
1992 [1984], 'Political Ecological Considerations in Marx', *Capitalism Nature Socialism*, 3(1): 37–48. © The Center for Political Ecology. Reprinted by the permission of Taylor & Francis Ltd., www.tandfonline.com, on behalf of The Center for Political Ecology.

'Paper for the Conference on Politics and Ecology'
1987 [1979], 'Comunicación a las Jornadas de ecología y política', in *Pacifismo, ecología y política alternativa*, edited by Juan-Ramón Capella, Barcelona: Icaria Editorial, S.A.

'The Political and Ecological Situation in Spain and the Way to Approach This Situation Critically from a Position on the Left'
1987 [1981], 'La situación política y ecológica en España y la manera de acercarse críticamente a esta situación desde una posición de izquierdas', in *Pacifismo, ecología y política alternativa*, edited by Juan-Ramón Capella, Barcelona: Icaria Editorial, S.A.

'Three Notes on the Clash of Cultures and Genocide'
1995 [1975], 'Tres notas sobre choque de culturas y genocidio', *mientras tanto*, 63: 77–87.

'On the Subject of Eurocommunism'
1985 [1977], 'A propósito del 'eurocomunismo', in *Intervenciones políticas. Panfletos y materiales III*, edited by Juan-Ramón Capella, Barcelona: Icaria Editorial, S.A.

'On Stalinism'
2005 [1978], 'Sobre el stalinismo', in *Seis conferencias*, edited by Salvador López Arnal, Barcelona: Ediciones de Intervención Cultural/El Viejo Topo.

'Marxist Parties and the Peace Movement'
1987 [1985], 'Los partidos marxistas y el movimiento por la paz', in *Pacifismo, ecología y política alternativa*, edited by Juan-Ramón Capella, Barcelona: Icaria Editorial, S.A.

'The Marxist Tradition and New Problems'
2005 [1983], 'Tradición marxista y nuevos problemas', in *Seis conferencias*, edited by Salvador López Arnal, Barcelona: Ediciones de Intervención Cultural/El Viejo Topo.

'"Gramsci is a classic, he is not a fad": Interview with the *Diario de Barcelona*'
2004 [1977], '"Gramsci es un clásico. No es una moda". Entrevista con *Diario de Barcelona*', in *De la Primavera de Praga al marxismo ecologista*, edited by Francisco Fernández Buey and Salvador López Arnal, Madrid: Los Libros de la Catarata.

'Manuel Sacristán Speaks with *Dialéctica*'
2004 [1983], 'Manuel Sacristán habla con *Dialéctica*', in *De la Primavera de Praga al marxismo ecologista*, edited by Francisco Fernández Buey and Salvador López Arnal, Madrid: Los Libros de la Catarata.

'Interview with *Naturaleza*'
2004 [1983], 'Entrevista con *Naturaleza*', in *De la Primavera de Praga al marxismo ecologista*, edited by Francisco Fernández Buey and Salvador López Arnal, Madrid: Los Libros de la Catarata.

'Interview with *Mundo Obrero*'
2004 [1985], 'Entrevista con *Mundo Obrero*', in *De la Primavera de Praga al marxismo ecologista*, edited by Francisco Fernández Buey and Salvador López Arnal, Madrid: Los Libros de la Catarata.

PART 1

On Marx and Engels

CHAPTER 1

Marx's Scientific Work and His Notion of Science

> Peut-on éviter de se laisser prendre à ces jeux stériles en parlant de Marx et de ses enseignements? Autrement dit, peut-on parler raisonnablement, en respectant les règles élémentaires de la logique et la vérité palpable des faits? Bref, une marxologie scientifique est-elle possible quand on se trouve en face des exhibitions fantaisistes de toute une corporation – universitaires y compris – d'intellectuels?
>
> MAXIMILIEN RUBEL (1978)

∴

It is opportune, in the best sense of the word, to take up Marx today, now that this author is being deprived of the extravagant attentions that he had enjoyed for the last two decades. In the most recent period of Marxist fashion, centred on 1968, some particularly deceptive illusions dominated the field in regard to the topic that we are considering today, namely, Marx's scientific work. This helps to explain the fact that over the last two years (approximately) discussion of the scientific calibre of Marx's work, or lack thereof, has been placed at the very centre of the description of the crisis, which explicitly Marxist political movements, and several currents of thought within the same tradition, have been undergoing. We may note that the authors raising the most critical voices on this question are philosophers who until very recently construed Marx's work in the most scientistic manner, as a thought that had undergone a rupture, break or *coupure* (to borrow a term widely used since the 1960s) with respect to its metaphysical origins. Doubts over the scientific calibre of Marx's work create less trouble for interpretations of Marx that are not scientistic. For example, we do not find any important disturbance because of such concerns among currents that interpret Marx as a social philosopher or a philosopher of culture, in the style of the Frankfurt School, or among those who read Marx primarily as a philosopher of revolution, what was once called 'Western Marxism', as in Lukács's school and other traditions. All of these, or almost all of these, currents now agree on the need for more or less important revisions of modes of thought present in Marx's work, or of Marx's theses.

---

* First published 1980. Republished as 'El trabajo científico de Marx y su noción de ciencia', in *Sobre Marx y marxismo. Panfletos y materiales I*, edited by Juan-Ramón Capella (Barcelona: Icaria Editorial, S.A., 1983).

 | DOI 10.1163/9789004280526_004

However, none of the currents mentioned perceive this state of theoretical and practical crisis as a collapse. For their part, the economists, whether or not they consider themselves Marxists, have long tended to see in Marx simply a classic author, as great an inspiration as any other for a tradition that some modern economists develop and others reject, but which no one should idolise and which all can consider interesting.[1]

On the other hand, the authors to whom I have alluded, intellectuals in crisis (examples include Althusser and Sollers in France, and Colletti in Italy), are philosophers who react with dramatic formulations to their recent discovery that Marx's work is not, contrary to everything that they had taught until a very short time ago, exact science, *scientia in statu perfectionis*, as the old philosophers said, let alone 'the only social science', as Philippe Sollers had proclaimed 'Marxism-Leninism' to be. Althusser's and Colletti's interpretations of Marx were as one in being based on the idea of a complete break between the mature Marx and his earlier philosophical training, which was primarily Hegelian. Sollers's is an extravagant case. In his period of infatuation with Marxist-Leninist-Mao Zedong thought, Sollers was bursting with amusing phrases, such as the one already mentioned about Marxism-Leninism being the only modern social science, or the memorable discovery that the essence of the Chinese Cultural Revolution was the destruction of the question of meaning: a good billion Chinese were converted, as if by missionaries, into an illustration of a mediocre semiotic of understanding ... Althusser and Colletti were, of course, always quite far removed from those sorts of things. They provide, involuntarily, a much more interesting example of the dangers that threaten Marxist navigation. Both are authors who not only satisfy the customary criteria of academic quality, but also easily go beyond them, to the point of presenting more the image of a master than of a professor. Nonetheless, viewed in light of the crisis besetting their earlier interpretations of Marx, which Althusser and Colletti themselves express, those earlier interpretations now appear to be a kind of hagiography, like the life of an intellectual saint. Their earlier interpretations in fact confused the history of ideas and philological

1 The work of Michio Morishima is a good representative of an intellectual atmosphere free of the philosophical and ideological tensions, whether Marxist or anti-Marxist, attending predominantly literary mental habits. Morishima writes: 'It is no exaggeration to say that before Kalecki, Frisch and Tinbergen no economist except Marx had obtained a macro-dynamic model rigorously constructed in a scientific way ... [O]ur approach to Marx is somewhat different from the so-called Marxian economics ... Our aim is to recognize the greatness of Marx from the viewpoint of modern advanced economic theory and, by so doing, to contribute to the development of our science' (1973, pp. 3, 5).

research (to put it pointedly) with the free development of the tradition of a classic thinker. It is one thing to study and explain Marx's thought; it is quite another to do Marxism today. Many (perhaps all) of the things that Althusser and Colletti were teaching five years ago are better studied as the Marxist thought (or thought in the Marxist tradition) of one of these authors than as the thought of Marx. This confusion between the philological treatment of a classic thinker and the productive continuation of his legacy is, moreover, common in traditions originating in a classic thinker, not only in the sense of being a paradigm of theoretical – in particular, scientific – thought, but also in the sense of being a moral, practical or poetic inspiration.

However, it is not my intention to engage in polemics, but merely to do what I have called philology, that is, to speak of *Marx's* thought, and not to present a continuation – whether good or bad, productive or sterile – of his thought. And it is not because of a desire to dodge this question, nor because I believe that a classic thinker must always be the object of a philological reading, but rather because I think that among the several good things that we can derive from a situation of crisis, from a change of perspective, is the possibility of restoring a sound historical basis to the study of ideas. This is a favourable moment for Marxists to undertake this effort, for the sterile ideologism from which they seem to be freeing themselves is now actually taking hold of the new anti-communist fashion – it, too, an *article de Paris*, as was the earlier swaggering Marxism – to which I am not going to refer, since it has nothing to say in relation to the modest and quite unspectacular questions pertaining to the philosophy of science that I intend to address here.

At any rate, it was necessary for me at the outset, even without any desire for controversy, to refer to the framework of the disputes, criticism, counter-criticisms and self-criticisms within which any question regarding Marxism will be situated. It had to be done, first of all, so as not to arrogantly ignore the situation, and secondly, because as far as the philosophy of science is concerned, the authors mentioned are – however odd one sometimes finds the unexpected fury with which they make a great to-do – notable philosophers, not 'semi-informed literati', *halbwissende literati*, to borrow a phrase from Marx.[2] They are notable philosophers who express, in a somewhat inappropriate manner, a set of problems that is new for them, but by no means imaginary. Consider, for example, Colletti. He finds a new difficulty for his reading of Marx in the need to acknowledge that, contrary to what he had always claimed, in Marx's work there are *two* concepts of science: the normal concept of science (let us call it that, without going into a lot of detail, using

2 Marx 1991d, p. 242.

the term made famous by a well-known historian and philosopher of science, Thomas S. Kuhn), the concept of science that scientists normally embrace; and the Hegelian concept of science, or *Wissenschaft*, a notion of Platonic origin encompassing the knowledge of essences and metaphysics.

There can be no doubt that Colletti's own formulation of the crisis of his earlier belief, which saw in Marx a pure, normal scientist, is on the mark. Colletti is quite right: so much so that one cannot but wonder why he took so long to become aware of something as obvious as the fact that neither Marx's thought nor any Marxism that can be truly related to Marx is pure science, nor are they merely science. Marx's own vocabulary suffices for one to realise as much. Marx speaks disparagingly about what he calls *science*, in a malicious Anglo-French, and speaks proudly about what he calls *deutsche Wissenschaft*, German knowledge, literally 'German science', just as the Nazis would say later on – among other things because he shares a tradition in common with the latter: that of German Idealism. When Bakunin complained about Marx's patriotism, he was quite right (as right as when Marx complained about Bakunin's pan-Slavism).

Authors not nearly as well known as these philosophers were aware long ago of this news, which undermines the scientistic and theoreticist Marxism of the structuralists and neo-Kantians. Paul Kägi, for example, an old Swiss union official who was never a professor at any university, stated the following in 1965: 'We will say: Marx found in Hegel a respect for empirical science, yet at the same time a concept of science that goes from empirical science to the doctrine of ideas'.[3]

So, to state my opinion briefly and clearly: the concepts of science governing Marx's intellectual work, the inspirations for his scientific mission, are not two but three: the notion of science that I have called 'normal', *la science*; the Hegelian notion, *Wissenschaft*, which Colletti now discerns and which Kägi discussed fifteen years ago; and a notion of Young-Hegelian inspiration, received from those circles [*ambientes*] which, in the 1830s, after Hegel's death, critically developed his legacy, circles in which Marx moved and in which the idea of science as *critique* flourished. *Science, Kritik* and *Wissenschaft* are the names of the three traditions that nourish the philosophy of science implicit in Marx's scientific work, as well as the work itself.

My intention here is to document in Marx's work the presence of the two philosophical traditions of the concept of science least common today, leaving aside the normal notion of science, which I take for granted and which, despite all the 'paradigm shifts', continues to enable us to string together in a

3 Kägi 1965, p. 54 [translated from Sacristán's Spanish citation (Ed.)].

single thread, however twisted, Euclid, Ptolemy, Copernicus, Galileo, Newton, Maxwell, Einstein and Crick, for example. I will then consider the weight that those notions have had in Marx's work, and point to what matters most: how the three notions of science are integrated into Marx's explicit philosophical-scientific programme, or implicit in his practice.

The Classical German Philosophical Tradition

Exposition as 'Development', or 'The Dialectical Method'

Louis Althusser observed that the notion of development is the centre of Marx's methodology. It must be said, however, that that factor is precisely what characterises the mature Marx as a Hegelian. 'Development' is the term most often used to translate the German word *Entwicklung*. Sometimes it is rendered as 'evolution', which is what it means in biological contexts. In general, when *Entwicklung* is translated into Romance languages it is necessary to bear in mind the sense of evolution.

The idea of grounding [*fundamentación*] as development, rather than as deduction or empirical validation, expresses the conviction that argumentation about something must not be a chain of reasoning indifferent to the thing, but has to consist in the presentation of the unfolding of the thing itself. ('Unfolding' [*despliegue*] is an acceptable translation of *Entwicklung*). According to this conviction, argumentation by means of necessities external to the object, which are not specifically its own – for example, general logic, or mathematical logic, or mechanical logic – is not scientific, since it is not truly necessary: 'External necessity is properly causal necessity':[4] this is how the metaphysical foundation of that methodology of development was expressed by its founder, Hegel.[5] The criterion of this Hegelian methodology is to only regard as scientific an explanation by means of what we might call the internal law of the object's development, understood as something that cannot be grasped from without. A good way of imagining what this means, when one does not have any great interest in studying Hegelian philosophy, is to think of an organic metaphor, the development of a living body, and to understand that this methodological ideal of development, of science as the development of the object, entails that a scientific treatise reproduce the development of that organism from germ to death and as seen from within, instead of explaining

4 Sacristán does not furnish any source for this quotation, which I have translated from the Spanish [Ed.].

5 'Founder' in a relative sense, as we shall see.

it by means of external necessities. Such a methodological principle would be a tautology if applied to knowledge of the whole – since there cannot be anything external to the whole – but in any other case (including biology itself, on account of Romantic philosophy's qualitative notion of 'the internal'), in common scenarios of scientific research, its application may bring us very close to the immoderation of the intuitionist philosophers, who (to paraphrase a joke from Einstein) demand that the chemical analysis of soup taste like soup.

At first glance, the methodology of development already appears quite consistent with Hegel's ontology. An idealist monism, like that of Hegel, can only regard as an explanation of being the *explicatio*, the unfolding or development of being. If there is only one point of reference in the world of knowledge, the explanation of that thing must also lie within it: there cannot be any explanatory argumentation concerning that thing other than the presentation of its development.

The truth is that, as often occurs in metaphysics, the structure in this case is more apparent than real. For Hegel, there was a need to invoke the methodological principle of development, of evolution or unfolding, only for being in the strict sense, the whole. Moreover, one of the most resounding poetic expressions of the philosopher's ideal of knowledge is the famous saying 'the true is the complete', or, as it is usually translated, 'the True is the whole' [*das Wahre ist das Ganze*],[6] which, taking the notion of completeness literally, did not require from him a methodology of development for specific research, or research on the incomplete. The fact that in Hegel and his tradition the methodology of development – which is the dialectic – is nevertheless also maintained for every specific kind of research is due to certain aspirations to knowledge that are not necessarily linked to Hegelian absolute idealism, even though they accord well with it. I shall say more about this later.

On the methodological level, the idea of explanation or grounding [*fundamentación*] as development yields a conception of scientific work that seems to be at odds with the common sense of people in the twentieth century. For Hegel, the developmental explanation is more or less isomorphic to the evolution of being and, starting from a generic emptiness, moves or unfolds toward completeness, totality, concreteness. When scientific work begins, its fruit is exceedingly abstract. In contrast to what common sense thinks today, knowledge of a thing does not start, according to Hegel, from the concrete and rise toward abstract generalities; it does not start, for example, from perceptible concrete things and then arrive at general laws that deal with abstract objects. According to the Hegelian methodology of development, things occur the

6 Hegel 1977, p. 11.

other way around; knowledge begins with the abstract and ascends to the concrete, for what it does (if it is true knowledge) is follow the unfolding of the object, its evolution toward its current concreteness, starting from the abstract indeterminacy that it is at the beginning. The logical-historical ambiguity of the word 'beginning' in that context is characteristic of Hegel's thought and of his tradition.

Marx accepted such a methodological ideal in broad outline. He too speaks of *ascent* from the abstract to the concrete, in opposition to the usage, common today, according to which we usually say that one ascends from the concrete to the abstract. Yet he accepts not only the general methodological approach, but also many of its elements. The notions of (self-)contradiction, mediation, and alienation are concepts that Hegel uses to construct development; since the being that evolves is the only one (it is being), the development must be the work of that selfsame being in development, which can only move by negating itself, contradicting itself, placing itself outside of itself (which is what 'alienating itself' means), and once again mediating itself toward itself. All of these concepts, so widely used sociologically within a Marxist framework, come from the Hegelian notion of unfolding, or the evolution of being, from the dialectic of being.

In incorporating the concept of the dialectical method, Marx undoubtedly abandoned the thematically idealist thesis that the being which thus develops shares the nature of the Idea. Here it is a matter of the well-known thesis according to which Marx's dialectical method consists of Hegel's method but with its ontology inverted. The naïve mechanical metaphor, suggested by Marx himself, does not explain much, but it is sufficient to continue with the question that concerns us here. By replacing Hegel's idealist ontology with one he deems materialist, Marx is obliged to take material or perceptual concreteness into account in his method. This is why, on inheriting the Hegelian idea of ascent from the abstract to the concrete, he must alter the idea in the following way: there is a material concrete and an intellectual concrete, of thought or knowledge. Knowledge starts from the material concrete and first obtains an abstract product. Thought then assembles the initial abstract simples until it achieves, *by ascending*, the concretes of thought. Hegelian *Entwicklung* thereby takes shape as a composition or synthesis with an empirical starting point, and the most interesting and sensible element of the Hegelian or dialectical methodology thus becomes obvious: the assessment of synthetic knowledge of the concrete, in opposition to the classical motto *non est scientia de particularibus*. This opposition to classical epistemology, an opposition that is self-conscious to the point of being theorised (in an abusive and unbridled manner, to be sure), is precisely what places Hegel among the half-dozen classic, eponymous currents found in Greco-European philosophy of knowledge.

Incidentally, the methodological variation effected by Marx with his 'overturning' [*Umstülpung*] of Hegelian ontology is very important for the critical understanding of Hegel reached by Marx in his maturity. In 1857, Marx thought that Hegelian absolute idealism was based on a poor understanding of the relationship between the abstract and the concrete. In the first Introduction to *A Contribution to the Critique of Political Economy*, Marx writes:

> [Hegel] accordingly arrived at the illusion that the real was the result of thinking synthesising itself within itself, delving ever deeper into itself and moving by its inner motivation; actually, the method of advancing from the abstract to the concrete is simply the way in which thinking assimilates the concrete and reproduces it as a mental concrete. This is, however, by no means the process by which the concrete itself originates.[7]

In speaking of the origins of Marx's 'dialectical method' it is necessary to mention, if only very briefly, the Spinozan and Leibnizian precedents of the aspiration to knowledge of the 'law of development' of single entities. The rejection of the classical thesis that the individual is not an object of science is already a motif in Spinoza's *explicatio* (one of the aims of the Hegelian term *Entwicklung* is to translate the Dutch philosopher's Latin), and above all it is the cornerstone of Leibniz's philosophy. The Leibnizian thesis concerning the existence of a *complete notion* of the singular substance is the strongest expression of this type of theory of knowledge that thrives on the passion for the intelligibility of the singular concrete. And one must not forget that the Leibnizian idea has had a wide and profound influence, thanks to the effective work of its promoters. Thus it appears, for example, in the 27th paragraph of the first chapter of a manual studied by three generations of highbrow Europeans, Christian Wolff's *Logic*:

> All that we conceive of in an *individual*, or all that we find in it, is determined in every respect; and it is precisely for this reason, because the thing is determined both in what constitutes its essence and in what is accidental in it, that it acquires the quality of *individual*.[8]

7 Marx 1986b, p. 38.

8 Sacristán does not furnish any source for this quotation, which I have translated from the Spanish [Ed.].

The 1857 Presentation

Marx twice wrote a thematic presentation of his 'dialectical method'. The first is found in a text that was not published, namely, the 1857 Introduction cited earlier, which today is usually published together with the *Outlines of the Critique of Political Economy* (the *Grundrisse*); the second is found in the Epilogue to the second edition of *Capital*, Volume I, in 1873.

The third section of the 1857 Introduction is devoted to method. It is entitled 'The Method of Political Economy'. It has two parts, one in which Marx talks about the method of political economy in general, and another in which he refers to his own work. The first part is of most interest to us here.

Marx begins by presenting the Hegelian idea that the good method ascends from the abstract to the concrete. He then expounds the critical observation regarding Hegel's idealism summarised earlier, based on the distinction between the material concrete and the intellectual concrete. The weight of idealist epistemology is, despite that criticism, so great in Marx that he shows no interest in the question of the origin of the initial abstract elements of the process of knowledge, and instead treats them as if they were 'immediate data of consciousness' or neo-positivist protocol statements. Finally, after partly illustrating his description of the scientific method as an ascent from the abstract to the concrete (for example, from the generic idea of labour to the peculiarity of labour in a certain society), Marx poses a question that absorbs the rest of his exposition: whether there exists a correlation between the 'ascending' logical order of the categories, of the concepts, and their historical order. The explicit and problematic historicisation of the method is another departure from the strictly Hegelian dialectic.

Marx answers the question stated by first saying, quite sensibly, that it depends; sometimes there is a correspondence between the logical development and the historical evolution, and other times there is not. Later, however, at the end of the text, he arrives at a much more categorical statement, claiming an 'inverse relation' between the logical and historical order. This is the paragraph that culminates rhetorically in the famous phrase: 'The anatomy of man is a key to the anatomy of the ape'.[9] Yet the thesis is also expressed more formally:

> It would … be inexpedient and wrong to present the economic categories successively in the order in which they played the determining role in history. Their order of succession is determined rather by their mutual relation in modern bourgeois society, and this is quite the reverse of what

9 Marx 1986b, p. 42.

> appears to be their natural relation or corresponds to the sequence of historical development.[10]

So as not to belabour the point, I will limit myself to noting that this implicit paralogical identification of the logical order among the categories with the order in which they appear in modern bourgeois society is brimming with Hegelian epistemological realism. We must not forget, in any case, that what we are reading is a draft, and that if Marx had prepared it for publication, he would probably not have maintained the Hegelian schema of the completion of eras, of the identity of the logical with the 'utmost' real of eschatological logic (as it were), just as no doubt he would have removed the contradiction between the empirical reply to the question of historical order/logical order ('Ça dépend') and the almost theological reply at the end. One of the causes of the eternalisation of Marx's work is probably the fact that – despite his extensive drafting of schemas and conspectuses – when he started to write, he did so in a steady stream (though sometimes quite slowly), rather than fleshing out a detailed [*desmenuzado*] schema of propositions, as does the researcher who writes a report or the educator who prepares a presentation. All of this lends credence to the tendency of Gramsci and Althusser to study above all the works of Marx that he himself published. However, the sheer mass of the posthumous manuscripts obliges us, in any case, to take them into consideration.

Economic scholars will notice at once that while the text under discussion speaks of the method of economic science, what it says nonetheless has little to do with their professional reading. A methodological discussion in economics in which the question is whether the logical order of the categories corresponds to the empirical order of their historical succession, and in which one reaches the conclusion that it does not and that they follow inverse orders, is simply not found in the methodological chapter of a normal book of economic science today. Marx's 1857 methodological text serves another intellectual project, and is plainly seeking something different or, at the very least, something different from what is sought in normal economics books.

It might seem that what Marx seeks is historical knowledge, and that the purpose to be served by the 'dialectical method' (1857 version) is not economic science in the sense most prevalent today, but history. Marx was, without question, very much a historian. Yet he was more of a historian (at least methodologically) in the years prior to 1857, which is the year of his rediscovery of

---

10 Marx 1986b, p. 44.

Hegel.[11] For example, he strongly insisted on the empirical historical point of view in 1846, when, in writing *Misère de la Philosophie*, he criticised

> the error of bourgeois economists who regard those economic categories as eternal laws and not as historical laws which are laws only for a given historical development, a specific development of the productive forces.[12]

As a matter of fact, what Marx puts forward in the methodological chapter from 1857 is neither 'normal' history, nor 'normal' historical methodology. The problem of the correlation between the logical and the historical does not belong to normal historical methodology, and still less the thesis that this is an inverse correlation. Nevertheless, it is an essential, central question for Marx's thought and has methodological standing. The same thing happens in the Marxian tradition, and also in the best works of Marxology, up to the essay by Zelený on 'The Logical and the Historical in *Capital*', a stage preceding his well-known study of the structure of Marx's main work.[13]

This science has its own type of abstraction: 'Although an abstraction, it is an historical abstraction and hence feasible only when grounded on a specific economic development [*Entwicklung*] of society'.[14] And it can apparently rely on a providential Hegelian logicality in the world, which common mortals are perhaps not always able to predict, given that this logicality sometimes swims up the river of history, as in the case of the anatomies of man and ape, and at other times occurs downstream, as in the case of the difference between money and credit: 'To state the *differentia specifica* is here both part of the *logical* development [*Entwicklung*] of the matter in hand and the key to understanding its *historical* development'.[15] And at other times, both developments – the logical and the historical – progress together, and not at cross-purposes, as in the origin of certain forms of capital:

> Implicit in money – as the elaboration [*Entwicklung*] of its definitions shows – is the postulate *capital*, i.e. value entering into and maintaining

11 This is the same year as Freiligrath's gift: see Marx 1983b, p. 249. I cite the main passage below.

12 Letter to Pavel Vasilyevich Annenkov, 28 December 1846; Marx 1982b, p. 100.

13 Zelený 1968.

14 Letter to Engels, 2 April 1858; Marx 1983f, p. 298.

15 Marx 1987a, p. 63, original emphasis.

> itself in circulation, of which it is at the same time the prerequisite. This transition [is] also historical.[16]

There is also a correspondence between the logical transition and the historical transition from capital to landed property, as is stated in the following passage, which is well-known because it is a commentary on the 'Outline' for *Capital*:

> The transition from capital to landed property is also historical, since landed property in its modern form is a product of the action of capital on feudal, etc., landed property. In the same way, the transition of landed property to wage labour is not only dialectical but historical, since the last product of modern landed property is the general introduction of wage labour, which then appears as the basis of the whole business.[17]

If one truly puts aside all reverential respect for the classic authors (without assuming the pettiness of ceasing to admire and learn from them, and without forgetting Eugenio D'Ors's warning, namely, that whatever is not tradition is plagiarism), one may notice that this whole question of the logical and the historical, undoubtedly important and of great interest, like all genuine metaphysical questions, can easily result in sterile extravagance when understood as a matter of scientific methodology. In this area it tends to lead to the Hegelian vices of insufficiency of logical abstraction – in order to enable the quasi-logical to stick fast to the historical (bad logic) – and excessive logicisation or rationalisation of experience, in order to enable it to prove logically necessary (a bad treatment of experience). In Marx's work too, this question is the framework within which paralogisms, pre-established harmonies between supposedly logical (dialectical) developments and apparent historical processes, appear most frequently. Among these paralogisms, or instances of inconclusive reasoning, we must include those that refer to correlations that are, at first glance, synchronic – between base and superstructure, for example – and that, for Marx, always have a diachronic side, that of their 'development'.

The 1873 Presentation

In the Afterword to the second edition of *Capital*, Volume I, Marx assembles those criticisms of the first edition that he regards as responses from compe-

16 Letter to Engels, 2 April 1858; Marx 1983f, p. 303. [All three interpolations of '*Entwicklung*' in this paragraph are Sacristán's (Ed.)].

17 Letter to Engels, 2 April 1858; Marx 1983f, p. 298.

tent people, and notes the discrepancies between the praise and the condemnation. He observes that some critics who have been favourable to him praise his method for its 'analytical' or 'deductive' rigour, while others criticise it for being 'dialectical'; some reproach him for his 'idealism', while others laud his way of discussing the empirical material. Marx attempts to resolve these discrepancies among the critics with a distinction between method of inquiry and method of presentation. The main, widely cited passage can be summarised in the following lines:

> [T]he method of presentation must differ in form from that of inquiry. The latter has to appropriate the material in detail, to analyse its different forms of development, to trace out their inner connection. Only after this work is done, can the actual movement be adequately described. If this is done successfully, if the life of the subject-matter is ideally reflected as in a mirror, then it may appear as if we had before us a mere a priori construction.[18]

The appearance of an a priori construction is due to the dialectical reconstruction. This is why the passage includes the well-known critical praise for Hegel:

> The mystification which dialectic suffers in Hegel's hands, by no means prevents him from being the first to present its general form of working in a comprehensive and conscious manner.[19]

The distinction, apparently so obvious, between mode of inquiry and mode of presentation, which, taken literally, is the common distinction between heuristic and didactic methods, proves quite problematic in Marx's case. By 'presentation' Marx does not understand a purely didactic, pragmatic discourse. The dialectic – and this is what is at issue here – has never been understood, either before or after Hegel, as a didactic instrument. In the letter to Engels of 16 January 1858, in which Marx announces his theory of profit, the dialectic appears as a 'method of treatment' [*Bearbeitung*].[20] He is no doubt using this

---

18 Marx 1996, p. 19.

19 Ibid.

20 The relevant passage reads as follows: 'What was of great use to me as regards *method* of treatment was Hegel's *Logic* at which I had taken another look by mere accident, Freiligrath having found and made me a present of several volumes of Hegel, originally the property of Bakunin. If ever the time comes when such work is again possible, I should very much like to write 2 or 3 sheets making accessible to the common reader the

term to refer to what he calls 'method of presentation' in the second edition of *Capital*, Volume I. What is the logical status of this 'method of presentation' or 'method of treatment'? It is not didactic in the ordinary sense, since for any pedagogy or presentation it is enough to present the facts that thorough research has prepared and, as Marx says, whose inner connection has been delineated. That is what is provided by a manual or treatise on mechanics, genetics or economics: the well-established facts and their inner connection, the data and their theorisation. What is the logical status of a treatment that is added to something that would already be sufficient to present a piece of knowledge? Let us look at the aim of this dialectical treatment, in which 'the actual movement [is] adequately described' so that 'the subject-matter is ideally reflected'. Marx admits that precisely when this outcome is achieved, 'it may appear as if we had before us a mere a priori construction'. This paradoxical concession is a sign of the methodological vacillation of the mature Marx, conscious, on the one hand, of all that he owes to Hegel, but already well versed in empirical and positive-theoretical methods and knowledge, both unknown in the mental universe of classical idealism. This Afterword's curious concession is rounded out, moreover, by insinuating that the reader could dispense with the Hegelian dialectical apparatus. Moved by the desire to give his favourable yet non-dialectical critics the key for translating a 'treatment' of Hegelian ancestry into the common language of normal scientific grounding [*fundamentación*], Marx reveals in this text – and not only in this text – the redundant methodological character of the dialectical presentation: *the dialectical treatment is something that is added to a piece of knowledge that has already been established.* The dialectical treatment is a grounding [*fundamentación*] or validation added to the 'normal' treatment.

Yet that redundancy appears as such from the point of view of science, not in the ensemble of Marx's work. The dialectical method that Marx describes as a method of treatment and presentation of the facts and of the connections among them is in substance the method of Hegelian development, yet rendered more complicated by the introduction of positive scientific methods in the stages of establishing data and the positive 'connection' (theorisation) among them. This method aims to present the facts – once they have themselves been established and their interconnection ascertained – by reflecting their 'life'. The organicist comparison suggests that this method – which seeks to present content in such a way that it is not only established empirically and endowed with theoretical consistency, but also has a superadded

rational aspect of the method which Hegel not only discovered but also mystified' (Marx 1983b, p. 249, emphasis in original).

connection – has a lot to do with an artist's way of working. Marx himself felt this way when he refused to publish his work in instalments:

> Whatever shortcomings they may have, the advantage of my writings is that they are an artistic whole, and this can only be achieved through my practice of never having things printed until I have them in front of me *in their entirety*. This is impossible with Jacob Grimm's method which is in general better with writings that have no dialectical structure.[21]

The dialectic is, however, not redundant for the aims of Marx's intellectual work, and not only because of the latter's organicist and artistic aims, which come to Marx from the tradition of Spinoza, Leibniz and Hegel. There is another reason, namely, that the dialectic establishes a relationship to reality, or practice, that differs from the usual one established by scientific theory.

Every scientific theory has, as is obvious, a relationship to practice. That relationship may be called 'technological'. It is a relationship of applicability in the technical sense: with the help of the theory, one can calculate, or manufacture tools or machines, and so on. In the case of Marx's socio-economic thought, there is without question a technological relationship to practice of the sort found in science in the normal sense. But there is, moreover, another relationship, as is also well known: a direct political relationship, which is served precisely by the dialectical treatment, by the reconstruction of reality as a systematic, individualised whole, a reconstruction that attempts to make the complex object of political intervention tractable.

The scientific redundancy of the so-called dialectical method (which is not a scientific method in the 'normal' sense) lends Marx's intellectual work its specific meaning and explains some of the difficulties in interpreting it. For example, the enigma of the 'preliminary chapters', the *vorchapters* of Marx's work to which he refers in letters and drafts, and which were to contain a generic presentation of universal economic categories. It is likely that as his mature idea of science came into being, with the methodological redundancy of its dialectic, which tends to singularise the object of study and arrange it in the same way as a work of art, those *vorchapters* of general abstract theory, of modest science without dialectic, came to hold less interest for Marx.

Let what I have said about the Hegelian (and, strictly speaking, Spinozan and Leibnizian) inspiration of Marx's notion of science suffice for this evening. This is, without a doubt, the most influential philosophical inspiration. Yet

---

21 Letter to Engels, 31 July 1865; Marx 1987d, p. 173, original emphasis.

the Young-Hegelian influence (the influence that Marx received from the left Hegelians of the 1830s) likewise bore great importance for his scientific work.

The Young-Hegelian Inspiration

Marx was himself a member of the Hegelian Left, a 'Young Hegelian', at least from the time of his explicit acceptance of Hegel's philosophy until he productively assimilated Feuerbach's influence and freed himself from it. The rest of the Young Hegelians – Bauer, Ruge, Strauss, Hess, Echtermeyer – were present in the world of the young Marx. The latter's main initiative as a publicist, the *German-French Annals* [*Deutsch-Französische Jahrbücher*] from 1844, can be considered a continuation of the group's journal that was banned in Germany in 1843, the *German Annals for Science and Art* [*Deutsche Jahrbücher für Wissenschaft und Kunst*], edited by Ruge himself, who was to be Marx's co-editor on the *Deutsch-Französische Jahrbücher*, and by Echtermeyer.

Young-Hegelianism gave Marx the idea of *science as critique*, and not as 'absolute' theory. In his 1843 correspondence with Ruge, published in the *German-French Annals*, Marx writes:

> Hitherto philosophers have had the solution of all riddles lying in their writing-desks, and the stupid, exoteric world had only to open its mouth for the roast pigeons of absolute knowledge to fly into it.[22]

Here, in contrast to the absolute knowledge of the old philosophy, is a philosophy that has become 'mundane' and indicates:

> what we have to accomplish at present: I am referring to *ruthless criticism of all that exists*, ruthless both in the sense of not being afraid of the results it arrives at and in the sense of being just as little afraid of conflict with the powers that be.[23]

In the literary practice of the Young Hegelians, criticism is not criticism of positively all that exists as much as it is criticism of all that exists in writing. The Young Hegelians were a group quite consumed with literary phenomena, and in the history of the world of print they constitute an intermediate link between the eighteenth-century *homme de lettres* and the twentieth-century intellectual. That makes the Young-Hegelian concept of science as critique an obstacle opposed to empirical research and scientific positivity. The concep-

22 Marx 1975f, p. 142.
23 Ibid., original emphasis.

tion of science as critique suggests that the data and even the connections among the data – the theory – are already available. From the Young-Hegelian point of view, to do science is to confront the pre-existing scientific edifice and criticise it.

Marx (and Engels) saw the epistemological risks of that conception and satirised it in 1845 in *The Holy Family*, which, it will be recalled, is subtitled 'Critique of Critical Criticism'. We must also remember, however, that the idea of science as critique is quite present in Marx's work during not only the 1840s – during which time critique is the essential characteristic of the Marxian notion of science – but also the 1850s, though by that time it is offset by a wealth of more positive studies. The critical remark about Lassalle that Marx makes in his 1 February 1858 letter to Engels is very interesting in this regard, for it combines the Young-Hegelian critical methodology with the Hegelian dialectic. Marx does this without giving the matter any importance, which suggests that it was, for Marx, then something quite obvious:

> It is plain to me from this one note that, in his second grand opus, the fellow [Lassalle] intends to expound political economy in the manner of Hegel. He will discover to his cost that it is one thing for a critique to take a science to the point at which it admits of a dialectical presentation, and quite another to apply an abstract, ready-made system of logic to vague presentiments of just such a system.[24]

If this is taken literally – which would not be a good idea, since the Marx of 1858 already knows that he has to work through a great deal of empirical material – one would have to infer that doing economic science consists in criticising at great length Smith and Ricardo, so as to carry them to the point at which it is possible to expound them dialectically.

Fortunately, Marx, as we know, did not construct his science in that way. In that same year of 1858 – and precisely in a letter to Lassalle – Marx distinguishes critical work from substantive or positive work with a naturalness freed from the Young-Hegelian and Hegelian manner of speaking seen in the letter to Engels just cited. The vocabulary and tone even suggest a methodology contrary to the Young-Hegelian methodology:

> I cannot, of course, avoid all critical consideration of other economists, in particular a polemic against Ricardo in as much as even he, *qua* bourgeois, cannot but commit blunders *even from a strictly economic viewpoint*.

24 Marx 1983c, p. 261.

> But generally speaking the critique and history of political economy and socialism would form the subject of another work ...[25]

Thus, in 1858 Marx had abandoned the Young-Hegelian identification of science with critique. He had overcome it on the level of methodological principles, but some remnants of it remain throughout his later work, including *Capital*. The method of quotation used in Volume I of that work is a remnant of the Young-Hegelian philosophy of science. There are quotations that often appear to be based on the cited authors' statements regarding non-literary facts, an appeal to authority [*procedimiento por autoridades*], which of course would be unacceptable in science. In the Preface to the third edition of *Capital*, Volume I, Engels gave a plausible explanation of this way of quoting used by Marx, attributing it to historical-doctrinal sifting.[26] This explanation is partly and perhaps largely correct, namely, in that the mature Marx's tendency in research led to a clear separation of criticism and theory. However, as I have said, I do not think that is the whole story: in the beginning, in his youthful project in economics, Marx had not distinguished between the positive treatment – the 'real treatment', as he put it – and the critical treatment, the study of the literature. And not only in the beginning: in the 22 February 1858 letter to Lassalle cited above, Marx wrote:

> The work I am presently concerned with is a *Critique of Economic Categories* or, if you like, a critical exposé of the system of the bourgeois economy. It is at once an exposé and, by the same token, a critique of the system.[27]

---

25 Marx 1983d, p. 270, original emphasis.

26 'In conclusion a few words on Marx's art of quotation, which is so little understood. When they are pure statements of fact or descriptions, the quotations, from the English Blue books, for example, serve of course as simple documentary proof. But this is not so when the theoretical views of other economists are cited. Here the quotation is intended merely to state where, when and by whom an economic idea conceived in the course of development was first clearly enunciated. Here the only consideration is that the economic conception in question must be of some significance to the history of science, that it is the more or less adequate theoretical expression of the economic situation of its time. But whether this conception still possesses any absolute or relative validity from the standpoint of the author [Marx] or whether it already has become wholly past history is quite immaterial. Hence these quotations are only a running commentary to the text, a commentary borrowed from the history of economic science' (Engels 1996, p. 29).

27 Marx 1983d, p. 270.

The system to which he is referring is that of economic science, and the book is going to be called *Critique*, as the 1859 publication was indeed titled. Marx had separated the two tasks – the critical task and the systematic task – to such an extent that it was possible in the end to publish separately the critical part of the manuscript (the *Theories of Surplus Value*), which most densely reveals the complicated fusion that existed in the initial project.[28] The Young-Hegelian motif will not form part of the title in 1867, as it had in 1859, although it will continue to be present as part of the subtitle on the cover of *Capital: A Critique of Political Economy*.

What Marx's Science Owes to Its Philosophical Inspirations

The best thing that Marx owes to his youthful Hegelianism and his 'rediscovery' of Hegel in the 1850s is the characteristic virtue of his intellectual work, that is to say, its totality [*globalidad*], that programme which aims at a complete comprehension of social reality, a complete comprehension of the social whole. Not only followers and disciples [*continuadores*], but also critics or writers engaged in the attempt to refute Marx's main theses have usually recognised an eminently systematic quality in Marx's work, a theorisation of exceptionally broad scope and depth. The best thing that Marx's epistemology owes to that of Hegel is his development of the philosopher's maxim mentioned above, 'the true is the complete'. Among Marx scholars who scarcely identify, if at all, with his philosophical and political thought, Schumpeter and Morishima are probably the ones who have most appreciated, in very different ways, the systematic grandeur of Marx's work. Joan Robinson too. She thinks, incidentally, that Marx learned from Ricardo the scientific ideal of the system, of theory in the strong sense. I find it impossible to be convinced of this, despite the devoted admiration with which I read Mrs. Robinson, for two reasons. First, and most important, because despite producing, in part of his work, theoretical science in the strict sense and with even greater systematicity than Ricardo, Marx nonetheless found himself, unlike Ricardo, obliged to blur the limits of the implicitly formal theoretical artefact, upon inserting it within a complete, inevitably hazier, social perspective. *Das Ganze* is more extensive than the theoretical system in the formal sense; Marx's *das Ganze* is more Hegelian than Ricardian. This is why it does not fit satisfactorily within the framework of theory in the formal sense, and lends itself much better to the historical-doctrinal category for which Schumpeter introduced the term 'vision', which is less bound up with structures and formalities, or the Kuhnian category of 'paradigm', as was noted at once by American economists of

28 See Marx 1988a; 1989a; and 1989b.

radical or Marxist leanings, who have probably been the claque most enthusiastic about the success of Kuhn's 1962 essay. The second reason is that Marx was convinced that Ricardo was an unsystematic writer, who for lack of sufficient systematicity gave rise to 'vulgar economics'.[29] The sweepingly systematising theoretical programme came to Marx from the Hegelian ideal of knowledge, enriched (and hindered) by the empirical inclination [*vocación*] of the 'normal' scientist, which, although it has not been studied here this evening, was one of Marx's two main gains in abandoning speculative philosophy (the other was his revolutionary commitment [*vocación*]). Ricardo's epistemological influence, and that of the English economists in general, probably had more of an effect on Marx's reaching the normal science of his age, the proper appreciation of experience, the acquisition of analytical habits, and so on. (However, Hegel's *Logic* is also visible in the qualitative analyses of the first section of *Capital*, Volume I).

Economists and historians of economic science have described the character of Marxian systematicity in terms of what it shares with 'normal' theory and in terms of how it goes beyond this theory, or is 'aberrant' – to repeat Joan Robinson's term – in comparison with the academic theoretical economics of the twentieth century.[30] Maurice Dobb wrote that in Marx:

> the boundaries of economic analysis were drawn more widely than in the narrower market-equilibrium studies to which we have grown accustomed in post-Menger, post-Jevonian economics, from which property relations and their influence are excluded because they are thought to belong to social rather than to economic theory.[31]

And Ronald L. Meek has spoken of 'a kind of *ménage à trois*' in which Marx brings together 'economic history, sociology and economics'.[32]

Meek's study of the excesses of Marxian science is, in my opinion, excellent: 'In Marx's hands', he writes:

---

29 'As you yourself will have discovered from your economic studies, Ricardo's exposition of profit conflicts with his (correct) definition of value, thus giving rise among his followers either to a complete departure from his basis, or to the most objectionable eclecticism' (Letter to Ferdinand Lassalle, 11 March 1858; Marx 1983e, p. 287).

30 Joan Robinson considers it an aberration on Marx's part to have connected the problem of relative prices to the problem of exploitation in the way that he did it (Robinson 1965, p. 176).

31 Dobb 1968, p. 450.

32 Meek 1967, p. 101.

> the theory of value is not simply a theory which sets out to explain how prices are determined: it is also a kind of methodological manifesto, embodying Marx's view of the general way in which economics ought to be studied and calling for a restoration of the essential unity between the different social sciences.[33]

He further remarks:

> If this interpretation of Marx's theory of value is correct, it follows that any criticism of the theory based on the assumption that it is a crude and primitive over-simplification is entirely misconceived. The only really valid criticism of it which can be made, I would suggest, is one of precisely the opposite type – that for our present purposes today it is unnecessarily complex and refined.[34]

One might even change Meek's 'our present purposes' to 'the purposes of science': the excessiveness or the 'aberration' of the Marxian programme of knowledge is the material correlate of what I have called the dialectic's methodological redundancy. The Marxian notion of system or theory contains, of course, the goal of a theoretical core in the positive-scientific sense, one that can be formalised or is formalisable (which justifies, in my view, undertakings like that of Morishima and the opinions of people like Godelier on Marx's economics and mathematics). But in its essence it is also a practical, historical vision, whose combination with the theoretical core in a strict sense yields an intellectual creation that is not entirely positive science, although it strives, at the same time, not to be mere speculation. It is a notion of scientific system that proceeds from the Hegelian epistemology of comprehensiveness [*globalidad*] and corrects it – attempting to rid it of speculation – through the reception of the positive concept of the 'normal science' of the age and of the practical concept of the contemporary labour movement.

This correction is not always complete. To repeat Marx's well-known metaphor, Hegel's feet do not always stay on the ground in Marx's philosophy of science. The patriotic enthusiasm for 'German science' has a great deal to do with this. The passages in Marx adequate for documenting this are not numerous, but they are indisputable. I will repeat, first of all, his comment in connection with Liebig in a letter to Engels:

---

33 Meek 1967, p. 105.

34 Meek 1967, pp. 104–5.

> You will understand, My Dear Fellow, that in a work such as mine, there are bound to be many shortcomings in the detail. But the *composition*, the structure, is a triumph of German scholarship, which an individual German may confess to, since it is in no way *his* merit but rather belongs to the *nation*. Which is all the more gratifying, as it is otherwise the silliest nation under the sun![35]

Marx then goes on to cite a few of Liebig's discoveries and some of the biochemist's words, which are as follows:

> The combustion of a pound of coal or wood restores to the air not merely the elements needed to reproduce this pound of wood or, under certain conditions, coal, but the process of combustion *in itself* (note the Hegelian category [Marx's interpolation]) transforms a certain quantity of nitrogen in the air into a nutrient indispensable for the production of bread and meat.

He then immediately adds: 'I feel proud of the Germans. It is our duty to emancipate this "deep" people'.[36]

This letter was written only one year prior to the publication of Volume I of *Capital*. We may note, with amusement, the ineffective modesty with which Marx attempts to cover up his patriotism, making himself, for this purpose, into an English writer. It is more important, however, to note the text's extravagance with respect to science. The faithfulness to Hegel in the 'composition' of his thought, in its organicism or dialecticality, leads Marx to irrelevant formulations that border on the absurdities of the nationalist theory of science. To be sure, he was even closer to these absurdities years earlier, when he opposed *Wissenschaft* to science.[37]

Yet even in later periods Marx did not completely free himself from the extravagant side of the dialectical theory of science, which consists in ignoring the scientific point of view's constitutive narrowness, as compared with the aim of the dialectic. Marx owes to the Hegelian heritage a curious susceptibility for succumbing to the spell of pseudo-science, as can be noticed in his unjustified

---

35 Letter to Engels, 20 February 1866; Marx, 1987h, p. 232, original emphasis.

36 Ibid. [The last line, as well as 'silliest nation' and a few other words from the first passage cited, appear in English in the original (Ed.)].

37 For example, in this passage from a 12 November 1858 letter to Lassalle: '[E]conomics as a science in the German sense of the word has yet to be tackled' (Marx 1983g, p. 355).

enthusiasm for the disoriented astronomer Daniel Kirkwood,[38] or his favourable opinion of the arbitrary evolutionism of P. Trémaux.[39] (Incidentally, contrary to a very widespread prejudice, it is Engels who judiciously corrects Marx's fanciful scientistic and pseudo-scientific remarks, preventing them from leaving a trace in Marx's main research).[40] And while Marx is enthralled by the pseudo-scientists, in the 1860s he actually regards Darwin – despite his admiration for him – as representative of crude English science, as compared with the complex completeness of 'German science'.[41]

The Marxian ideal of 'German science', which is fundamentally the dialectical legacy of Hegel, helped Marx by facilitating access to his mature goal for knowledge, and even the notion of systematic theory (through the quest for the complete, the 'Whole'). At the same time, however, this legacy brought with it the risk of never coming to recognise the essential characteristics of 'normal' science. The idea of 'German science', the interpretation of the dialectical system as positive science, or as *the* science, suggests contempt for what Hegel calls, in the Preface to the *Phenomenology*, 'genius' or the learnable

38 Marx 1987e, p. 184; 1987f, p. 187. On this point too Marx allows himself to be carried away by his twofold weakness for nationalism and Hegelianism: 'Hegel's polemic amounts to saying that Newton's "proofs" added nothing to Kepler, who already possessed the "concept" of movement, which I think is fairly generally accepted now' (Marx 1987e, p. 185).

39 Letter to Engels, 7 August 1866; Marx 1987i, pp. 303–5. Trémaux's 1865 work, *Origine et Transformation de l'Homme et des autres Etres*, strikes Marx as 'a *very significant* advance over Darwin', 'progress, which Darwin regards as purely accidental, is essential here [in Trémaux's fanciful work] on the basis of the stages of the earth's development' (Marx 1987i, p. 304, original emphasis).

40 'I have not quite finished reading the latter [Trémaux's book] yet, but I have come to the conclusion that there is nothing to his whole theory because he knows nothing of geology, and is incapable of even the most common-or-garden literary-historical critique. That stuff about … the whites turning into Negroes is enough to make one die of laughing.… The book is utterly worthless' (Engels's letter to Marx, 2 October 1866; Engels 1987a, p. 320). Marx maintains his mistaken point of view (Letter to Engels, 3 October 1866; Marx 1987j, p. 322). Thus he earns a conclusive rejoinder from Engels (Letter to Marx, 5 October 1866; Engels 1987b, pp. 323–4).

41 'In the course of my ordeal – during the past four weeks – I have read all manner of things. *Inter alia* Darwin's book on *Natural Selection*. Although developed in the crude English fashion, this is the book which, in the field of natural history, provides the basis for our views' (Letter to Engels, 19 December 1860; Marx 1985a, p. 232). Or again: 'Darwin's work is most important and suits my purpose in that it provides a basis in natural science for the historical class struggle. One does, of course, have to put up with the clumsy English style of argument' (Letter to Ferdinand Lassalle, 16 January 1861; Marx, 1985d, pp. 246–7).

'knack' [*der erlernbare Pfiff*].[42] Very well: the knack (or 'trick') that can be learned is an essential element of any validation in science. There is science in the usual sense, not wisdom reserved for idealist titans, when one uses a knack that can be learned and taught, and whose use can be consequently verified by any colleague. What is not verifiable by means of any learnable knack may be of greater interest than any kind of science, but this is precisely what it will not be – science.

It also seems clear that apart from that fundamental disorientation in connection with the 'knack' that can be learned, the Hegelian element in the Marxian philosophy of science is responsible for paralogisms and errors of detail of little systematic importance, but these are relatively frequent in Marx's work and of a greater speculative arbitrariness than such errors in Engels's work. For example, Engels also adduced, in connection with hydrocarbons, the Hegelian law of the transformation of quantity into quality. This phrase, like many other expressions from the history of metaphysics ('idea', 'matter and form', 'potency and act', 'entelechy', 'negation of the negation', and so on), is a magnificent receptacle for life's wisdom, and may even be so for poetry. But when one attempts to subject those phrases to a positive, scientific usage, they become pompous trivialities, by which nothing is explained. Engels, who was not especially meticulous in this regard either, was nevertheless never as crude as Marx in a note to Chapter 11 of *Capital*, Volume I. In the main text, Marx writes:

> The possessor of money or commodities actually turns into a capitalist in such cases only where the minimum sum advanced for production greatly exceeds the maximum of the middle ages. Here, as in natural science, is shown the correctness of the law discovered by Hegel (in his *Logic*), that merely quantitative differences beyond a certain point pass into qualitative changes.[43]

He then adds in a footnote: 'The molecular theory of modern chemistry first scientifically worked out by Laurent and Gerhardt rests on no other law'.[44] The terrible paralogism – which critics have analysed many times, as I myself did in an old piece (and for this reason will not dwell on it now) – is made even worse here on account of the excessive merits that Marx ascribes to Laurent and Gerhardt, which Engels later corrected.

42 Hegel 1977, p. 30.
43 Marx 1996, p. 313.
44 Marx 1996, p. 313, n. 2.

On other occasions, the lapses into speculation are more serious and serve to discredit Marx's method, to some extent, for the arrogant epistemological optimism of Hegelianism demands or expects unattainable results from the method. One example: In the most recent complete Spanish translation of *Capital*, the translator, Pedro Scaron, holds that a passage in Volume I must be a misprint or mistake, and he notes as much. The passage in question says the following:

> It is, in reality, much easier to discover by analysis the earthly core of the misty creations of religion, than, conversely, it is, to develop from the actual relations of life the corresponding celestialised forms of those relations. The latter method is the only materialistic, and therefore the only scientific one.[45]

The least of the mistakes in this passage is its denial of scientific status to the reductive sociological analysis of cultural facts, in this case religious facts. (Let us note in passing that texts such as this one allow us to form an opinion of the knowledge of those critics who severely condemn Marx's 'reductionism'). The worst error is the claim that the scientific method is capable of 'developing', starting from the socio-economic basis of a society, nothing less than its theology. Pedro Scaron is quite right in thinking that this text affirms something that is impossible. He is mistaken, however, in considering this a mistake or misprint. It is neither a mistake nor a misprint, but Hegel, objective idealism, 'German science'. If one believes that to know is, for the human species – and no longer for God, an irreplaceable assumption in sociological reflection – to contemplate the unfolding of being itself, of the thing itself, then it makes sense to think that, if one has a good command of the 'real' method, it is possible to remove from the basic seed, with organic necessity, the theological fruit.

Another harmful effect of the Hegelianising philosophy of science consists in the fact that it makes it more difficult for Marx to specify the epistemological status of his intellectual work, whose core, as I have indicated, has a strictly scientific structure (to put it formally, without assessing its validity for now). It is not the case that Marx always ignores the fact that he is working by means of the composition of abstractions. This is sometimes expressed through an adaptation to the kind of device used within the theoretical edifice, and even to the conditionality of the theoretical discourse, something that is not always found among his followers. In many passages, Marx knows that he is working with what would today be called a model. Louis Althusser's development of an

45 Marx 1996, p. 375, n. 2.

exact concept of 'mode of production' can claim that justification. It is natural for Marx to work with theoretical models, as does anyone devoted to theory. And his models are neither less artificial nor less abstract than those used by what Dobb calls 'post-Jevonian' economics.[46] What distinguishes them from the latter is the fact that Marx's models refer to a much broader empirical area, one that is 'sociological' from the point of view of today's academic economics.[47]

At any rate, the optimism of idealist epistemology clouds Marx's perception of the fact that theory is inevitably a construct, a perception he sometimes loses altogether. Without entering into the debate as to whether or not what Marx calls 'the falling tendency of the rate of profit' was an empirically justified notion, we can state, in any case, that, methodologically considered, the notion of a 'law of tendency' is an obscure expression of the relation between a necessary connection in the theoretical model and the much greater complicatedness of the reality studied. The notion of a 'tendential law' must be understood as an epistemologically rather uncritical expression – essentialist in the 'material manner of speaking' – of the fact that reality does not behave in exactly the same way as the model (which is not always proof of a model's inadequacy). The Hegelian dialectical idea that the law 'operates' 'when cir-

46 Let the following passage, from a letter to Engels of 9 August 1862 in which Marx refers to theory in the most formal and abstract sense (and actually underlines the term), serve as an example of this: 'All I have to prove *theoretically* is the *possibility* of absolute rent, without infringing the law of value. This is the point round which the *theoretical* controversy has revolved from the time of the physiocrats until the present day' (Marx 1985c, p. 403, original emphasis). The following passage from *Capital*, Volume II, whose context is a discussion of the circulation of surplus value, is perhaps even more suggestive of the theoretical modelling: 'Apart from this class [the capitalists], according to our assumption – the general and exclusive domination of capitalist production – there is no other class at all except the working-class' (Marx 1997, p. 346).

47 Of course, Marx would not have considered them 'sociological'. It is also true, however, that he himself sometimes distinguished between economics without qualification and what he called 'pure economics'. He did not clearly thematise the distinction, but it is operative even in *Capital*. For example, when he cites the famous phrase from Ferguson about the 'nation of Helots' – a formulation, we may note in passing, which had a great influence on Marx – it is to make clear that he is only going to concern himself with the economic effects of the division of labour in a narrow sense. 'It is not the place, here, to go on to show how division of labour seizes upon, not only the economic, but every other sphere of society, and everywhere lays the foundation of that all engrossing system of specialising and sorting men, that development in a man of one single faculty at the expense of all other faculties, which caused A. Ferguson, the master of Adam Smith, to exclaim: "We make a nation of Helots, and have no free citizens"' (Marx 1996, p. 359).

cumstances allow the law to operate',[48] can reasonably be interpreted in two ways: either it means that in order for the conditional statement of a law to be regarded as confirmed in an interesting sense, the antecedent must have been verified (and then it is a matter or a sensible triviality), or rather it claims to say something more, to really talk about the world, and then it is only an archaic description of work with abstract constructs.

All of this can also be said, however, in the form of praise, instead of saying it with the nit-picking pedantry used until now. For example, consider these two passages from Volume III of *Capital*:

> This factor [i.e. a given element of disturbance] does not abolish the general law. But it causes that law to act rather as a tendency, i.e., as a law whose absolute action is checked, retarded, and weakened, by counteracting circumstances.[49]

A statement is confirmed 'as a tendency, like all other economic laws'.[50] Regarding methodological reflections like this, it can be said that they are one step away from the full awareness of work with theoretical models, and that, in any case, they leave unresolved the same problem that arises with any theoretical explanation, namely, whether it is possible to explain by means of the theory in question (or by means of the general theory of which it forms a part, or by means of another theory compatible with them) the operation of 'counteracting circumstances'. Yet what needs to be underscored here is that even on a benevolent view of such expressions of thought as that of a 'tendential law', the most that can be seen in these expressions is a respectable, yet imprecise, philosophy of science, and of course no dialectical 'overcoming' of common methodological concepts.

There are reasons for thinking that the weight of Hegelianism increased, rather than declined, in Marx's mature years. At the very least, some of Marx's most metaphysical and least scientific Hegelian schemas appear precisely in writings from the last period of his life. The following, curiously Hegelian passage from Volume II of *Capital* derives from Manuscript V, which means that it is from 1877:

> Commodity capital, as the direct product of the capitalist process of production, is reminiscent of its origin and is therefore more rational and

48 Marx 1996, p. 522.

49 Marx 1998, p. 233.

50 Marx 1998, p. 173.

> less incomprehensible in form than money capital, in which every trace of this process has vanished, as in general all special use forms of commodities disappear in money.[51]

The idea that wherever there is memory of the origin there is a concept is pure Hegelianism. That consideration has no importance with regard to science.

Also from the final period of Marx's life are the mathematical manuscripts that are now available (without, however, all of the reading excerpts) in two Western European paperback editions.[52] Apart from the fact that they have little importance within Marx's oeuvre,[53] the manuscripts essentially reproduce the anti-analytic thought of the Hegelian and Goethian tradition, as well as the useless metaphors regarding the notion of the differential already familiar from Engels's *Anti-Dühring*. I must say that not all readers of these manuscripts are of the same opinion, and that two very distinguished readers, Mrs. Janovskaia, the manuscripts' editor, and Lucio Lombardo Radice, author of the Introduction to the Italian edition, find in them merits which they do of course possess. The main merits, in my view, are the critique of the notion of infinitesimal and the forging of a notion of variable very close to operationalist criteria. In acknowledging this, I must somewhat correct my article from 1964, 'Engels's Task in *Anti-Dühring*'[54] in which I ventured the conjecture, based on the facts that I had at my disposal at the time, that Marx's mathematical manuscripts were probably not interesting. Yet Marx's rejection of the notion of limit,[55] the traditional algebraic path that he follows and some other matters of detail (such as his laboured understanding of Leibniz) do not allow me, for now, to completely change my old opinion, although I do consider myself obliged to study the subject again. However, it will be another time and not this evening, when we are already sufficiently weighed down with other tasks.

---

51 Marx 1997, p. 54.

52 Marx 1974; 1975g.

53 'The [mathematical] manuscripts represent... primarily Marx's assimilation of auxiliary mathematical science, and lack importance in comparison with the epochal significance of Marx's social theory' (Endemann 1974, p. 8; translation from Sacristán's citation in Spanish [Ed.]).

54 See Chapter 3 below.

55 Jesús Mosterin suggested to me, after the discussion following this lecture, that one would have to determine whether Marx's notes on calculus, and in particular his rejection of the concept of limit, have any affinity with non-standard analysis. I believe that we need to consider Mosterín's observation, but up to now I have not been able to trace this question in the text of the manuscripts.

We have surely reviewed enough aspects of the bad influence of Hegelianism in Marx's philosophy of science (after having considered the good influences) to venture an assessment. It is a favourable assessment, for the obscurity, the logical confusions, the discrepancy between scientific work and the ideological vision of it – all of these bad consequences of the Hegelian dialectic are of much less importance than it would seem, and even more importantly, the bad philosophical or methodological consequences can often be eliminated without any loss to the actual scientific work. An example of this can be found in the Hegelian use of metaphor, so intense in Marx's work. The violent metaphor from Volume I of *Capital*, 'the metamorphosis of commodities', expressed by Marx with the formula C–M–C (commodity-money-commodity), which does not refer, as is obvious, to any physical change in the commodities, is a confusingly Hegelian expression. It is clear that the metamorphosis pertains not to the commodity, but to the value (and I put it this way to stay within Marx's mystical or entomological Hegelian lexicon):

> If we now consider the completed metamorphosis of a commodity, as a whole, it appears in the first place, that it is made up of two opposite and complementary movements, C–M and M–C.[56]

Clearly, it would be much more sensible to say 'movements of value' rather than 'movements of the commodity', since it does not seem absurd to say about the first that it is sometimes linen and other times money, whereas to say that linen is sometimes money and other times linen proves rather inadvisable. Marx's way of speaking involves a vice typical of Hegel (which the latter regarded as a virtue): the insufficient abstraction, the abstraction of that which is confused, the abstraction of various concepts presented as a single concept, lumped into one, an imprecise abstraction which is a technique that comes from the arbitrariness of derivation through 'development', and which makes this derivation a great trick that it is unnecessary to learn. In the example cited, the arbitrariness consists in maintaining that the commodity in question (linen) returns to its seller (the weaver). However, this bad Hegelianising abstraction rhetorically masks a correct abstraction with the concept of value, as is made clear a few pages further on:

> The change of form, C–M–C, by which the circulation of the material products of labour is brought about, requires that a given value in the shape of a commodity shall begin the process, and shall, also in the shape

56 Marx 1996, p. 120.

> of a commodity, end it. The movement of the commodity is therefore a circuit.[57]

And even more explicitly in Volume II: 'Intrinsically both C–M and M–C are mere conversions of given value from one form into another'.[58]

On many other occasions, confused discussions [*desarrollos*] that seem ambitiously 'profound' (we know that this is the characteristic of 'German science') can be reduced to elementary questions of logic. A notable example of this is the long history of the specificity or determination or overdetermination of the dialectical contradiction, a history that has engaged the efforts, to little avail, of people as estimable as Engels himself, Lukács, Gramsci and Althusser. It turns out that in the Hegelian dialectic there is no exact and reproducible canon – no 'learnable knack' – for finding which is the contradictory notion of a given notion, in contrast to what obtains in common logic, in which it is clear that the contradictory of 'Every A is B' holds that 'Some A is not B'. The Hegelian, dialectical contradictory is either specific (Engels), determinate (Gramsci), or overdetermined (Althusser). The same thing occurs with other relations of opposition, which, moreover, Hegel has no interest in clearly distinguishing from a contradiction. Marx quite often adds to a determination the indication of the opposition from which he takes it. For example, he adds to 'commodity-capital' the indication 'as opposed to productive capital'.[59] That way of speaking – typical of the 'determinate', 'specific' or 'overdetermined' opposition of the Hegelian dialectic – implies lack of sufficient formalisation, lack of theory and even lack of definition. (The romantic methodological principle that it is not necessary to define, but only 'determine', is preserved from Hegel to Lukács). The valuable dialectical objective of not losing the flow of being is falsely achieved by renouncing precise concepts, which are inevitably definite.

The procedure is used broadly: the '*avances annuelles*' are such over against and as 'distinguished from the *avances primitives*'; 'circulating' capital is such 'as distinguished from fixed capital'.[60] The constant clarifications suggest that the person speaking is reserving the option of other meanings, of using the concept in another opposition. The criticism of Ricardo's work, with its use of the categories of fixed and circulating capital, is of interest in this regard, for Marx undertakes his analysis precisely with the instrument of this determinate

57 Marx 1996, p. 124.
58 Marx 1997, p. 131.
59 Marx 1997, p. 207.
60 Marx 1997, p. 214.

opposition. Here Marx is explaining why Ricardo neglects the capital invested in labour material:

> From one of these points of view [that of production] the material of labour is classed in the same category with the instruments of labour, *as opposed to* the capital-value laid out in labour power; from the other viewpoint [that of circulation] the part of capital laid out in labour power ranges with that laid out in material of labour, as opposed to that laid out in instruments of labour.
>
> For this reason the part of the capital value laid out in material of labour (raw and auxiliary materials) does not appear on either side in Ricardo. It disappears entirely; for it will not do to class it with fixed capital, because its mode of circulation coincides entirely with that of the part of capital laid out in labour power. And on the other hand it should not be placed alongside circulating capital, because in that event the identification of the antithesis of fixed and circulating capital with that of constant and variable capital, which had been handed down by Adam Smith and is tacitly retained, would abolish itself. Ricardo has too much logical instinct not to feel this, and for this reason that part of capital vanishes entirely from his sight.[61]

This text (one example among many others) is of interest for two reasons. First of all, it illustrates how the methodology of the contrasts that 'are taken' from some process or movement is a nomadic, inexact, pre-theoretical methodology, with only a general philosophical framework that has not been positively realised. Marx makes a virtue of necessity, just as Hegel always does, claiming that he thus captures life. He does not define. He believes that he reconstitutes the concrete of thought better by not analysing the real concrete. He fears that definition will reduce and that division will sever.

At the same time, however, it is also clear in the text that what lies below the apparent confusion of oppositions and determinate or overdeterminate contradictions is a simple and reasonable question *de fundamento divisionis*, which can be approached with all the elementariness of classical logic. Marx is saying simply that, in his opinion, Ricardo, following Smith, confuses two principles of division, namely, that which derives from the division between constant and variable capital, and that which is produced by the division between fixed capital and circulating capital. Incidentally, at times Marx actually expresses himself on these matters using the vocabulary of classical logic.

---

61 Marx 1997, pp. 218–19, emphasis added.

Yet his consciousness of the simplicity of the problematic is unsteady. Three successive pages in Chapter 11 of Volume II of *Capital* – whose context is the criticism of Ricardo mentioned above – comprise such a complete illustration of the suspicions and hesitations of Marx's rough drafts in these logical matters that it is worth reviewing them. Marx begins by observing that confusion of the difference between constant and variable capital with the difference between fixed and circulating capital obscures the 'differentia specifica' (his words) that is of most importance for understanding the capitalist mode of production:

> Once the part of capital invested in labour differs from that invested in instruments of labour only by its period of reproduction and hence its term of circulation … all *differentia specifica* between capital invested in labour power and capital invested in means of production is naturally obliterated.[62]

Here Marx is criticising a confusion in the division that invalidates or blurs the definitions that are based on it: the passage from one principle of division to another. He expresses the same idea a few lines later with a Spinozan and Leibnizian vocabulary:

> [T]here is a confusion of the definition according to which the part of capital invested in labour [power] is variable capital with the definition according to which it is circulating capital, as opposed to fixed capital.[63]

This expression is a perfect parallel to the possible traditional formulation, which would read: there is confusion between principle of division A and principle of division B. The correspondence is reinforced immediately afterwards through the reappearance of the language of the traditional theory of the definition:

> It is evident at the outset that the definition of capital invested in labour power as circulating or fluid capital is a secondary one, obliterating its *differentia specifica* in the process of production.[64]

Two pages later, however, Marx's state of mind and intention are different (and gauging the two things is important for understanding drafts, which is what

62 Marx 1997, p. 225.
63 Marx 1997, p. 226.
64 Ibid.

these texts are). The view that sees the instruments of labour in production as fixed capital (rather than constant capital) is a 'scholastic definition, which leads to contradictions and confusion'[65] (which could be translated thus: it is the product of a superfluous division that leads to contradictions and confusion). This puts him in an anti-scholastic frame of mind that does not like to use terms from medieval logic, which he himself had used two pages earlier. And then, in the end, he begins to speak Hegelese to present his topic, treated in such a tiresome way in the drafts that Engels would publish as Chapters 10 and 11 of Volume II of *Capital*: 'It is not a question here of definitions, which things must be made to fit. We are dealing here with definite functions which must be expressed in definite categories'.[66] The 'specific differences' about which he was still speaking just a few paragraphs earlier now vanish (verbally) and, along with them, classical logic, in the interest of 'dialectical' logic. This is the verbal path (Hegel's arbitrary reading of the first *Critique*) followed by the majority within the Marxist tradition.

It will not be necessary to remind anyone that from a substantive point of view, the pages from Marx that I have cited here as one of the best illustrations of the vacillations and vague remarks that give rise to the 'dialectical method' are shrewd and true. It is true, as Marx says, that the use of a single classification from Smith to Ramsay, the neglect of one of the principles of division seen by Smith, led to the loss of the notions of constant and variable capital. However, this substantive truth does not cancel out the formal inadequacy, which at bottom stems from essentialism, from the tendency to reification characteristic of traditional metaphysics and epistemology: it is the realism of intuition to believe that division severs and definition cuts up not the concepts but the things themselves, and therefore that in order to avoid using force on things we must neither define nor divide concepts.

The key point in assessing all of this is that in every important instance it is possible to translate the Hegelian esoterica into precise reasoning (whether it is true or false is another matter). Moreover, and more importantly, as I have already said, it was the Hegelian dialectic (the confused notion of 'development', among other things) that taught Marx systematicity, and thereby gave him a feeling for theory, enabling him to rise above the mere 'critique' of the Young Hegelians. Without his return to Hegel – in particular the *Logic* – in the 1850s, Marx would have remained stuck with a much poorer scientific programme. In order to document this point, it is enough to consider for a moment the philosophy of science implicit in Marx's works from the 1840s.

65 Marx 1997, p. 227.

66 Marx 1997, pp. 227–8.

In a notebook of extracts from 1844, Marx writes, in connection with MacCulloch, a comment on G. Prévost's praise for the Ricardians, which noted the fact that Ricardo worked with averages. Marx writes:

> What do these *averages* prove? That one abstracts more and more from mankind, that one dismisses more and more real life, and that one considers the abstract movement of material and inhuman property. *Averages* are real offences inflicted upon real, particular individuals.[67]

This critical Marx is still unaware of what constitutes theoretical science. Marx's transition to science implies, among other things, an inversion of his position regarding Ricardo in the passage cited. This is even clearer in the continuation of the passage:

> Prévost praises the Ricardians' discovery that *price* is represented by the costs of production, without being *influenced by supply* and *demand.* First: the good man disregards the fact that the Ricardians only prove this principle by means of calculations of *averages*, that is, by abstraction from reality.[68]

When Marx discovers (aided by Hegel) that there is no science without abstraction and begins to do science, he turns precisely to Ricardo and to average rates.[69]

Marx will overcome the scientific inviability of Young-Hegelian philosophical critique in the 1850s, with the rediscovery of Hegel's system of logic and his subsequent comprehension of the scientific value of classical economics (chiefly Petty, Quesnay, Smith and Ricardo). The effort required of Marx was considerable, since his philosophical training had left him with an ignorance of facts and a dearth of tools, which are the occupational ills of the profession.[70]

---

67 The passage cited, which accompanies extracts from some of Marx's early reading in economics, is not included in the English-language edition of Marx and Engels's *Collected Works*; the original can be found in Marx 1981, p. 480. The translation used here is adapted from Hollander 2008, p. 171, original emphasis [Ed.].

68 Marx 1981, pp. 480–1, original emphasis [my translation from the German (Ed.)].

69 The appeal to Ricardo at that moment explains the fact that Joan Robinson sees Marx's school of theory in Ricardo's work. I have already explained above why I can only partly endorse this view.

70 In the *Grundrisse* and the manuscripts for *Capital*, Marx repeats exercises with fractions *ad nauseam*, and without succeeding in freeing himself from errors in calculation. Everything suggests that he is attempting to give himself the skill that the university had

However, while it proved unfruitful for science, the critical philosophy was, on the other hand, going to be a permanent element of Marx's general vision. 'The critical criticism' helped to provide Marx with a perception of the limitations of a non-sociological economic theory, limitations he would try to overcome with the broad range of the dialectic. In the 1844 extracts on MacCulloch, Marx perceives those limitations of 'pure economics' inadequately, for he regards them as an 'infamy' (as does later vulgar Marxism) instead of the inevitable schematism of abstraction. But the critical motivation will not be lost later, when he ceases his sterile opposition to theory:

> The infamy of economics consists in speculating, after taking for granted the antithetical interests caused by private property, as if interests were not antithetical and property were communal. It can thus be proven that if I consume everything and you produce everything, consumption and production are well-ordered in society.[71]

Criticism, Metaphysics, Science

It has perhaps become clear by now that Marx's transition to science and his definitive reception of Hegelianism in the 1850s occur in parallel. That Marx reached the most theoretical core of his thought thanks in large part to Hegel (as a result, above all, of the intensification of the latter's influence in the 1857 *Grundrisse*) is a good indication of the convolutedness of the heuristic problems that Popper excludes, with an astute caution, from the philosophy of science. Of heuristic problems and their gags, for it was precisely the most anti-scientific element in Marx's training – Hegelianism – that led him to the most scientific part of his work. Until the recovery of Hegel, the other elements of Marx's intellectual outlook [*horizonte*] – the Young Hegelians' critical philosophy, Feuerbach's philosophy and French socialism – prevented him from producing his own conception of science from his study of the classics of political economy, for these elements made the science of economics, with its averages, strike him as an infamy.

The problem of the relationship between metaphysics and science is lurking behind the Hegelian inspiration for Marx's theoretical science. The

---

incapacitated. This sometimes seems pathetic, as when Marx has moments of great satisfaction because he gets the right answer to some elementary calculations and exclaims, as in the *Grundrisse*, 'That is it!' (Marx 1986c, p. 265).

71 Marx 1981, p. 482. [This text, which I have translated from the German, is not included in the English edition of Marx and Engels's *Collected Works* (Ed.)].

metaphysical motivation was fruitful for Marx's science. His methodological mistake – which consists in regarding an attitude (the dialectic) as a method in the formal sense, and in regarding the vision of a goal for knowledge (the 'concrete totality') as scientific theory – is due to the Hegelian version of an ancient aspiration: the desire for scientific knowledge of an individual or concrete thing, in defiance of the classical rule according to which *there is no science of the particular*. In Hegel, that aspiration, also quite central to Leibniz's philosophy, took the form of a putative logic of the individual thing, of the historically concrete, from which one could 'develop' being up to its current concreteness, thereby articulating at one and the same time its history and its structure. This arrogant, pre-critical programme frames the success and failure of Marx's contribution to social science and revolutionary knowledge.

The attempt to rid Marx of his Hegelian heritage in order to view him as a scientist is flimsy. Naturally, all who develop Marx's legacy in their own work can do as they please, and some will do well to practice a scientistic Marxism (or to lose interest in Marx upon realising the importance of the tradition of Hegelian metaphysics in his mature work on the whole), and others will do Marxist metaphysics, as is their right. Yet for anyone who wishes to portray him as he was and not turn him into an infallible super-scientist, Marx was in fact an original metaphysical author of his own positive science; or to put it the other way around, he was a scientist who was also, and this is uncommon, the author of his own metaphysics, of a general explicit vision of reality. This cannot be said of all metaphysicians, nor can it be said of all scientists. Among Marx's precursors, it is Leibniz, not Hegel or Spinoza, who has the greatest affinity with Marx from this point of view.

The critical inspiration was much less fruitful for the birth of Marx's social science. It might even have prevented it from coming into being, as I have sought to show, if Marx's return to Hegel in the 1850s had not facilitated a good reading of the classics of political economy. On the other hand, however, that inspiration is relevant to the fact that Marx can be considered one of the founders of the sociology of knowledge and the sociology of science. I trust that it will not be taken merely as a joke with which to end this long lecture if I say that Marx's naïve phrase from 1844, according to which political economy is an infamy, is the first milestone in the sociology of science. The idea of science as critique (mainly as critique of previous science) facilitated Marx's inauguration of the ideological analysis of scientific creations and also the sociological consideration of science as a force of production.

Regarding the first chapter of Marx's sociology of science, that which concerns itself with the relationship between science and ideology, I believe that the Marxist tradition abounds in debilitating schematisms, whether because, as in some cases, it tends to separate in material reality – and not merely logically – the scientific from the ideological within cultural creations (which normally contain both elements at the same time), or because, in other cases, it practices a universal ideologism, regarding as 'idealist' any recognition of the effective presence of disinterested science in the history of the ideal. One must note that this sociologistic thesis is not Marx's. According to this thesis, Marx is an idealist, for the first conviction of his sociology of science is that true science consists in disinterested knowledge or, as he says in Volume I of *Capital*, knowledge with no other interest than 'disinterested thinking'.[72]

The other great chapter of Marx's sociology of science – his consideration of science as a force of production and of its effects on work and daily life – derives less from the critical philosophy than from Ferguson and the Ricardian socialists.[73] In my opinion, it is the chapter of greatest interest from the standpoint of today's social problems. It is also the area in which a revision of Marx's legacy is most necessary, for the sake of revolutionary Marxism's intellectual needs for the end of the century. In this very series of lectures, Professor Fetscher cited, a few days ago, an eloquent text by Marx that suffices to show

---

72 Marx 1977, p. 269, n. 24. [The Vintage translation of *Capital*, Volume I, is used here because it diverges much less from the original German – '*interesseloses Denken*' (Marx 1962, p. 180, n. 37) – and from Sacristán's Spanish translation than the translation included in Marx and Engels's *Collected Works*. Indeed, Sacristán's point is lost if one uses the latter translation (Ed.).] Many other passages are as telling as this one. For example: 'Political economy can only be turned into a positive science by replacing the conflicting dogmas by the conflicting facts, and by the real antagonisms which form their concealed background' (Letter to Engels, 10 October 1868; Marx 1988c, p. 128). 'Since the reasoning process itself arises from the existing conditions and is itself a *natural process*, really comprehending thinking can always only be the same, and can vary only gradually, in accordance with the maturity of development, hence also the maturity of the organ that does the thinking. Anything else is drivel' (Letter to Kugelmann, 11 July 1868; Marx 1988b, p. 69, original emphasis). Also relevant here are the various passages in which Marx speaks of 'disinterested research'. The *locus classicus* is the Afterword to the second edition of Volume I of *Capital*. Disinterested research is the norm for Marx even in political economy, so long as the class struggle is merely latent. Any class that disposes of the necessary material and intellectual means (leisure and education) and is not threatened by another rising class can do political economy. This implies that not all scientific activity represents class interests. Not even all critical activity (Marx 1996, pp. 13ff).

73 During the discussion following this lecture, Ezequiel Baró and Juan Ramón Capella drew my attention to the fact that this influence is not given sufficient consideration in this exposition. This is, indeed, one of its several defects. On the other hand, the topic of science as a force of production in general could only be dealt with fleetingly under the title of this lecture.

that his thought concerning science contains none of the progressive naïveté reflected in Lenin's famous phrase, according to which communism is Soviet power plus electrification; instead, it is a considerably more cautious and complicated conception. Yet Iring Fetscher could also have cited scores of passages from Marx brimming with an excessive optimism as regards the liberating power of science as a force of production. Marx barely sees, for example, the interdependence between modern science and capitalism, which prevents him from perceiving, in particular, the earliest beginnings of 'big science';[74] and from the 1850s on, he repeatedly lapses into excessively sociological treatments of the relationship between science-technology and the social order.[75] This is not an appropriate time to begin a discussion of the problem, which would do well to start from Chapter 15 of Volume I of *Capital*. I believe that the questions of greatest interest and difficulty for a productive development of Marxism as communist thought lie within this tangle of problems, while the debates on Hegelianism, on the epistemological break, on the two notions of science present in Marx's work, etc. – all of those things which Marxist philosophers dealt with during the sixties and seventies – are questions of secondary importance, whose treatment has often produced bad philology mistaken for an autonomous development of Marx's legacy.

---

74 Thus, in Chapter 24 of *Capital*, Volume I: 'Like the increased exploitation of natural wealth by the mere increase in the tension of labour power, science and technology give capital a power of expansion independent of the given magnitude of the capital actually functioning' (Marx 1996, p. 601).

75 'Communists must demonstrate that technological truths already attained can only become practicable under communist relations' (Letter to Roland Daniels, May 1851; Marx 1982a, p. 368). The letter containing this statement has not been preserved, but this passage survived because Daniels included it in his reply to Marx on 1 June 1851. The fact that the letter precedes the *Grundrisse* by six years is of great interest, since it is in this text that people usually see the beginning of Marx's assimilation of questions of science and technology. (For example, this is how Ernest Mandel sees things).

CHAPTER 2

Karl Marx as a Sociologist of Science

Introduction

By 'sociology of science' we usually understand a derivation from, rather than a part of, the sociology of knowledge, whose primary aim is the sociological study of communities of scientists, even if, as a result of several influences (among which we may include, together with the obvious influence of T.S. Kuhn's work, the period of the Marxist renaissance in the 1960s, and even the speculations of Marxist structuralism), research in this field has gone beyond the framework of the subject matter with which it was established. The academic discipline that we know today as the sociology of science can be regarded as having been established toward the middle of the twentieth century, and mainly within the area of functionalist sociology.[1] But the roots or beginning of the sociology of science in the sociology of knowledge naturally leads one to think of Marx, who is one of the earliest authors in whose work we find an overall view of and general theses about the relationship between knowledge and social reality. Indeed, Marx's work, above all the part written between 1857 (*Outlines of the Critique of Political Economy*, the *Grundrisse*) and 1863 (*Theories of Surplus Value*), offers a systematic conception of that relation, organised around two large questions: the ideological connection between science (mainly social science) and reality; and the efficacy of science (mainly natural science) in the production, reproduction, and transformation of the foundations of society.

These two questions may seem too ambitious from the point of view of the research programmes most common today in the sociology of science, which are frequently limited to the micrological study of the relationships between scientists and groups of scientists through their citations, their interaction at

* First published in 1983. Republished as 'Karl Marx como sociólogo de la ciencia', in *Lecturas de filosofía moderna y contemporánea*, edited by Albert Domingo Curto (Madrid: Editorial Trotta, 1997). Reprinted by permission of the publisher.

1 Merton's *Science, Technology and Society in Seventeenth Century England* (Merton 2002) dates from the year 1938, and his *Social Theory and Social Structure* (Merton 1968), Part Four of which is also a fundamental contribution to the sociology of science, is from 1949. At first, Merton, still close to the sociology of knowledge of German origin, understood his research more broadly than, for example, in his *The Sociology of Science* (Merton 1973). A detailed review of the origins and present state of the sociology of science can be found in Medina 1982.

 | DOI 10.1163/9789004280526_005

congresses and symposia, and so on. If we add to this the fact that Marxian considerations on the sociology of science also often have a philosophical dimension, and almost always a historical dimension, the result is the well-known picture of excess, so to speak, characterising the Marxian approach to any social question. (Excessive from the point of view of the specialised research that is common in the organisation of contemporary academic institutions, yet very plausible as far as the aspiration to knowledge is concerned, as is generally admitted by everyone in their frequent rhetorical laments regarding specialisation). It is possible that, if we follow Merton's systematics literally, we shall have to call many of Marx's contributions to the subject that concerns us 'sociological theory of science', and not 'sociology of science'. But not all of them; far from it. For Merton's idea holds that the sociological theory of science is a special type of epistemology, and this is not the case with Marx's main analyses, which it would be more appropriate to call 'macrosociology of science'.

Moreover, despite the natural absence in Marx's work of microsociological analyses (such as those to which I have alluded) and, to an even more extreme degree, of quantitative studies, and despite the fact that in many cases we could say that Marxian considerations on the sociology of science only offer an initial and speculative or highly abstract consideration of the problem, Marx's basic ideas in this area are nonetheless not so far removed from those guiding contemporary research, and his 'macrosociological' approach cannot be reasonably contrasted with one that is 'microsociological'. Rather, we would have to hope that the development of the latter would concretely substantiate, or correct, or refute, the former. The cultural continuity between Marx's texts that are of interest for the sociology of science and that which is practiced under this name today indicates that both cases share the same elementary assumptions, which do not entirely accord with those of other periods in the history of the knowledge of the educated. Marx would no doubt accept the four values that define the activity of Merton's scientist: universalism, communism, organised scepticism, and disinterestedness. Leaving aside the first two, which are in principle obviously acceptable (although the militarisation of science, with its natural consequence of secrecy, is reducing the second criterion to mere hypocrisy), it will be recalled that organised scepticism – in the radical form of Bacon's exhortation, *De omnibus dubitandum* – was Marx's favourite motto,[2] and that 'disinterested interest' was, in his opinion, the defining value of science, adherence to which led him to write:

---

2 In response to a questionnaire given to him by his daughters, Marx chose Bacon's motto *De omnibus dubitandum*, 'Doubt everything' (Marx 1987c, p. 568).

> But when a man seeks to *accommodate* science to a viewpoint which is derived not from science itself (however erroneous it may be) but from *outside*, from *alien, external interests*, then I call him '*base*' ('*gemein*').[3]

In what follows, Marx's thought on the sociology of science is studied alongside his intellectual development, broadly speaking. This style of exposition is probably less effective than a direct, systematic presentation of the most mature version of Marx's ideas in this regard. I choose it, in spite of its disadvantages, because I think it is interesting to register the continuity of Marx's positions on this subject. In the sociology of science, Marx's work shows a continuous development of thought, without a single rupture, at least from the very early moment – which can be dated back to the completion of his doctoral dissertation in 1841 – in which he ceases to take an interest in speculations of a Hegelian and Young-Hegelian sort as regards the philosophy of science.[4]

The Appearance of a Sociological Point of View on Science in Marx's Writings from the 1840s

A sociological point of view on science appears in Karl Marx's writings from the first years of the 1840s. It was a time of important changes in the life of their author, in his projects (both private and public), and in his ideas. Shortly

3 Marx 1989a, p. 349, original emphasis. On 'disinterested thought' as a feature of scientific behaviour, see Volume I of *Capital*; Marx 1977, p. 269, n. 24; [see Chapter 1, n. 70 (Ed.)].

4 Had Marx not abandoned this sort of speculation, he would have been incapable of practicing modern science, for the Hegelian and Young-Hegelian ideas on science guiding such speculation are inconsistent with modern scientific activity. Thus, for example, in his thesis Marx believed that Epicurus had established atomistics because he had succeeded in objectifying the 'contradiction' between essence and existence in the concept of atom, whereas Democritus was not scientific because he limited himself to formulating hypotheses for assembling experience, that is, he limited himself, according to this conception, to practicing what we would today call science: 'The consideration of the properties of the atoms leads us therefore to the same result as the consideration of the declination [of the atoms], namely, that Epicurus objectifies the contradiction in the concept of the atom between essence and existence. He thus gave us the science of atomistics. In Democritus, on the other hand, there is no realisation of the principle itself. He only maintains the material side and offers hypotheses for the benefit of empirical observation' (Marx 1975a, p. 58). Hegelian science and its Young-Hegelian derivation are incompatible with science with a small 's'. The fact that the influence of Hegel was, in spite of this, beneficial for Marx's scientific work is examined in my 'Marx's Scientific Work and His Notion of Science'; [see Chapter 1 of the present volume (Ed.)].

after finishing his doctorate, Marx renounced an academic career, impossible for him in the political circumstances prevailing in Germany at the time. For a while he devoted himself to journalistic work, as editor-in-chief of the *Rheinische Zeitung* [*Rhenish Gazette*]; when that job also became unfeasible for him, Marx finally emigrated to Paris, with new scientific and political-literary projects. At the same time, he had begun to separate himself from the Young-Hegelian 'critical philosophy', and by the middle of the decade, above all in *The German Ideology* (1845–6), he had reached the outlook customarily called 'historical materialism'. These vicissitudes produced a writer in whom it was already possible to recognise, in different phases of development, almost all the motifs of the classic Marx. However, the changes his thought underwent in the five years that stretch from the writing of his doctoral thesis to that of *The German Ideology* do not exclude the persistence of ideas and intellectual characteristics present in Marx from the time of his early education. Thus, he continues to have the eighteenth-century Enlightenment spirit of his father and father-in-law, in the form of, for example, his dislike of the Historical School;[5] and certain operative ideas also persist in Marx, ideas which he will perhaps cloak in metaphysics over the course of his life, yet which are recognisable as functionally identical beneath all the garb. The idea of the unity of science stands out among them, an idea that is expressed with an occasionally obscure Feuerbachian vocabulary and language in this period, but which is already consistent with that which governs the research in *Capital*.[6] Equally persistent – as in the entire evolution of Marx's thought, even in the periods in which it seems least apparent – is Hegel's influence, above all in the preservation of the idea of development of the concept as the basis and point of departure for the method.[7] On the other hand, ideas that appear for the first time in Marx's writings from these years, and which at first have a more radical formulation than in later years (to the point of misleadingly suggesting to a hasty or tendentious [*intencionada*] reading their ultimate abandonment), characterise the Marxian notion of science throughout the rest of his work and

5 'It is commonly held that the *historical school* is a *reaction* against the *frivolous spirit* of the *eighteenth* century. The currency of this view is in inverse ratio to its truth. In fact, the eighteenth century had only *one* product, the *essential character* of which is frivolity, and this *sole frivolous* product is the *historical school*' (Marx 1975b, p. 203, original emphasis).

6 'History itself is a *real* part of *natural history* – of nature developing into man. Natural science will in time incorporate into itself the science of man, just as the science of man will incorporate into itself natural science: there will be *one* science' (Marx 1975d, pp. 303–4, original emphasis).

7 See, for example, the comment on Say's concept of wealth (Marx 1975d, p. 247).

are of importance for our considerations. Among these ideas, the naturalism of Feuerbachian origin, so vividly expressed in the *1844 Manuscripts*, stands out.[8]

Above all, the rupture with the speculative philosophising of the Young-Hegelian criticism and also probably the journalistic work – about which Marx would later say that it was his first contact with social reality – accompany a budding interest in empirical questions, which places Marx at quite a remove from the philosophy of science professed in his doctoral thesis and predisposes him to a positive view of science itself. Regarding the Young-Hegelian critical philosophy, Marx will write that it signals the culmination in comedy of the 'distort[ion] [of] reality … through philosophy'.[9] Shortly before that, in his criticism of Hegel, he had written about the 'perversion' of empirical questions by the philosopher's metaphysics.[10] In the same year, 1843, and still in a rather Young-Hegelian 'critical' style, Marx had taken leave of Absolute Knowledge, of idealist *Wissenschaft*, at least in intent:

> Hitherto philosophers have had the solution of all riddles lying in their writing-desks, and the stupid, exoteric world had only to open its mouth for the roast pigeons of absolute knowledge to fly into it. Now philosophy has become mundane …[11]

And in *The German Ideology* (1845–6), that intellectual evolution, now complete, issues in classic formulations:

> Where speculation ends, where real life starts, there consequently begins real, positive science, the expounding of the practical activity, of the practical process of development of men. Empty phrases about consciousness end, and real knowledge has to take their place. When the reality is

8 'Nature is man's *inorganic body* – nature, that is, insofar as it is not itself human body. Man *lives* on nature – means that nature is his *body*, with which he must remain in continuous interchange if he is not to die. That man's physical and spiritual life is linked to nature means simply that nature is linked to itself, for man is a part of nature' (Marx 1975d, p. 276, original emphasis).

9 Marx and Engels 1975, p. 7.

10 'Hegel converts all the attributes of the constitutional monarch in the Europe of today into the absolute self-determinations of *the will*. He does not say "the monarch's will is the final decision", but "the will's final decision is the monarch". The first proposition is empirical. The second perverts the empirical fact into a metaphysical axiom' (Marx 1975c, p. 25, original emphasis).

11 Marx 1975f, p. 142.

> described, a self-sufficient philosophy [*die selbständige Philosophie*] loses its medium of existence.[12]

That complete epistemological change, thanks to which Marx perceives positive science in a normal fashion, free of the distorted, Hegelian speculative view of knowledge, makes possible in turn the perception of the social roots and functions of science.

Science as a Social Category

The idea of the historicity of the category of 'science' itself appears very early in Marx's writings: the social position of what a given society calls science has to do with the concrete reality of scientific activity and scientific results. In the 1843 *Contribution to the Critique of Hegel's Philosophy of Law*, that idea is still expressed in a rather obscure manner, in which echoes of the Hegelian Objective Spirit remain; but the notion is stated: modern science is 'the universal science', since it has ceased to be a matter for individuals and has become the work of society as a whole; and that transformation has changed not only the form of science, but its content too.[13]

One year later, in the *Paris Manuscripts*, during Marx's first period of intensive study of political-economic questions, that thought took concrete form in the precise idea of science as a form of production (just like the other 'objectifications' of culture): 'Religion, family, state, law, morality, science, art, etc., are only *particular* modes of production, and fall under its general law'.[14]

Science as a Force of Production

The dedication to the study of capitalist economics and society, Marx's primary intellectual objective since the beginning of the 1840s and above all since his first stay in Paris (1843–5), narrowed the scope of his attention to questions pertaining to the sociology of science (always within the context, as is characteristic of Marx, of considerations that were also epistemological and philosophical), virtually limiting it to the science of the bourgeois era of the eighteenth and nineteenth centuries. No doubt, it is possible to understand

12 Marx and Engels 1976a, p. 37.

13 Marx 1975c, p. 64.

14 Marx 1975d, p. 297, original emphasis.

many of Marx's ideas in this regard in a broader sense, as referring to all known science; however, his theses and analyses appear far more concrete and display far greater adherence to the facts if they are understood as basically referring to the science of the bourgeois epoch. So, for example, in the *Paris*, or *1844*, *Manuscripts*, we read propositions that are apparently 'categorial', as it were; that is, propositions that apparently refer to features of all science, of the science of any culture. Yet even the propositions of this sort contain a certain historical precision, and although the words employed lend themselves to a universal use, it nonetheless remains clear that they connote capitalist culture. For example, '*industry*', we read, 'is the *actual*, historical relationship of nature, and therefore of natural science, to man'.[15] Admittedly, in this context 'industry' can be correctly construed as including prehistoric European lithic industries and the basketweaving industry of Amerindian prehistory. However, the thesis clearly has a privileged context, which is European capitalism. That is why the paragraph speaks of 'the natural sciences', and why all of the illustrations of this philosophical and sociological idea are situated within the modern European era. Marx thus states that mechanics is one of the conditions of large-scale industry, the 'third period' of private property since the Middle Ages,[16] and when he alludes to the inverse relation of industry to natural science, he does so within an unmistakably modern framework:

> Feuerbach speaks in particular of the perception of natural science; he mentions secrets which are disclosed only to the eye of the physicist and chemist; but where would natural science be without industry and commerce?[17]

As a result of considerations such as this one, in *The German Ideology* Marx will formulate one of his main notions regarding the sociology of science, namely, the subsumption of natural science under capital in modern culture. No matter how many useful suggestions – as documented by his reading extracts – Marx may have found in the writings of Babbage, Ferguson, Tooke, Ure, Thompson, Hodgskin, Whately, Senior, etc., for arriving at this concept, the coherence [*integridad*] of this view and its conceptual precision are all his own: 'Large-scale industry … made natural science subservient to capital'.[18]

15 Marx 1975d, p. 303, original emphasis.
16 Marx and Engels 1976a, p. 72.
17 Marx and Engels 1976a, p. 40.
18 Marx and Engels 1976a, p. 73.

Within the framework of the view of science as a force of production it is natural to look within science for specific signs of processes that affect all other forces of production and labour as a whole. In this way Marx reaches observations of a narrowly sociological nature in connection with modern scientific activity, as, for example, when he proposes to study the division of labour's influence on science,[19] or when he takes notice of the fact that modern research is organised in teams,[20] or when he notes the wage-labourer status of the modern scientist.[21]

Science in 'The Bad Side of the Movement'

The oddest proposition of the young Marx's 'macrosociology' of science, a thesis derived directly from the conception of science as a force of production, is an idea that is going to precisely define, for the rest of his work and up until his final writings, the place of science in his social theory. The formulation of the thesis is made possible because in these years Marx had already built the essential part of his dynamic or dialectical model, his conception of social change. This is particularly evident in *The Poverty of Philosophy* from 1847, although the formulation in *The Communist Manifesto*, from the end of the same year, is doubtless more powerful, having much greater rhetorical force. Yet the exposition contained in *The Poverty of Philosophy* presents nuances of particular interest for our topic when the criticism of Proudhon's doctrine – which Marx regards as a rhetorical, pseudo-dialectical embellishment of petty-bourgeois common sense, eager to preserve 'the good side' and dispense with 'the bad side' of social 'contradictoriness' – obliges Marx to formulate concisely and on a fairly abstract level his own conception of the dialectical dynamism of change. For Marx, the dialectic of Hegelian origin is an undisputed good, even in this period, that of his most pronounced anti-Hegelianism. The Alpha and Omega of the Hegelian dialectic, however, is the productive function of negativity; and negativity, in the case of history, is 'the bad side of the social movement', admits Marx, without distancing himself on this score from the anthropocentric, evaluative and metaphorical thinking characteristic of the Hegelian dialectic, or from its naïve domestication by Proudhon. It is not possible, as Proudhon wishes, to seek the solution to social problems by means of an attempt to suppress or mitigate 'the bad side' of the existing reality, for that

19 Marx and Engels 1976a, p. 92.

20 Marx and Engels 1976a, p. 394.

21 Marx and Engels 1976b, p. 487.

bad side, and not the subjective, reformist desire of a well-intentioned individual, is precisely what makes change possible:

> It is the bad side that produces the movement which makes history, by providing a struggle. If, during the epoch of the domination of feudalism, the economists, enthusiastic over the knightly virtues, the beautiful harmony between rights and duties, the patriarchal life of the towns, the prosperous condition of domestic industry in the countryside, the development of industry organised into corporations, guilds and fraternities, in short, everything that constitutes the good side of feudalism, had set themselves the problem of eliminating everything that cast a shadow on this picture – serfdom, privileges, anarchy – what would have happened? All the elements which called forth the struggle would have been destroyed, and the development of the bourgeoisie nipped in the bud. One would have set oneself the absurd problem of eliminating history.[22]

Enriched by an analysis that makes it – already in the period of *The Communist Manifesto* – something much more vivid and realistic than a simple 'application' of the Hegelian dialectic, that dynamic schema will be preserved over the course of Marx's thought. Within its framework, science occupies a very prominent position as a force of production in the capitalist mode of production. And it occupies this position precisely on the bad side of the movement, since it is a force stolen from the power of the immediate producers, that is, to use Marx's words, it is 'alienated' or 'estranged': the natural sciences have developed with enormous energy and have appropriated more and more material. Above all:

> [science] has invaded and transformed human life ... *practically* through the medium of industry; and has prepared human emancipation, although its immediate effect had to be the furthering of the dehumanisation of man.[23]

It was an effect that was to be expected from a force of production that has become 'the basis of actual human life', yet 'in an estranged form'.[24]

22 Marx 1976, pp. 174–5.
23 Marx 1975d, p. 303, original emphasis.
24 Ibid.

The Critique of Ideology in Social Science

In the young Marx, there is not a single consideration regarding natural science in which the critique of ideology plays an important role. I believe that it can be said that the same thing occurs in the late Marx, for his observations on the relationship between English capitalist society, with its ideology, and Darwin's work do not, I think, constitute a charge of ideology against the latter, a charge which Marx did indeed make against the Social Darwinists.[25] By contrast, analyses of and observations on the ideological substance of a great deal of social-scientific output abound. It is not merely a matter of opinions about specific authors – the interpretation of Ricardo as a crude representative of the industrial bourgeoisie,[26] or of Proudhon as a representative of the petty bourgeoisie[27] – but also and primarily his insistence on the classist nature or connotation of the origin of certain research. So, for example, English political economy is 'the most definite expression of the English view of pauperism – we are speaking always of the view of the English bourgeoisie and government'.[28] The critical-ideological consideration of political economy elicited from Marx many brilliant formulations and sometimes magnificent explosions of indignation, like his description of what he calls 'the infamy of economics',[29] that is to say, the disappearance of concrete misery under statistics and averages. However, such passages as these are not the best part of Marx from the point of view of the philosophy and sociology of science, not even for these years. Marx's complete conception regarding those problems is richer. That he describes as 'cynicism' a certain feature of Ricardo's work, or even 'political economy' as a whole, and that he expresses himself so forcefully with regard to ideological elements does not mean that he reduces the social science of bourgeois culture to those ideological elements, let alone to apologetic intentions. The English bourgeoisie's understanding of pauperism did not just have truth content; it was even epistemologically correct, a science, 'the scientific

25 A letter from Marx to Laura and Paul Lafargue of 15 February 1869: 'Darwin was led by the struggle for life in English society – the competition of all with all, *bellum omnium contra omnes* – to discover competition to [...] as the ruling law of "bestial" and vegetative life. The Darwinism, conversely, considers this a conclusive reason for human society never to emancipate itself from its bestiality' (Marx 1988d, p. 217).

26 Marx 1976, p. 121.

27 Marx 1976, p. 178; Letter to Pavel Vasilyevich Annenkov, 28 December 1846; Marx 1982b, p. 105.

28 Marx 1975e, p. 192.

29 Marx 1981, p. 482. [This passage, which I have translated from the German, is not included in the English edition of Marx and Engels's *Collected Works* (Ed.)].

reflection of English economic conditions'.[30] And the 'cynicism' of not only Ricardo but of 'political economy' as a whole is actually a function of the consistent, true development of that science:

> There is not merely a relative growth in the *cynicism* of political economy from Smith through Say to Ricardo, Mill, etc., inasmuch as the implications of *industry* appear more developed and more contradictory in the eyes of the last-named; these later economists also advance in a positive sense constantly and consciously further than their predecessors in their estrangement from man. They do so, however, *only* because their science develops more consistently and truthfully.[31]

Karel Kosík identifies the 1857 Introduction to *A Contribution to the Critique of Political Economy*[32] as the point in Marx's works at which he lays down the distinction between the social origin of a product (in this case, Greek art) and its validity or enduring value [*vigencia*].[33] The conception that we have just studied, according to which the birth of English political economy was linked to a class (of which its best authors, notably Ricardo, are an expression), without ceasing to be science, a product without any interest other than that of disinterested thought, allows us to substitute the early 1840s for the date proposed by Kosík.

The Articulation of Marx's Sociology of Science in the Writings from 1857–9

Karl Marx's ideas on questions pertaining to the sociology of science were developed to the point of constituting a systematic conception during the period in which he reaped the results of his decision to begin his studies and reflections again 'from the beginning', that is to say, in the second half of the 1850s. In expressing himself in these terms, Marx was referring precisely to his economic studies, but it was a new beginning in every sphere, including philosophy: it was in these years that he recovered Hegel, from a maturity that is not yet 'formal' – the crystallisation of Marx's thought from this period will appear in a book, *A Contribution to the Critique of Political Economy*, which

30 Marx 1975e, p. 192.

31 Marx 1975d, p. 291, original emphasis.

32 That is, the Introduction to the *Grundrisse* [Ed.].

33 Kosík 1976, pp. 77–8.

despite its importance will ultimately remain, within the whole of his corpus, a publication at the wrong moment, its results being restated anew in the first pages of *Capital* – but which had already taken shape in a research programme and in the core of a theory.

The main document from this period, the *Outlines of the Critique of Political Economy*, the *Grundrisse* from 1857–8, is a fascinating text precisely on account of its unripeness, that freedom of composition characteristic of a manuscript which the author must have known, very early on, to be unpublishable as a book and destined to remain a draft. In the 1857–8 manuscript, a vital lack of intellectual inhibition, which not infrequently culminates in openly speculative tirades, with abundant, undisguised value judgements, forms the backdrop for precise analyses and tensely argued syntheses, which present the essential elements of the Marxian macrodynamic model. And often, especially in the nodal points of the exposition, the manuscript states matters with great power, sometimes with as much force as we find in *The Communist Manifesto*.

The Philosophy of History Framework: Prediction and Politics

The *Grundrisse* again uses a Hegelian vocabulary in the philosophy of knowledge: the 'dialectical' aim of capturing reality in its 'organic totality' dominates the entire manuscript, and the economists' intellectual coarseness and failure to understand social events are attributed to the fact that they haphazardly assemble, or in more Hegelian language, bring 'into a merely speculative connection',[34] elements forming an 'organic whole'. No less Hegelian-sounding are certain extreme abstractions common in the manuscript, especially the ones that can be said to comprise a philosophy of history centred on the triadic schema that summarises the process of the individual's disalienation:

> Relationships of personal dependence (which originally arise quite spontaneously) are the first forms of society, in which human productivity develops only to a limited extent and at isolated points. Personal independence based upon dependence *mediated by things* is the second great form, and only in it is a system of general social exchange of matter, a system of universal relations, universal requirements and universal capacities, formed. Free individuality, based on the universal development of the individuals and the subordination of their communal, social

34 Marx 1986b, p. 26.

> productivity, which is their social possession [*Vermögen*], is the third stage. The second stage creates the conditions for the third.[35]

The high level of abstraction, so high that it is actually speculative (both in the Hegelian sense and in the common sense of 'speculation'), in addition to the statement of the thesis in an absolute fashion, without any historical or geographical relativisation, are typical of the Hegelian legacy in the 1857–58 manuscript. But suggestions of a much less speculative nature may also have come from Marx's re-reading of Hegel in the second half of the 1850s. For example, the first editors of the *Grundrisse* rightly used a citation from Hegel to annotate the passage in which Marx says that machines are '*organs of the human mind which are created by the human hand*, the objectified power of knowledge'.[36]

Although the late Marx will end up abandoning a philosophy of history that is of Hegelian inspiration and governed by a Hegelian method, his adoption of this perspective in the 1850s, and in general his new immersion in Hegel's work lend Marx's thought from this period an intellectual impetus that undoubtedly helped to prevent him from definitively abandoning his theoretical project in what were particularly adverse circumstances. This philosophical-historical picture, which is highly abstract and speculative, is, at any rate, merely the formal-dialectical formulation of a rather more concrete idea (which is rich in empirical historical material), of an analysis of the same thing, and of a more positive, less speculative theorisation. Yet it is also nourished by both implicit and explicit value judgements. All of these components appear in the *Grundrisse* in expositions whose main point seems to be to provide the basis for revolutionary political action, and in which we can distinguish a quasi-predictive aspect, based on a particular vision of historical development, and another patently evaluative aspect, reflected in the application of descriptions like 'better' or 'preferable' to processes and situations. In the section on 'Money as a Social Relation' in the *Grundrisse*'s 'Chapter on Money', there is a magnificent verbal formulation of this complex of thought. Marx has just questioned the Proudhonist labour certificates, arguing that such a solution cannot work if commodity exchange continues to obtain. The triadic formulation that I have just mentioned appears in this context. After this, Marx notes how, within the framework for creating the conditions of the third stage of individuality, immediate personal relations characteristic of:

35 Marx 1986c, p. 95, original emphasis.

36 Marx 1987a, p. 92, original emphasis.

> patriarchal conditions and those of antiquity (likewise feudal ones) therefore decline with the development of trade, luxury, *money, exchange value,* in the same measure in which modern society grows with them step by step.[37]

In this society, individuals find themselves placed in:

> an *objective* relationship *independent* of them. In the *world market* the *connection of the individual* with all others, but at the same time the *independence of this connection from the individuals,* has itself developed . . .[38]

Suddenly, Marx interrupts his analysis of bourgeois society and inserts a very interesting parenthesis in which he gives greater historical positivity to his schema, at the same time as he introduces certain assessments that suggest its politicisation. Lukács appropriately cited the last paragraph of this page in his polemic against irrationalism, and it is worth considering this passage in more detail, for it summarises many other passages but in a more robust language. 'It has been said, and may be said', the parenthesis begins, 'that the beauty and greatness lies precisely in this spontaneously evolved connection' typical of capitalist culture, typical of the second stage of individuality, 'in this material and spiritual exchange, which is independent of the knowledge and wishes of individuals and presupposes their mutual independence and indifference'.[39] At this point Marx introduces a value judgement which, given the context, can only be described as political, namely, that this inter-individual connection within capitalism, whether purely material-objective or forged through things [*sachliche*], 'is to be preferred to the lack of any connection or to a purely local connection based on primitive blood ties, nature, and relationships of lordship and bondage'.[40] This enlightened *preference* for capitalism as compared with the absence of society or ancient societies is supplemented with a dose of Hegelianism, though the kind that is closest to good common sense: an appearance of the concept that history advances along its bad side, as Marx had stated in *The Poverty of Philosophy*. In this case, it is only through capitalism's creation of certain social relations and conditions which individuals will be able to appropriate later on. It is important, however, not to confuse capitalism's spontaneity with an individual's naturalness, with natural

37 Marx 1986c, p. 95, original emphasis.
38 Marx 1986c, p. 98, original emphasis.
39 Ibid.
40 Ibid.

individuality, in the manner of bourgeois political economy. The purely material or 'thing-based' connection between individuals in capitalism 'is a product of history', not something natural; 'it is the connection, the spontaneously evolved one, of individuals within certain narrow relationships of production',[41] precisely those of capitalism. The same historicity is (or will be) characteristic of the 'third stage' of individuality, of universally developed individuals, whose social relations are subject to their own communal control. The preparation of these relations among individuals in an earlier stage – without which every attempt to overcome this stage would be 'quixotic'[42] – presupposes production on the basis of exchange values, which causes on the one hand (on the 'bad' side), the alienation or estrangement of the individual with regard to himself and others, but on the other (on the 'good' side), the generalisation and all-sidedness of individual relations and capacities. Before studying the way in which Marx filled out this schema – which is at once speculative, theoretical and political – with historical, social and economic positivity, it is worth giving in to the temptation to cite the parenthesis's beautiful final paragraph:

> During earlier stages of development, the single individual seems more fully developed because he has not yet worked out the fullness of his relations and has not yet set them over against himself as independent social powers and relations. It is as ridiculous to long for a return to that original fullness as it is to believe that the present complete emptiness must be permanent. The bourgeois view has never been more than the opposite of that Romantic view, and so the Romantic view will accompany it as a justified opposite till its blessed end.[43]

Building the Theory

As is well known, the general idea considered here is concretised in Marx's later work, and in part in the *Grundrisse* of 1857–8 itself, and consists in a macrodynamic model whose core is a certain mechanism which, if we are to be as faithful as possible to Marx's thought and vocabulary, we would have to call 'grounding' [*fundamentador*] or 'enabling' [*posibilitador*], and not specifically causal:

41 Marx 1986c, p. 99.
42 Marx 1986c, p. 97.
43 Marx 1986c, p. 99.

> [T]he tendentially and potentially universal development of the productive forces – of wealth in general – as basis, likewise the universality of intercourse, hence also the world market as basis. The basis as the possibility of the universal development of the individuals . . .[44]

It is a universal development which is at one and the same time the possibility of the later overcoming of the initial basis, etc.[45] It cannot be a question of reviewing, on the present occasion, the whole of Marx's thought, since what we want to examine is only that part of his thought relevant to a sociology of science. On the other hand, however, it is impossible to study this without bearing in mind the theoretical core of Marx's work. This is why we inevitably had to begin by reviewing it, and also why we must inevitably add a few points of clarification.

The thesis of the basic contradiction between the development of the forces of production and the existing relations of production is presented in the 1857–8 *Grundrisse* by means of formulations that underscore its technical aspect: in keeping with the point of view characteristic of this manuscript, which combines a certain Enlightenment optimism (reinforced by an increasingly detailed study of advances in technology during the eighteenth and nineteenth centuries) with the Hegelian faith in the efficacy of the internal logicalness of real processes, those formulations appear at a level that might well seem purely technical, were it not for the fact that, as we shall see, the keystone of the solution to the basic contradiction, the *punctum saltans* of emancipation, is the very opposite of a technical fact: it is the transformation of the individual, his or her conversion, as it were: 'By striving to reduce labour time to a minimum, while, on the other hand, positing labour time as the sole measure and source of wealth, capital itself is a contradiction-in-process'.[46]

This technical-structural consideration is the *Grundrisse*'s most general statement of the basic contradiction between the forces of production and the relations of production. Naturally, the *Grundrisse* studies the immediate resolution (the capitalist resolution) of that contradiction, the transformation of what it still calls 'superfluous labour' into necessary labour – and in the analyses in question the manuscript presents surprising anticipations of dynamic aspects of capitalist culture which did not become pervasive until much later – as well as the revolutionary resolution of that contradiction, after the latter has

---

44 Marx 1986c, p. 465. [The Greek equivalent of 'potentially' is used in the original. The editors of Marx and Engels's *Collected Works* have added 'potentially' in a footnote (Ed.)].

45 Marx 1986c, pp. 465–6.

46 Marx 1987a, p. 91.

been magnified by means of the many partial solutions within the system. The reduction of labour time characteristic of capitalism is due to the following fact: to the extent that industry develops, the creation of wealth depends less on the labour time applied than on the power of the agents placed in motion during work time, whose efficacy likewise does not depend on the labour time that it takes to produce them, 'but depends, rather, upon the general level of development of science and the progress of technology, or on the application of science to production'.[47] This reflection illustrates a peculiarity present in Marx's thought from the *Grundrisse* until the end of his work: on the one hand, science (technology, the interpretation of which as applied science – as modern technology, and certainly not as something opposed to science – is clear in the paragraph cited)[48] is the main agent responsible for labour's new productivity; on the other hand, however, science is viewed as standing outside the system of labour: its production, the production of science, seems to be based on the scientist's almost infinite productivity, and the efficacy of science will not depend on the labour time needed to produce it. This idea, deeply rooted in Marx, suggests that neither his statement that science has been subsumed under capital and thus turned into a direct productive force, nor his astute perception of the fact that modern science requires teamwork, and so on, were sufficient for him to 'prophesy' the organisation of capitalist or pseudo-socialist big science as merely one more branch of production, with the corresponding criteria of profitability in the allocation of resources. Marx's acute and anticipatory observations concerning the organisation of scientific work within mature capitalism (within the model of it that he himself builds) appear alongside features that pertain to a conception of science characteristic

47 Marx 1987a, p. 90.

48 This makes the interpretation of Marx's thought as a culmination of Western humanity's technical 'fate' [*Geschick*] in relation to Being irrelevant, at the very least, for understanding his intellectual intentions. That Heideggerian vision is the basis of Kostas Axelos's *Alienation, Praxis, and Technē in the Thought of Karl Marx* (Axelos 1976). None of this will probably matter very much to the Heideggerian interpreter of Being, who can continue to think that Marx was unaware of the fate which that sublime authority was sending him. Yet even Axelos's version of what Marx said, leaving aside the mysterious question of who inspired it, is quite implausible: for Axelos, 'technique, the secret of the modern era under various forms, also operates in Marx's work, and the objective of his effort is simply a dealienated and total deployment of the power of technique' (1976, p. 20). The least that one can say in countering this is that not even in the Marx of 1857–8, the Marx most awestruck, shall we say, by the possibilities of technology [i.e. 'technique' (Ed.)], do we by any means read that the task of socialism is to liberate technology, but rather that technology contributes to the task of making socialism possible.

of the age of the great solitary pioneers, the productivity of whose work was, admittedly, enormous, even when calculated in accordance with modern criteria of measurement. Still, for both the abiding revolutionary effects of nineteenth-century technology and the daily revolutions wrought by twentieth-century technology, Marx's lapidary statement in the *Grundrisse*, contained in his analysis of the basic contradiction, remains valid:

> The *theft of alien labour time, which is the basis of present wealth*, appears to be a miserable foundation compared to this newly developed one, the foundation created by large-scale industry itself.[49]

The technical basis of the basic contradiction is the transformation of labour within large-scale industry. Labour gradually ceases to be included in the production process and 'man relates himself to that process as its overseer and regulator'.[50] This brings about an important change for the worker; the conception of this change, here much more 'basic' in the Marxian sense than in earlier writings, positively articulates and brings to fruition the far more speculative vision of 'species being' and the 'disalienated' individual from the 1840s:

> No longer does the worker interpose a modified natural object as an intermediate element between the object and himself; now he interposes the natural process, which he transforms into an industrial one, as an intermediary between himself and inorganic nature, which he makes himself master of. He stands beside the production process, rather than being its main agent.[51]

The same idea is expressed a year later, in the *Contribution to the Critique of Political Economy*, with the distinction between 'simple labour' and labour with a scientific basis.[52] Yet the formulation there does not have the anticipatory, almost visionary force of the texts in the 1857–8 *Grundrisse*.

The transformation of 'society's general science, knowledge', as scientific productive technology, into an '*immediate productive force*' has an indicator, which is 'the development of fixed capital'.[53] And that transformation has as its *consequence* the fact that the *conditions* of the social process fall

49 Marx 1987a, p. 91, original emphasis.
50 Ibid.
51 Ibid.
52 Marx 1987b, pp. 272–3.
53 Marx 1987a, p. 92, original emphasis.

under the control of the general intellect and are 'remoulded according to it'.[54] Formulations with this almost scientistic tone, produced under the umbrella of Enlightenment discourse, are not uncommon in the *Grundrisse*. In these formulations Marx ignores the revolutionary moment, which is elsewhere presented as a condition of that passage whereby the social process comes under the general intellect.

On the other hand, following the transformation of labour by large-scale industry, the product ceases to be a product of direct individual labour, and 'the *combination* of social activity'[55] becomes the real producer. In this way, while the law of value (labour), a basic foundation of the capitalist mode of production, ceases to operate, the other basic foundation, the market – the realisation of the human species' general labour solely through the market – is also destroyed:

> In immediate exchange, the isolated immediate labour appears as realised in a particular product or part of a product, and its communal social character – its character as the objectification of general labour, and satisfaction of general need – is only posited by exchange. By contrast, in the production process of large-scale industry, we see, on the other hand, that the productive power of the means of labour developed to an automatic process presupposes the subjection of the natural forces to the social intelligence, *and, on the other hand, that the labour of the individual in its immediate existence is posited as superseded individual, i.e., as social, labour. Thus the other basis of this mode of production is abolished.*[56]

The socio-economic result of these processes is capital's tendency to constantly create free time and to transform it into surplus labour time. On the basis of this tendency, the *Grundrisse* introduces the Marxian schema of crises of overproduction, which occur when capital promotes that tendency 'too well'. In this case, it is impossible to employ [*realizar*] the value produced and reproduced, and even necessary labour is interrupted:

> The more this contradiction develops, the more obvious it becomes that the growth of the productive forces can no longer be tied to the appropriation of alien surplus labour, and that the working masses must, rather, themselves appropriate their surplus labour.[57]

---

54 Ibid.

55 Marx 1987a, p. 95, original emphasis.

56 Ibid., original emphasis.

57 Marx 1987a, p. 94.

This entire process and its resolution proceeded along the 'bad side' of the socio-historical movement: it is capital 'which has subjected historical progress to the service of wealth',[58] and consequently the creation of non-labour time appears as free time for only some individuals. Indeed:

> what capital adds is that it increases the surplus labour time of the masses by all the means of art and science, because its wealth consists directly in its appropriation of surplus labour time; for its *direct aim is value*, not use value.[59]

That the basic contradiction advances along 'the bad side' is what determines the revolutionary nature of its resolution, according to the Hegelian conception that Marx professes on a philosophical level. Nonetheless, the treatment of these questions in the *Grundrisse* often unfolds on a more typical level, which underscores the technical-structural aspect of the process and, at the same time, that of the evolution of the individuals' situation and the evolution of the individuals themselves. In the section subtitled 'Contradiction Between the Foundation of Bourgeois Production (Value as Measure) and Its Development', we find a synthetic formulation of this conception that may serve to illustrate this point, and also to complete this inevitable review of the thesis regarding capitalism's basic contradiction, as presented in the 1857–8 manuscript:

> As soon as labour in its immediate form has ceased to be the great source of wealth, labour time ceases and must cease to be its measure, and therefore exchange value [must cease to be the measure] of use value. The *surplus labour of the masses* has ceased to be the condition for the development of general wealth, just as the *non-labour of a few* has ceased to be the condition for the development of the general powers of the human mind. As a result, production based upon exchange value collapses, and the immediate material production process itself is stripped of its form of indigence and antagonism. Free development of individualities, and hence not the reduction of necessary labour time in order to posit surplus labour, but in general the reduction of the necessary labour of society to a minimum, to which then corresponds the artistic, scientific, etc., development of individuals, made possible by the time thus set free and the means produced for all of them.[60]

58 Marx 1987a, p. 509.

59 Marx 1987a, pp. 93–4, original emphasis.

60 Marx 1987a, p. 91, original emphasis.

The Social Function of Science

The importance of the role of science in the conception presented in the *Grundrisse*, which I have just summarised, is striking, and not merely because science explicitly occupies a prominent position in the last passages cited, so prominent that Marx proposes that it be used as the privileged example of this theory.[61] The decisive point is that science is a force of production with a leading role in producing change, along with labour power. Modern science alone would have sufficed to break up ancient societies, Marx believes, if it had been able to exist in isolation from the other forces of production. That is impossible, however, for science that has already been produced, that is to say, scientific results, shape the other forces of production, to the point at which science can also be regarded as a form of all other productive forces. As both producer and product of wealth, science is ideal, and not merely practical, wealth, and is consequently also subject to the laws governing the ideal. The 1857–8 manuscript expresses this ensemble of thoughts in condensed form:

> The *development of science alone*, i.e. of the most solid form of wealth, both product and producer of wealth, was sufficient to dissolve this [pre-capitalist] community. But the *development of science*, this notional and at the same time practical form of wealth, is only one aspect, one form, in which the *development of human productive powers*, i.e. of wealth, appears.[62]

Modern science, or science in the capitalist age – which is what we are dealing with, since we have mentioned its capacity to break up the old society – possesses an obvious efficacy when it comes to bringing the basic contradiction into being: it is the force of production most directly responsible for overcoming labour time as the main factor in the creation of real wealth, thanks to the process of automating production, which Marx examines with such prescience.[63]

All of this proves quite obvious as a direct consequence of Marx's basic model for the social idea of science, and it will all be preserved with a small amount of

61 At the end of the passage cited, in which Marx makes a parenthetical remark about the 'ridiculous' nostalgia for the fullness of the past and the 'ridiculous' attachment to the emptiness of the present capitalist society, he adds: 'Here the relationship of the individual to science can be taken as an example' (Marx 1986c, p. 99).

62 Marx 1986c, p. 464, original emphasis.

63 Marx 1987a, p. 95.

retouching, some of which is important, in the major Marxian works from the 1860s, 1870s and throughout Marx's final years. A more specific and less widely noted idea is Marx's notion, in the *Grundrisse* and *Contribution*, of the role of science in the constitution of disalienated labour, which is the basis for the possibility of the disalienated individual and the emancipated society. Marx acknowledges, along with Adam Smith, that labour always appears, in the forms of labour known up to now (slave, serf and wage labour), as something repulsive, and non-labour as liberty and happiness. Yet this is due to the fact that in its historical forms labour has been external, coerced labour, since the 'subjective and objective conditions' necessary for labour to be attractive – the individual's self-realisation – have yet to be created, while on the other hand, labour has already lost the features that lent such a quality to 'pastoral labour'. When these conditions do exist, however, labour will not be purely a game, as Fourier thought. Truly free and self-realising labour requires a very serious and intense effort; Marx mentions the work of composing music as an example of such labour. A central thesis of the *Grundrisse* holds that labour that is free, serious, and intense is also possible in material production, provided that it satisfies two conditions: first, 'its social character is posited'; and second:

> it is of a scientific character and simultaneously general [in its application], and not the exertion of the worker as a natural force drilled in a particular way, but as a subject, which appears in the production process not in a merely natural, spontaneous form, but as an activity controlling all natural forces.[64]

In order for labour to be 'socially posited', such that the workers' sociability as individuals is not produced blindly and solely through the market, and in order for the disalienated social individual to be able to realise him- or herself, it is necessary that labour be 'scientific' (as we likewise read in the *Contribution*),[65] yet based on a disalienated scientificity, that is, one befitting a science that does not entail, alongside the leisure of a few (the wise), the alienation of the working masses with regard to knowledge.[66] A disalienated science is possible, as is a disalienated and social worker, for as the masses' surplus labour has ceased

64 Marx 1986c, p. 530.

65 Marx 1987b, pp. 272–3.

66 'The barrier to *capital* is the fact that this entire development proceeds in a contradictory way, and that the elaboration of the productive forces, of general wealth, etc., knowledge, etc., takes place in such a way that the working individual *alienates* himself …' (Marx 1986c, p. 465, original emphasis).

to be the condition for the development of general wealth, 'the *non-labour of a few* has ceased to be the condition for the development of the general powers of the human mind'.[67] The possibility of the disalienation of science, and at the same time that of the individual worker and even the old do-nothing, consists in this development. In this way, the 'subjective conditions' of free, self-realising labour are satisfied, along with the objective conditions centred on the collapse of 'production based upon exchange value'.[68] In short, the 'development of individuals' is made possible, because the aim of reducing necessary labour time is no longer the creation of surplus labour, but is instead the promotion of 'the artistic, scientific, etc., development of individuals, made possible by the time thus set free and the means produced for all of them'.[69]

The disalienation of science – joined to but distinct from technology, in accordance with the social position of modern science – is part of the cornerstone of the new way of producing and constituting wealth. The disalienated social individual who shapes him- or herself on the basis of that possibility is a more positive, less speculative (at least conceptually) vision of the generic individual of the *1844 Manuscripts*:

> Once this transformation has taken place, it is neither the immediate labour performed by man himself, nor the time for which he works, but the appropriation of his own general productive power, *his comprehension of Nature* and domination of it by virtue of his being a social entity – in a word, the development of the social individual – that appears as the cornerstone of production and wealth.[70]

This disalienated individual is the cornerstone of the new society, and science performs an important function in the constitution of that individual. The individual's foundational position is implicit even in the *Grundrisse*'s formulations, which seem not to suggest this, since they consider things from another point of view. For example, when it establishes that the development of fixed capital indicates the degree to which general social knowledge has become an immediate productive force and, as a result, the conditions of the process of social life have come to fall under the control of the intellect:[71] a decisive part

67 Marx 1987a, p. 91, original emphasis.
68 Ibid.
69 Ibid.
70 Ibid., emphasis added.
71 Marx 1987a, p. 92.

of what can be considered fixed capital is the free time of the disalienated, knowledgeable individual.[72]

The fact that a period of much scientific, technological, and agricultural reading – the years spent preparing the drafts of *Capital*, the first of which is the one that we are examining – also saw the renewal of Marx's Hegelianism was a coincidence with major ramifications. These studies must have bolstered Marx's Enlightenment tendency to historical optimism, affording it the necessary elements to be developed in a positive and detailed fashion. The revival of Marx's Hegelianism prevented his enthusiasm for the revolutionary efficacy of modern techno-science from yielding a simple progressivism. The productivity of negativity in the Hegelian dialectic enabled him to insert within the framework of historical optimism all of the horrors due to the fact that movement advances along its bad side. The result of these two influences – that of the progress of science and technology, and that of Hegel – was an almost infallibilist and ethnocentric (Eurocentric) vision of the historical process of emancipation, which gives the *Grundrisse* a captivating vigour, but which also often turns it into a merely partial reflection of the ideas which its author had already reached in that period. Thus, for example, despite the fact that, as we have seen, the individual's action and transformation are the cornerstone of the new society, the passages in the *Grundrisse* in which there is an explicit mention of the revolutionary moment, of a political rupture in the relations of production, are few and far between; rather, it is tacitly presupposed in almost every development. And when it is mentioned, Marx limits his remarks to just a few words, which, moreover, lack the resonance of those he had used in 1847 in the *Communist Manifesto* and those which he will later use in *Capital*. The most that the *Grundrisse* says in this connection is that 'the working masses must ... themselves appropriate their surplus labour', and that:

> once they have done so ... society's productive power will develop so rapidly that, although production will now be calculated to provide wealth for all, the *disposable time* of all will increase. For real wealth is the developed productive power of all individuals. Then wealth is no longer measured by labour time but by disposable time.[73]

The 1857–8 *Grundrisse* is a purely theoretical text. It is the first attempt at writing *Capital*. This fact coupled with the text's abrupt interruption during the 'Chapter on Capital' explain that questions such as the revolutionary

72 Marx 1987a, p. 97.

73 Marx 1987a, p. 94, original emphasis.

intervention of the working masses in the resolution of capitalism's basic contradiction are not subjects that receive a separate treatment. On the other hand, the *Grundrisse* sketches in more detail, as compared with the majority of Marx's texts, the picture of the emancipated society that is contrasted with capitalist society, which the Marx of the late 1850s plainly views as being on the verge of succumbing to its own contradictoriness. The *Grundrisse* is probably the best place in Marx's works as regards what we nowadays call 'communism of abundance'. And the place of science in that society is extremely important. Communism does not involve renouncing the enjoyment of anything, given that the saving of labour time on which it is based, since it is due to techno-scientific progress, 'is identical with the development of the productive power'.[74] However, one must not interpret those words as they might sound in a 'consumerist' society, as one used to say in the 1960s. Marx is thinking of individuals who have learned to develop 'the capacity for enjoyment' that '*is created by the development of an individual disposition, productive power*',[75] so that the main aim of that enjoyment is not superfluous stuff of any sort (for example, private automobiles), but rather free time 'for the full development of the individual'.[76] Such a goal for production does not result in its complete paralysis because the development of the individual 'as the greatest productive force ... reacts upon the productive power of labour'.[77]

Unlike Fourier, whom he admired, Marx does not believe that work in the emancipated society can be play; we have already seen his disagreement on this score with regard to a writer whom he held in high esteem. Instead, he thinks that free time and work time cease to oppose one another in an 'abstract antithesis',[78] as is the case in pre-communist societies. The new relation between them, their interpenetration, is due to the fact that free time – understood at one and the same time as 'leisure' and 'time for higher activity' – has, in the communist society, '*transformed its possessor into another subject*'.[79] The Marxian conception of communist work in the 1857–8 *Grundrisse* is clearly based on the transformation of the individual, the cornerstone of his doctrine. The manuscript specifies to some extent the individual worker's process of transformation, and even, more implicitly, that of the old do-nothing, whether direct exploiter or intellectual. That process is discipline, as seen from the

---

74 Marx 1987a, p. 97.
75 Ibid., emphasis added.
76 Ibid.
77 Ibid.
78 Ibid.
79 Ibid., emphasis added.

viewpoint of the individual undergoing transformation, and is 'application, experimental science, material creative and self-objectifying science',[80] as seen from the viewpoint of the individual who has already been transformed. The specification of science as the characteristic quality of the transformed individual represents something more than an understanding of the technical process as being the source of the transformation of the material and instrumental basis of production. It is an acknowledgment of the revolutionary social value also possessed by science as 'ideal wealth', and it sounds like an ethos not too far removed, in its spirit (though quite distant in its realisation), from the ancient hope of ethical intellectualism, or the traditional reciprocal convertibility of the transcendental *bonum* and *verum*, or, stated in more folkloric terms, the cruel saying, 'There are no good fools' ['*No hay tonto bueno*'].

The image of disalienated labour, so intimately related to the transformation of the individual through knowledge, is completed with a vision heralding Marx's assessment (in the period of *Capital*) of the 'proletarian of the primitive forest' and its contrast to Roscher's progressivism:[81]

> So far as labour demands practical manual exertion and free motion, as in agriculture [i.e., to the extent that it has not been mechanised or automated], the production process is for both of them [i.e., for both the individual undergoing transformation and the one who has already been transformed], at the same time, exercise.[82]

Here 'exercise' means 'experimental' science as well as physical exercise. Since Marx has no guarantee whatsoever that the cleaning of sewers is going to be automated any time soon, we have to accept that hard and disagreeable work is also viewed as 'exercise'. It seems clear that individuals will need to be socialised to quite a considerable extent in order to experience it that way, quite apart from the fact that task rotation will have to be a routine that has already

80 Ibid.

81 '"The sickly proletarian of the primitive forest", is a pretty Roscherian fancy. The primitive forester is owner of the primitive forest, and uses the primitive forest as his property with the freedom of an orangoutang. He is not, therefore, a proletarian. This would only be the case, if the primitive forest exploited him, instead of being exploited by him. As far as his health is concerned, such a man would well bear comparison, not only with the modern proletarian, but also with the syphilitic and scrofulous upper classes' (Marx 1996, p. 609, n. 1). While more impassioned, the paragraph is more cautious and acceptable than Marshall Sahlins's Sunday tripper vision of the picnics in the Palaeolithic 'society of abundance'; cf. Sahlins 1968.

82 Marx 1987a, p. 97.

been assimilated. Science and technology are decisive factors in that transformation of individuals, which is the cornerstone of the conception presented in the 1857–8 *Grundrisse*.

The Sociology of Science in Karl Marx's Mature Works

The main contributions to the sociology of science deriving from Karl Marx's writings after *A Contribution to the Critique of Political Economy* can be classified under two headings: the study of intellectuals and scientists found in the 1861–3 manuscript (which contains the *Theories of Surplus Value*), and the clarifications and revisions of the conception from the *Grundrisse*, which appear in that manuscript, in *Capital*, and in Marx's statements (primarily letters) contemporaneous with the final manuscripts for *Capital*.

Intellectuals and Scientists in the 1861–3 Manuscript

The 1861–3 manuscript begins as a direct continuation of the *Contribution*; its first five notebooks address what a continuation had to address: the transformation of money into capital, absolute surplus value, and relative surplus value. In reaching that point, however, the manuscript embarks upon an extensive critical exposition of the history of the theories of surplus value, which takes up notebooks VI to XV. It is mainly in this context that we find those considerations regarding intellectuals in general, and scientists in particular, which constitute the chief enrichment of Marx's thinking on the sociology of science during first half of the 1860s.

The general framework in which those analyses are presented then is obviously the question of the production of surplus value: the discussion of intellectuals starts with the distinction between productive and unproductive workers in the capitalist mode of production's sense (namely, in terms of whether they do or do not produce surplus value). Those categories are indeed, in the Marxian approach, historical categories, so that in his analysis productivity means exclusively capitalist productivity. In this sense, only the worker who produces surplus value for the capitalist, or who serves capital's self-expansion, is productive.[83] In the *Theories*, Marx discusses, in connection with several authors (Jones, Storch, Smith, etc.), the criteria for distinguishing between productive and unproductive workers within capitalism: according

83 Marx 1996, p. 510.

to Marx, the distinction between workers who live on (are paid by) capital, and workers who live on (are paid out of) revenue, refers to the form of labour, and this is the difference between the capitalist and non-capitalist mode of production. But within the truly capitalist mode of production, Marx establishes the difference between productive and unproductive labour in terms of the difference between labour that enters into the production of a commodity (from the first step of its production to the final step of being put on the market), and labour that does not enter commodity production. Marx considers the distinction indispensable, despite acknowledging that every type of activity has an impact on material production and *vice versa*.[84]

The discussion of intellectuals, and of scientists in particular, is placed within this framework. 'A writer', for instance, 'is a productive labourer', in the capitalist sense, 'not in so far as he produces ideas, but in so far as he enriches the publisher who publishes his works, or if he is a wage labourer for a capitalist'.[85] Or, as *Capital* illustrates this point, paraphrasing material from the 1861–3 manuscript:

> a schoolmaster is a productive labourer when, in addition to belabouring the heads of his scholars, he works like a horse to enrich the school proprietor. That the latter has laid out his capital in a teaching factory, instead of in a sausage factory, does not alter the relation.[86]

The connection between 'material' production and 'spiritual' or 'intellectual' production [*materielle und geistige Produktion*] is historical, since both forms of production are historical. 'Thus for example different kinds of intellectual production correspond to the capitalist mode of production and to the mode of production of the Middle Ages'.[87] Indeed, it turns out that it is not only a specific organisation of society that results from the form of material production. The latter also yields a specific relationship of society to nature, and consequently a certain kind of intellectual view of nature, and reality in general,[88] among the members of said society, and lastly, a predominant type of specific intellectual production.[89]

84 Marx 1991a, p. 354.

85 Marx 1989a, p. 14.

86 Marx 1996, p. 510.

87 Marx 1989a, p. 182.

88 For the natural sciences 'form the basis of all knowledge', as Marx writes in Notebook 20 of the *Economic Manuscript of 1861–3* (Marx 1994, p. 34).

89 Marx 1989a, p. 182.

That general characterisation of the historicity of the category of 'intellectual production' is fleshed out in the *Theories* manuscript by means of interesting examples and moments of clarification, some of which are required for the coherence of Marx's theoretical system. For example: the idea that whether or not it is necessary to regard as intellectual production the professional activities of all the different strains within the ruling class which carry out social functions as their business (administrators, governors, etc.) is a question that must be resolved bearing in mind the structure of the relations of production in each individual case.[90] Other examples, to be sure, may well be romantic prejudices, deeply ingrained in Marx since his adolescence as a reader of the *Sturm und Drang* and *Junges Deutschland* poets, such as the assertion, repeated almost *ad nauseam*, that the capitalist mode of production is unfavourable for artistic and poetic production. In the course of a discussion of Storch's work, we encounter one of the most complete formulations of that capricious thesis:

> [C]apitalist production is hostile to certain branches of intellectual production, for example, art and poetry. If this is left out of account, it opens the way to the illusion of the French in the eighteenth century which has been so beautifully satirised by Lessing. Because we are further ahead than the ancients in mechanics, etc., why shouldn't we be able to make an epic too? And the *Henriade* [by Voltaire] in place of the *Iliad!*[91]

As so often happens with the romantic sensibility, this residual prejudice in Marx is sustained by narrow horizons, as is shown by what it fails to see, namely, the novel, which is the bourgeois era's epic, bourgeois theatre, and nothing less than a democratising explosion of refined music in the age of capitalism. Marx's Lessingian example thus reduces to the tautology that the Greek epic is not the bourgeois novel. The prejudice assumes that poetry is Greek poetry. It is a nice prejudice, but false; one could parody the historian and say: all modes of intellectual production are equal before the Muses.

Nonetheless, there is an additional level of analysis, on which Marx works out another version of his idea of the limited relation between the capitalist mode of production and a specific type of intellectual production, yet without arriving at the macrosociological considerations from the 1857 Introduction concerning the incompatibility between Greek mythological figures and the technological foundation of modern society. 'Capitalist mode of production' in this context means, quite precisely, a capitalist way of doing things. There are

90 Ibid.

91 Marx 1989a, pp. 182–3.

two possibilities, writes Marx, in non-material production. First, it can produce commodities, objects separable from the producer, like books, paintings, and so on. In this case, capitalist production, the capitalist way of doing things, can only be applied on a very limited basis, for example, to the extent that a writer exploits a certain number of other writers as executors of a collective work (an encyclopaedia, for instance); this is a kind of transition (in which there is maximum exploitation, Marx adds, perhaps recalling his own work for the *New American Cyclopedia*) toward truly capitalist production, which involves various scientific or artistic producers, artisans or professionals, working for the joint commercial capital of book dealers. The second possibility is that non-material production is not separable from the act of production, as happens with 'all executant artists, orators, actors, teachers, doctors, clerics, etc.'[92] In this case too, Marx thinks that capitalist production hardly occurs, which was surely true in his era. However, Marx generalises that experience to the point of coming up with the thesis that what prevents the capitalist mode of production from arising often in the sphere of non-material production is something 'in the nature of things'.[93] In the thesis that the capitalist mode of production is hostile to certain branches of intellectual production there is, besides the Goethean and Heinean prejudice, probably a hasty generalisation from the facts of the age. Incidentally, it is in this context that Marx adduces for the first time the example of the teacher that he will use four years later in *Capital*: in some spheres of intellectual production, he says, the capitalist way of producing can in fact operate normally:

> E.g. teachers in educational institutions may be mere wage labourers for the entrepreneur who owns the institution; there are many such education factories in England. Although they are not *productive workers* vis-à-vis the pupils, they are such vis-à-vis their employer. He exchanges his capital for their labour capacity, and enriches himself by this process. Similarly with enterprises such as theatres, places of entertainment, etc. Here the actor's relation to the public is that of artist, but vis-à-vis his employer he is a *productive worker*.[94]

92 Marx 1994, p. 144.

93 Ibid.

94 Ibid., original emphasis. There is something to this association of ideas. What professor has not felt like an actor on more than one occasion? Surely, it could only be one who is exceedingly naïve.

By 'productive worker', Marx means a producer of surplus value, which is the goal of capitalist production. However, after giving his examples, he considers them exceptional, and ends his analysis by repeating, as a summary and conclusion: 'all the phenomena of capitalist production in this [intellectual] area are so insignificant in comparison with production as a whole that they can be disregarded entirely'.[95] I have already remarked that the thesis strikes me as a false generalisation, ignoring its romantic roots. On the other hand, it is obvious that he does not include *scientific* intellectual labour, since from the time of the *1844 Manuscripts* (and with more precision since the 1857–8 manuscript), Marx has viewed that labour as subsumed by capital.

Scientists do indeed find themselves in another situation once the capitalist mode of production has incorporated science into its production process. Thus, just as reciprocal relations are established between science and capitalist production (relations through which capitalist production offers science, which supplies an extraordinary productive force, a new possibility of producing costly 'philosophical instruments', i.e., the powerful material requirements of modern research),[96] so too the interaction between the scientist and the system situates the former within a peculiar ambiguity. On the one hand, the scientist's work continues to have the special quality of being 'universal' [*allgemeine Arbeit*],[97] as Volume III of *Capital* says, using an expression which, coming from the pen of one of Hegel's disciples, has the most flattering echo. On the other hand, the scientist becomes accustomed to viewing science, as do his or her bosses, as a way of acquiring wealth, and in fact enters into competition with colleagues to find '*practical applications*'[98] before they do. Within capitalist production, all these interactions together make possible a utilisation and organisation of science 'on a scale which earlier epochs could not have imagined'.[99] (This is one of Marx's observations that seem to discern most

---

95 Ibid.

96 'It is the capitalist mode of production which first puts the natural sciences to the service of the direct production process, while, conversely, the development of production provides the means for the theoretical subjugation of nature' (Marx 1994, p. 32).

97 'Incidentally, a distinction should be made between universal labour and co-operative labour. Both kinds play their role in the process of production, both flow one into the other, but both are also differentiated. Universal labour is all scientific labour, all discovery and all invention. This labour depends partly on the co-operation of the living, and partly on the utilisation of the labours of those who have gone before. Co-operative labour, on the other hand, is the direct co-operation of individuals' (Marx 1998, p. 106).

98 Marx 1994, p. 34, original emphasis.

99 Ibid.

clearly the later development of technological research as a branch of production and the 'big science' associated with it).

However, the 'ideological castes' (whether or not they consist of scientists) are soon absorbed by the already dominant bourgeoisie as 'its functionaries'.[100] The intellectual labourers succeed in drawing a 'large share ... out of material production',[101] but that does not spare them a certain fear that the capitalists are not sufficiently convinced of their productivity,[102] nor does it imply (more importantly) that all intellectual labour is ideology, let alone apology: not only in the specific field of natural science, but even in that of the literary imagination, there is in addition to ideology 'free intellectual production'. Criticising Storch's lack of historical vision, Marx observes that as a result of this deficiency:

> he deprives himself of the basis on which alone can be understood partly the ideological component parts of the ruling class, partly the free spiritual production of this particular social formation.[103]

The context leaves no doubt that such free spiritual (intellectual) production for the most part comes from the ruling class itself.

The Peculiarity of Capitalism and Science

The subsumption of science under capitalism supplies the justificatory model for the great mass of so-called 'higher grade' workers – such as state officials, military people, artists, doctors, priests, judges, lawyers, and so on. Some of these are not merely non-productive but in essence destructive; however, they know how to appropriate to themselves a very great part of the 'material' wealth, partly through the sale of their 'immaterial' commodities and partly by forcibly imposing the latter on other people.[104] As the subsumption of the natural sciences – understood in this context in a strict sense, not as technology

100 Marx 1989a, p. 197.

101 Marx 1989a, p. 192.

102 The fear is justified, since 'even the most sublime intellectual productions should merely be granted recognition, and *apologies* for them made to the bourgeoisie, that they are presented as, and falsely proved to be, direct producers of material wealth' (Marx 1989a, p. 184, original emphasis).

103 Marx 1989a, p. 182.

104 Marx 1989a, p. 30.

but as 'those spheres of production not directly related to the production of material wealth'[105] – is completed, and to the extent that the pure natural sciences thus become utilisable as means of material production, the figure of the scientist furnishes an analogous model for improperly asserting the (capitalist) productivity of all the 'intellectual workers'.[106] Marx is plainly enjoying himself as he reconstructs the historical parable of the cleansing of the intellectuals' capitalist honour, starting from the moment in which the bourgeoisie, already the ruling class, perceives its need to reconstruct the hierarchy of classes which it had criticised when the state was in the service of others:

> [A] section of the agents of production (of material production itself) were declared by one group of economists or another to be 'unproductive'. For example, the landowner, by those among the economists who represented industrial capital (Ricardo). Others (for example Carey) declared that the *commerçant* proper was an 'unproductive' labourer. Then even a third group came along who declared that the 'capitalists' themselves were unproductive, or who at least sought to reduce their claims to material wealth to 'wages', that is, to the wages of a 'productive labourer'. Many intellectual workers seemed inclined to share the skepticism. It was therefore time to make a compromise and to recognise the 'productivity' of all classes not directly included among the agents of material production. One good turn deserves another; and, as in the *Fable of the Bees*, it had to be established that even from the 'productive', economic standpoint, the bourgeois world with all its 'unproductive labourers' is the best of all worlds. This was all the more necessary because the 'unproductive labourers' on their part were advancing critical observations in regard to the productivity of the classes who in general were '*fruges consumere nati*', or in regard to those agents of production, like landowners, who do nothing at all, etc. Both the *do-nothings* and their *parasites* had to find a place in this best possible order of things.[107]

Marx's interest in a matter such as productive and unproductive labourers – which he himself notes is almost a pseudo-problem only of the interest to 'second-rate fellows' and, above all, vulgarisers and authors of school manuals, along with literary dilettantes[108] – is surely due to the fact that it relates to the

105 Marx 1989a, p. 31.

106 Ibid.

107 Marx 1989a, pp. 30–1, original emphasis.

108 Marx 1989a, pp. 29–30.

important question of the functions that will be either necessary or superfluous in a communist society. However, this question can be better examined in another context.

In the context of the subsumption of the intellectuals, and in particular that of the scientists and science, under capital, the writings from Marx's maturity complement rather than correct the conception [*cuadro*] he had reached in the 1850s, revealing the other side of the coin, as it were. In the 1857–9 *Grundrisse*, driven by the more or less dramatic optimism (if we can combine these words) deriving from the spirit of the Enlightenment and the Hegelian force of negation, 'the bad side of the movement', Marx had underscored how capital 'captures' science for all of society, for 'historical progress', and how capital places science in the service of wealth, it being the case that in earlier cultures 'historical development, political development, art, *science*, etc., are located in the higher spheres above them [the labourers]',[109] above material production. By contrast, in *Capital*, Marx stresses that the capture of science for capitalist production results in, for one thing, the separation of manual labour from productive knowledge, since the old productive knowledge of the peasant or artisan is displaced by a new knowledge, which they do not possess. The knowledge of the traditional peasant or independent artisan was applied, as was that of the savage, in a personal manner, in each moment of a productive process, which they themselves executed and controlled. But since the advent of manufacture, and much more in large-scale industry, knowledge is only required for the plant as a whole, while the individual worker's operations can be blind. 'What is lost by the detail labourers, is concentrated in the capital that employs them', writes Marx, basing himself on Ferguson.[110] The manufacturing division of labour consists in, among other things, opposing the intellectual powers of the production process to the workers:

---

109 Marx 1986c, p. 509, emphasis added.

110 Marx 1996, p. 366. This analysis shows the extent to which André Gorz (misled by his own writings from another period) distorts Marx's idea of the industrial proletariat; see Gorz 1982. Gorz seems to believe that Marx based his perspective concerning the disalienation of labour on the rise of 'skilled workers … [and] their power in the factory', and he states that today Taylorism, 'scientific work organisation', and automation, by putting an end to that type of worker once and for all, have ruled out Marx's perspective (Gorz 1982, p. 28). As an interpretation of Marx, this is crazy: it was precisely Marx who based his revolutionary perspective on a proletariat that had been 'drained', totally dispossessed, 'with nothing to lose', as *The Communist Manifesto* puts it, and which was counting on automation for its emancipation. The Gorz of 1980 confuses Marx with the Gorz of 1960.

> This separation begins in simple co-operation, where the capitalist represents to the single workman, the oneness and the will of the associated labour. It is developed in manufacture which cuts down the labourer into a detail labourer. It is completed in modern industry, which makes science a productive force distinct from labour and presses it into the service of capital.[111]

This point of view had already been worked out in detail in the *Theories*. In the 1861–3 manuscript, Marx had written several well structured expositions and some especially illuminating general formulations:

> This contrast between wealth that does not [materially] labour and poverty that labours in order to live also gives rise to a contrast of knowledge. Knowledge and labour become separated. The former confronts the latter as capital, or as a luxury article for the rich.[112]

In this connection, Marx makes abundant use of Ure's book of 1835, *The Philosophy of Manufactures: or, an Exposition of the Scientific, Moral, and Commercial Economy of the Factory System of Great Britain*, from whose third volume he had written down one of the most categorical and jubilant proclamations from that enthusiastic apologist of the manufacturing system: 'When capital enlists science in her service, the refractory hand of labour will always be taught docility'.[113] Marx repeatedly uses the philosophical term 'alienation' or 'estrangement' [*Entfremdung*] in the 1861–3 manuscript when describing the relation between science and the labourer within capitalism.[114] That alienation is a factor 'directed ... against the individual worker';[115] just as the machinery is the 'master's machinery', so the science embodied in that machinery is 'the master's science', something strange and hostile that dominates labour.[116] The hostility is not only a structural or objective relation, but also often represents a deliberate action by the capitalist class against the workers' resistance to exploitation:

111 Marx 1996, p. 366. The paragraph is accompanied by a note with a citation from W. Thompson.

112 Marx 1989a, p. 202.

113 Marx 1988a, p. 342.

114 For example, Marx 1994, pp. 29, 34.

115 Marx 1994, pp. 29–30.

116 Marx 1994, p. 34.

> Self-actors, wool-combing machines in the spinning industry, the so-called 'condenser' which replaces the hand-turned 'slubbing machine' (in the woollen industry as well), etc., are all machines invented in order to defeat strikes.[117]

Still, the basic fact in this whole constellation is the separation or alienation of positive science from manual labourers, whose intellectual and professional development is suppressed,[118] whereas in earlier phases there was 'no separation of hand from brain'.[119]

However, this accentuation of the separation of manual labour and productive science in capitalism does not contradict the characterisation of capitalism in terms of the incorporation of science into production; rather, it explains the form of that incorporation. As Marx writes, in a very condensed fashion, in the course of his discussion of Jones's ideas: 'Capitalist production leads to separation of *science from labour* and at the same time to the application of science to material production'.[120] The simultaneity of the two phenomena need not surprise us:

> *[I]t is indeed the peculiarity of the capitalist mode of production that it separates the different kinds of labour, hence also brain and hand labour – or the kinds of labour in which one or the other aspect predominates – and distributes them among different people …*[121]

It is the peculiarity of capitalism that shapes [*constituye*] science in a situation that the 1861–3 manuscript continues to call 'alienation', without dismissing the possibility that other mechanisms produce analogous effects in other cultures. Despite the fact that science is 'the product of general historical development in its abstract quintessence',[122] as the 1861–3 manuscript over-intellectually puts it, the same thing happens to it within capitalism as happens to any other '*social* characteristics of … labour', namely, it is opposed, in its '*capitalised*' form, to the working class: 'vis-à-vis the workers, realised science appears in *the machine* as *capital*'.[123] All applications of science, like those of the forces of

117 Marx 1988a, p. 340.
118 Marx 1994, p. 34.
119 Marx 1994, p. 33.
120 Marx 1991a, p. 364, original emphasis.
121 Marx 1994, p. 145, emphasis added.
122 Marx 1994, p. 124.
123 Ibid., original emphasis.

nature or the social combination of individuals, appear as means of exploiting labour, as 'means of appropriating surplus labour, hence, vis-à-vis labour, as *forces* belonging to capital'.[124] Yet none of this contradicts the fact that capitalism is the mode of production which, through the 'bad side' of the historical movement, has created scientific culture as a universal social fact (as Marx had written since his youth), the bourgeoisie having produced 'the intellectual prerequisites' for 'the regeneration of science in general', starting with the printing press.[125]

Although the process starts from simple cooperation, it is not completed until the emergence of large-scale industry, the phase in which the systematic application of science to production makes it possible to transform the means of labour into an automaton. Trapped within this automaton, possessed and controlled by capital, the intellectual forces of production become detached from and opposed to manual labour.[126] Given this historical evolution, it is understandable that the complete view of science as a productive force does not yet appear in older authors, not even in those whose insight Marx most admires, such as Petty,[127] but instead only appears in later authors, even though their work is on the whole, as in Jones's case, of less importance. The reason for this is that 'the development of chemistry, geology and physiology, the sciences that *directly* form the specific basis of agriculture rather than of industry, does not take place till the nineteenth century and especially the later decades'.[128]

In the *Theories* and in *Capital* Marx maintains the idea, inspired by the circumstances of the era, that science, as a force of production, does not cost the individual capitalist anything, at least to the extent that it teaches him how to replace human labour performed by natural agents without the help of machinery; and in this case, Marx adds, if we ignore the production costs of scientific labour power, it does not cost society anything either.[129] That notion assumes that the scientist's personal productivity depends on his or her inventiveness alone, and it does not count costs of preparation and training over and above the ordinary costs incurred in the education of the cultured classes. 'Science, generally speaking, costs the capitalist nothing', we read in Volume I

124 Ibid., original emphasis.

125 Marx 1991a, p. 403.

126 Marx 1996, pp. 425–6.

127 Marx cites a passage from Petty in which the latter places '*the improvement of natural* knowledge' among 'the arts and exercises of pleasure and ornament' (Marx 1989a, p. 35, original emphasis).

128 Marx 1989a, p. 341, original emphasis.

129 Marx 1989b, p. 179.

of *Capital*,[130] in an annotation to a phrase which presents, in a reasonable fashion, this view of the basic science of pioneers, which scarcely needs any development for its application:

> Once discovered, the law of the deviation of the magnetic needle in the field of an electric current, or the law of the magnetisation of iron, around which an electric current circulates, cost never a penny.[131]

Stated with such precision and restricted to basic science, the proposition remains defensible today. Taken without restrictions, however, it suggests free, public research, devoid of secrets and accessible without major investments, something that hardly corresponds to the main line of development followed by technological research since Marx's day. In Volume III of *Capital*, we find a partial – and 'obvious', in Marx's opinion – explanation for the fact that scientific progress has been free for the individual capitalist: the development of productive power in one branch of production ('development ... which may ... be partly connected with progress in the field of intellectual production, notably natural science and its practical application') has an impact on one aspect of the production costs of other branches that have nothing to do with the gestation of that progress.[132] In general, however, since the development of productive power always, in the last analysis, extends to the social character of labour, the division of labour and the development of intellectual labour, 'especially in the natural sciences', by taking advantage of scientific progress the individual capitalist is making use of the effects of the entire system of the social division of labour.[133] This is why Marx contends, in Volume I of *Capital*, that science and technology constitute a power for the expansion of individual capital, independently of the latter's actual magnitude.[134] And in the later parts of the second volume, he continues to maintain that 'methods and scientific developments ... cost the capitalist nothing'.[135] Science is one of the three great productive forces that cost Marx's individual capitalist nothing; the other two are the division and combination of labour, and the increase in population.[136]

---

130 Marx 1996, p. 390, n. 1.
131 Marx 1996, pp. 389–90.
132 Marx 1998, p. 85.
133 Ibid.
134 Marx 1996, pp. 600–1.
135 Marx 1997, p. 354.
136 Marx 1994, p. 17.

Yet although science costs the individual capitalist nothing, according to this conception, it nevertheless greatly influences his fate. For one thing, the unequal progress of different sciences causes different states of investment in the various branches of the economy.[137] And the great influence of scientific progress in the organic composition of capitals within the different branches of the economy partly causes the resulting differential depreciations of the capitals in operation.

Most of those effects of science on the economy are measured by machinery in large-scale industry. Between science and machinery there is, moreover, an interesting economic analogy: both science and machinery have reproduction costs that are considerably lower than their 'original production' costs. There is a 'great difference in the cost of the first model of a new machine and that of its reproduction',[138] while, for its part:

> the product of mental labour – science – always stands far below its value, because the labour time needed to reproduce it has no relation at all to the labour time required for its original production. For example, a schoolboy can learn the binominal theorem in an hour.[139]

This question of the costs of 'original production' (which has had no bearing on the question of the free cost of science for the individual capitalist) is closely related to that of inventions and technological innovation, in relation to which some authors claim to find the outline of a theory in Marx's work, especially

---

137 'Hence, if the average composition of agricultural capital is e.g. C [constant capital] 60, V [variable capital] 40, while that of not agricultural capital is C 80, V 20, this proves that agriculture has not yet reached the same stage of development as industry. (Which is easily explicable since, apart from anything else, a prerequisite for industry is the older science of mechanics, while the prerequisites for agriculture are the completely new sciences of chemistry, geology and physiology)' (Letter to Engels, 2 August, 1862; Marx 1985b, p. 397). Or, as we read in *Capital*, Volume III: 'If the composition of capital in agriculture proper is lower than that of the average social capital, then, *prima facie*, this expresses the fact that in countries with developed production agriculture has not progressed to the same extent as the processing industries. Such a fact could be explained ... by the earlier and more rapid development of the mechanical sciences ... compared ... with the later and in part quite recent development of chemistry, geology and physiology, and ... in particular, their application to agriculture' (Marx 1998, pp. 746–7). These passages and others make me think that Bolchini's statement in his Foreword to *Capitale e tecnologia*, according to which Marx neglects chemistry, has little justification (Bolchini 1980, p. 19).

138 Marx 1998, p. 106.

139 Marx 1994, p. 87.

in the 1861–3 manuscript.[140] According to this theory, there is a first phase of social stimulation of innovation, owing to the needs of production; then there is a phase of intuitive responses to the stimulus; and lastly, there is a truly scientific phase of trial and error. Whether or not those ideas constitute the core of a theory of technological innovation, the suggested interpretation is quite in keeping with the mature Marx's way of presenting the relations between social and technological evolution, accentuating, with certain variants, the esteem for technology found in the *Grundrisse*. Marx makes it clear that what he is studying is not 'a precise technological separation', but rather 'a revolution in the means of labour employed',[141] and he projects that point of view onto his historical analyses, with results that are expressed without ever suggesting any ideas relating to technological determinism. Thus, for example, he shows how only the development of the economic relations in England (among which its agricultural circumstances and colonial possessions stand out) made possible the capitalist utilisation of the scientific advances in the fields of mathematics, chemistry, and technology that were being produced simultaneously, but without yielding the same socio-economic results, in France, Sweden, and Germany.[142] Piero Bolchini has pointed out, indeed, that certain omissions that Marx ought not to make, from the point of view of a true history of technology, are just what allow Marx:

> to propose the factory as a central structure and nodal problem of the Industrial Revolution, integrating aspects of the development of technology into the transformation of the relations of production.[143]

That is to say, they enable Marx to continue to focus on the economy (in the Marxian sense), rather than on technology.

Science and Mechanisation

Mechanisation is technology with a scientific basis. More precisely, it is the means of working which, until well into the twentieth century (and hence in the era in which Marx was writing), most eminently represented modern

140 See Rosenberg 1976.

141 Marx 1991a, p. 389.

142 Marx 1994, p. 58.

143 Bolchini 1980, p. 19 [I have translated Sacristán's Spanish translation from the Italian (Ed.)].

technology: a technology based more on theoretical science than on pre-theoretical experience, as is the case with many traditional technologies. In mechanisation, the routine 'definitely settled by experience' is replaced by the 'systematic applications of natural science'.[144] The beginning of the operation of mechanisation consists in analysing the process of production into its constitutive parts and resolving the problems thus defined 'by the application of mechanics, of chemistry, and of the whole range of the natural sciences'.[145]

The social reality of mechanisation, that outstanding embodiment of the productivity of science, is contradictory, to state things with the Hegelian vocabulary familiar to Marx. In this regard, from the 1840s on, Marx maintained the general idea that appears in a complete and organised form in the 1857–8 *Grundrisse*. However, depending on the period, Marx pays more or less attention to each of the two 'sides' of the movement, at times because of chance factors (as in the case of the long chapter in *Capital*, Volume I, on the lengthening of the working day),[146] and at other times because one or another aspect had recently revealed its special importance or certain structures of interest (as occurs, I believe, in the *Grundrisse*, as I have already suggested). In the 1861–3 manuscript, in *Capital*, and in what he wrote during the last years of his life, we can discern a revival of Marx's feeling for the 'bad side' of capitalist – and also scientific-technological – progress, which despite not leading him to correct the 'dialectical' model articulated in the second half of the 1850s, nonetheless evokes the political and moral tone of the writings from the 1840s.

The 1861–3 manuscript insists that mechanisation does not directly liberate the labourer; quite the contrary. Machinery produces an overpopulation of workers, not because the population increases more rapidly than the food supply, but rather precisely because the rapid increase of the latter due to the introduction of machinery allows in turn for the introduction of more machines, which diminishes the demand for labour, producing the overpopulation of workers, and so on. With 'the alienated form which the objective conditions of labour ... assume',[147] the social powers of labour (among which we find science) present an appearance of destructive efficacy to the workers:

144 Marx 1996, pp. 488–9.

145 Marx 1996, p. 464.

146 'I could make no progress with the really theoretical part. My brain was not up to that. I therefore elaborated the section on the "*Working-Day*" from the historical point of view, which was not part of my original plan' (Letter from Marx to Engels, 10 February 1866; Marx 1987g, p. 224).

147 Marx 1994, p. 29.

they toss the workers into the gutter; they turn the workers into 'superfluous'[148] human beings; they deprive them of the dignity of professional specialisation which the earlier division of labour afforded them; and they subject them to 'the thoroughly organised despotism of the factory system and the military discipline of capital'.[149] The labourers who continue to work with the machines, those who are not cast into the darkness of the redundant population, endure a new servitude scarcely more desirable than the misery that engulfed the artisans whom they have displaced. The bourgeois 'apologetics' familiar to Marx counter this picture with two scenarios, or rather they offer two ways out of this process: the increase in jobs in activities that are not directly productive, and the increase in jobs within the same industry, thanks to the expansion of accumulation made possible by the increase in surplus value, industrial profits in particular. In regard to the first argument, Marx states, in a style that recalls that of his youth, full of indignation at the 'the infamy of economics': 'this is indeed a fine result of machinery, that a considerable section of the female and male labouring class is turned into servants';[150] and he responds to the second one, likewise in a tone rather different from the most cheerful passages in the *Grundrisse*, with the claim that the expansion of production is not always something desirable in itself:

> [A] portion of the increased net revenue [augmented surplus value, according to Marx's reading of Ricardo] is transformed into capital … Thus the workman must constantly enlarge the power of capital, and then, after very serious disturbances, obtain permission to repeat the process on a larger scale.[151]

And since the machine always creates relative overpopulation, a 'reserve army of labourers',[152] capital's contractual power increases. For this reason, the sector of the population with work lives under conditions that are not at all superior to those of the 'sickly proletarian of the primitive forest' for whom the smug Wilhelm Roscher felt sorry. Marx uses some statistics from the General Dispensary of Nottingham, which cover the years 1852–61, to document the rise

148 Marx 1994, p. 28.

149 Marx 1994, p. 29.

150 Marx 1989b, pp. 195–6.

151 Marx 1989b, p. 198. The *very serious disturbances* are those produced by the loss of work, unemployment and the search for other work in new branches of industry or expanding industries (Marx 1989b, pp. 196–7).

152 Marx 1997, p. 315.

in tuberculosis among the young workers in the mechanised lace industry, and remarks: 'This progress in the rate of consumption ought to suffice for the most optimist of progressists'.[153] By increasing capital's contractual power, machinery puts an end to even the appearance of a contract between free persons, which is the juridical superstructure of the relationship between the worker and the capitalist.[154] Once the consequences of the process of mechanisation have become obvious, 'the worker... justifiably regards the development of the productive power of his own labour as hostile to himself'.[155] For this reason, although the struggle between the capitalist and the wage-labourer begins as soon as the capitalistic relationship is formed, only after the introduction of machinery does the worker fight against the means of labour itself. We can in fact follow the history of workers' rebellions against machines since the seventeenth century.

Still, 'the bad side of the movement' remains only one side of the dialectical model, albeit one that receives more intense attention in both the *Theories* and in *Capital* than in other texts. The workers managed to discover the complexity of the situation, although:

> it took both time and experience before the workpeople learnt to distinguish between machinery and its employment by capital, and to direct their attacks, not against the material instruments of production, but against the mode in which they are used.[156]

It is necessary to make this distinction, for mechanisation 'in itself' represents the possibility of abolishing the traditional, perpetual assignment of one function to an individual worker.[157] Indeed, given the fact that it opens up the possibility of overcoming the settled manufacturing division of labour (as well as the even greater rigidity of older social divisions of labour), and given its structurally cooperative mode of operation,[158] mechanised production offers a basis for socialism. In *Capital*, Marx followed this train of thought to the very

153 Marx 1996, p. 469.

154 Marx 1996, p. 400.

155 Marx 1989b, p. 198.

156 Marx 1996, p. 432.

157 Marx 1996, p. 739. [The reference that Sacristán provides may well be an error, as it seems to make little sense here (Ed.)].

158 'Machinery, with a few exceptions... operates only by means of associated labour, or labour in common. Hence the co-operative character of the labour-process is, in the latter case, a technical necessity dictated by the instrument of labour itself' (Marx 1996, p. 389).

end, though in few words: the mechanised factory offers the possibility of overcoming the worker's subjection to a fixed task because in this mode of production the movement of things starts not from the worker, but from the machine itself. On the other hand, as machinery also allows for the reduction of necessary labour time and the simplification of the worker's operations, and consequently a reduction of the time required for the latter's *professional* training, it greatly increases the possibility that cultured, multifaceted individual workers will develop within production. In a society that consistently universalised the cooperativism rendered technologically possible by machinery, toil would still be necessary, as would the tough and disagreeable jobs involved in the maintenance of life in society [*la vida civil*], but their simplicity and the reduction of necessary labour time will allow for 'a rapid and constant change of the individuals burdened with this drudgery'.[159] It is worth noting that this vision of work in a liberated society based on mechanisation is essentially consistent with that of *The German Ideology* of 1845–6 or that of the *Grundrisse* of 1857–8.[160] It is useful to bear this in mind when considering the question of the continuity and discontinuity of Marx's thought in relation to our present concerns.

Marx's insistence on the saving of labour power and labour time due to machinery, and technological innovations in general, has been criticised by many economists. They normally criticise it in order to refute the law of the falling rate of profit, a central aspect of which is the increase in the organic composition of capital through the relative decrease in variable capital as a result of the relative decrease in labour power employed, a decrease that Marx explains by the saving of labour. Thus, for example, Blaug argues that because Marx disregarded the technological innovations that tend to save capital (using Marx's vocabulary, one would have to say: those that tend to save constant capital), and only paid attention to those that save labour, 'his predictions failed to materialize'.[161] Leaving aside the question of whether or not subsequent events have contradicted Marx's predictions – an issue which does not concern us here – the fact is that the idea of technological innovation on the one hand, and the saving of labour on the other, constitute a more complicated picture in Marx's thought than is suggested by Blaug's observation; and they certainly do not stand merely in the relation claimed by Blaug. It is true that Marx attributes to machinery two socio-economic effects that are of the greatest importance for him, one of which is the saving of labour (the other is the elimination of the need for the old division of labour): 'the machinery replaces

159 Marx 1996, p. 424.

160 Compare the text that corresponds to note 60 above.

161 Blaug 1968, p. 233.

labour',[162] as does, in general, science applied to production.[163] However, this thesis comes with various restrictions and points of clarification; moreover, it is contained within another, more general thesis. The restrictions, for example, refer to cases in which new branches of social production are created on the basis of new technologies, cases in which we naturally cannot speak of workers' replacement by machines or of variable capital's replacement by fixed constant capital;[164] they also refer to the fact that although machines expel labour power previously needed for a specific kind of production, they also subsequently attract labour for other, new functions created by mechanised technology itself. As such, machinery can act in both directions (except, says Marx, within agriculture, in which 'the predominant tendency of machinery [and, in general, the implantation of scientific techniques] must be to make the population redundant not only temporarily but absolutely'.[165]

With respect to the broader thesis, which includes the saving of labour by means of scientific techniques, and in particular through machinery, those new factors merely complete a tendency which, for Marx, is proper to the capitalist mode of production in itself. Scientific technical innovation is not the root of the phenomenon, as Blaug suggests, following a biased interpretation of Marx that has a long history, namely, one that goes back to Loria's stress on the importance of the *strumento di lavoro*. In Marx's opinion, the reduction of necessary labour time for the production of commodities, and consequently of the number of workers necessary for the production of a given quantity of commodities, 'is characteristic of all *social forms* and combinations of labour developed within capitalist production'.[166] Mechanised technology, developed on a scientific basis, completes this tendency, replacing salaries with fixed and circulating constant capital and generating a surplus of workers; and this completed form of the phenomenon is an important novelty, owing to its magnitude. As a result of it, the dominance of dead labour over living labour ends up being, in addition to a social fact, 'a *technological* validity'.[167] However, the root of the phenomenon is social in a restricted sense, and not purely technological. It is technological in its mature form.

The saving of necessary labour time as a general tendency of capitalist production and its culmination in technified production is the main thesis of this

162 Marx 1994, p. 20.

163 Marx 1994, p. 38.

164 Marx 1994, p. 27.

165 Marx 1994, p. 31.

166 Marx 1994, p. 24, original emphasis.

167 Marx 1994, p. 31, original emphasis.

idea, its 'axis' or 'pivot', as Marx puts it at some point, bringing Fourier to mind. The other question – the fact that this mechanism also attracts labour power or introduces it for the first time in new areas of production, and so forth – consists of a set of secondary theses. And it is not so obvious that the Marxian stress on the saving of labour is a mistake that distorted Marx's predictions, when one reads, in recent studies of the evolution and tendency of the labour market under the impact of computerisation and roboticisation, conclusions such as the following:

> [T]he conclusion is the same for all: within the next ten years, computerization will result in considerable manpower reductions in the large service organizations.... Given the increasing automation of industry, most industrial managers state that growth in the coming years will be accomplished without increases in manpower – in fact, that manpower will decrease slightly, unless demand rises at an unusual rate.... [S]uch a hypothesis has important consequences: it means that the only industrial jobs created from now on will be in small and medium-sized businesses.[168]

Surely the point from which a critical review of Marx's thought on these questions must begin is precisely the consideration of the future of small businesses, and not so much his vision of the evolution of large-scale industry and the great public or private service-providing organisations. However, that question need not concern us here.

The conviction that communist society will realise or actualise the emancipatory possibilities opened up by machinery is based on an analytical consideration of the question within the Marxian economic model, but it is developed by adding two other elements to it. The analytical basis is the idea that the margin for the application of machinery in a capitalist economy is determined by the difference between the machine's value and the value of the labour power it replaces, which in practice means that given a capitalist foundation, machinery is only utilised when massive, large-scale production is possible.[169] The difference between the machine's value and the value of the labour power it replaces can vary a great deal from one country to another, depending on the period, and so on, even if the difference between the amount of labour necessary to produce the machinery and the quantity of labour that it replaces remains the same. But this latter difference is the only one that matters in

168 Simon and Minc 1980, pp. 37–9.

169 Marx 1994, pp. 20–1.

communist production, whose goal is the saving of total labour time and not the increase of surplus value.[170]

The other elements that enter into the explanation of the contradiction between the emancipatory potentialities of mechanisation and its capitalist reality [*actualidad*] are of a rather political-philosophical nature. Borrowing some of Ure's formulations, Marx writes that whereas any application of machinery on a large scale implies the 'combined co-operation of many orders of workpeople, adult and young, … tending with assiduous skill … a system of productive machines, continuously impelled by a central power', the capitalist application of machinery, the modern manufacturing system, in contrast is characterised by its being:

> a vast automaton, composed of various mechanical and intellectual organs, acting in uninterrupted concert for the production of a common object, all of them being subordinate to a self-regulated moving force.[171]

Satisfied with having found these descriptions in the work of an enthusiast of the manufacturing system, Marx comments, with a use of the concepts of subject and object that suffice to show the ethical and philosophical continuity between *Capital* and the youthful Marxian criticism of Hegel or the *1844 Manuscripts*:

> These two descriptions are far from being identical. In one, the collective labourer, or social body of labour, appears as the dominant subject, and the mechanical automaton as the object; in the other, the automaton itself is the subject, and the workmen are merely conscious organs, co-ordinate with the unconscious organs of the automaton, and together with them, subordinated to the central moving-power.[172]

This capitalist transformation of the thing into an intelligent subject, and of the human being into an object lacking initiative, a vision in which it is possible to identify a fairly widespread motif from classical-humanist and Romantic criticism of English capitalism,[173] encapsulates Marx's thought, on a more philosophical level, in its critical relation to the capitalist application of

170 Marx 1996, pp. 395–6.

171 Cited in Marx 1996, p. 421.

172 Marx 1996, pp. 421–2.

173 It was already present, for example, in the poet Heinrich Heine, with whom Marx maintained a friendship for years: 'Yes, wood, iron, and brass, these seem to have usurped

machinery. Marx states the same thing, likewise in Volume I of *Capital*, on an economic level (in the Marxian sense), in explaining that although machinery overcomes the traditional division of labour *from the technical point of view*, making possible the constant rotation of individuals who are more universally and harmoniously developed and trained, capitalism nevertheless systematically reproduces and consolidates the old system of division of labour in order to facilitate the worker's exploitation: by fastening the worker to a machine for life, the costs of reproducing labour power are lowered, and moreover, the labourer remains in a 'helpless dependence' on the factory as a whole, that is, on capitalism.[174] It is very interesting that Marx thus finds himself obliged to admit that there is an increase in productivity due exclusively to the capitalist over-exploitation of the worker, and distinguishable from that which is due to the development of the social process of production; natural science is very important for the latter type of increase in productivity, but it has no bearing on the first type, on Marx's view. The first type of increased productivity is something of a police measure, since society already has the possibility of advancing in another way.

The maintenance of the old system of the division of labour prevents us from offsetting the evils that machinery *in itself* causes (for machinery does not just contain emancipatory potentialities), evils that can only be confronted through the reduction of total labour time and the rotation of functions. The most fundamental of these evils is the fact that machinery must be served, whereas the artisan makes his tool serve him. In addition, the machine attacks the nervous system 'to the uttermost'; it upsets the balance of muscular activity; it 'confiscates' mental activity; and it tortures the worker owing to the simplification of work itself, burdening him or her with tasks lacking in variety and sometimes devoid of any apparent sense.[175] And science reigns over this deplorable picture:

> The special skill of each individual insignificant factory operative vanishes as an infinitesimal quantity before the science, the gigantic physical forces, and the mass of labour that are embodied in the factory mechanism and, together with that mechanism, constitute the power of the 'master'.[176]

the spirit of humanity, and often to be raging with fullness of intelligence, while Man, with his soul gone, attends like a machine to his business and affairs'; Heine 1891, pp. 51–2.

174 Marx 1996, p. 425.

175 Marx 1996, pp. 425–6.

176 Marx 1996, p. 426.

Apart from this, capitalist society not only prevents the realisation of the emancipatory potentialities that the science of mechanisation brings with it, but also, in order to offset mechanisation's contribution to the falling rate of profit, seeks to prolong the working day with the machines, thus completely inverting the technological potentiality of mechanised production.[177]

The Most Mature Version of the Revolutionary Model

In both the 1861–3 manuscript and *Capital*, there are fairly numerous occasions in which the thread of the argument leads Marx to write very simple, even crude, condensed versions of the model of revolutionary social change that he had maintained since the second half of the 1840s. This occurs in a very interesting way in a certain passage from the *Theories*, in the course of a discussion of Ricardo's thought from a point of view opposed to that of Marx's first reading of Ricardo in 1844. Now, in 1861, Marx distances himself from Sismondi's criticism of Ricardo. Ricardo is right in wanting production for production's sake, since production for production's sake means nothing other than the development of the human productive forces that will make possible the disalienation of both work and worker. By opposing the development of production for the sake of production to individuals' wellbeing, as Sismondi does, one ignores the fact that:

> the development of the capacities of the *human* species takes place at the cost of the majority of human individuals and even classes, in the end it breaks through this contradiction and coincides with the development of the individual; the higher development of individuality is thus only achieved by a historical process during which individuals are sacrificed.[178]

177 'Hence, the application of machinery to the production of surplus value implies a contradiction which is immanent in it, since of the two factors of the surplus-value created by a given amount of capital, one, the rate of surplus value, cannot be increased, except by diminishing the other, the number of workmen. This contradiction comes to light, as soon as by the general employment of machinery in a given industry, the value of the machine-produced commodity regulates the value of all commodities of the same sort; and it is this contradiction, that in its turn, drives the capitalist, without his being conscious of the fact, to excessive lengthening of the working day, in order that he may compensate the decrease in the relative number of labourers exploited, by an increase not only of the relative, but of the absolute surplus labour' (Marx 1996, p. 410).

178 Marx 1989a, p. 348, original emphasis.

Marx rounds off the crude and schematic synthetic version of the model (to finish putting it in order) with a consideration that evokes, in an anticipatory way, late twentieth-century sociobiological points of view:

> [T]he interests of the species in the human kingdom, as in the animal and plant kingdoms, always assert themselves at the cost of the interests of individuals, because these interests of the species coincide only with the *interests of certain individuals*, and it is this coincidence which constitutes the strength of these privileged individuals.[179]

The way that Marx reads Darwin – namely, as 'the detailed refutation, based on natural history, of the Malthusian theory'[180] – reinforces his categorical commitment [*afirmación*] to the model. Even so, it is worth recalling a decisive difference between Marx's notion and the Social Darwinist or sociobiological visions that sound like they have a certain affinity with his view: Marx believes in the possibility (whose realisation he seeks) of humanity's definitive departure from the 'animal kingdom', while reproaching the Social Darwinists for opposing that emancipation of the species.[181]

Such simplistic versions of his thought, however, are only brief and abstract formulations of a model that is a good deal more complicated, even in its general features, and stamped by an important indeterminacy, which Marx seems to have felt no need to eliminate by clarifying its conditions. The indeterminacy lies in the 'assumption' that 'capitalist production has already developed the productive powers of labour in general to a sufficiently high level for this *revolution* to take place'.[182]

We are familiar with the 'good' and 'bad' sides of the worker's 'all-around mobility' imposed by modern industry through the capitalist perpetuation of the old division of labour. The catastrophic way in which large-scale capitalist industry resolves that contradiction, through unemployment and the cruel jostle of workers in pursuit of capital, makes it a 'a question of life and death for society' to replace 'that monstrosity, an industrial reserve army, kept in misery in order to be always at the disposal of capital' by the individual 'fit for a variety of labours, ready to face any change of production', and:

179 Ibid., original emphasis.

180 Marx 1989a, p. 351.

181 See the letter from Marx to Laura and Paul Lafargue cited in note 25.

182 Marx 1989b, p. 204, emphasis added.

> to replace the detail-worker of to-day, crippled by life-long repetition of one and the same trivial operation, and thus reduced to the mere fragment of a man, by the fully developed individual … to whom the different social functions he performs, are but so many modes of giving free scope to his own natural and acquired powers.[183]

This transformation of the labouring individual is the decisive element in complicating the abstract schema of the revolutionary model. The key productive force is the individual labourer, and in his or her transformation – viewed since 1844 in an increasingly positive and less metaphysical manner, but constituting a clear continuity throughout Marx's works – *the political revolution and the revolution of science* play the main roles: 'when the working class comes into power, as inevitably it must, technical instruction, both theoretical and practical, will take its proper place in the working-class schools',[184] in order to produce a worker who is 'enlightened' and 'trained more universally and harmoniously'.[185] It is again worth noting, on the other hand, that the notion of the new individual's mobility in the system of social work continues to follow the conception from *The German Ideology*.

The transformation of the individual obviously implies a revolution in the way of living in communist society. This is not a question that Marx addressed at any length in his mature works, but he did write in some places – chiefly in *Capital* (above all in Volume I, Chapter 15, section 10, which is of special interest for this topic) – a few things that suffice to give us an idea of the extent to which he had considered the problem. These considerations can be assembled in two groups; both consist of critical assessments that refer in contrasting ways to a positive vision of the new life, as it were, the life of the transformed individual. Yet they do so on two different levels. On the one hand, the new form of life will have to eliminate 'a vast number'[186] of functions that have arisen only because of the capitalist mode of producing, not because of production *per se*. This thesis plainly suffers from the same indeterminacy noted above, which it may not be worth criticising, for in order to avoid it in this case Marx would have needed to engage in detailed speculation, which Gramsci would say is the essence of utopianism. However, the fact remains that Marx's reflections in this regard prove incomplete. A passage from Chapter 17 of *Capital*, Volume I,

183 Marx 1996, pp. 490–1.

184 Marx 1996, p. 491.

185 Sacristán does not provide a reference for the word and phrase quoted here [Ed.].

186 Marx 1996, p. 530.

is probably the most detailed expression of its author's thinking in this regard, but it does not go beyond saying the following:

> From a social point of view, the productiveness increases in the same ratio as the economy of labour, which, in its turn, includes not only economy of the means of production, but also the avoidance of all useless labour. The capitalist mode of production, while on the one hand, enforcing economy in each individual business, on the other hand, begets, by its anarchical system of competition, the most outrageous squandering of labour power and of the social means of production, not to mention the creation of a vast number of employments, at present indispensable, but in themselves superfluous.[187]

Since the number of functions superfluous in themselves is 'vast', it must not be the case that it is only a matter of state functions and those that have to do with repression.

Related to the motif of superfluous functions to be abolished in communist social life is the possibility that the need for surplus labour will diminish. This seems to imply the possibility of a reduction of needs, yet as Marx always thought, as did Larfargue, that the increase of needs is concomitant with the progress of individuals, it is probably necessary to understand this implication in the sense of a global decrease of total needs in communist society, but with a selective increase in some of them (the 'spiritual' – *geistige* – needs and those involving 'exercise', judging by Marx's numerous statements in which he speaks about free time). In any case, the text does not suggest much more than what it says explicitly about this topic:

> It is, however, clear that in any given economic formation of society, where not the exchange value but the use value of the product predominates [as occurs in Marx's communist society], surplus labour will be limited by a given set of wants which may be greater or less, and that here no boundless thirst for surplus labour arises from the nature of the production itself.[188]

The most important thing about this formulation is the term 'boundless', which suggests that the constant and boundless creation of all types of needs is not

187 Ibid.

188 Marx 1996, pp. 243–4.

an inevitable consequence of the progress of production in itself, but only of its use by capitalism.

The other group of considerations that are of interest for the study of Marx's mature conception of revolutionary change and communist society start from a criticism of the effect of science and large-scale industry on agriculture under capitalism. On the one hand, large-scale industry acts on agriculture in the most revolutionary manner, since it destroys the bulwark of the old society, which is the peasant, and because it introduces scientific methods in what was precisely the most traditionalist type of production,[189] once the sciences capable of technifying agriculture, which emerge later than mechanics, are developed.[190] The uprooting which thereby breaks the old bond between agriculture, traditional craftsmanship, and manufacturing, fully realised by the development of the capitalist mode of production, is the transitory 'bad side' and asset which:

> creates the material conditions for a higher synthesis in the future, viz., the union of agriculture and industry on the basis of the more perfected forms they have each acquired during their temporary separation.[191]

However, the 'bad side' of the process has a deep dimension that affects the very roots of the life of the species. That dimension gives rise to an ecological analysis that does not exactly correspond to the kind of analysis most commonly associated with Marx's thought (the analysis of the living conditions of the new industrial working class), but which encompasses it. Capitalist production leads to the preponderance of the urban population, which it amasses in large centres;[192] it thereby stores up revolutionary potential and yet at the same time 'disturbs the circulation of matter between man and the soil' and 'violates the conditions necessary to lasting fertility of the soil'.[193] The process parallels that which occurs in capitalist industry. In the latter, the increase of labour's productivity and the facilitating of the workers' mobility result in the

189 Marx 1996, p. 506.

190 Marx 1989a, p. 341.

191 Marx 1996, p. 506.

192 When Engels proposes, in *Anti-Dühring*, the dissolution of large cities in a communist society, he is without a doubt in agreement with Marx, who, as is well known, closely followed the writing of this work and collaborated with Engels on it. 'It is true that in the huge towns civilisation has bequeathed us a heritage which it will take much time and trouble to get rid of. But it must and will be got rid of, however protracted a process it may be' (Engels 1987c, p. 283).

193 Marx 1996, pp. 506–7.

exhaustion of the workers themselves. In agriculture, the price of capitalist progress is the degradation of the land and of the farming wage-labourer:

> [A]ll progress in capitalistic agriculture is a progress in the art, not only of robbing the labourer, but of robbing the soil; all progress in increasing the fertility of the soil for a given time, is a progress towards ruining the lasting sources of that fertility.... Capitalist production, therefore, develops technology, and the combining together of various processes into a social whole, only by sapping the original sources of all wealth – the soil and the labourer.[194]

This ecological analysis, the most extensive one produced by Marx, is the basis for a programme within the framework of the new society. As capitalism will have obliterated the purely spontaneous conditions for the interchange between the human species and nature beforehand, in the new society it will be necessary to bring about 'its restoration as a system, as a regulating law of social production, and under a form appropriate to the full development of the human race'.[195] This single thesis in the mature Marx's ecological programme leaves many questions open, but it seems clear that while he regards the cause as lost under capitalism, he continues, as in 1844, to centrally locate a 'disalienated' science within the communist project, in which it will be necessary to consciously regulate the metabolism between human being and nature. It is even possible that the importance ascribed to an immaterial factor, like science, in a revolution that is to begin by producing, in a systematic manner, the interchange between nature and the species, constitutes a bridge of continuity and consistency between this mature or classic Marx and the Marx who will write, several years later, the letters to the editorial staff of *Otechestvennye Zapiski* and to Vera Zasulich. But this question deserves to be studied separately.

---

194 Marx 1996, pp. 507–8.

195 Marx 1996, p. 507.

CHAPTER 3

Engels's Task in *Anti-Dühring*

Why *Anti-Dühring* was Written

On 3 January 1877, *Vorwärts* [*Forward*], the organ of the German Social Democratic Party, began to publish a series of articles by Engels under the general title 'Herr Eugen Dühring's Revolution in Philosophy'. The series ended with the article of 13 May of the same year. Yet on 27 July, the first article of a new series appeared, entitled 'Herr Eugen Dühring's Revolution in Economics'. Part of this series – Chapter 10 of the second section of the book – is Marx's work. The last of these articles was published in *Vorwärts* on 30 December 1877. Finally, a third series began to be published on 5 May 1878 and concluded on 7 July of the same year. The general title of this last series was 'Herr Eugen Dühring's Revolution in Socialism'. In their publication in book form (three editions appeared during Engels's lifetime: 1878, 1886, and 1894), the three series of articles appear as three sections. The title of the book – *Herr Eugen Dühring's Revolution in Science* – parodies, as do the titles of the series of articles, that of a book by Dühring on the economist Carey.

Eugen Dühring was a *Privatdozent* at the University of Berlin, who in 1868 had published a review of Volume I of Marx's *Capital*. Shortly thereafter, Dühring declared his embrace of socialism and began to exercise a certain influence within the German Social Democratic Party. Dühring's influence struck Liebknecht, Marx and Engels as quite negative. From Germany, Liebknecht urged Engels to take a stand with regard to Dühring. Engels consulted Marx, who believed that taking a stand could only be done 'by criticising Dühring without any compunction'.[1] On the other hand, in the same letter Marx points out that Dühring's writings lacked importance in themselves, to such an extent that a critique of his works by Marx and Engels would be 'too paltry'.[2] Marx viewed Dühring's danger, which was of little importance, in the satisfaction that he elicited among, as Marx puts it, the 'artisans' – that is, among the trivial socialist writers without any scientific preparation – and the flattering reception

* First published in 1964. Republished as 'La tarea de Engels en el Anti-Dühring', in *Sobre Marx y marxismo. Panfletos y materiales I*, edited by Juan-Ramón Capella (Barcelona: Icaria Editorial, S.A., 1983).

1 Letter to Engels, 25 May 1876; Marx 1991c, p. 119.

2 Marx 1991c, pp. 119–20.

 DOI 10.1163/9789004280526_006

Dühring afforded them, which they could hardly fail to contrast with the severity with which Marx had always treated semi-educated figures bereft of any scientific spirit.

Dühring was indeed small potatoes. Today, as at the time of the second edition of Engels's book, nothing remains of the work of the rhetorical Berlin pedagogue, who seems to have been fated to rack his brains on account of major scientific figures like Marx or the physicist Helmholtz. Given Dühring's scientific incompetence, Engels himself was at first surprised by the success of his critique of Dühring. Yet he soon understood the source of *Anti-Dühring*'s success: this book was the first comprehensive exposition of the communist worldview inaugurated by Marx. Of course, we must not lose sight of the fact that an exposition as thematically diverse as *Anti-Dühring* can be no more than a manual of popularisation, considering that it hardly exceeds 300 pages in octavo format. Yet despite – or perhaps precisely because of – this fact, it was of great importance for the entire labour movement.

Anti-Dühring was in fact written with an immediate political and polemical motivation, and against an obscure muddler who is now forgotten. During the course of his work, however, Engels also found himself led to polemicise against an ideological current, perhaps always present in the socialist movement, which in his day was briefly represented by Dühring. From the point of view of the history of socialism, Dühring actually represents, despite his smug contempt for the utopian socialists, a return to a utopian, idealist foundation for the labour movement. For all socialist theory is based, according to Dühring, on abstract moral categories, such as Justice, Equality, the rejection of 'violent property', and so forth. While polemicising with Dühring, Engels goes about providing an exposition, as required by his arguments, of the bases of what is usually called 'scientific socialism', that is to say, a socialism that finds its support in historical reality, in actual human life, and not in a mere morally sanctioned desire.

Of course, the point is not that Marxism is devoid of moral motives. In criticising Feuerbach, Marx said that the word *communist* does not have a merely theoretical content, since it means being an active member of a specific party, which itself implies a moral element in anyone who has a right to call him- or herself a *communist* in Marx's sense, for active party membership is the result of a choice, something belonging to morality. But in this regard Marxism is characterised by the claim that the content of moral postulates must be sought in reality. A clear example of the dialectic of morality and reality in Marxist thought can be found precisely in *Anti-Dühring*, in Chapter 10 of Part One, where Engels defines the moral concept of equality's content for the labour movement and scientific socialism. Equality, for Marxism, is not an abstract postulate independent of reality, but the postulation of something with a real historical viability and a content determined by it, that is to say, by the abolition of social classes: 'the real content of the proletarian demand for equality is the demand for the *abolition of classes*. Any demand for equality which goes beyond that, of necessity passes into absurdity'.[3] Moral ideas are, like all of culture (superstructure), a function of the socio-economic base, of the real life of men and women. These ideas are determined by that base, albeit in a complicated and mediated way, and thus are either rationalisations of it, or pessimistic justifications for it, or a protest against it. In the latter case – which is that of the labour movement – moral ideas only truly make sense if they contain a rationally justified critique of the reality which they confront, if their content expresses a foreseeable future reality, and if they are placed within the framework of a worldview which is capable, on a scientific basis, of first explaining and then organising the realisation of those contents.

Engels's task in *Anti-Dühring*, aside from criticising Dühring himself, consists in clarifying this point: how the basis of modern socialism is not a moralistic desire, but knowledge of reality. 'To make a science of socialism', we read in Chapter 1 of the Introduction, 'it had first to be placed upon a real basis'.[4] This requires Engels to attempt – with all the risks of prematureness attending the effort to summarise something newly emerging – an exposition of the worldview that was to be the basis of scientific socialism. This motivation was also behind the writing of *Anti-Dühring*, although Engels may not have been completely aware of it at first, absorbed as he was by the 'paltry work' of stemming Dühring's influence within the German Social Democratic Party.

What is a Worldview?

A worldview is not knowledge in the sense of positive science; it is not learning. It is a series of principles that account for a subject's behaviour, at times without the subjects having explicitly formulated them. This is a fairly common situation: sympathies for or aversions to certain ideas, facts or persons; rapid, uncritical reactions to moral stimuli, viewing certain relations among men and women as if they were facts of nature; in short, a large part of the consciousness of daily life can be interpreted in terms of principles or beliefs that are often implicit or 'unconscious' in the subject who acts and reacts.

3 Engels 1987c, p. 99, original emphasis.

4 Engels 1987c, p. 21.

It is often the case, however, that those principles or beliefs that inspire everyday behaviour, while not always stated by the subjects themselves, are explicit in the culture of the society in which they live. This culture normally contains a set of claims regarding the nature of the physical world and life, as well as a code of values [*estimaciones*] for conduct. The contemplative or theoretical part of a worldview is intimately related to the practical part, to the code or system of value judgements, through questions such as those pertaining to the meaning of human life and death, the existence or non-existence of an ideal or spiritual principle which is the cause of the world, and so on. For example, from the theoretical claim that the human being has a defective nature [*naturaleza herida*], as Catholic theology holds, it is quite natural to arrive at the rule that postulates submission to authority. That rule is indeed consistent with the theoretical belief in question.

However, the existence of an explicit formulation of a worldview in a society's culture does not allow us to readily determine, on the basis of officially stated beliefs, which worldview is truly operative in that society, for the superstructural character of a worldview does not consist in being a direct, naïve, mechanical reflection of the lived social and natural reality. The reflection always contains a great deal of ideology, and behind the principle of charity, for example, there may be, in the society that apologetically invokes this principle, a rather cynical belief, just as behind the Rights of Man there have historically been other actual beliefs, morally far less universal. Yet it is possible to overlook this point in clarifying the role of a worldview with regard to positive-scientific knowledge (which is the main problem posed by *Anti-Dühring*), even if it is in itself indispensable for a full comprehension of cultural formations. For the study of the relationship between a worldview and positive science, however, it suffices to consider the formal aspects of each.

In cultures within the Greco-Roman tradition, worldviews tend to display certain features [*puntas*] of a very conscious and condensed sort, in the form of a religious-moral belief or philosophical system. The latter form in particular was quite characteristic until the nineteenth century. Born, in fact, from a clash with religious belief on the eve of the classical period of Greek culture, systematic philosophy, philosophy as a system, watched as one thematic field after another was taken away by the positive sciences; it ended up trying to preserve its substantialness [*sustantividad*] in a repertoire of truths that were supposedly superior to those of the whole of science. In the most ambitious cases – those of Plato or Hegel, for example – systematic philosophy exhibits more or less openly its pretension to produce through reasoning the content of the positive sciences. In this case, as in that of positive religious beliefs, the worldview wishes to be a form of knowing, real knowledge of the world, with the same positivity as that of science. This pretension can be regarded as having definitively failed by the middle of the nineteenth century, precisely with the disintegration of the most ambitious philosophical system in history, namely, Hegel's. His system, which seeks to develop the truth of the world systematically and by means of material claims, was, according to Engels's expression in the *Anti-Dühring*, 'a colossal miscarriage, but it was also the last of its kind'.[5]

There are several reasons why the pretension of systematic philosophy ends up being invalid. On a formal level, the level of the theory of knowledge, the primary cause is the conscious and definitive constitution of positive scientific knowledge during the modern era. This is a kind of knowledge formally characterised by intersubjectivity, and in practical terms by its capacity for making possible exact predictions, even if increasingly at the cost of constructing and handling exceedingly artificial concepts, veritable mental machines that do not speak at all to the imagination, unlike the meaty and intuitive concepts of the philosophical tradition. That a piece of knowledge is intersubjective means that all people with adequate preparation understand its formulation in the same way, in the sense that they are equally informed regarding the operations that would allow for the verification or falsification of said formulation. The theses of the old systematic philosophy, religious dogmas, and worldviews lack these features. And since those features afford us a considerable security and return, the positive-scientific knowledge that possesses them succeeds in dethroning, as a form of knowledge of the things of this world, the more vague and less operative thought of traditional systematic philosophy.

That worldviews lack these two characteristic features of positive knowledge is not an accident or something remediable, but rather inevitable: it is due to the fact that worldviews by their very nature contain claims about questions that cannot be resolved by the decision methods of positive knowledge, which are empirical verification or falsification and analytical argumentation (whether deductive or inductive-probabilistic). For example, an authentic worldview must contain – either explicitly or in a sense that can be made explicit – statements concerning the existence or non-existence of God, the finiteness or infiniteness of the universe, the meaning or meaninglessness of these questions, and so on, and these statements will never be open to empirical proof, demonstration or refutation in the same sense as in the sciences. This does not mean that positive knowledge – and, above all, its methodological requirements – does not lend more credence to one worldview than to

5 Engels 1987c, p. 25.

another. But to lend credence to, or to render plausible, is not the same thing as to prove in a positive sense.[6]

These features enable us to correctly pose the question of the relationship between a worldview and positive-scientific knowledge. A worldview that takes science as the only body of real knowledge will be visibly – to use a simplifying spatial comparison – both ahead of and behind positive research. Behind because it will attempt to build itself in accordance with the course and results of positive research; ahead because as a general view of reality, the worldview inspires or motivates positive research itself. For example, if the modern scientist's worldview were truly dualist on the question of soul and body, science would never have undertaken the kind of research that constitutes psychology, and the psychologist would never have taken an interest in the physiology of the central nervous system from a psychological point of view. This is true independently of the fact that the society's dominant ideology makes the scientist profess, when he is not engaged in research, a dualist conception of the world.

In reality, the worldview's quality of inspiring research is poorly captured by the spatial comparison just mentioned, for that inspiration is constantly produced, throughout research, in combination with its internal, formal-dialectical needs. It is important to realise that when, in accordance with the positivist programme, science moves to and fro in the illusion of having nothing to do with any worldview, the scientist runs the risk of submitting unconsciously to

---

6 An excessively common vulgarisation of Marxism insists on using loosely and anachronistically (as in the days of the Romantic and idealist 'philosophy of nature') the terms *demonstrate, prove* and *refute* for arguments whose plausibility corresponds to that of a worldview. Thus, for example, we repeatedly find the inept phrase that the course of science 'has demonstrated the non-existence of God'. This is literally nonsense. Science cannot prove or demonstrate anything regarding the universe as a whole, but only statements regarding isolated and (in some sense) abstract sectors of the universe. Empirical science cannot prove, for example, that a being called *Abracadabraing Abracadabra* does not exist, for faced with any positive-scientific report declaring that this being has not been found, it is always possible to answer that the Abracadabra in question is to be found beyond the reach of telescopes and microscopes, or to claim that Abracadabraing Abracadabra is imperceptible, and not even positively conceivable by human reason, and so forth. What science can establish is that the claim that the Abracadabraing Abracadabra exists does not serve any explanatory function at all regarding known phenomena, and therefore is not suggested by them.

Moreover, the vulgar phrase 'demonstration of the inexistence of God' is a naïve blunder that burdens materialism with the absurd task of demonstrating or proving instances of non-existence. Instances of *non-existence* cannot be proven; instances of *existence* are proven. The one who asserts an instance of existence bears the burden of proof, not the one who does not assert such an instance.

the worldview prevailing in his or her society, which is that much more dangerous to the extent that it is not recognised as such. And it is no less important to maintain, in spite of that complexity, the distinction between positive knowledge and worldview.

The Marxist Worldview

The 'materialist and dialectical conception of the world', referred to by Engels at other times more loosely as the 'communist world outlook',[7] is motivated, as is everything in Marxism, by the aim of putting an end to the clouding of consciousness, to the presence in human conduct of factors that are unacknowledged or idealised. It follows from this that it is an explicit worldview, or that it presents itself with the task of becoming explicit in every respect: to believe that consciousness can become the master of itself through mere theoretical effort is an idealist attitude foreign to Marxism. The liberation of consciousness presupposes the liberation of practice, the liberation of the hands. And from this we can infer a second feature of the Marxist worldview, one that is important, if unfortunately barely respected, on account of the prevalence of simplifying and trivialising tendencies. This second feature consists in the fact that the Marxist worldview cannot regard its explicit elements as a system of knowledge superior to positive knowledge. The new materialism, writes Engels in *Anti-Dühring*,

> is no longer a philosophy at all, but simply a world outlook which has to establish its validity and be applied not in a science of sciences standing apart, but in the real sciences. Philosophy is therefore 'sublated' here, that is, 'both overcome and preserved'; overcome as regards its form, and preserved as regards its real content.[8]

This concise and expressive formulation by Engels implies a conception of philosophy not as a system superior to science, but as one level of scientific thought: that of the inspiration for research itself and for reflection on its development and results, in accordance with the description given in the preceding section. But it is worth noting – and we shall return to this later on – that Engels's formula remains very general; depending on how this formula is

7 Engels 1987c, p. 8.
8 Engels 1987c, p. 129.

fleshed out in the exact elaboration of a worldview, there may arise the risk of confusion between the positive and philosophical levels.

For now, it will be more interesting to examine in greater detail the wisdom of this general formula. To begin with, it contains the rejection of all systematic philosophy: there is no 'separate' knowledge above positive knowledge. Recalling one of Kant's celebrated phrases, we could say that there is no philosophy for Marxism either, only philosophising. Secondly, given that both its starting point and end point are 'real science', this worldview cannot seek anything more than to develop the motivation for science itself. This motivation can be called, in classical philosophical terminology, *immanentism*: the principle – often implicit, more visible in scientists' behaviour than in their words – that the explanation for phenomena must be sought in other phenomena in the world, and not in occurrences alien to or above the world. This principle lies at the basis of scientific activity, which would lose all meaning and be reduced to absurdity if at any given time it had to allow for the action of non-natural causes, which would necessarily destroy the web of this-worldly relations ('laws') that science strives to discover and to construct in order to understand reality.

The Marxist worldview is based on this postulate of immanentism, which defines the possibility of scientific knowledge. The first principle of the Marxist conception of the world – materialism – is fundamentally a statement, at an explicit philosophical level, of the immanentist postulate: the world must be explained by itself. Materialism is, even historically, the first thing in Marxism, that is, in the history of its gradual composition in Marx's and – to a much lesser degree – Engels's thought.

However, materialism is but one of the two fundamental principles of what Engels calls the 'communist world outlook'. The other one is the principle of the dialectic. The latter finds its inspiration not so much in positive-scientific activity as in its limitations. A study, however brief, of the place of the dialectic in Marxist thought requires (if this place is to be understood without paying an excessive tribute, unnecessary today, to the Hegelian historical origin of the Marxist concept of dialectic) a brief detour though the realm of the method of positive science.

Positive science fulfils the principle of materialism through a reductive-analytic methodology. Its elimination of irrational factors in the explanation of the world proceeds through an analytical reduction of complex and qualitatively determined formations to less complex (in a sense to be specified in every case) and qualitatively more homogeneous factors, with a tendency to a reduction so extreme that the qualitative aspect loses all importance. This way of proceeding – so visible, for example, in physical chemistry – has characterised all scientific work through its very different phases, from ancient mechanics to the modern search for 'elementary particles'. More generally, the reductive analysis practiced by science even tends to leave aside concepts with qualitative content altogether, so as to limit itself in the main to the handling of quantitative, or at least materially empty, formal relations. This is clearly noticeable in the beginnings of modern positive science. Thus, for example, what we today call 'atmospheric pressure' was for some time dealt with by early modern science by means of the old name of 'nature's horror of a vacuum', without the use of this notion causing major problems, for what was truly of interest for the reductive analysis of the phenomenon (form Galileo to Torricelli) was to obtain a number that measured the force in question, whatever its nature.

The reductive analysis practiced by science succeeds on a regular basis. Its success can be broken down into two aspects. On the one hand, the reduction of complex phenomena to more elementary, homogeneous notions, wholly devoid, in the ideal case, of qualitative connotations, enables us to fathom reality quite materially and effectively, since it makes it possible to pose very precise questions to nature (questions that are quantified and bear on 'elementary' phenomena), and to make exact predictions which, if proven correct, confirm to a greater or lesser extent the hypotheses on which they are based, and which, if proven incorrect, falsify them definitively. On the other hand, in the long run reductive analysis makes possible the formation of more adequate concepts, if only through the destruction of the old, inadequate concepts. Thus, although the concept of atmospheric pressure does not yet appear in Galileo, as it does in Torricelli and Pascal, Galileo had already relativised and minimised the qualitative content of the traditional concept of nature's horror of a vacuum.

However, precisely because they are based on a reductive analysis that by means of abstraction dispenses with the qualitative peculiarity of the complex phenomena analysed and reduced, the concepts of science in the narrow sense – modern positive science – are invariably general concepts whose place is in statements that are no less general, 'laws', as we usually say, which provide information about entire classes of objects. With this knowledge, a part of concrete things is lost: precisely that part that is decisive for the individualisation of objects. This is the case not because of any accidental limitation, but rather as a result of the defining assumption of the analytic-reductive methodology, which is simply motivated by the materialist principle of explaining all complex, qualitatively distinct formations by the same, more or less homogeneous factors.

Complex and concrete 'wholes' do not appear in the discourse of positive science, even though the latter supplies all of the reliable elements for any rational comprehension of said wholes. What it does not supply is their totality, their concrete consistency. The relevant field or range for dialectical thought is precisely that of concrete totalities. Hegel expressed this motivation in his poetic language by saying that 'the True is the whole'.[9]

A worldview must of necessity yield a specific comprehension of concrete totalities. For human practice is confronted not merely with the need to fathom reality analytico-reductively, but also with the need to understand and deal with real concrete phenomena [*concreciones*], which positive science cannot grasp. According to this view, the task of a materialist dialectic consists in recovering what is concrete without bringing to bear anything other than the materialist data of reductive analysis, and without conceiving the qualities lost in reductive analysis as entities that must be added to the data, but rather as the new result of the structuring of these data in the individual or concrete formation, in the 'natural wholes'. 'The living soul of Marxism', according to Lenin's phrase, is 'a concrete analysis of a concrete situation'.[10] However, the word 'analysis' does not have the same meaning here as in positive science. Marxist analysis seeks to understand the concrete, individual situation (in this regard it is dialectical thought) without postulating any components of the situation other than the results of abstraction and reductive scientific analysis (and in this regard Marxism is a materialism).

In this sense, the level or world of discourse within which it really makes sense to speak of dialectical thought or analysis would seem to be clear: it is at the level of understanding concrete phenomena or totalities, not that of the reductive analysis of positive science. Concrete phenomena or totalities are, in this dialectical sense, first and foremost living individuals and particular historical formations, the 'concrete situations' of which Lenin speaks, that is, the locally delimited historical presents, and so on. They are also, in a much emptier sense, the universe as a totality, which cannot be thought, as is obvious, in terms of positive-scientific analysis, but dialectically, on the basis of the results of said analysis.

The Presentation of the Marxist Dialectic in *Anti-Dühring*

There is no shortage of passages in *Anti-Dühring* specifying, with more or less detail, the scope of the dialectic's relevance, the level at which it makes sense to pass from the abstract, analytical, reductive scrutiny of reality by positive

9 Hegel 1977, p. 11.

10 Lenin 1966, p. 166.

science to the synthetic, reconstituting language proper to the dialectical, materialist worldview. For example, Engels explains that with the general language of the dialectic it is not possible to fathom analytically any '*particular* process of development',[11] and also that the dialectic is not 'a mere proof-producing instrument',[12] like reason in positive scientific theory, but must be understood as inspiring research. Several of his examples clearly suggest the comprehension of concrete structures, and not the formulation of general positive laws. In this regard, his use of the Hegelian terms 'contradiction' [*Widerspruch*] and 'antagonism' [*Gegensatz*] are very illuminating. Engels does not use them as synonyms – in contrast to what tends to happen in many didactic expositions of Marxism. In general, Engels speaks of 'contradiction' when the subject is some real structure, for example, the structure consisting of the web of relations that constitutes the capitalist mode of production. A real structure, the structure of some existing formation, is, indeed, not like a mathematical or formal structure, something free of inconsistencies by design. For the structure of a real formation is the structure of something historical, with elements of diverse origin and no guarantee of consistency. Antagonism is, on the other hand, a relation between elements of a real structure. Hence what is empirically observable, such as clashes and interaction, are antagonisms: the antagonisms develop structural contradictions. This process of development may require a stretch of historical development:

> [M]odern industry has developed the contradictions lying dormant in the capitalist mode of production into such crying antagonisms that the approaching collapse of this mode of production is, so to speak, palpable.[13]

But whether or not its development requires time, it is always a question of the same thing: antagonisms embody contradictions; real elements of a concrete situation oppose one another because they occupy contradictory positions in a real structure. For example, 'the contradiction between socialised production and capitalistic appropriation manifested itself as the antagonism of proletariat and bourgeoisie'.[14]

Nonetheless, still more frequent in *Anti-Dühring* are examples of an inappropriate application of the dialectic outside of its scope of relevance. In the Introduction, Engels writes, 'every new theory … [has], at first, to connect

---

11 Engels 1987c, p. 131, original emphasis.
12 Engels 1987c, p. 125.
13 Engels 1987c, pp. 253–4.
14 Engels 1987c, p. 259, original emphasis.

itself with the intellectual stock-in-trade ready to its hand, however deeply its roots lay in economic facts'.[15] Engels and Marx had to connect themselves with Hegel's repertoire of concepts, no matter how much the roots of their new theory lay elsewhere, namely, in socio-economic reality and the labour movement. And this obligatory connection with Hegel often results, on account of this great thinker's profound ambiguity, in an unjustified invasion of the terrain of positive science, in a sterile, purely verbal application of the dialectic to the level of abstract and reductive analysis. The well-known and unfortunate example of the grain of barley – which in its sowing, germination, and growth is to be understood in accordance with the time-honoured Hegelian formula of the 'negation of the negation' – is typical in this regard. Scientific knowledge begins to count in human life precisely when it frees itself from such approximate and imprecise descriptions, mere paraphrases of crude experience (like the scholastic-Aristotelian 'actuality' and 'potency'), and grasps analytically-reductively the germinating grain of barley.

This inappropriate application of the dialectic to levels and for tasks proper to the reductive analysis of science sometimes has consequences that contradict basic principles of Marxism. The most incontestable example in this regard is perhaps Engels's interpretation of infinitesimal calculus. As is well known, infinitesimal calculus was born of intuition, as a mere practical operation of computation, over a long period of evolution that began with the 'methods of exhaustion' of the ancients, and which has important milestones in the seventeenth century with Leibniz and Newton. In its Leibnizian-Newtonian state, infinitesimal calculus is still without a theory, that is to say, there is no clarity with regard to its logical grounding or justification. It functions with absurd notions, like that of infinitesimal ('infinitely small quantity'), or others that are vague and imprecise, like the Newtonian 'fluxion'. Owing to Hegel's influence, Engels delights in taking that unresolved state of science as a 'proof' of the reality of contradiction in mathematics. Nowadays, the old antinomies of infinitesimal calculus have been overcome in mathematics, and those 'contradictions' prove to be a mere consequence of the improper mix of two levels of thought: that of calculus itself, which is *an intellectual artefact*, and that of its application to natural reality, specifically the calculation of surfaces. To integrate is not to 'sum infinitesimals' in order to find a total; rather it is to go from one equation to another by means of operations that are now logically clear. One can then apply this technique for passing from one equation to another to calculate surfaces, for example, or distances, and so forth. And the variables of calculus are simple signs that save, in a formula, a place for values of a certain

15 Engels 1987c, p. 16.

kind, and not, as Engels views them (in a Hegelian fashion), 'contradictory' quantities that can be made 'infinitely small' and then 'enlarged'. The latter notion is not dialectically contradictory; it is simply absurd. What may vary is the real object measured by the quantities that can occupy the place of a variable in the formulas, but not the quantities themselves, which express the result of each measurement. These do not change, but rather are simply different in each case. When a person gains weight, going from 50 to 60 kilos, it is not the number 50 that changes, but rather the person. The number 50, a *conceptual construct* of science, is always the same.

In all of his observations on infinitesimal calculus (in Chapter 13 of Part One), and on mathematics in general, Engels fails to see something that is essential from the Marxist point of view: the importance of practice to all aspects of human life, and therefore also to the internal structure and function of scientific activity. This is why he conceives of science's constructs statically, as copies of nature, rather than as human beings' responses to the problems posed by nature.[16] A calculation or algorithm, or even, in large measure, a positive scientific theory, are constructs, as are machines; they are the fruit of a determinate practice, the practice of science, of positive knowledge. This practice is dialectically joined to all other practices in a *concrete totality* of human life within a given society. The dialectical treatment of that practice consists in seeing it as an element of this concrete totality, and not in replacing its own internal functioning. Just as it would be absurd to seek in every piece of a machine a direct and unmediated reflection of reality, so too is it inappropriate to seek in every piece of knowledge the full dialecticity of human life and nature. This is what Engels frequently does – whenever he attempts to grasp dialectically the analytical operations of science – and the Marxist reader must not hide this fact from him- or herself, since it results from forgetting the principle of practice, which is the principle of work, at the level of intellectual work. And the fact that this principle is forgotten is enough to make us realise that Engels's exposition [*desarrollos*] offers a Marxism that remains undeveloped [*no realizado*], one that is still not entirely conscious of itself.

The most serious consequence of the relative absence of the principle of practice in *Anti-Dühring* – and of the resulting Hegelian confusion of the

16 When he makes general statements, Engels tends to be above this way of seeing things – thus he says, for example, that the needs of mathematics are far from being the needs of nature. For the most part, he only lapses into this view in his specific interpretations of pieces of knowledge, theories or notions. Yet these specific interpretations are precisely the touchstone for assessing the extent to which the general statements are borne out in *Anti-Dühring*.

analytical (positive-scientific) and synthetic (dialectical) levels – is the idealist solution that Engels formulates for the problem of the chasm between world-view (or philosophising) and science:

> Only by learning to assimilate the results of the development of philosophy during the past two and a half thousand years will it [empirical natural science] rid itself on the one hand of any natural philosophy standing apart from it, outside it and above it, and on the other hand also of its own limited method of thought, which is its inheritance from English empiricism.[17]

It is a basic principle of Marxism that no division within culture – such as that between scientific reductive analysis and philosophical synthesis – can be overcome by means of ideas (for example, by learning to assimilate a three-thousand year old tradition), but only by the revolutionary, material overcoming of that aspect of the natural division of labour that establishes the division in question. With the idealist procedure of anticipating by means of ideas the real overcoming of the divisions in human life, we can obtain nothing more than utopian and, in a certain formal sense, 'reactionary', regressive solutions. Engels's results regarding these critical points in *Anti-Dühring* might serve as examples of both things: in saying that the logical difficulties of Leibnizian-Newtonian infinitesimal calculus were fundamental and would never be solved in mathematical theory, Engels assumes a regressive epistemological attitude, which was later overcome by the efforts of mathematicians; and with his version of the fusion of scientific analysis and dialectical synthesis, Engels reproduces the utopia of Goethe, Hegel or Leopold von Henning concerning the integration of 'experiment' and 'faculty of judgment', 'science' and 'poetry'.[18]

Finally, when the inadequacy of the direct dialectical treatment of the abstract analytical themes of science makes it plain to him that he manages to say absolutely nothing new of cognitive value in connection with positive analysis, Engels takes refuge in a definition of the dialectic that is scarcely relevant and quite empty, since it fails to capture what is essential to dialectical thought: the recovery of the real, concrete phenomena that science's reductive analysis forsakes, because of its premises. (Moreover, this recovery of real totalities is the serious question underlying the Hegelian paradox of the 'concrete universal'). That definition, perpetuated by the manuals, refers to

---

17 Engels 1987c, pp. 14–15.

18 Some information relating to this point can be found in my article, 'La veracidad de Goethe' ['Goethe's Truth'] (Sacristán 1963, pp. 12–29).

only one of the fields to which the dialectic is relevant – the universe – and without even suggesting that the dialectical consideration of the universe is that which regards it as a totality that must be understood solely by means of immanent principles, as a totality which is, to be sure, the emptiest of all of the dialectically concrete phenomena. The definition can be found in Part One, Chapter 13, and reads as follows: 'Dialectics, however, is nothing more than the science of the general laws of motion and development of nature, human society and thought'.[19] The surprising expression 'is nothing more than' seems to reflect a certain perplexity on Engels's part (if we bear in mind its context in that chapter), for Engels must have known, even if he did not clearly express [*realizado*] it, that the Marxist dialectic is much more than that, namely, in the words of Lenin cited earlier, the 'concrete analysis of a concrete situation', an attempt to comprehend the concrete realities that human beings face, which are not the differential equations of classical mechanics or the Dirac equation, but other human beings, other concrete, structured wholes composed of humans, concrete states of nature, and the concrete support and resistance of nature: in a word, life.

The Question of 'Engelsism'

The evident underdevelopment [*inmadurez*] of the exposition of the Marxist dialectic in *Anti-Dühring* and in the *Dialectics of Nature*, the fact that Hegel is not only the inspiration for Engels's dialectical thought but at times its idealist lord [*dominador*], as well as the fact that as a result of this, Engels assumes some of science's regressive, paralysing methodological attitudes (the cited example regarding infinitesimal calculus is not the only one), together form the basis for a vague spirit of opposition to Engels's works. This spirit is found above all among existentialists and neo-positivists interested in Marxism, and also among Marxists interested in existentialism and neo-positivism.

It is true that this may be to trace back to Engels one of the worst features of the Marxist tradition, which consists, according to Roger Garaudy's euphemistic expression, in 'anticipating' the results of science.[20] Yet this is only partially true. Engels, who in *Anti-Dühring* repeatedly displays the chief virtue for an intellectual, namely, modesty, cannot be held responsible for a certain inveterate piety that insists on regarding his modest manual of popularisation as

19 Engels 1987c, p. 131.

20 Garaudy 1960.

'an encyclopedia of Marxism'.[21] The primary cause of this paralysing effect of positive scientific thought[22] is not Engels's Hegelian limitation, but certain circumstances that could hardly be avoided and were inevitable in the past, and which concern the relationship of the labour movement to its classic texts.

As a general rule, for those who practice the same science, a classic author – for example, Euclid – is no more than a source of inspiration that defines, with more or less clarity, the basic motivations of their thought. However, the classics of the labour movement have defined, in addition to some basic intellectual motivations, the foundations for the movement's practice, its general objectives. The classics of Marxism are classics of a worldview, not classics of a special positive-scientific theory. As a result, there exists in the labour movement a relationship of militant adherence to its classics. Given this necessary relationship, it is quite normal for the lazy, uncritical tendency, the tendency to worry about nothing other than one's own moral security, to frequently prevail in the reading of these classics, unjustly conferring on any historical state of the theory the same inviolability as is found in the programmatic objectives that define a socio-political movement. If we add to this the fact that the struggle against Marxism – from outside the labour movement as well as within it, through what is usually called 'revisionism' – combines, for its part and for reasons that are easy to understand, the criticism of theoretical developments that are more or less outmoded with the betrayal of the labour movements' objectives, one immediately understands why a lazy and dogmatic interpretation of the classic texts of Marxism has had an easy time of it up to now. And the triumph of this interpretation was absolute, thanks to the concurrence of the requirements of invariably simplifying popularisations and the tight machinery built by Zhdanov and Stalin for the organisation of Marxist culture. It is probably fair to admit that the simplification of Marxism could perhaps scarcely have been avoided during the impressive process of teaching adult literacy and the introduction of scientific techniques into the archaic Russian society of fifty years ago. But today, when the productive forces have grown to a much higher level in both socialist and capitalist countries, the task of

21 Insitut für Marxismus-Leninismus beim ZK der SED 1975, p. viii.

22 Garaudy, in the book cited, includes some words from the distinguished Soviet physicist, D.I. Blohinzev, which prove that the expression used above is no exaggeration: 'In order for some fact or other or some or another theory to be connected to idealism or positivism, or interpreted in the spirit of these philosophies, it was enough that the content of that fact or theory be completely rejected'. [Sacristán does not provide a page number for this reference, which I have translated from his Spanish translation (Ed.)].

liberating Marxism from a dogmatic, clerical reading of the classic works is urgent enough for us to face any risk.

However, the Marxist path that leads to that goal does not involve a rejection of Engels. The thesis – old enough, but which has been revitalised today, above all by French existentialism – that it is necessary to liberate Marxism from a naïve, 'naturalist' 'Engelsism', descriptively superadded to the social or humanistic 'wisdom' of Marx, is historically false. The underdevelopment [*inmadurez*] of Engels's dialectical thought, at least as far as the relationship between the communist worldview and the positive science of nature is concerned, can without a doubt also be found in Marx (albeit to a lesser extent in Marx's works). Yet this is mainly due to the 'division of labour' that governed the actions of Marxism's two founders, as Engels himself indicates in *Anti-Dühring*. Owing to this division of labour, Marx was not faced with the need to present general, compendious popularisations of his thought (indeed, the one time that he did so, in *The German Ideology*, he surrendered the manuscript 'to the gnawing criticism of the mice'),[23] and could concentrate on the elaboration of factual material (*Capital*) and on the 'concrete analysis of the concrete situation' (his articles and historical studies). It is true that one must look for the essence of Marxism more in Marx's immense effort to understand concrete phenomena than in Engels's premature general expositions. However, if Marx had been required to write such expositions, he would surely have lapsed into the same inevitable submission to Hegel, given the need to cling to the 'intellectual material' available for expressing an initial awareness of one's own intellectual motivations. In any case, Marx supervised Engels's work on *Anti-Dühring*. Engels attests to this in his preface to the second edition of the book:

> [I]nasmuch as the mode of outlook expounded in this book was founded and developed in far greater measure by Marx, and only to an insignificant degree by myself, it was self-understood between us that this exposition of mine should not be issued without his knowledge. I read the whole manuscript to him before it was printed, and the tenth chapter of the part on economics ('From *Kritische Geschichte*') was written by Marx ... [W]e had always been accustomed to help each other out in special subjects.[24]

It is even quite likely that the confused conception of infinitesimal calculus that Engels presents in *Anti-Dühring* comes directly from Marx. More than a

23 Marx 1987b, p. 264.

24 Engels 1987c, p. 9.

thousand pages of calculations and mathematical reflections by Marx have been preserved, but the Soviet Institute of Marxism-Leninism has not published them up to now (probably with good reason).

The thesis, then, that posits a naïve, naturalist, and at times idealist 'Engelsism', which has nothing to do with Marx, is in the first place historically scarcely defensible. But in addition, it is not at all Marxist, for Marxism is an explicit worldview, and so necessarily it must also contain a vision of the relationship between humanity and nature, and consequently a vision of nature itself and of the science that studies it. A disregard for the need to make explicit that aspect of the worldview is not a refined Marxism, but rather positivism or existentialism: positivism, when the attitude is based on the opinion that there is no possibility of rational thought other than that which consists in collecting perceptible-empirical data, and at most ordering them, for economy of thought; and existentialism when avoidance of the task of making explicit one's own conception of nature, scientifically known through the compartmentalised abstractions of science, is based on the idea that the true relationship of human beings to nature has nothing to do with science, faith in which ought to be destroyed, according to Sartre's expression.

The first attitude, that of neo-positivism, results in the surrender of a worldview – of the questions which, as Kant saw precisely as he was inaugurating critical philosophy, are ineliminable from thought – to non-rational authority, which protects itself, thanks to this disqualification, from the progressive destruction to which it has been subjected by science, while social change was weakening its roots in human life. The second attitude, that of existentialism, is related to a conception of freedom as a pure empty space of consciousness. For this conception of freedom, all that is not an 'authentic' decision of the individual, all that is not his or her 'own' decision, is unfreedom. And it is clear that positive scientific knowledge is not the individual's own decision.

However, it is a decision of human beings to undertake science, and to hold that the only data from which to begin the attempt to understand even that which can never be a scientific fact – the universal totality and the particular totalities in their real, concrete qualities – are the data of science. This decision is indeed characteristic of Marxism, and is programmatically laid out by Engels in *Anti-Dühring* precisely in the various passages in which he denies that the Marxist worldview can be a philosophical system.

The fact remains that, if it cannot be a system, it cannot be immutable either, but rather must change its language and factual starting point to the extent that knowledge, and the human society with which it is concerned, change over time. Marxism is, in its concrete totality, the attempt to consciously formulate the implications, assumptions, and consequences of the effort to create a communist society and culture. And just as the specific data of that effort – its assumptions, implications, and factual consequences – change, so too must the assumptions, implications, and particular theoretical consequences – the intellectual horizon of each era. The only thing that cannot change in Marxism without vitiating Marxism is its general materialist, dialectical outlook [*planteamiento*], which can be summarised in a rather limited set of principles, with the following two – the most general and also the most formal – at the top: that all being is material, and that its various qualitative states (for instance, consciousness) are compositions of matter in motion; and that this constant movement and change of being, with its real creation of new qualities, acts on its own, owing to its dialectical composition. From these two maximally general principles of the Marxist worldview, we can derive two methodological necessities, which are also the most general and unchanging methodological necessities of Marxist thought: (1) to only admit as genetic data that of positive-scientific explanation, in whatever state of development the latter finds itself in each era; and (2) to recover, on the basis of these data, the concreteness of higher, complex formations. We achieve the latter not by admitting otherworldly causes that could confer on matter, from without, the new defining qualities of every higher, complex formation, but by considering every one of these formations, once it really occurs, in its activity and movement, and above all in three of its manifestations [*despliegues*]. Though imbricated in reality, these manifestations can be distinguished as intra-action (internal dialectic) of the formation, re-action of each complex formation vis-à-vis genetically earlier instances (as revealed by the reductive analysis of science), and inter-action, or the reciprocal action of the formation vis-à-vis the various formations at the same reductive-analytical level.

These essential features of the Marxist worldview and dialectical method *must* exclude any dogmatic adherence to the results of its concrete application, since this application must take the analytical data of science as its starting point at every moment. It is clear, moreover, that only in this way can Marxism fulfil the task which Engels deems essential, and which is of course more important than any passive speculative moment: to raise socialism to a high scientific level and keep it there.

That all of this was insufficiently clear in the development of the theory – but not in its general formulation, as is proven by Engels's insistence, in *Anti-Dühring*, on denying that it makes any concrete sense to speak of 'absolute, eternal truths' – by Engels, and certainly by Marx as well, seems beyond question. It should likewise be beyond question, on the other hand, that the harmful consequences that this has had for Marxism are attributable less to Engels than to the vicissitudes of the labour movement and the construction of socialism in the USSR. Yet Engels's task in *Anti-Dühring*, which consists in making explicit, starting from his own historico-cultural situation, the communist worldview, is a task essential to Marxist thought, a task that it must constantly undertake anew. Indeed, it must do so more in connection with the 'concrete analysis of a concrete situation', a framework within which the materialist dialectic becomes operative, than with the lax, expository overviews, which become progressively emptier the more they distance themselves from positive science and concrete phenomena. Yet it must also perform this task, without any great pretensions to major changes in content, at the greatest remove from positive research, that is to say, in the realm of a general view of reality, which is in fact an inspiration (though not the only one) for science itself.

Barcelona, 1 May 1964

CHAPTER 4

Marx on Spain

Analysis and Tambourines[1]

I think it continues to be true that if, as I wrote in the 1960s, the reading of Marx's articles on Spain may be interesting for people today, it is because those articles are a good illustration of his method, his intellectual style.[2] Even so, one might also wish to read them less out of a desire to learn than for entertainment, for those journalistic pieces (correspondent's reports and in-depth articles for the *New York Daily Tribune* written in 1854 and 1856) allow us to glimpse a backdrop of experience or perception [*vivencia*] of all things Spanish, composed of both common clichés and Marx's own shrewd observations. This backdrop also reflects a familiarity with the ethical and poetic motifs of the Schillerian *Sturm und Drang*, the young Goethe and the old Goethe, the sensibility of the Young Germany in regard to the assonance of Castilian romance verse, and the sensibility of German romanticism in regard to our Baroque drama. All of this adds interest, between aesthetics and the wisdom of life, to the value of the methodological example, which is without doubt the most important thing in Marx's writings on Spain.

* First published in 1983. Republished as 'Marx sobre España', in *Lecturas de filosofía moderna y contemporánea*, edited by Albert Domingo Curto (Madrid: Editorial Trotta, 2007). Reprinted by permission of the publisher.

1 An allusion to 'the Spain of the tambourine' ['la España de pandereta'], i.e. the 'typical' Spain geared to tourists [Ed.].

2 Marx's articles on Spain consist of the following: 11 relatively brief correspondent's reports on the June 1854 O'Donnell and Dulce uprising; nine in-depth articles, or small essays, on Spanish history, of which the newspaper for which he wrote them (along with his correspondent's reports), the *New York Daily Tribune*, only published eight; two more correspondent's reports on the occasion of O'Donnell's 1856 coup; and the 'Bolivar' article for the *New American Cyclopedia*, which is from 1858. Engels also wrote articles on Spanish affairs for the *New York Daily Tribune*: three articles in 1860, titled 'The Moorish War', on O'Donnell's capture of Tetouan. Besides that, he wrote about the Spanish Army for *Putnam's Magazine* (1855) and the articles 'Badajoz' and 'Bidosa' for the *New American Cyclopedia* (1858). However, Engels's most important and influential text on Spain is the set of four articles titled 'The Bakuninists at Work' ['Die Bakuninisten and der Arbeit'], published in 1873 in *Der Volksstaat*, the organ of the German Social Democracy. The present article only considers Marx's articles on Spain.

 | DOI 10.1163/9789004280526_007

The sensibility that these readings and experiences, which were not always well developed, awoke in Marx reveals a certain affinity with things Spanish, often in contrast to a certain scorn, no less a German Romantic cliché, toward a large part of French literature, as in this passage from a letter to Engels of 3 May 1854, a sample of the taste – and good taste, one must say – of German Romanticism:

> At odd moments I am going in for Spanish. Have begun with Calderón from whose *Mágico prodigioso* – the Catholic Faustus – Goethe drew not just a passage here or there but whole settings for some of scenes in his *Faust*. Then – *horribile dictu* – I am reading in Spanish what I'd found impossible in French, Chateaubriand's *Atala* and *René*, and some stuff by Bernardin de St-Pierre.[3]

The affinity in question has its odd moments, as when, referring to the Castilian War of the Communities, Marx speaks of Carlos I and explains to his American public: 'or Charles V, as the Germans call him' (*New York Daily Tribune* [NYDT], 9 September 1854).[4] When he transforms himself into a Spaniard, Marx can become as moving as on orator on 12 October;[5] thus he comments, for example, on the defeat of the *Comuneros* [Communitics rebels]:

> If after the reign of Carlos I the decline of Spain, both in a political and social aspect, exhibited all those symptoms of inglorious and protracted putrefaction so repulsive in the worst times of the Turkish Empire, under the Emperor at least the ancient liberties were buried in a magnificent tomb. This was the time when Vasco Núñes de Balboa planted the banner of Castile upon the shores of Darien, Cortés in Mexico, and Pizarro in Peru; when Spanish influence reigned supreme in Europe, and the Southern imagination of the Iberians was bewildered with visions of Eldorados, chivalrous adventures, and universal monarchy.[6]

And the attraction of things Spanish is not limited to the brilliant period in which 'Spanish liberty disappeared';[7] also: 'an appreciation of ... all she [Spain] has done and suffered since the Napoleonic usurpation ... [is] one of the most

---

3 Marx 1983a, p. 447.
4 Marx 1980d, p. 392.
5 Spain's national holiday [Ed.].
6 Marx 1980d, p. 395.
7 Ibid.

touching and instructive chapters in all modern history'.[8] It is precisely when he speaks of the Spanish War of Independence that Marx expresses himself most emotionally, with accents that are quite reminiscent of Heine's verses about Riego and Quiroga. The War of Independence is a 'great national movement' with 'heroic episodes', a 'memorable exhibition of vitality in a people supposed to be moribund'.[9] And it is quite remarkable that the action of the Napoleonic armies is not, for Marx, fundamentally a means of completing the ascent of the bourgeoisie, but 'the Napoleonic assault on the nation'.[10] 'On the one side', writes Marx with rather surprising conviction, 'stood the *Afrancesados* (the Frenchified), and on the other the nation'.[11]

Naturally, among Marx's Spanish clichés there are some that reflect the Central European's surprise vis-à-vis what he views as a somewhat ridiculous southern exuberance: 'where is imagination greater than in the south of Europe?', wonders Marx,[12] thereby explaining everything from the prestige of the guerrilla caudillos to the bombast of the military proclamations. Yet foremost in his own imagination are images projected by a nostalgia for that South, which is not so much the Goethean nostalgia for the lands 'where the lemon trees bloom' as one of a different, moral and political sort, that which is felt for the noble farmers who – 'a feature peculiar to Spain' – 'if poor and plundered, did never groan under that consciousness of abject degradation which exasperated them in the rest of feudal Europe'.[13]

Cervantes Between Homer and Shakespeare

As is well known, Marx's literary tastes were solid to the point of bordering on the conventional. 'Thus to me, as to my sisters before me', recalled his daughter Eleanor, 'he read the whole of Homer, the whole *Nibelungen Lied, Gudrun, Don Quixote*, the *Arabian Nights*, etc. As to Shakespeare he was the Bible of our house'.[14] And Lafargue recounts in his 'Reminiscences of Marx' that Marx's favourite novelists were Cervantes and Balzac. The main literary critic from the first generation of Marxists, Franz Mehring, made an observation that enables

8 Marx 1980d, p. 399.
9 Marx 1980d, p. 400.
10 Ibid.
11 Marx 1980d, p. 402.
12 Marx 1980c, p. 343.
13 Marx 1980g, p. 657.
14 Marx-Aveling n.d., p. 252.

us to see in those utterly canonical literary tastes a motivation that is deep and quite in keeping with Marx's intellectual personality. Mehring observed that all of Marx's bedside authors – Homer, Dante, Shakespeare, Cervantes and Balzac – were in fact:

> minds which have recorded the image of an entire age so objectively that every subjective residue more or less vanishes, and sometimes so completely that the creators disappear, behind their creations, into a mythical darkness.[15]

Moreover, all of them document in depth and in great detail social states and processes. *Don Quixote* in particular is, for Marx, as his son-in-law Lafargue recalled, 'the epic of dying-out chivalry whose virtues were ridiculed and scoffed at in the emerging bourgeois world',[16] but which *The Communist Manifesto* evoked as 'patriarchal' and 'idyllic'.

Don Quixote obviously lends himself to Marx's understanding. Marx frequently refers to the hidalgo and in a variety of registers, depicting his anachronistic eccentricity, recalling accidents of his character and life, and also applying to him the complete key to the Marxian conception of the history of Europe: as can be gathered from his criticism of Lassalle's *Franz von Sickingen*, Marx believes Don Quixote's pathetic eccentricity is due to the fact that a struggle like his, directed against the unjust powers of his age, in order to have any good prospects, needed 'to appeal … to the towns and the peasants, i.e. the very classes whose development = the negation of knighthood'.[17]

Yet Marx's relationship to Don Quixote – and to Cervantes – is also established on a less theoretical level, and one that is more immediate, imaginative, and characteristic of the simple wisdom of life. Marx often cites the *Quixote* and Don Quixote in such non-theoretical contexts, for example, by comparing the anti-Napoleonic guerrillas to the knight (NYDT, 30 October 1854), or by telling – from memory, in commenting on the relationship between Queen Cristina and Muñoz – the history of the rich widow who married a simple boy (NYDT, 30 September 1854). Marx's final reference to Don Quixote has a different tone: Marx, already dying, was in Algiers, and wrote to Engels, on 1 March 1882, that he had 'no sleep, no appetite, a bad cough, [and was] somewhat perplexed, not without an occasional bout of *profunda melancolía*, like the great

15 Mehring 1980, p. 574 [my translation (Ed.)].

16 Lafargue n.d., p. 75.

17 Letter to Lassalle, 19 April 1859; Marx 1983h, p. 419.

Don Quixote'.[18] The allusion is plainly to the sane, moribund knight for whom in last year's nests there are no birds this year;[19] and this may be added to several other indications of Marx's frustration at the very end.

History and System

As with Marx's other specific studies – that of the civil wars in France, for example, or that of the Russian village commune – the articles about Spain show an author who wields his own theoretical system quite freely and practices a broad methodological flexibility. I noted this earlier in connection with his description of the Napoleonic invasion as an 'assault on the [Spanish] nation', which leaves completely out of account his theoretical model. On the one hand, using his Spanish data Marx approaches things with a very empirical attitude, and on the other, he is very attentive to the country's 'peculiar features', while the interpretive schemas deriving from his system are merely a subordinate background presence. He sometimes makes vague, clichéd, more or less puerile remarks about Spanish peculiarity – as when he states that the Spanish guerrilla fighter has always been something of a bandit 'since the time of Viriathus' (NYDT, 9 September 1854).[20] In his articles on Spain, Marx also frequently makes explanatory links that are not an essential part of his theoretical model, and this is of importance in determining how Marx understood the explanatory function of his theory, as well as its scope. As in the case mentioned earlier, in which he attributes importance to the action of favourites and cabals in the involuntary incitement of insurrections, Marx always approaches the problems that he poses for himself on a level that we would have to call, using the most time-honoured Marxian vocabulary, 'superstructural': a political or military vocabulary, or that of national psychology. Accordingly, the more 'basic' considerations – regarding relations of production, forces of production, social classes – only appear (if at all) in the last analysis, as a general framework containing the conditions of possibility of what has already been explained 'superstructurally'.

Thus, Marx offers explanations from political-military causes that would surely leave many Marxists sceptical; for example, the explanation given for the peculiarity of the Spanish Cortes on the basis of certain consequences of the so-called 'Reconquest':

18 Marx 1992c, p. 213.

19 An allusion to *Don Quixote*, Part II, Ch. 74; Cervantes 1998, p. 1168 [Ed.].

20 Marx 1980e, p. 374.

> [N]either the French States General, nor the British Parliaments of the Middle Ages, are to be compared with the Spanish Cortes. There were circumstances in the formation of the Spanish kingdom peculiarly favorable to the limitation of royal power. On the one side, small parts of the Peninsula were recovered at a time, and formed into separate kingdoms, during the long struggles with the Arabs. Popular laws and customs were engendered in these struggles. The successive conquests, being principally effected by the nobles, rendered their power excessive, while they diminished the royal power. On the other hand, the inland towns and cities rose to great consequence, from the necessity people found themselves under of residing together in places of strength, as a security against the continual irruptions of the Moors.[21]

That explanation conceives of the Reconquest in the very manner it was understood by the most traditionalist and conservative of Spanish historians, as 'an obstinate struggle of almost eight hundred years',[22] as Marx writes. However, the most interesting thing about Marx's use of such concepts is their methodological implication: a great freedom of historical explanation with regard to the theoretical model, and the methodological principle of proceeding in research according to an order that is the inverse of the actual order of development [*fundamentación*] asserted by the theory.

Spanish Orientalism

Marx was quite interested in registering Spanish peculiarities; it often seems that he amuses himself in doing so: the smugglers, he observes, are the only force that has never become disorganised in Spain (NYDT, 1 September 1854); the dismissal of civil servants appointed by a government that has lost power 'is, perhaps, the only thing rapidly done in Spain. All parties show themselves equally quick in that line' (NYDT, 4 September 1854).[23] Yet he also tries, more seriously, to assemble a certain number of those peculiar features in a category that would situate them within his system: the category of orientalism. In the article from the *New York Daily Tribune* for 9 September 1854, Marx claims that the similarity between the Spanish absolute monarchy and the absolute monarchies in the rest of Europe is merely superficial, and that the Spanish

---

21 Marx 1980d, p. 393.

22 Ibid.

23 Marx 1980e, p. 375.

monarchy is actually one of the 'Asiatic forms of government': 'Spain, like Turkey, remained an agglomeration of mismanaged republics with a nominal sovereign at their head'.[24] According to Marx, the Spanish monarchy's nature as an oriental despotism explains the persistence of Spanish diversity, with its 'different laws and customs, different coins, military banners of different colors', and even different tax systems.[25] For:

> the oriental despotism attacks municipal self-government only when opposed to its direct interests, but is very glad to allow those institutions to continue so long as they take off its shoulders the duty of doing something and spare it the trouble of regular administration.[26]

In any event, this stress on what he views as Spanish peculiarities – including orientalism – does not lead Marx to think in metaphysical categories referring to the 'national spirit', or to completely separate Spanish processes from European processes. On the contrary, on more than one occasion he thinks that in Spanish events he has found representative realisations of general features of modern European history. So, for example, after writing that in O'Donnell's 1856 coup Espartero abandoned the Cortes, the Cortes abandoned the bourgeois leaders, the leaders abandoned the middle class, and the latter abandoned the people, Marx generalises as follows:

> This furnishes a new illustration of the character of most of the European struggles of 1848–49, and of those hereafter to take place in the Western portion of that continent. On the one hand there are modern industry and trade, the natural chiefs of which, the middle classes, are averse to the military despotism; on the other hand, when they begin the battle against this same despotism, in step the workmen themselves, the product of the modern organization of labor, to claim their due share of the result of victory. Frightened by the consequences of an alliance thus imposed on their unwilling shoulders, the middle classes shrink back again under the protecting batteries of the hated despotism. This is the secret of the standing armies of Europe, which otherwise will be incomprehensible to the future historian.[27]

---

24 Marx 1980d, p. 396.

25 Ibid.

26 Ibid.

27 Marx 1986a, p. 102.

The Spanish War of Independence also leads Marx to one of those generalisations that situate the history of Spain within the history of Europe. Marx shows that the movement for independence begun in 1808 seems 'on the whole' to be directed against the revolution rather than being in favour of it, but the principles that it expressed and sought to establish were revolutionary. He remarks: 'All the wars of independence waged against France bear in common the stamp of regeneration, mixed up with reaction; but nowhere to such a degree as in Spain'.[28]

Spanish Independence and Revolution

There can be little doubt that what motivated Marx to study and write about Spain was the Vicalvarada unrest: the popular participation in the *pronunciamiento* was the first sign of the awakening of European peoples since the commotion of 1848, which, of course, for Marx was more the defeat of the working people than the consolidation of the bourgeois national states. Although all of the articles written for the *New York Daily Tribune* were the product of both the need to earn some money in circumstances of great penury and an interest in Spain's revolutionary prospects, they can be divided into two groups: mere reports on developments as they occurred (the 1854 Vicalvarada, O'Donnell's uprising in 1856), and short essays that are historical and analytical. The latter are clearly the result of Marx's studies and reflections, whose aim is to understand the fate of 'revolutionary Spain'.

Marx's studies soon convinced him that Spain was a little-known country, perhaps the most poorly known and most misjudged country in Europe, 'except Turkey' (NYDT, 21 July 1854). 'The numberless local pronunciamentos and military rebellions have accustomed Europe to view it on a level with Imperial Rome at the era of the pretorians'. However, that opinion is a superficial error for which, Marx observes, Napoleon received a bitter surprise:

> The secret of this fallacy lies in the simple fact that historians, instead of viewing the resources and strength of these peoples in their provincial and local organization, have drawn at the source of their Court almanacs.[29]

28 Marx 1980d, p. 403.
29 Marx 1980f, p. 285.

If the historians had paid attention to the bowels of history and not merely the events of the court, they would have been able to identify the true enigma of Spanish history:

> How are we to account for the singular phenomenon that, after almost three centuries of a Habsburg dynasty, followed by a Bourbon dynasty – either of them quite sufficient to crush a people – the municipal liberties of Spain more or less survive? That in the very country where of all the feudal states absolute monarchy first arose in its most unmitigated form, centralization has never succeeded in taking root?[30]

The explanation that Marx suggests for the 'singular' Spanish 'phenomenon' essentially consists in adducing a series of 'political or economical' circumstances that ruined commerce, industry, navigation, and agriculture in Spain, preventing the Spanish absolute monarchy from carrying out the structural function it fulfilled in Europe – to put an end to the privileges of the nobility and the power of the cities, and to establish in their place 'the general rule of the middle classes, and the common sway of civil society'.[31] Yet, as I have said, that very failure of the Spanish monarchy, or actually one of its consequences, the preservation of decentralisation and the medieval diffusion of power, is the best explanation for the surprising efficacy of the Spanish resistance to the Napoleonic armies. And as the history of the Spanish revolution begins, according to Marx, with the War of Independence, the explanation of the latter is for him a first step in understanding the former.

Revolutionary Spain

The first great opportunity for modern revolution in Spain was, according to Marx, within reach of the Supreme Central and Governing Junta of the Kingdom:

> Exclusively under the reign of the Central Junta, it was possible to blend with the actualities and exigencies of national defense the transformation of Spanish society, and the emancipation of the native spirit.[32]

30 Marx 1980d, p. 395.

31 Ibid.

32 Marx 1980d, p. 418.

The revolutionary ineffectiveness of the Central Junta, paralysed, according to Marx, by its formalism and the impossibility of settling the conflict between its two wings (which Marx identifies with the ideas of Floridablanca and Jovellanos, respectively), at the same time sealed its military fate: 'The Central Junta failed in the defense of their country, because they failed in their revolutionary mission' (NYDT, 30 October 1854).[33] (Incidentally, the extreme Marxist and libertarian Left defended an analogous thesis during the Spanish Civil War, over against the predominantly military conception of the Republican government). On the other hand, the Cortes in Cadiz had no revolutionary possibilities; pent up in the most remote corner of the territory, the Cortes were merely 'ideal Spain', whereas 'real Spain' was to be found in the war's upheavals or had already been subjugated by the invader. 'At the time of the Cortes Spain was divided into two parts. At the Isla de Leon, ideas without action – in the rest of Spain, action without ideas'. In conclusion:

> [T]he Cortes ... failed, not, as French and English writers assert, because they were revolutionists, but because their predecessors [the Central Junta] had been reactionists and had missed the proper season of revolutionary action.[34]

Marx sympathises with the Cadiz legislators, about whom he writes in an epic tone (which is not exactly refined from a literary point of view), and with a very good understanding of the synthesis of tradition and revolution undertaken by those Cortes. Marx perceives the very genuine [*castiza*] roots of those who were in Cadiz: 'From the remote angle of the *Isla Gaditana* they [the Cortes] undertook to lay the foundation of a new Spain, as their forefathers had done from the mountains of Covadonga and Sobrarbe' (NYDT, 24 November 1854).[35]

The Constitution of 1812 had 'sprung up from the head of old monastic and absolutionist [sic] Spain at the very epoch when she seemed totally absorbed in waging a holy war against the Revolution', but that very Constitution would be 'branded by the crowned heads of Europe, assembled at Verona, as the most incendiary invention of Jacobinism' (NYDT, 24 November 1854):[36] this is how Marx frames what he calls 'the curious phenomenon of the Constitution of 1812'.[37] (As we see, for Marx Spain is the land of curious phenomena). Marx's

33 Marx 1980d, p. 419.
34 Marx 1980d, p. 418.
35 Marx 1980d, p. 424.
36 Ibid.
37 Ibid.

way of explaining this latter curious phenomenon is quite remarkable for an author from the 1850s: 'The truth is that the Constitution of 1812 is a reproduction of the ancient *Fueros*, but read in the light of the French Revolution, and adapted to the wants of modern society'.[38] At the end of his analysis of the Constitution, he expresses a competent, highly favourable opinion:

> [F]ar from being a servile copy of the French Constitution of 1791, it was a genuine and original offspring of Spanish intellectual life, regenerating the ancient and national institutions, introducing the measures of reform loudly demanded by the most celebrated authors and statesmen of the eighteenth century, making inevitable concessions to popular prejudice.[39]

The part about the concessions to popular prejudice refers primarily and explicitly to Article 12 of the Constitution ('The religion of the Spanish nation is, and ever shall be, the Catholic Apostolic Roman and only true faith; the State shall, by wise and just laws, protect it and prevent the exercise of any other'). The tenor of that article is at odds with the anti-religiosity of the ultra-Feuerbachian Marx, and above all proves inconsistent with his idea of a religious policy befitting a genuinely bourgeois state, such as he had conceived of it since the time of his essays on the Jewish question.

Marx reconstructs a continuous Spanish revolutionary tradition since the War of Independence, in contrast to the image of a praetorian Spain, the disconcerting setting of unconnected and unforeseeable insurrections. This history begins with Mina's failed coup, and is built around Porlier, Richard, Lacy, Vidal, Solá, and finally, Riego: 'The Isla de Leon conspiracy then was but the last link in a chain formed by the bloody heads of so many valiant men from 1808 to 1814' (NYDT, 2 December 1854).[40] The Revolution of 1820, of such great importance for the moral recomposition of the European Left prior to 1848, still inspires moving language in the Marx of 1854; yet what dominates his writings on that revolution is the desire to explain its defeat. And he thinks that explanation is easy: the Spanish liberals of 1820 attempted a bourgeois revolution, 'more especially, a town revolution', in which the peasantry was a passive spectator of a struggle among parties, which it found barely comprehensible. For this reason, the farmers acted on behalf of the counter-revolution in the few provinces in which they intervened: 'the revolutionary party did not

38 Marx 1980d, p. 429.
39 Marx 1980d, p. 433.
40 Marx 1980d, p. 445.

know how to link the interests of the peasantry to the town movement' (an article from 21 November 1854, not published by the NYDT).[41]

In the pronunciamento that prompts Marx's first reports on Spain – that of O'Donnell and Dulce in 1854 – an important feature of Spanish revolutionary history is quite visible, namely, the army's decisive presence in politics. Marx believes that two causes explain this Spanish peculiarity: first of all, the state, in the modern sense of the word, is almost nonexistent in the political life [*la vida civil*] of the Spanish people, which is essentially local and provincial, and the army alone is present there; secondly, the War of Independence had created conditions in which the army proved to be the natural place in which to concentrate the vitality of the nation:

> Thus it happens that the only national demonstrations (those of 1812 and of 1822) proceeded from the army; and thus the movable part of the nation has been accustomed to regard the army as the natural instrument of every national rising.[42]

Marx also recognises other causes for the Spanish army's political importance. Among them he includes the institution of the Captaincies General, whose title holders he compares to the Turkish pashas; the military origin of all of the 1815–18 liberal conspiracies; and above all and most significantly, the meagre political clout [*fuerza civil*] of the social classes and groups immersed in decisive struggles:

> [T]he isolation of the liberal bourgeoisie forcing them to employ the bayonets of the army against clergy and peasantry in the country; the necessity for Cristina and the camarilla to employ bayonets against the Liberals, as the Liberals had employed bayonets against the peasants; the tradition growing out of all these precedents; these were the causes which impressed on revolution in Spain a military, and on the army a pretorian character.[43]

At the beginning of his studies on Spain, Marx had already noted the 'superabundance of military places and honors', as a result of which 'out of every three generals only one can be employed on active service'.[44] He would soon

41 Marx 1980g, p. 657.
42 Marx 1980b, pp. 309–10.
43 Marx 1986a, p. 107.
44 Marx 1980a, p. 458.

understand this as one consequence of the praetorian state of the Spanish army. Another, much more important consequence was the increasing prevalence of the counter-revolutionary, conservative or reactionary orientation in the army's prounciamentos, its separation from 'the cause of the nation' (NYDT, 4 August 1854).[45] Marx believes that between 1830 and 1854 (a period of Spanish life he deems particularly difficult), the army, while increasingly powerful politically, applied its power in a petty fashion by resolving dynastic rivalries and exercising military authority over the court. Lastly, Marx thinks that in O'Donnell's 1856 uprising, the complete separation between the people and the army was sealed:

> This time ... the army has been all against the people, or, indeed, it has only fought against them, and the National Guards. In short, there is an end of the revolutionary mission of the Spanish army.[46]

For a Spanish reader one hundred years later, some of these last reflections by Marx on the 1856 coup may sound like a disturbing call to remember the dusty, old-fashioned motto 'Historia magistra vitae'; let these lines from 18 August 1856 serve as an example of this:

> On the one side – the army – everything was prepared beforehand; on the other everything was extemporized; the offensive never for a moment changed sides. On the one hand, a well-equipped army, moving easily in the strings of its commanding generals; on the other, leaders reluctantly pushed forward by the impetus of an imperfectly-armed people.[47]

45 Marx 1980b, p. 310.

46 Marx 1986a, p. 108.

47 Marx 1986a, p. 104.

CHAPTER 5

What is Dialectic?

You will have noticed that I did not mention Marx's name in discussing the Historical School, but that nonetheless more than one of the features I stated in connection with this school bears a resemblance to some passages from Marx's methodology. I did not mention him within the Historical School because Marx is rather a separate case, relatively isolated in that era. Yet this is nonetheless a good moment to consider Marx, for in my opinion there is, without a doubt, a clear kinship between him and the Historical School. Not in the sense that one may view Marx as a descendent of the Historical School. That is impossible for chronological reasons. Marx began to write earlier, but he was basically one of their contemporaries. On the other hand, the fact of the matter is that Marx was obviously an heir to the English classics, while the German Historical School was the adversary of those classics. One cannot imagine Marx without Smith and, above all, Ricardo, before him.

So it is that we cannot place Marx's economics and that of the Historical School in the same lineage. However, there is, to put it straightforwardly, a clear kinship with regard to the period and the explanations. For example, the idea of totality, characteristic of the Historical School, is likewise present in Marx. Marx's work as a whole is not pure economics in the sense that he also incorporates, as does the Historical School, political, cultural, institutional and historical factors. That kinship is obvious. The trouble is that Marx never denies the existence of a core of pure economics, of the deductive sort and in the style of Smith and Ricardo, while the Historical School denies that it has any validity.

Marx's methodological attitude evolved quite a bit over the course of his life. For example, the young Marx much more resembles the Historical School than does the mature Marx. By 'young Marx' I mean Marx up until 1856–7, those being the years in which his methodological change of outlook in economics occurs. The young Marx is convinced that classical English economics, as it appears to him in the author he knows best, namely, Ricardo, is a fictitious, even immoral discipline. It is an infamy because it works with abstractions, with averages, and with these it conceals socio-economic reality. This is a

* Transcription of a lecture delivered in 1984 or 1985. First published as, '¿Qué es la dialéctica?', in *Sobre dialéctica*, edited by Salvador López Arnal (Barcelona: Ediciones de Intervención Cultural/El Viejo Topo, 2009).

 | DOI 10.1163/9789004280526_008

view that any member of the Historical School would have shared. It is in that period when Marx's method is most akin to the Historical School's method. For example, 1843 is the year in which Roscher's course appears; the manuscripts in which Marx says that English economics is an infamy are also from 1843.[1] They truly are contemporary intellectual products. The mature Marx, however, is a very Ricardian Marx, as it were. He constantly works with concepts related to averages: average rates, average figures, etc.; some of the fundamental concepts of Marx's system are based on the calculation of those average rates. Therefore, there was a clear inversion, though perhaps not in his inspiration. The mature Marx continues to aspire to create an intellectual product that is what we today would call, at one and the same time, economics, history, sociology and politics. Yet he does not go about this through the procedure of dissolving pure economics, but rather by integrating economics into this totalising whole, which today we would consider, from the point of view of the academic divisions, proper to several scientific fields at the same time. So, the inspiration did not change, but the method did.

And what is that totalising methodological conception? There are a couple of *loci classici* for the study of Marx's methodological conceptions, and both have been translated. One is the 'Introduction', which he wrote in 1857 and then did not publish, to *A Contribution to the Critique of Political Economy*, a work from 1859 that is usually published with all of his introductions; the other passage worth studying is the epilogue to the second edition of Volume I of *Capital*, from 1873.

Marx's methodological programme changed a great deal over the course of his intellectual life. Besides an important evolution, however, there is the fact that his methodological ideas were always rather confused and obscure (in saying this I am not passing any judgement on the quality of the work, but rather making a judgement concerning the philosophical appraisal of his method), and in my opinion this is due to the fact that in Marx's scientific mindset there are three different concepts of method and science that are operative: (i) the Hegelian concept of science and method; (ii) the Young-Hegelian notion of science and method; and (iii) the concept of science and method current in that period (for example, that of Ricardo). The fact that there are these three concepts of science and scientific method present in his work is a statement that we can make today, *a posteriori*, but it is a fact of which Marx himself, in my opinion, was unaware, and hence the scant clarity of his expositions regarding method.

1 Marx 1981, p. 482. [The text to which Sacristán refers is not included in the English edition of Marx and Engels's *Collected Works* (Ed.)].

As often happens in intellectual life, this does not always lead to dead ends. Rather, it sometimes enables Marx to achieve keen, interesting insights. But when it is a matter of studying his methodological conceptions, it does create a rather considerable obscurity. The chief reason is the influence of Hegel. He was a great metaphysician, an admirable philosophical writer and, moreover, very learned. He had read many scientific texts, yet without adhering, in my opinion, to the modern idea of science. For Hegel, science continues to be an absolute knowledge, as it was for the Greeks, an indisputable knowledge, certain for all time, whereas the truly modern idea of science – real, not formal, science (i.e. that which deals with the world, from physics to economics) – is characterised by the very opposite idea. In the modern sense, science is characterised rather by being a form of knowledge that is constantly revisable, uncertain by definition. By contrast, the Hegelian idea of science is the idea of absolute, certain, secure knowledge.

That non-scientific idea of knowledge is actually quite understandable in an idealist philosopher. If we try to get into the mind of an idealist philosopher, who believes that being is of the same nature as thought, that there is no difference between real being and thought, then the idea of an absolute knowledge does not turn out to be so excessive or extravagant; for if all of reality truly has the same nature as our thinking, one may accept that there is complete correspondence between well-trained, well-bred thought and reality itself. And Marx is a disciple of Hegel in everything except the latter's idealism; thus, an absolute notion of knowledge in Marx proves much more obscure and much less justifiable, since he is not an idealist.

Marx never openly claimed that science was an absolute knowledge, and yet some remnants of this conception can be found in Marx. What remnants? For example, the following and very interesting one: in the 1857 'Introduction', Marx repeats a straightforwardly Hegelian idea of scientific method, the idea that the scientific method is a method that ascends from the abstract to the concrete. It is obvious from the everyday use of language that none of us says this. We say, rather, that we ascend from the concrete to the abstract. That is to say, we hold that when one goes from the perception of some dog or other to the idea of mammal, one ascends, we think that there is an increase in generality; we would not say that there is a rise from mammal to Rover, but, to the contrary, that there is a drop. For a Hegelian, however, one ascends from the abstract to the concrete.

In a realist and scientific-realist philosopher like Marx, this sounds odd. In Hegel, it sounds quite normal, since he thinks that the history of reality is the history of the Idea; thought began with the general idea of Being, which is what there was at first. The first Being was Being as such, without any further determination, Being in the abstract, and the history of Being, its evolution over time, has consisted in its becoming more concrete. First there was the pure idea of Being; then that pure idea of Being causes Nothing to arise out of it; then there is synthesis of Being and Nothing, and the product is Becoming. Thus begins an ontological race that is, in truth, of no value to you either as economists or as sociologists; but if we do want to understand a bit of what happened with this idea of dialectic in the social sciences, we have no choice but to review it briefly, even if it is not of direct interest to us. It is of greater interest for the sociologists because it is a type of thought that was quite widespread in that era. For example, it is also found in Comte. Very well: if thought is of the same nature as Being or vice versa, then, since the path of Being has been and is a path from the abstract to the concrete, thinks Hegel, with a certain idealist coherence, knowledge must follow the same path, and likewise go from the abstract to the concrete, rising from the empty and abstract to the concrete.

Marx inherited this idea, literally restating it in this Introduction from 1857, but for him it has a different character. It cannot be pure Hegelianism, since it is not accompanied by the ontology of idealism. Rather, in Marx, and also less consciously in Hegel, what we find is a reformulation of this idea very much along the lines of the Historical School. In Marx, the Hegelian idea that the scientific method of economics must proceed from the abstract to the concrete has a kinship with the Historical School; they resemble each other in their ambition to have historically or economically concrete phenomena, which are always historical realities, as an object of knowledge. A model can be atemporal, but a singular economic phenomenon cannot be atemporal – it must correspond to an existing society at a given time and place. Therefore, between the Hegelian idea, at least as Marx restates it, that method in political economy must ascend from the abstract to the concrete, and the Historical School's ambition to have knowledge refer to the historically singular, understanding this as meaning any unrepeatable historical presence, there is a family resemblance.

At any rate, Marx still faced the problem of coherently formulating, in a non-idealist context, that Hegelian idea of knowledge as a transition from the abstract to the concrete. To that end, he introduces a distinction, which is not in Hegel, between the real-concrete and the concrete of thought. The starting point for knowledge is the real-concrete, but thought obtains something abstract from that real-concrete, and from that abstract thing, it achieves, by means of an accumulation of pieces of knowledge and analysis, a concrete of thought. For an idealist philosopher, the real-concrete and concrete of thought would be the same thing. Marx avoids an idealist ontology by means of a procedure that says: the real-concrete is at the beginning of thought, and at the end there is a concrete, yet not the real-concrete, but rather the concrete of thought, the intellectual version of the historical concreteness from which one had begun. And so, the idea leaves its idealist mould, becomes a common sense idea, and characterises quite well the aspirations to knowledge of Marx's economics. In the course of his acquiring knowledge, of his accumulation of data and analysis of these data, he will come to have a more concrete notion. That is the content of common sense that underlies the idea when it is stripped of its idealist metaphysics. Yet, all the same, for someone who does not come from Hegel's metaphysics, as is my case, the idea naturally has a weak spot, and it is that it identifies 'general concept' with 'vague concept'. That in beginning to study, one knows very little, has a very vague idea, is one thing; but general concepts, which can be exceedingly clear and can be obtained on the basis of a certain knowledge, are another thing altogether. That what one knows is vague, poor, and imprecise is not the same thing as one's knowledge being very general. For example, the very general notion of mammal need not be any more vague than the notion of Rover – to the contrary, it is clearer. 'Mammal' is a well-defined technical term.

Thinkers in the Hegelian tradition, on the other hand, tend to identify the general with the vague. In my opinion, there is only one case in which this has a certain justification, which is when it is a question of historical subjects. For example, if what one really intends, when confronted with the idea of the pendulum, is to know intimately, intuitively, and aesthetically a specific, old pendulum in the house of one's grandmother, one will no doubt be unsatisfied with the laws of the pendulum in physics, among other reasons because the laws of the pendulum do not work for every pendulum and, moreover, they specifically do not represent any single pendulum: there is no pendulum that has all of its mass concentrated in a point. So, if there truly is an aesthetic interest in a specific pendulum, what is essential is not the law of the pendulum, although it is also important to know how a pendulum works.

For the entire Historical School and, in a parallel fashion, for Marx, it turns out that the object of knowledge resembles, to a great degree, the pendulum in the grandmother's house, so to speak. Its real interest is in individualised knowledge of certain historical moments. The difference is that, in Marx's case, in the case of the mature Marx, it is understood that even to know the grandmother's pendulum one needs the physical theory of the pendulum; in other words, for his research he also needs classical economics and mathematics. At forty-plus years of age he started to study mathematics again, and at fifty he wrote an essay on infinitesimal calculus, at a time when there was still no theory of this universally accepted calculus. He repeatedly tried to get his mathematician friends to mathematise and formalise his theory of crisis for him. They told him that for the time being it was impossible. But he tried. Which means that, unlike the Historical School, Marx had assimilated the methodological need for pure theoretical work as well; still, his aim greatly resembled that of the Historical School: it was the comprehension of concrete, well-defined historical presents and pasts. In Marx's case, in the case of his main work, *Capital*, this meant the comprehension of capitalism.

Against this background I can try to say, modestly, a little bit about the idea of the Marxian dialectic, in a way that does not entirely agree with the two principal interpretations of the Marxist dialectic found today in considerations of methodology. There are those who consider that the Hegelian-Marxian dialectic is a method for higher, more complete knowledge than the usual methods in science, and at the other extreme there are those who believe that it is empty talk devoid of scientific interest.

I think that the idea that there exists a dialectical method distinct from the usual methods of science is false, if by 'method' we understand a succession of controlled and repeatable operations. If by 'method' we understand merely an intellectual style, then it is a valid idea. In my opinion, the idea of dialectical method or dialectic is one of the last great metaphysical metaphors. After philosophy, it is above all in the theory of knowledge, but also in mythology, that we find an abundance of ideas that bring together – actually, metaphorically – pre-scientific experience and experience from everyday life, thereby helping, without a doubt, to structure people's lived experience. It is not that they are useless ideas, but in my opinion they are not scientific ideas, they are not exact ideas. I will give a few examples. In Aristotle's philosophy, the pair of concepts 'potentiality' and 'actuality' explains that natural beings can change because they are a composite of potentiality (i.e. capacity) and actuality (i.e. realisation), so that when a given being goes from state *A* to state *B*, it already had state *B* in potentiality and has now actualised it. In my view, this is not an explanation, but rather describes in cultured language what we already know: to say that an object was in potentiality *B* when we know that it has gone from *A* to *B* is plainly a truism. If it has become *B*, it is without a doubt because it could become *B*. As classical logic put it: the consequence goes from being to being able to be. If something is, it is because it could be what it is.

Yet those philosophical metaphors order lived experience, at times with a certain poetic charm and at others with no charm at all. For example, in Aristotle himself there is this charming phrase, which has a certain poetic quality, to explain the fact that the human being is capable of understanding material objects. This happens because 'the soul is in a way all existing things'.[2] Of course, this does not explain anything, yet it is suggestive, has poetic qualities, and is even suggestive for lines of research. If someone tells us that the soul is in a way all existing things, that is, that there is a real community between soul and thing, the way is open to begin studying what that community consists of, whereas if we think that they are absolutely heterogeneous, we will rather tend to explain knowledge of material things by means of a miracle, as did some Renaissance and idealist philosophers.

In my opinion, then, the fundamental ideas of the dialectic – for example, the idea that the 'negation of the negation' is useful for explaining reality – are just that, pre-scientific philosophical metaphors. In Engels, for example, we can read that a barley plant, with its seed, is the negation of a grain of barley, which means the following: that the grain of barley, once sown, is destroyed, negated, but then germinates, and that what germinates from that grain is the negation of the death of the grain, is the negation of the negation of the grain. Like the soul of Aristotelian potentiality, this may have its charm as a purely intuitive and metaphorical codification of pre-scientific experience, but one begins to understand what occurs when one does chemistry, not when one says that the stalk is the negation of the negation of the grain.

As a method and as a logical category, the dialectic is therefore on the same level as the great metaphors from the philosophical tradition. At the same time, however, there has always existed, at least since Hegel's day, and since even before Hegel, including an ancient precedent in Plato, an idea that goes under the name of 'dialectic' and that refers not to a hypothetical type of knowledge, but one that includes everything, that interpenetrates everything, which is what the word means, among other things, in Greek: it passes through everything. The etymology of 'dialectic' quite probably means – although these things are passed over by the philologists – precisely 'to bring everything together through everything'. One could not call this either method or logic in a strict sense; rather, it would have to be considered an intellectual programme. It is, so to speak, a logicist version the Historical School's aim, as we have seen it described by Schumpeter.

I have pointed out, as a fundamental fact about the Historical School, its aim of global comprehensiveness [*globalidad*], including sociological, institutional, and strictly economic points of view. Now it turns out that this feature is also key to the dialectical tradition, with the difference that the Historical School tends to conceive of that aim, of that programme, as being fastened together intuitively and empirically, while in the Marxist dialectic the aim is

2 Aristotle 1984, p. 686.

to carry out this programme by means of logical-scientific analysis, employing the usual methods.

Other historians of the method would contest this point. It must not be taken as something obvious; far from it. Every traditional Marxist on the one hand, and every analytical philosopher on the other, would contest this interpretation, would disagree. Yet as this what I think, I have allowed myself to state it.

In support of this interpretation one can summon the second text to which I referred, Marx's epilogue to the second edition of *Capital*, Volume I, for it is precisely there where Marx faces the need to answer critics who praise him and yet criticise his method. It is above all two critics – one anonymous, and the other a Russian economist from that era – who prove to be quite right in their criticism of what Marx specifically does, i.e. the practice of his method, and who, on the other hand, are quite opposed to his Hegelian dialectical language. Faced with these critics, who are, on the one hand, two people who have appreciated his book and the two critics who have been most positive, yet who, on the other, tell him that the Hegelian method is useless and counterproductive, Marx feels obliged to justify what he has done. He then explains that one must distinguish between the method of exposition and the method of research. The research must be done with the usual methods, gathering empirical data, analysing it, using deduction and induction like any other scientist; but in the method of exposition, on the other hand, it is possible to fashion a vivid ensemble that reflects the authentic life of the material, and he then says that the more he attains that goal of presenting a vivid picture of reality, the more it seems to his critics that he has used this method.

Marx then begins a comparison between his own method and that of Hegel that is completely confused, useless, and which demonstrates that, in my opinion, he is defending his text with little conviction. He reminds us of the criteria for distinguishing between method and system in Hegel; the method is valid for everyone and the system is idealist, which is an untenable claim and Hegel himself knew as much – Hegel had written that his method was his system and his system was his method – and, in my opinion, it is an excuse sought out by Marx in order to deceive himself about the combination of his Hegelianism and his scientific outlook [*carácter*], with the aim of reconciling the two facets of his work. He then says that he inverts Hegel's method, which is a metaphor that, in my view, is likewise absurd. A method cannot be inverted, and we do not know what inverting a method means. I can think about what inverting a system of theorems means. If I have, for example, three theorems and consider the first one the principal theorem, the second one the secondary theorem, and the third one the tertiary theorem, I can invert them and consider the third one fundamental. I would understand what that means, but inverting a method does not mean anything at all.

So, that part of the epilogue is, in my opinion, quite useless; however, his distinction between doing research, for which the only methods are the ones always used, and presenting an exposition, for which the dialectic can be used in order to recompose the life of the whole, strikes me as very useful. This is closely related to the fact that Marx refused to publish the first edition of *Capital* in, as we would say today, 'instalments', as his editor had proposed. For the reason that he gave for not publishing in that form was, literally, 'my writings ... are an artistic whole'.[3] And this is an idea of great interest, which once again relates his work to that of the Historical School, which also had an artistic notion of knowledge, and I believe that it partly confirms my way of interpreting this question, enabling us to see that the dialectical object as a goal for thought is very similar to the aesthetic-historical object – it is a programme that consists in seeking reconstruction as the product of knowledge.

'Dialectic' is a word highly charged with ideological passions and in regard to which it is difficult to form a very clear idea. I will summarise what one can say in view of, on the one hand, Marx's works as a whole and, on the other, his own idea of what he had done. The claim that the dialectic is a logic is false, in my opinion. There is no set of dialectical rules of exact operation. Rather, dialectic is a quality of certain intellectual creations, not a method in the rigorous sense of 'method'. *Dialectical* is an adjective applicable to a type of intellectual product that can be characterised by various features, and primarily by its global comprehensiveness [*globalidad*] and totality, and the very internal, endogenous character of the explanation that it offers (an object is explained dialectically when it is explained by elements and factors that are internal to it, not exogenous), which itself implies to a greater or lesser extent a historical point of view. Atemporal social objects do not exist.

In this sense, we can say that a theory or some conceptions are more or less dialectical to the extent that they are more or less encompassing, more or less self-explicable, and more or less historical. However, we cannot say that there exists a logic called 'dialectic', whose rules do not appear in a respectable form anywhere, for when they do appear they turn out to be, at bottom, metaphors that refer rather to everyday experience.

---

3 Letter to Engels, 31 July 1865; Marx 1987d, p. 173.

CHAPTER 6

One Hundred Years On: To What 'Literary Genre' Does Marx's *Capital* Belong?

Reading Capital, the title chosen by Louis Althusser a few years back in presenting a collection of studies, was a phrase intended provocatively: as a protest against the fashion of the 'young Marx', against the growing tendency to read Marx as a pure philosopher. Yet 'reading *Capital*' is also a problem from another point of view, beyond any strong feelings in favour of or against a fashion. In order to avoid such feelings and for the sake of brevity, I am here going to pose the problem of interpreting Marx in a non-polemical manner.

One of the oddest characteristics of the literature on *Capital* is the array of extreme opinions aroused by its interpretation. This is well known and not worth emphasising here. However, it is appropriate to point this out, for the climate that characterises the interpretation of Marx itself suggests something about the nature of Marx's work.

It is probably of more interest to consider for a moment the kind of assessment of *Capital* – much more concerned with objective, academic decency – typical of major authors who cannot allow themselves, given their scientific stature, a straightforward apology for capitalism by means of a crude refutation of Marx's book. Yet given their class position, nor can they dispense with an indirect apology for that social order by means of an intelligent justification for the thesis that *Capital* is outmoded. Schumpeter is probably the highest authority in this distinguished category. However, it is not a good thing to invade other specialists' field and, on the other hand, the distinguished category of authors that I have mentioned also includes prestigious philosophers whom the author of these notes can approach with less risk of misunderstanding due to technical inadequacy. The philosopher Benedetto Croce – Schumpeter's contemporary and for a time the holder of the high ideological throne in Europe later held by such authors as Bergson and Heidegger – offers a good starting point. Moreover, Schumpeter's historical-cultural affinity with Croce is considerable: Croce also went through the experience of an extensive reading

* Written, to all appearances, in 1968 for an underground university magazine. Republished as 'Cien años después. ¿A qué «género literario» pertenece *El capital* de Marx?', in *Lecturas de filosofía moderna y contemporánea*, edited by Albert Domingo Curto (Madrid: Editorial Trotta 2007). Reprinted by permission of the publisher.

 DOI 10.1163/9789004280526_009

of Marx; he too decided to take Marx to task; and he likewise explains Marxism (at times) as deriving from an – erroneous to his mind – overestimation of Ricardo, etc. But above all, Croce expresses in a typical way the problem that I am discussing. He expresses it, of course, as an anti-Marxist. In several of his books, and mainly in his *Storia della storiografia italiana nel secolo decimonono* [*The History of Nineteenth-Century Italian Historiography*], Croce notes, in the context of a general criticism of Marxism, and as a basic objection to Marx's economic writings and especially *Capital*, that those texts do not comprise a homogeneous treatise on economic theory – or 'political economy', as it was traditionally called – but a set of 'canons' or methods for the interpretation of the past, plus a few analyses and propositions of a truly theoretical sort, as well as a 'prophetic' or 'elliptical' impulse toward another kind of society, to which political action leads.

This kind of criticism cannot be directly reduced to the common propaganda, according to which *Capital*, as an analysis of capitalist reality, became outdated long ago. Yet it does move indirectly in the same direction, since this criticism amounts to saying that the science of economics has attained forms of pure theory – like physics or biology – that are neutral with respect to any socio-political programme or undertaking. Marx's work, like that of Ricardo, is prior to this theoretical standard; it is, therefore, an outmoded work.

There is something to be learned from that subtle liquidation of *Capital* and, in general, of the writings of the mature Marx. It is necessary to learn something from this because it captures a certain fact, even if only to turn it into the axis of an indirect apology for capitalism. The fact in question is accessible to any reader without excessively unconscious prejudices: it seems clear that in reading most of the pages from the most mature Marx – including many from *Capital* – we immediately have the impression that we are reading *a different type of literature* from that which we have in front of us when reading a treatise of economic theory or a monograph on some economic problem. And the difference cannot be explained solely by ideological factors, that is, by the fact that the majority of the economic, educational or research texts that we read in the here and now are unmistakably rooted in a bourgeois foundation and bourgeois culture. That explanation is inadequate, since we also notice a great difference in *genre* of reading between a large part of *Capital* and the expositions of Lange, Strumilin or Dobb concerning, for example, the functioning of socialist economies. (This is why Althusser's use of the word 'theory' to refer to all of the writings from Marx's maturity also proves so incorrect and confounding).

Words are not as innocent as they may appear. To begin with, words never appear, or never count, alone, individually; they only count within structures, languages (whether technical or everyday language), which appear and function as an elemental, implicit reproduction of reality, because they are themselves the articulation of more general concepts with which human beings perceive and think about reality. One of those structures, the one that interests us here, is formed with the technical terms that are names for intellectual activities: the names of the sciences, the partial theories, technologies, the arts, etc. Their structured set can be called – to use a classic term in methodology – a *systematics of intellectual labour*. The systematics of intellectual labour corresponds, in the last analysis, to the division of that labour and in this sense has its rationality: that rationality justifies, for example, the increasing creation of neologisms for new specialities, etc. However, since every rationality is relative to a system (or, at most, relative to a set or succession of systems), we cannot be surprised by the fact that such basic rationality serves ideologically as an instrument for stifling the sensibility of the men and women who live within a social system when it is a matter of intellectual creations that in some way break the systematics of the existing order. It is then common to hear or read criticisms of those creations as confused, ascientific, non-artistic, etc. A typical example in another field is the old denial of the theatrical-artistic character of Bertolt Brecht's work, or of one part of it (the didactic pieces).

What I am suggesting here is that this is also the case with that criticism of Marx's mature writings which could be called 'formal' or 'methodological': these writings indeed do not fit within the intellectual systematics of contemporary academic culture, and Althusser is indeed mistaken in simply calling them 'theory'. The 'literary genre' of the mature Marx is not theory in the strong or formal sense that attaches to the word today. Yet nor is it the literary genre of Ricardo, as Croce would have it. And that is because Ricardo never sets out to do what Marx essentially sets out to do: *rationally lay the foundations, and formulate a project, for the transformation of society*. This special activity of scientifically laying the foundations for a revolutionary practice – which could perhaps be called 'revolutionary praxeology' – is the 'literary genre' to which all of the works of Marx's maturity, and even a large part of his correspondence, belong. This is why it is useless to read the works of Marx as pure theory in the formal sense of university systematics, and useless to read them as if they were pure programmes for political action. Nor are they both things 'at once', combined, as it were. Rather, they are a continuous, uninterrupted discourse, which constantly goes from the programme to scientific grounding, and vice versa.

It is obvious – and to ignore this would be to confuse Marxian 'revolutionary praxeology' with pragmatism – that this intellectual activity requires Marx to command and clarify scientifically the greatest possible amount of material, and that the purely scientific criticism of the purely theoretical elements of Marx's work will therefore always be an acceptable operation and always make sense. So too will the operation that consists in continuing, developing, and completing the purely theoretical aspects of that work (as Hilferding did), or the whole of its revolutionary praxeology (as Lenin did). The only thing that is truly pointless is to make Marx's work into something that must necessarily be classifiable in accordance with the academic intellectual systematics: to force his discourse into that of pure theory, as the social democratic interpretation did and as the Althusserians do today, or to force it into being pure philosophy, into being a mere postulation of ideals, as numerous intellectuals and Catholics (as well intentioned as they are one-sided in their reading of Marx) do today.

Having suggested this interpretation of Marx's mature work, one must add a caveat in order to prevent, to the extent that this is possible, this concision – which is always unintentionally emphatic and categorical – from also suggesting a disdain for pure, formal theory: Marx's attitude, the attitude that I have here proposed calling 'revolutionary praxeology', is not, nor can it be, one of disdain toward or ignorance of pure theory. The relation between the revolutionary praxeological 'literary genre' and that of pure theory (in the strong or formal sense) is not one of antagonism, but is rather one of superordering: aside from its non-instrumental value as knowledge, theory is the most valuable instrument for the clarification and grounding of a rational revolutionary practice. Marx knew this very well – his erudition still amazes us today – and that is precisely what makes him a unique figure in the gallery of history's great revolutionaries.

The most academic manner of posing this question would in all likelihood consist in taking seriously *Capital*'s subtitle: *A Critique of Political Economy*. An interesting doctoral thesis in economics (in the history of economic doctrines) could set out to take seriously that 'authentic interpretation', as the philologists and jurists say, that is to say, Marx's self-interpretation. It could study the extent to which he paraphrases Kant's *Critique of Pure Reason* (and could venture, as an initial hypothesis, that he intentionally paraphrases it, albeit through 'Left Hegelianism'); one could then study the extent to which this means that Marx does not think that he is doing political economy, but rather something else (his critique), just as Kant was not doing traditional 'pure reason' (metaphysics), but something else, without for this reason abandoning the subject matter whose traditional conception he criticises, etc. Let us leave this suggestion for a scholar of economics interested in the ideological history of his or her discipline.

CHAPTER 7

On the Centenary of Karl Marx's Death

Reader: to devote an issue of *mientras tanto* to discussing Marx on the occasion of the centenary of his death is surely to participate in the academic party dedicated to 'a Marx for everyone'. The truth is that there is no reason to deny that there is a Marx for everyone, or almost everyone: for liberals and democrats, for social democrats and Stalinists, for Trotskyists and Eurocommunists... And, of course, the academics' Marx, the Marx as topic for competitive examinations. Not even the bruised narcissism – for which they were themselves responsible – of all the Collettis or former apologists for Marx who now hold him responsible for the Siberian concentration camps (although they still have enough good sense not to hold Christ responsible for the events in Santiago de Chile's National Stadium, probably because they had not previously held that Christ was a pure scientist without any connection to the Old Testament) renounces its annual share of publications, with some article or other on the fallen saint.

It is likewise true that if there is a Marx that all can accept, it is because he has been more or less exorcised and people no longer fear his evil effects. The exorcism of Marx is a complicated matter, and to say that it has already been achieved is to lapse into error: as Gramsci noted, it was already believed on earlier occasions that Marx had been exorcised. Gramsci was thinking of the Russian upper bourgeoisie from the end of the past century and beginning of the present one, for whom, he said, *Capital* must have been a bedside book, since it promised them, with its schema of philosophy of history, the unfailing advent of a perfect capitalism. However, the members of the upper bourgeoisie were mistaken in taking literally the laws and necessities they found stated categorically in *Capital* and in other writings by Marx that could be called 'classic'. The Bolsheviks were mistaken in the very same way, likewise believing in all of those necessities and infallible conclusions. If the error of the members of the bourgeoisie mainly concerns the facts, for they could never have overseen an English capitalism in Russia, the Bolsheviks' error is confirmed by documentation bearing Marx's autograph: the letters, now famous but at

* First published in 1983. Republished as 'En el primer centenario del fallecimiento de K. Marx', in *Escritos sobre El Capital (y textos afines)*, edited by Salvador López Arnal (Barcelona: Fundación de Investigaciones Marxistas/Ediciones de Intervención Cultural/El Viejo Topo, 2004).

 | DOI 10.1163/9789004280526_010

that time unknown, to *Otechestvennye Zapiski* (*Annals of the Fatherland*) and to Vera Zasulich, in which Marx relativised the most speculative part of his system, limiting it to the countries of Western Europe and, above all, explicitly renounced the philosophy of history. At the end of his life, Marx was not predicting anything 'necessary' or 'determined' for either the great Russian bourgeois or Bolshevik, as a result of which we can assume that his thought ended up leading beyond the comforting certainties with which the bourgeoisie and despots exorcised him.

When one reads Marx without continuing to believe in any 'historical necessity' from which certain predictions were derived, predictions whose fulfilment was doubtful if not clearly contradicted by the facts, what is the main merit that we find in his texts? First and foremost: that of being *loci classici* of the revolutionary tradition. Marx's work is situated within the succession of those figures who, in the name of God or of reason, have been against the 'realistic' acceptance of the grim waterwheel that is the history of the human species, one turn after another of suffering that is not simply 'natural' and of injustices that are socially produced. Within that tradition, Marx is notable for having carried out extraordinary scientific work. However, there is no scientific work whose fruits are destined to last forever, unless it is a question of the sciences that do not directly talk about the world.

When, at the end of the 1870s, Marx was relativising the results of his research, he admitted that it was possible for there to be processes of communist development that did not pass through 'the capitalist mode of production', processes that were, so to speak, 'para-capitalist'; however, the uncertainty [*indeterminación*] in which we find ourselves today with regard to the communist path is characteristic of a situation that could be called post-capitalist, if by 'capitalism' we are thinking of what Marx was familiar with. It is not because we are beyond capitalism, but because we already find ourselves faced with the urgent need to solve problems that Marx thought would only prove tractable after capitalism. The most important of those problems foreseen by Marx is the ecological problem, from its aspects related to agriculture to those caused by megalopolises. To Marx, the solution to those problems seemed to belong to the socialist future. He could hardly have imagined that the growth of the productive-destructive forces was going to pose those problems, and with real urgency, before we could discern a revolutionary change in daily life, or even just in politics.

While that is the main sphere in need of revision as far as Marx's forecasts, certainties, and articles of faith are concerned, it is not the only one. There are many others, beginning with the verbal expression of the most elementary ideas of communist thought. The only explanation for the preservation of a metaphysical jargon from the end of the eighteenth and beginning of the nineteenth centuries when speaking of communism is the emotional efficacy of the ritual formulas (as in the case of people who remain loyal) and the usefulness of mastering them for advancement in an academic or political career (as in the case of the scholars).

When one thinks – as we in the *mientras tanto* collective think – that the chief and most enduring merit of Marx's work is its status as a link in the revolutionary tradition, critically revising that work means attempting to maintain or reconstitute its effectiveness as a communist programme. To engage with Marx's work while separating it from its author's communist intentions makes no Marxist sense, although it may make conservative-political sense or academic sense. To separate from that intention motifs that are scientifically untenable or that are inapplicable to a new reality is to follow Marx's tradition: it is exactly what he sought to do with authors like Owen or Fourier.

To contribute to that task, it is not bad to stop every now and then to reread Marx in light of current problems. And why not on his centenary?

CHAPTER 8

Which Marx Will Be Read in the Twenty-First Century?

In the twenty-first century, Marx will continue to be read. By that time it will be clear that the contempt for Marx of the 1970s and 1980s, born of the hyper-Marxism of 1968, was merely, like the latter, another mistake due to the same petit bourgeois instability. It will be clear, as it is today, that Marx is a classic author. He will continue to be read, if anything is still read – if there does not first occur that catastrophe whose presentiment so many people are trying to repress, with the help of the angelical Tofler or the sinister, obese Kahn. At any rate, even that catastrophe would not lead to a definitive discarding of Marx. Rather, some extraterrestrial Marxologist present at the spectacle could claim that the denouement was foreseen in the 'common ruin of the contending classes'[1] from *The Communist Manifesto*.

Yet it is by no means easy to foresee which Marx will be read in the twenty-first century. Hermann Grimm had it much easier in asking himself which Goethe we would take the most pleasure in reading in the twentieth century; he predicted that it would not be *Werther*, let alone the *Theory of Colours*, which he did not even consider, but *Faust*, and he was right. The question cannot be posed in this way for Marx, even though there are similarities between the two cases. In the works of Marx there is likewise science along with other things, as in the case of Goethe, but these other things are different and, moreover, are organised in a different way: the relationship between poetry and truth is not the same for the two men. The pages from Marx that might survive as classics offer texts of various kinds: systematic scientific writings, historical studies, works of sociological and political analysis, programmatic pieces. On the other hand, none of those texts – perhaps with the exception of *The Communist Manifesto* and some bits of *Capital* – is literarily so good as to last on the basis of its perfection alone.

Twenty years from now, there will be no difficulty in recognising the scale and limits of the formally theoretical core of Marx's works (that which is pure

* First published in 1983. Republished as '¿Qué Marx se leerá en el siglo XXI?', in *Pacifismo, ecología y política alternativa*, edited by Juan-Ramón Capella (Barcelona: Icaria Editorial, S.A., 1987).

1 Marx and Engels 1976b, p. 482.

 DOI 10.1163/9789004280526_011

economics, as Marx said, but also sociology and history); but the illusion of the Della Volpeans and Althusserians, who turned Marx's works into pure theory, without any trace of Hegelian speculation, will have been dispelled. The period in which Marx considered himself and was in fact least Hegelian was between 1845 and 1855, that is to say, at the threshold of his maturity as an author, which begins with the recovery of Hegel. That is precisely the circumstance that makes the question of the scientific element in Marx's work so complicated and obscure. On the one hand, the Hegelian inspiration ignores the nature of *modern* science, despite the breadth of Hegel's scientific reading (and in spite of the enthusiastic efforts of the Hegelians to convince both themselves and others of the contrary, with the same tenacity with which the Vatican maintained, until well into the pontificate of Pius XII, the pretence to scientificity of geocentrism *today*, in the form of a prize to whoever could justify it). On the other, the Hegelian inspiration permitted Marx to reconcile himself to the idea of theory (through the idea of system), and to go beyond his earlier intellectual programme of mere criticism of theory.

But the speculative inheritance of Marx – who was born intellectually as a romantic philosopher and took twenty years to make his way to a clear notion of what scientific work is in the modern sense of the term, and who, moreover, began to practice that work without abandoning speculation – is not the only reason why his work is not pure theory, even granting that the core of his work is pure theory. There is another, more interesting reason, which is Marx's intellectual project, his ideal of knowledge, the idea, so to speak, that arises from his work. The knowledge Marx seeks must be comprehensive, containing what in today's academy we call economics, sociology, politics, and history (history being, for Marx, the knowledge most worthy of that name). Yet, in addition, the Marxian ideal of knowledge includes a projection that is not only technological, but also globally social, oriented toward practice. An intellectual product with those two features cannot be positive scientific theory in the strict sense, but must very much resemble common, or even artistic, knowledge, and become incorporated into an ethical, or more precisely political, discourse. Allow me to repeat – because in speaking about Marx one always runs the risk of ruffling someone's feathers: this does not exclude the central presence of strictly positive-scientific content in Marx's works. This is indispensable in his conception and distinguishes it from other eras of the revolutionary tradition.

A word as *camp* as 'revolutionary', which will perhaps be viewed as a stain on this page (above all in this age of the apotheosis of watered-down sherry with soda), is the one which most adequately describes Marx's personality and the central theme of his works and practice. Let us stick to his works since we are asking which Marx will be the most read in the twenty-first century.

The most important and problematic thing that 'Hegel turned right side up' yields in Marx's works is the objectivism of the 'laws of history' that appears in his idea of social revolution. The reading that sees in that idea a fatalist determinism is, without question, a bad one; more justified is the reading that regards as unresolved the tension, which is at the centre of the Marxian outlook, between the action of objective or objectified and subjective factors, between the transformational efficacy, which the 'development of the forces of production' shows in its tendential clash with the 'relations of production', and the stated need for the subjectively revolutionary development of the exploited class. To appreciate the complicated nature of this conception – or 'theory' – of social revolution, it is necessary to bear in mind that the subjective factor is already present, before it emerges [*sobrevenga*] in a political form, among the objective factors, in the productive forces that consist of labour power and scientific knowledge.

It is precisely the development of the forces of production far beyond anything that Marx could imagine which allows us to pose this question today in a much more exact fashion than in the old debates between 'economistic' Marxists and 'dialectical' Marxists. It not only allows us to do so, but it also, unfortunately, requires us to do so. The development of the productive forces – notably that of certain military technologies (atomic, biological, and chemical weapons), yet also, and equally so, that of technologies for civilian life (from the production of energy on a large scale, with its strongly centralising effect, to genetic engineering) – can be seamlessly incorporated into a political perspective that tends to eternalise exploitation and oppression, giving yet another spin to the sad wheel of universal history. Those perspectives already exist, and some of them have already been translated into Spanish, for example, Adrian Berry's *The Next Ten Thousand Years*. If Berry's perspective on the conquest of the cosmos – based on nuclear energy and the authoritarian unification of humanity (presumably by means of one or several atomic wars aimed at the destruction of the USSR and the subjugation of non-White peoples) – is combined with the horizon opened up by the 'productive force', almost in existence today, that Aldous Huxley dreamt up in *Brave New World*, we develop a picture in which the triumph of progress consists of billions of little Epsilon slaves working in a servile manner on the moon, on parts of Jupiter and even much further afield, without their masters (who will no doubt speak a simplified English in the Hudson Institute) even having to whip them. The 'dialectical synthesis', the emancipatory 'negation of the negation', would wait in vain, nestled in Hegel's *Logic*, for the movement of history (since it cannot be that of the Idea) to carry out all of the prior disasters that are supposedly necessary.

Not all that is real is rational; rather, almost nothing is.

I will not attempt to argue here for the value of the Marxian conception of the role of the development of the productive forces. For one thing, I believe that it is theoretically consistent and plausible from an empirical standpoint; for another, this would take me too far afield from the question posed here. In order to know how Marx will be read in the twenty-first century, it is of interest to consider what he wrote about the social change that mattered to him most: the transition to socialism. In so setting things out, it may seem that I am dividing history into two realms – the past and the present – with a very arbitrary boundary, as Croce did in another time, and precisely in his critique of Marxism. But this is not the case. Granting that Marx's dynamic schema is not deterministic (as regards either the present or the past), today's changes do not affect the theoretical question concerning the sense in which the schema is valid, but rather the political question of how one must act on the data that today satisfy the schema for promoting the realisation of socialist values. And to answer that question we must bear in mind the peculiarity and novelty of a productive force that had barely been born in Marx's day: contemporary techno-science.

In Marx's works we find, above all starting in the manuscripts from 1857–8 (as Ernest Mandel has pointed out), fairly symmetrical and complete considerations regarding the influence of the science of nature on modern social change. It is possible to classify these considerations into three groups. There are reflections that are plainly inspired by a peculiar blend of the infallibilism of the Hegelian dialectic and the eighteenth-century Enlightenment optimism that Marx's father and father-in-law instilled in him; these are found especially in the *Grundrisse* manuscripts that I have cited and in other texts up until the end of the 1870s. Then there are other reflections opposed to these, in which Marx studies and expounds the oppressive and destructive effects of technical progress not only among the working class, but also in nature; these statements are dispersed throughout Marx's works, but are primarily to be found in Volume I of *Capital* and in the manuscripts from the period in which he read the most about chemistry and agronomy (the preparation for Volume III of *Capital*); and we can add to this group some melancholy and doubtful reflections from his final years, for example, regarding the dissolution of the Russian village community or the penetration of the railroad into the Rhine's tributary valleys. Lastly, there is a third, characteristically 'dialectical' register, which springs up in *The Communist Manifesto* of 1848, and which can be found fully formulated in the 1857–8 manuscript, in a passage, often cited in recent years, that describes the conflict between machine-based progressivism and medievalist reaction, claiming that the struggle between those two equally partial notions will only be resolved with the overcoming of capitalism.

The recurrent Marxian observation that within capitalism every productive force is at the same time a destructive force likewise belongs to this 'dialectical' line of thought.

There have always been interpretations of Marx – in connection with this crucial question of the relation between *revolution* and *progress* – that accentuate, with more or less consistency and one-sidedness, the eighteenth-century Marx of his most confidently progressive moments or statements. That interpretation was dominant in the Second International and is dominant in the political culture of Soviet society, to the extent that the latter lives with the aspiration of 'catching up to and overtaking America', to use Khrushchev's slogan. If we continue advancing down the road of devastating the earth, which the right-wing futurologists see with much more lucidity and coherence than do the Soviets, one can imagine that when the twenty-first century Epsilons are taking their nutritional pills in the refectory, they will hear verses from the Marx who extols the Ricardian idea of 'production for production's sake'.

It is highly unlikely that the pages containing a prophetic condemnation of capitalist progress will ever prevail in the interpretation of Marx's work, despite the fact that they are the best ones, from a literary point of view. No economics or sociology professor who is not more than a little odd will want to explain texts that bear more of a resemblance to Isaiah than to Durkheim or Walras. Pure moralism, as they say.

There remains the interpretation that is most faithful to Marx's system and to his intellectual style, that which is guided by the dialectical perspective articulated for the first time in the 1857–8 manuscripts, though anticipated in *The Communist Manifesto*: the tension between creation and destruction, both caused by the capitalist development of the productive-destructive forces, as well as the tension between the corresponding ideologies, can only be resolved with socialism. With regard to known societies, or to the degree that it is merely negative, the thesis sounds realistic and seems to tally with the facts. However, it does not give us even a vague clue as to how or why those tensions are going to be overcome under socialism. One might suspect that the logicism of Hegelian origin, 'turned right side up' and transformed into a faith in the 'laws of history' and the 'rationality of the real', is the cause of that gap. (It was not until after Marx's death that Engels, in responding to some of Kautsky's concerns, began to suspect that maybe Malthus was right in part; and only then did he stop trusting in the dialectic of historical laws, start doing research on the demographic problem, and begin to argue that, 'if it occurs', it will be easier to solve under socialism than under capitalism.)

That this most complete Marx – even with this important gap – will be the one read in the twenty-first century presupposes that his readers have abandoned the progressives' faith in the supposedly necessary goodness of every increase in reproduction, and even of the passage of time itself. And for twenty-first century Marxists to be aware of the gap that exists even in this interpretation, which is the best one, presupposes that they have also abandoned the Hegelian faith in the rationality of the real (and, incidentally, goodness knows what that means).

The real issue lurking behind so much interpretation is the political question of whether the nature of socialism consists in doing the same thing as capitalism, only better, or whether it consists in living in a different way.

Mexico, D.F., 6 February 1983

PART 2

On Political Ecology, Communist Politics, and the New Social Movements

CHAPTER 9

Political Ecological Considerations in Marx

One can be nearly sure today, as opposed to what would have occurred two or three years ago, that a talk with this title needs no justification. I do not doubt that there are still circles that consider our concern for the subject to be somewhat frivolous, but in general there are so many people today who are well-informed about the importance of political-ecological problems that we can dispense with a lengthy justification. The issue is not a passing fashion; on the contrary, it intensifies daily. Nor is it an aesthetic question, as some critics have disdainfully and condescendingly suggested. And nor is it an idyllic affirmation of an alleged harmony that is being violated. Those who seriously grapple with political-ecological issues know it is not a question of cultivating nostalgia for happier and more stable days gone by. The hypothesis that the animals that we anthropocentrically call 'superior', such as ourselves, owe our conditions of existence to pollution is enough right there to eliminate all aesthetic or nostalgic overtones. We breathe because there is currently enough oxygen in the atmosphere, and that oxygen was pollution from the point of view (in a manner of speaking) of the algae and other organisms which perhaps produced it: those organisms breathed carbon dioxide.

Therefore one cannot identify a political-ecological consciousness with nostalgia, which would posit a false and anthropocentric pure initial state. The first documented or hypothetical earthly environment was not at all beneficial to the human species. Political-ecological problems are neither ideological nor are they characterised by aesthetic longing: they are pragmatic problems. When one laments, for example, that oil tankers pollute the seas on their return voyages (because they carry salt water as ballast and then release it, with all the oil mixed in, as they return to port), one does so not for aesthetic reasons (which would, in any case, be fully justified), but rather because the gradual pollution of the ocean threatens the primary productive source of oxygen on this planet. For the same reason, and for many others, one may protest without any necessarily aesthetic motives against radioactive waste that threatens

* First published in 1984, and translated by Ruth MacKay: 'Political Ecological Considerations in Marx', *Capitalism Nature Socialism*, 3, 1: 37–48.

© KONINKLIJKE BRILL NV, LEIDEN, 2014 | DOI 10.1163/9789004280526_012

human beings and other animals with centuries of problems for which we can today imagine no solution. A similar case can be made for the gradual disappearance of tropical forests, which in some cases, such as that of south-eastern Mexico, have been reduced to foliage of just eight to ten metres alongside the riverbanks, as if they were decorative festoons, while the former forests have been turned over to cattle raising so that meat may be exported to industrialised nations. Tropical forests are also important producers of oxygen, and once they are destroyed they will probably be lost forever because their fertile ground tends to be rather weak.

Ecological-political problems are practical, not ideological. They are furthermore global, international to a greater or lesser extent. It is obvious that the problems of the oceans or the atmosphere are international issues. In this regard, one often mentions the harm done to the Scandinavian countries by London's 'clean-up' operation by which pollutants were simply displaced or emitted at higher levels. Both the fact that these are practical problems which were previously not perceived as such, and the fact that they must be treated in a global fashion, serve to seriously challenge the modern traditional conception of politics, bound by the idea of the bourgeois national state. There is no way of treating these questions with nationalist criteria. Old-fashioned political common sense, and what General Franco called 'the sacred egotism of nations', turn out to be at times absurd, at times suicidal, and often criminal.

The Marxist tradition has not dealt with these problems, or at least has dealt with them insufficiently. However, there are interesting points raised in the work of Marx, and to a lesser extent in that of Engels, which have been taken into account in various ways throughout the century since Marx wrote. For example, Marx and Engels's critique of the living conditions of the labour force, particularly industrial workers, but also peasants and the lower classes in general, has always been taken into consideration. With 'afterknowledge', as the Italians say, this critique can be seen as elementary human ecology, particularly labour ecology, in ascendant capitalism. Insofar as it has political-ecological importance, Marx's treatment of these issues is quite profound because it gets to the root of the matter. Marx tried to explain what he at times called, in an ecological fashion, the depredation of the worker in capitalist society. One does not have to search among the obscure works; in his most frequently read work (it is said), Volume 1 of *Capital*, Marx describes how during its heroic phase, the capitalist production of surplus value, when it is driven by the need to obtain the maximum level of what Marx called absolute surplus value, continually searches for the prolongation of the working day with which, Marx says, human labour power atrophies, is exhausted, and eventually dies. This would be the ultimate cause of what is often called the depredation of labour power, in an interesting parallel to the depredation of the earth in capitalist agriculture. This point is often expressed in *Capital* in strong language, as evidenced by this passage from Chapter 10 of Volume I, which concerns the working-day:

> But in its blind unrestrainable passion, its were-wolf hunger for surplus labour, capital oversteps not only the moral, but even the merely physical maximum bounds of the working-day [by 'moral maximum' he means the customary limits]. It usurps the time for growth, development, and healthy maintenance of the body.
>
> It steals the time required for the consumption of fresh air and sunlight. It higgles over a meal-time [a premonition of Chaplin's *Modern Times*], incorporating it where possible with the process of production itself, so that food is given to the labourer as to a mere means of production, as coal is supplied to the boiler, grease and oil to the machinery.[1]

This grave and even slightly pathetic tone is often found throughout Volume I of *Capital* when Marx examines the causes for the depredation of labour power or when he describes it, several times using the noted correspondence between worker and land. For example, also from Volume I:

> The same blind eagerness for plunder that in the one case exhausted the soil [Marx is referring to the first 30 years of the nineteenth century], had, in the other, torn up by the roots the living force of the nation. Periodical epidemics speak on this point as clearly as the diminishing military standard in Germany and France.[2]

This question, to which Marx conceded great importance, but which is rarely remembered when considering his work, indicates a fairly accurate assessment of the social importance of what might be called biological indicators; Marx had carefully studied military statistics from Central Europe (mainly Germany) and England. With them he obtained a significant curve of the diminished height of young conscripts and correlated it with the initial stages of capitalism in those regions. It is true that all Marx's observations in this regard exude a moralistic tone, because his analyses were rarely purely descriptive and were laden with political and ethical passion. In Volume I of *Capital*, again in Chapter 10, one finds the famous metaphor according to which the treatment

1 Marx 1996, pp. 270–1.

2 Marx 1996, p. 247.

meted out to the labour force in capitalism, the depredation of labour power, can be compared to that given cattle in the River Plate, where the abundance of cattle often led to the practice of slaughtering cows for their hides and discarding the overabundant meat. Searching through the English government's blue books and other statistical or descriptive sources, Marx found documentation of the degradation and depredation of labour power; for example, the English custom, up until the 1850s, of calling workers 'full-timers' or 'half-timers' according to their age and the hours they could work in accordance with limitations on child labour.

Marx did not study only this facet of human ecology, which we can term the ecology of labour power in early capitalism. He also considered several aspects of daily life from the same perspective. Among them, housing and food stand out. Engels conducted a more systematic study of housing than did Marx, whose observations are more impressionistic and superficial. But regarding nutrition, Marx seems to have been the first social scientist to treat the issue of adulterations not from an exclusively medical perspective but rather from a political one, thus bringing together two separate traditions: governmental action and the latest advances in bromatology. Marx based his work on previous studies of the adulteration of food, primarily in England, France, and Germany, but he gives a new socio-political twist to the data. For example, he studied the adulteration of bread in early nineteenth-century England, when there were 'full-price' and 'half-price' bakers; the former sold bread made from pure flour while the latter mixed their flour with heavy substances such as sand and alum. (It is interesting to note that Marx's analysis of the adulteration of food for the working-class market in England and Central Europe during early capitalism offers some clear comparisons with the adulteration of rape seed oil in Spain during the early 1980s. In both cases, the motive is the same: to obtain products that cheapen the cost of labour, products which, being aimed at the working-class budget, permit the worker to subsist on the lowest salary possible. That was the purpose of 'half-price' bread in England and of the authorisation of the sale of oil other than olive oil in Spain during the 1950s, also a period of industrialisation.)

All these points raised by Marx make up a political-ecological critique, and when his observations were presented as a thesis, rather than being merely descriptive or analytical remarks, they were even more radical. For example, both Marx and Engels considered it obvious that large cities would have to be abolished in a socialist society. Here one begins to come up against classical theses that the Marxist vulgate, contaminated by bourgeois progressivism, would consider non-Marxist. Vulgar Marxists resist the idea that their classic texts ever said that large cities, the residence of the industrial proletariat, must be destroyed. But the thesis is there, and again it is contained not in any obscure or abstruse text known only to the erudite, but rather in one of the easiest and most widely read books written by Marx and Engels, *Anti-Dühring*: 'It is true', wrote Engels, doubtless in agreement with Marx, who collaborated on the book:

> that in the huge towns civilisation has bequeathed us a heritage which it will take much time and trouble to get rid of. But it must and will be got rid of, however protracted a process it may be.[3]

But these considerations, and many others, some of which we will consider later on, have not had much continuity in the Marxist tradition except in a few notable cases, of which two stand out. The first is Kautsky's concern with demography, which was particularly praiseworthy given that he wrote during the last 25 years of the nineteenth century, when there was little awareness of the problem. As in so many other instances, Kautsky's observations, which were shared by the old Engels, despite some hesitation, have been forgotten in the mainstream Marxist tradition, to the point that the supposedly Marxist governments of Eastern Europe unanimously voted in international gatherings, along with the Vatican, to oppose any measure of population control.

The second exceptional and brilliant case I would like to mention is that of a Polish Marxist who wrote in the late nineteenth century, who is far less known than Kautsky. His name was Sergei Podolinsky and he published a fascinating two-part essay in the journal of the German Social Democrats about the Marxist concept of labour value and the second law of thermodynamics, the principle of entropy. The law of entropy says that in a closed system the amount of usable energy, or the differences of potential, to put it another way, steadily diminishes. The law refers to a closed system, which it is clear the Earth is not, given that it constantly receives energy from the sun. Therefore, there has always been a debate about whether or not the law of entropy is useful for understanding human processes, particularly productive processes. But the question is not a simple one because one may counter the objection that the Earth is an open system by replying that the sources of life for the human species are perhaps not so open. The discussion is similar to that recently carried out by what we would call 'vulgar Prigoginism', the idea that there is no need to worry about the imbalance of a given environment since there are many other possible dynamic equilibria in nature. But the pragmatic question for the human species is knowing in which of these states we may survive and

3 Engels 1987c, p. 283.

in which we cannot; the dinosaurs can derive little consolation from knowing that they died, but that the human race arose.

Podolinsky was meritorious in recovering the naturalist point of view that Marx expressly abandoned (in order to dedicate himself to political economy) in the first pages of *The German Ideology*. Podolinsky re-cultivated it and tried to reconstruct the idea of labour value within the framework of thermodynamics. It is just, then, that we honour the memory of Kautsky and Podolinsky, but at the same time we must repeat that the classical thinkers' efforts in the direction of an ecological-political perspective have had practically no continuity in the Marxist tradition. Anything we today might call ecological-political issues were put under the heading of 'The Evils of Capitalism' in traditional Marxism with no attention given to the specificities of the risks involved in civilisation's treatment of nature. Thus was constituted a problem-free progressive tradition that contained more traditionally bourgeois elements than socialist novelties.

Before we ask ourselves why this is the case, we should turn to the lesser-known political-ecological ideas in Marx. These observations do not concern the ecology of industrial labour power, but of agriculture. The classical source of ideas on the subject is the tenth section of Chapter 15 in Volume I of *Capital*. It is a well-known, mature text that nevertheless demonstrates a manner of thought that does not necessarily fit in well with the usual image of Marxist doctrine. Marx thought, due to his philosophical education, that history advances 'on its bad side'. But in the passage referred to, Marx's dialectical model, this advance through the bad side, appears to be suspended. Marx believes and says that the advance through the bad side may not characterise the dynamic of progress in the case of agriculture because capitalist exploitation 'disturbs the circulation of matter between man and the soil, ... it therefore violates the conditions necessary to lasting fertility of the soil'.[4] This was written a century before the fanatics of the 'Green Revolution' launched upon their exploits.

Marx's thinking here is interesting in that it does not fit in well with his usual train of thought. All progress in capitalist agriculture, Marx writes, 'is a progress in the art, not only of robbing the labourer, but of robbing the soil; all progress in increasing the fertility of the soil for a given time, is a progress towards ruining the lasting sources of that fertility'. He ends with a general affirmation:

4 Marx 1996, pp. 506–7.

> Capitalist production ... develops technology, and the combining together of various processes into a social whole, only by sapping the original sources of all wealth – the soil and the labourer.[5]

Thus Marx's writings contain considerations (more than mere indications) that go beyond the ecology of labour under capitalism. But, in addition, Marx tried to use these ideas to understand what socialist society would be like. The attempt is brief and not very precise, but is nonetheless interesting. He starts with the very pessimistic conviction that capitalism will have completely destroyed the correct relationship between the human species and the rest of nature by the time socialism is to be constructed, understanding the word 'correct' in a pragmatic sense, the appropriate relationship for the sustenance of the species. He then assigns to society the task of 'systematically producing' this exchange between the human species and the rest of nature, which is understood as a basic regulatory law of production in a form that conforms with what he calls (in an ideological vein typical of the era and which is still present in terms such as 'evolutionary psychology', etc.) 'full human development'. Socialist society thus is characterised as that which establishes the ecological viability of the species. The development is very brief; the entire tenth section of Chapter 15 of Volume I of *Capital* is short; depending upon the edition, it takes up between three and five pages. But it is very interesting. Why is it that such a categorical and stimulating text was not followed up on, given that it expresses the hypothesis that capitalism will not extinguish itself until it has entirely destroyed the lasting metabolism between the human species and nature? Sensibility regarding any problem is a historical question. Generations upon generations of Marxists and Marxologists have read these pages and paid heed to the other things Marx said concerning, for example, the fact that capitalism technologises agriculture, that it reduces the agricultural population, etc. But they never stopped to study what he said about the relationship between the human species and nature.

One of the reasons for this lack of interest is probably found in the Hegelian philosophical base beneath Marx's thought. From Hegel, Marx inherited a peculiarly deterministic mode of thinking based on the idea that events are produced with internal logic and with absolute necessity, the idea that there is no distinction between the logical and the empirical, that facts are in and of themselves logically necessary. This is what he meant in the famous and oft-repeated phrase: 'All that is real is rational'. In addition, the logic or necessity that Hegelian philosophy attributes to events, to history, operates through

5 Marx 1996, pp. 507–8.

negativity: it constructs a dynamic in which the motor of change, the motor of the historical process, is what Hegelians call 'negation'. This negation does not coincide with what we in everyday speech call negation but is what some Marxists have called a 'determinate' negation or even, to elaborate further, 'overdetermined'. It is a negation which one cannot construct through what we commonly call logic. When we are asked, in everyday speech, to deny the affirmation, 'This table is gray', we respond: 'This table is not gray'. We all know how to deny an affirmation given to us in the common speech we all share. But denying an affirmation in the Hegelian system or in any Hegelianised system is something only the Hegelians know how to do. Only they know that the negation of 'bourgeoisie' is 'proletariat', or something like that, whereas the rest of us believe that the negation of 'bourgeoisie' (its complement) is 'non-bourgeoisie'.

In any case, the Hegelian idea that the historical process depends upon this internal and necessary dynamic of negation, which is (seen anthropocentrically) the bad side of the process and also the motor of the process, decisively leads one to worry little about the problems of development and to concern oneself almost exclusively with what is seen as the fundamental direction of development. Marx proposed a common-sense version of this Hegelian speculation, such as in his classical exposition of the function of negation, of the 'bad side' of historical progress, in *The Poverty of Philosophy*. But the results are frequently as arbitrary as Hegel's. Thus, for example, communism would be the negation of the negation of primitive communism, or, on an even more sterile and ridiculous level, the grain of barley that grows on a stalk would be, according to Engels's example, the negation of the negation of the sown barley grain. This type of imaginative thought, very traditional in philosophy, is very similar to other trivial speculation of the tradition, such as explanation through the ideas of act and potency, or of substance and form. They are more or less poetic codifications of everyday common experience, but taken as explanations of reality they halt the inquisitive spirit with the appearance of comprehension which is nothing more than a paraphrase of what is already known. In the case of the 'negation of the negation', the inhibition of the investigative spirit leads to a certain fatalism that awaits the necessary development of events through, precisely, the 'bad side': it is the negativity of a given social stage, its bad side, which permits progress. The idea is presented very clearly in the following passage from *The Poverty of Philosophy*:

> It is the bad side that produces the movement which makes history, by providing a struggle. If, during the epoch of the domination of feudalism, the economists, enthusiastic over the knightly virtues, the beautiful

> harmony between rights and duties, the patriarchal life of the towns, the prosperous condition of domestic industry in the countryside, the development of industry organised into corporations, guilds and fraternities, in short, everything that constitutes the good side of feudalism, had set themselves the problem of eliminating everything that cast a shadow on the picture – serfdom, privileges, anarchy – what would have happened? All the elements which called forth the struggle would have been destroyed, and the development of the bourgeoisie nipped in the bud. One would have set oneself the absurd problem of eliminating history.[6]

This idea of unavoidable progress through the 'bad side' is the philosophical basis for the typically adolescent and falsely revolutionary claim that the worse things are today, the better for the future. And as concerns the matter before us, it paradoxically favours the unconditional acceptance of the given, being that it is precisely the maintenance of what exists, particularly the bad side, that will permit us to overcome this stage. There is plenty of documentation indicating that the old Marx did not believe this was the case, but it is certain that the mature Marx (the orthodox Marx, if one allows the joke) did indeed think like this, at least until he wrote Volume I of *Capital*. He thought so in a radical fashion, at times approaching what is today one of the worst right-wing tendencies, political sociobiology. In an 1863 manuscript, he wrote:

> ... [A]lthough at first the development of the capacities of the *human* species takes place at the cost of the majority of human individuals and whole human classes, in the end it breaks through this contradiction and coincides with the development of the individual; the higher development of individuality is thus only achieved by a historical process during which individuals are sacrificed, for the interests of the species in the human kingdom, as in the animal and plant kingdoms, always assert themselves at the cost of the interests of individuals, because these interests of the species coincide with the *interests of certain individuals*, and it is this coincidence which constitutes the strength of these privileged individuals.[7]

There is, however, an important difference between the social Darwinists of the past (the rightists) or today's reactionary sociobiologists, on the one hand, and Marx's thought, on the other. The difference is that Marx believed that human

---

6 Marx 1976, pp. 174–5.

7 Marx 1989a, p. 348.

beings must 'abandon the animal realm', an absurd proposition from a zoological point of view, obviously, but one which has political meaning. But acceptance of the model of advance on the bad side is, at any rate, hardly consistent with a programme of political ecology. If things must advance on the bad side, one could say, we should just let them get worse. This strain of thought is more widespread than one might think, and not just among Marxists. More than one authoritative academic ecologist believes in more or less the same practical consequences, though starting from different premises: that if human nature leads us to destroy our habitat, all the worse for humans, but all the better for the laws of nature. If a self-destructive technical development takes root in the nature of the species, we should let it continue on with its smoke, its noise, and its radioactive waste because they are all fruits of the species's potential. Furthermore, insects, many of which can resist doses of radiation far too high for human beings, will continue living and multiplying on the planet. The Franciscan tone of the reasoning is odd, and one must wonder if Saint Francis of Asisi would have been willing to favour the insects over the survival of the human race.

I am sure this is not a full explanation, but I think it is likely that the reason for the scant attention paid to Marx's observations on political ecology has a great deal to do with the Hegelian element of his philosophy. Any useful continuation of the Marxist tradition must start by abandoning the Hegelian dialectical schema regarding the philosophy of history. Marx himself appears to have realised this more or less clearly after the mid-1870s. In 1877, for example, he wrote a now-famous letter to a Russian newspaper asking that people stop considering his thought as a philosophy of history. The same need was present in a variety of different contexts. Each one needs to be studied.

CHAPTER 10

Paper for the Conference on Politics and Ecology

In the following paragraphs, I intend to present some general considerations on the problems posed by the ecological crisis to the revolutionary Left. I trust that the second and third sections of the list of topics may leave room for some rather philosophical reflections, probably useless except for the person stating them, who, in stating them, will be obliged to test the solidity of his beliefs. I am grateful to the organisers of the conference for having given us the opportunity for this test, and hope to be able to confine myself, more or less, to the time limit that they have recommended.

1. The main transformation of revolutionary thought suggested by ecological constraints [*condicionamientos*] involves abandoning the wait for the Last Judgement, abandoning utopianism and eschatology, and ridding oneself of millenarianism. Millenarianism is the belief that the Social Revolution is the peak of all time, an event after which all the tensions among people, and between people and nature, will be resolved, for then the objective laws of being, which are good in themselves but have until now been deformed by the sinfulness of the unjust society, will operate free of any hindrance. The eschatological attitude is found in all currents of the revolutionary Left. Nevertheless, as this reflection is inevitably self-critical (at least on a collective, if not personal, level), it is appropriate for each of us to refer to his or her own tradition, and to improve it and help it advance with one's own tools.

In Marxism, the eschatological utopia is based on an understanding of the real dialectic as a process in which all tensions or contradictions come to an end. What we have learned about planet Earth confirms the need (which always existed) to avoid that chiliastic vision of a harmonious future paradise. There will always be contradictions between the powers of the human species and nature's constraints [*su condicionamiento natural*]. The dialectic is open-ended. In the cultivation of the classic theorists of Marxism, it is worth paying attention to those places in which they themselves view the dialectic as a process that cannot be consummated.

* First published in 1979. Republished as 'Comunicación a las Jornadas de Ecología y Política', in *Pacifismo, ecología y política alternativa*, edited by Juan-Ramón Capella (Barcelona: Icaria Editorial, S.A., 1987).

 | DOI 10.1163/9789004280526_013

One of the three most interesting attempts up to now in Marxist milieus to assimilate (among other things) ecological-social knowledge, the theory of radical needs proposed by Agnes Heller, has, along with some valuable, correct ideas, the defect of not admitting without reservation the need to abandon eschatology. Heller's theory, based on a philosophical anthropology that metaphysically presumes to know the human 'essence', nourishes the hope that the final harmony is attainable, once the radical or authentic needs have been identified and the present alienation of desires has been removed. That idea can inspire a good ideology, a good politics, a good education, a good way of posing the question of the 'new man' or new culture (an unavoidable question in the revolutionary movement), but it is not good anthropology. It is a programme, not knowledge of what exists. There are no radical needs, except in a trivial sense. In general, the species in its evolution has developed, for better or worse, a practically inexhaustible plasticity as regards its powers and needs. We must recognise that our natural capacities and needs are capable of expanding to the point of self-destruction. We must see that we are *biologically* the species of hubris, of original sin, of arrogance – the species of excess.

2. In order to overcome the eschatological utopia it is necessary to revise our understanding of the role of society's objective processes in achieving revolutionary prospects. That role seems more problematic today than in other times.

It is of particular importance in this connection to get an idea of the complexity, now visible, of the operation of two of those processes that are especially crucial: the class struggle and science as a force of production. It would be a mistake to believe that in the Marxist labour movement's past, people saw in the class struggle an infallible agent of communism. To the contrary, Marx and Engels themselves, citing examples from history, had considered the possibility that an era of intense social struggles might end in disaster for all classes involved in the battle. Analogously, the traditional view of science as a productive force was not purely and naively progressive either. The movement knew from its very beginning that, according to Marx's words, every one of capitalism's productive forces is at the same time a force of destruction.

However, that knowledge, aside from often being forgotten, is not sufficient to solve some of the recently perceived problems. Today we notice not only that the working class in the industrial countries (which is the context in which I offer these reflections) can become dispersed within a new social structure, in which automatisation, the plundering of the Third World, and the pillaging of the earth would confirm the hypothesis (already known to Marx) of a parasitical proletariat, without having produced the revolution that Marxists expected from them; we also notice that in those countries the working classes can respond poorly to ecological problems, showing a subaltern solidarity with the interests of capital, submitting to the reality of imperialist capitalism, and losing revolutionary motivation and imagination. There is no lack of signs indicating that this process of transformation is already underway, reinforcing the working class's corporativist tendencies and, in turn, becoming stronger itself. On the other hand, to generally acknowledge that every productive force is a destructive force under capitalism is not the same thing as perceiving the novelty of the prospect of complete tyranny opened up by, for example, the nuclear state or genetic engineering.

3. The new assessment, which is necessary, of the play of objective social forces in the revolutionary process leads to a more nuanced and more complete appraisal of the agent, the subject of the process. This new assessment must solve two main problems. The first follows directly from the loss of confidence formerly placed in objective factors: the problem of finding out what it is that the revolutionary subject is supposed to do now takes on even greater importance.

Owing to the way that we have finally learned to look at the earth, we know that the agent cannot regard 'liberating society's forces of production', supposedly fettered by capitalism, as a fundamental task. We have ceased to give credence to the mystical correspondence between society's objective development and communist objectives, a correspondence in which Lenin, for example, still believed. We now know that we must earn the new earth entirely with the work of our own hands. (We could retain the idea or phrase 'liberating society's forces of production', but only on the condition that we redefine those forces and underscore the primacy of labour power over all the rest. That task is not possible in a brief presentation, even if done dogmatically, in the same way that it is possible to say other things briefly and without too much reasoning.)

On the other hand, the revolutionary agent's fundamental task cannot consist simply in hindering the productive forces either. First, because that is probably unattainable in a voluntary manner: it is possible that the only agent capable of hindering, in a general fashion, the vitality of the productive forces is a social catastrophe of great proportions. Second, because even if it were attainable, it would not yield a society compatible with the aspirations to justice, freedom, and community, which is the motivation for the communist tradition. An aristocracy of inquisitors may perhaps aim at such a Platonist and bureaucratic ideal; but a communist movement cannot be on the side of the censors. In the administration of knowledge, for example (an important example, given that it is one of the two motifs that make up the threads of this discussion), it is inconceivable that a movement could be communist while having to grapple with a Galilean nostalgia for forbidden knowledge.

The complexity of what the revolutionary subject has to do – neither simply 'liberate society's productive forces', nor simply hinder them – entails a change in the traditional image of the agent. The agent was thought of as a shackled, mutilated force, whose liberation was understood as an unlimited expansion of inclinations, powers and operations. That was consistent with the idea that the revolution would break the social dike that prevented the 'free flow of the springs of common wealth'. Judging by the complicatedness of the fundamental task described, the revolutionary agent's action [*operación*] will have to be described in a manner that is much less Faustian and inspired more by the rules of conduct characteristic of the archaic tradition. So archaic that it can be summarised in one of the Delphic maxims: 'Nothing in excess'. The fact of the matter is that the maxims of insatiability are just as old, yet they had a greater presence in the modern revolutionary movement ('Be realistic, demand the impossible' was widely repeated in May 1968). So, if this reflection is not completely off the mark, we ought to aim at an inversion of some of the values of the modern revolutionary tradition.

4. The second problem refers to the revolutionary agent's self-consciousness. Since 1848, Marxism has proposed to the industrial working class a self-understanding (a class self-consciousness) based on the negativity of its social being, the notion that it would have nothing to lose. Reformism saw that the situation of the proletariat in the imperialist countries was no longer a mere negative of bourgeois existence and acted accordingly. The result is the class consciousness of the imperialist labour aristocracy, which in practice identifies with the economic values of capitalism in the West, and the corrected version of those very same values in the East.

We cannot ignore the fact that the economic and cultural values of modern capitalist society powerfully attract the most backward populations from the point of view of this culture, as is shown by the current awe among a considerable part of the Chinese people after catching a glimpse of what those of us who live in this culture know to be the illusion of a reality that is becoming more and more sinister. The adherence of a large part of the workers of the industrialised countries to the values of predatory economic growth and the hierarchical, despotic structure that, in different forms, often organises that growth, led Rudolf Bahro (the author of another of the main Marxist attempts to articulate the crisis) to what is probably the chief weakness of his study, *The Alternative in Eastern Europe*: proposing intellectuals as the revolutionary subject, while conceiving of the working class (in the countries of the East) as a passive weight whose gravity stabilises that bureaucracy which, in the East, conducts the delayed response to the material world of capitalism, touched up with some good collectivist or communitarian features. Bahro's thesis is implausible because the intellectuals, whether scholarly or technical, are a social group that benefits from the system to the extent that it is based on the fundamental division between manual labour and intellectual labour. The efficacious publicity for intellectuals who consider themselves critical, diligently spread by the mass media of the system criticised (from television to the most distinguished press organs), cannot hide the fact that this social stratum is, in production and consumption, an appendage of the ruling classes, as much in the East as in the West. This stratum's specific privileges, language, and science make it easier for individuals to frequently separate themselves from the group of intellectuals and situate themselves on the other side, with the exploited and oppressed classes. That is, however, not a new development that would confirm Bahro's thesis.

The necessary revision of our conception of the revolutionary subject in industrial societies must not base workers' class consciousness solely on the negativity which a part of that class has overcome in those societies, thanks to struggle and the evolution of the system; it must also be based on the positivity of its status as sustainer of the species, conserver of life and indispensable organ of society's metabolism with nature. The era of capital has added to that positivity of the working classes of all these societies the capacity for scientific knowledge and its habits, and as a result of this, versatility at work and the potential awareness, largely blurred today, of global problems (ecological problems being among them). The working classes, and most importantly the working class in the industrial countries, must continue to view themselves as a revolutionary subject, not because the absolute negation of humanity is perfected among them, a negation through which the utopia of the finale will burst forth, but because they are the part of humanity that is completely indispensable for survival.

Wolfgang Harich – the author of the third Marxist project for overcoming the social-ecological crisis to which I want to pay tribute here – has also drawn our attention (in different words) to the requisite revision of our conception of the revolutionary subject. What I have presented as a shift from a formal dialectic of pure negativity to an empirical dialectic that includes considerations of positivity involves, for Harich, a feminisation of the revolutionary subject and of the very idea of a just society. I think that he is right, for the values of positivity, of nourishing continuity, of measure and equilibrium – 'compassion' – are mainly feminine within our cultural tradition.

5. Several of the problems mentioned and several of the proposed solutions stated here can be viewed as leading to dead ends and, moreover, ones with

which we are already familiar and which, if apparently always tempting, are flanked by the ruins of the revolutionary movement: the two most dangerous dead ends are reformism and authoritarianism.

The false, reformist solution seems to benefit from the need to abandon the Mephistophelian dialectic of pure negativity, of 'the worse, the better', in order to advocate a revolutionary ethics of good sense. That is just a false appearance, however, caused by the vagueness of a very general description. In the concreteness of life, the struggle for good sense and survival has to be as revolutionary and radical as the struggle for justice and freedom. It is not possible by means of reforms to turn a system whose essential dynamic is growth and irreversible depredation into a friend of the earth. That is why what is reasonably reformist is, in this regard as well, irrational. Those left-wing parties and publicists who adopt lines that are supposedly reasonable and apparently sensible, yet which owe this appearance solely to the fact that they have not been thought out to the very end, act irrationally. Thus, for example, the thesis of 'few nuclear reactors and all of them controlled by the people' is an impossible solution, since no gigantism (including, indeed, that of huge solar energy stations) can be subordinated to the will of the community, but rather demands a concentration of despotic power. The concealed insanity of the reformist parties reproduces the petty-bourgeois ideology of Proudhonian anarchism, which believes that it is possible to have a society of small property owners in competition with one another without there arising a concentration of capital and power. The publicists who in their editorial articles reject the 'passion' and 'emotion' of environmental and anti-nuclear groups must be made to see that the emotion with which one defends the truth is more rational than the tepidity with which falsehoods are advocated in their newspapers.

The authoritarianism proposed by Wolfgang Harich as a revision of Marxist communism in light of socio-ecological problems is more reasonable than reformism. One can imagine a revolutionary aristocracy despotically guaranteeing, in the aftermath of a true revolution (that is, after the destruction of the capitalist state and the abolition of the old property relations), a healthy metabolism between society and nature. That vision is not self-contradictory, as is the vision of reformism. On the other hand, however, it has three defects that doom it as a communist hypothesis. First of all, it is implausible, if we bear in mind historical experience, including that which is most recent, which is the experience presented by the aristocracy in the countries of so-called 'really existing socialism'. Secondly, despotism belongs to the very culture of excess that needs to be overcome. Thirdly, it is highly unlikely that a communist movement will fight for such an aim. A communist consciousness will think, rather, that for that purpose the revolutionary struggle is a fat lot of good. To the objection (repeatedly insinuated by Harich) that the instinct for conservation must prevail over a repugnance for authoritarianism, we can at least advance a doubt in regard to what can be done by a humanity lacking in enthusiasm and frustrated in its millennial aspiration to justice, freedom, and community.

6. We need not inevitably remain stuck on these discouraging facts [*comprobaciones*]. Harich's programme has a methodological defect arising from the closed dialectic of negativity: the attempt to derive a definitive solution. (Harich's programme would deserve even more attention than it no doubt deserves if it were presented merely as a transitional programme, although I do not find it entirely convincing in that sense either).

The most rational policy for the revolutionary movement consists in recognising that it is too risky to aim, in the manner of the idealist dialectic, at an immediate deduction of the socio-ecological solution. Instead, it must combine two types of revolutionary practice, whose scientific-communist nature rests not on the possession of a deductive model of the liberated society, but on the systematic practice of research by trial and error, guided by the communist goal. The two complementary practices must be revolutionary, not reformist, and they refer to state political power and daily life, respectively. One conviction common to all Marxist attempts to assimilate the socio-ecological problematic is that the movement must try to lead a new daily life, without postponing the revolution in daily life until 'after the Revolution', and that it must not lose its traditional, realistic vision of the problem of political power, and state power in particular.

On this score too, the reformist abandoning of certain elements of the Marxist tradition proves counterproductive. For example, the ecological crisis increases the validity and importance of the principles of global planning and internationalism, principles which the labour parties tend to abandon under a bourgeois ideological influence that is truly anachronistic, since capital is meanwhile becoming even politically internationalised and is planning a disaster for humanity on a planetary scale, in the belief that it is ensuring 'Progress'.

In this paper I have tried (in a condensed and dogmatic manner, since there was not time to include all of the necessary reasoning, or all of the remaining doubts) to make the philosophical points that strike me as indispensable for a renewal of revolutionary consciousness today. I do not think it possible, within these constraints, to attempt to go any deeper into the question that the sixth point raises: the old '*What is to be done?*'

CHAPTER 11

The Political and Ecological Situation in Spain and the Way to Approach This Situation Critically from a Position on the Left

In regard to the situation here, I think that we can dispense with data, which we all have. This will allow me to move forward and stimulate – without provocation – a discussion or reflection, and to talk about what can be done given our situation, beginning with the clarification of one of the fundamental problems, probably *the* fundamental problem, confronting initiatives from the classical, and mainly (but not exclusively) Marxist Left, in the face of this new situation.

This problem is the following: an idea has appeared, on various occasions and among authors of some importance, even authors with a socialist background, to the effect that the demands imposed by ecological-social problems were, to begin with, hardly foreseeable, on the basis of the labour movement's classical assumptions [*planteamientos*]: the labour movement was generally based on the prospects of a deployment of the productive forces and not on the desirability of restricting them. And secondly, the immediate solution to these problems also seems to clash with the basic traditions, so to speak, of the trade union movement. Hence, for example, Bahro and some other authors who think that the crucial question of revolutionary political thought, the question of who is the subject or agent of social transformation, needs to be changed altogether. For this author, for example, we need to look for the agent of the new change, of the socio-ecological revolution, to use a term that is already rather well established, not in the industrial working class (in accordance with the Marxist schema), nor even in the most dispossessed, deprived, exploited strata, as in the tradition of the labour movement as a whole (including the anarchists), but in the stratum of intellectuals in production, technicians, scientists, and critical humanist intellectuals, supported, at best, by the most enlightened sectors of the working classes.

* Transcription of a talk given in 1979, first published in 1981. Republished as 'La situación política y ecológica en España y la manera de acercarse críticamente a esta situación desde una posición de izquierdas', in *Pacifismo, ecología y política alternativa*, edited by Juan-Ramón Capella (Barcelona: Icaria Editorial, S.A., 1987).

 | DOI 10.1163/9789004280526_014

My opinion in this regard, which I would like to propose merely as a basis for discussion, is that this is fairly superficial thinking. First of all, for a negative reason: it is inconceivable that the agent of social change should be, on the one hand, a minority and, on the other, a beneficiary, to a large extent, of the existing situation. And this is, in my view, equally true in regard to East and West; I mean that the stratum of intellectuals in general, and that of the technical intellectuals in particular, cannot be counted among those who are directly harmed in a classical sense. If anyone can benefit from the technical products and at the same time avoid their worst consequences, it is the social strata that include at least a large proportion of the intellectuals. And secondly, for a positive reason: because the social class which is most productive in terms of survival is, in my opinion, indispensable for change, so I do not view the stratum of intellectuals as an adequate agent, nor do I see the possibility of making an important social change without the class that most decisively maintains society's subsistence.

Of course, there is a possibility of getting around my two objections: the possibility of those intellectuals having a despotic power that could force the working classes to continue working and, at the same time, to accept, under conditions of domination, a new austerity, a new type of daily life.

Without elaborating any further, I will simply state my opinion. I believe that the new set of problems does not alter the revolutionary labour movement's old conviction that the agent of social change is found in the working classes, primarily in the industrial proletariat. Having said this, it is in any case worth reviewing schematically the new problems, which may lead us to think, according to Lukács's famous *boutade*, that we are worse off than in 1848 from that point of view, from the point of view of the active self-consciousness of those who ought to be the material agent of social change.

The new problems are cultural and material. The cultural problem is the entire tradition of the labour movement: it will surely be very difficult for the labour movement, in, for example, its most direct expression, the trade union movement, to perceive any time soon the need to consider the satisfaction of its needs in a new way. All of us who work in the labour milieu have had experience of just how difficult it is. For example, I myself have faced the following, spontaneous response from militant, combative worker cadres when they heard the idea that the private automobile is surely something whose elimination is necessary: 'now that the workers can own a car you theorists discover that the car is bad'. Laura Tremosa has had an experience even more dramatic than this one: in a workers' environment in which she was employed, they went so far as to forbid her from saying, or to threaten to interrupt her if she said, anything against the automobile during her work. And it is in the

German trade unions, in West Germany, that the only fairly broad foundations have been laid for demonstrations in favour of nuclear power.

Here there is, therefore, an important cultural difficulty, not to mention the problem with the top officials themselves. Some of you will surely remember the terrible lead article signed by L.C. in *Mundo Obrero* a few years ago, in which the core sector of the PCE – there are naturally other sectors as well – argued for the healthiness and advisability of nuclear-generated electricity in a way that was probably more radical and crude than that of the General Manager of ENHER[1] in his most recent declarations. It is not that this is the state of mind of all of the labour officials, not even within the PCE's leadership – far from it. Yet it does exist within the leadership of all labour parties.

This cultural difficulty is aggravated – I suppose this is obvious – by the worsening of life circumstances as a result of the economic crisis. When there is, for instance, an entire debate as to why business people are not investing, and one comes out and categorically observes that it is necessary, in addition, to lower and hinder an indicator that for fifteen years had been considered an indicator of proximity to paradise, namely, energy consumption per capita, there is a very high possibility that both the business people and their employees will react with intolerance.

What to do when confronted with this situation? First of all, it seems to me, we must avoid reactions along the lines of simple individual complacency. This is happening everywhere: even in the Comité Antinuclear de Catalunya one constantly notices the departure [*abandono*] of people who seek refuge in environments that are culturally more hospitable, as they leave the Comité Antinuclear – where comprehensive work is done for all of Catalonia, work that is very bland and therefore disagreeable – for a neighbourhood athenaeum, where all are friends and all are against pollution: there they find themselves emotionally more protected. This is not a merely negative development: they may do great work on this basis, without a doubt; it all depends on the state of mind with which they do the work. If they leave in order to start actively working from there, it is certainly a good attitude. But I fear that in many cases it is rather a matter of giving up [*abandono*], of taking refuge in environments that are warmer, more tolerable.

This is quite understandable, since at this point it is very difficult to control the indignation produced by the spokespersons for the major electric companies when they speak about these questions. In spite of everything, there have been few things more sinister than the statement from the President of ENHER

1 Empresa Nacional Hidroeléctrica del Ribagorzana, a company involved in the construction of nuclear reactors [Ed.].

from a week ago, which you will perhaps remember, according to which the accident at Three Mile Island shows how healthy nuclear reactors are, given that no one has died in this most serious public accident. He thereby ignores the spreading of tumorous diseases and the tremendous psychic harm caused to the evacuated population, primarily to children. For him, none of this matters at all when compared to his career in a major electric company. One therefore understands reactions that involve a total break. However, they seem to me to be the ones that most fundamentally need to be prevented.

I would like to propose the following positive policies for discussion. First and foremost: spur on and defend the action of those sectors in the labour parties and unions who are sensitive to these problems. This nudging should be done in two ways. Those who are militants in parties or unions should do so from within. Those of us who are not in any party or unionised in any union should act on the basis of external organisations: the CANC for the nuclear question, DEPANA, AEPDEN, and all of the other environmental associations in other spheres.

Let me stress that I think this should be the main policy if one is realistic and does not forget that there has been no social change that could ignore the question of power. While it probably sounds almost 'camp', or at least old-fashioned, to say so, since this is the straightforward Leninist lexicon for every revolutionary question, here nothing has changed: the fundamental question continues to be Leninist question, the question of power.

Consequently, and no matter how unhappy one is with the conduct of the major labour parties and the unions, there is no doubt that the fundamental action for social, ecological change lies in the movement of those major class bodies, which are at least objectively class organisations. No matter how little one can stand them personally, as sometimes happens, and even if one must remain on the outside. They are still the major figures in all of the transformations.

I would place specific, practical actions on a secondary level, secondary only in terms of their feasibility and not because of their importance. And precisely not 'more Goma-2 for Lemoniz',[2] which may prove more dangerous than Lemoniz itself, but actions which, being direct, like this one, are more cautious in terms of their physical consequences and more vast in terms of the number of people who carry them out.

Thirdly, but second in importance, the Left needs to assimilate a strategic line that was always scorned to an extreme degree under the name of Gandhi. Here it is necessary to say some rather harsh things; and the fact is that at this

2 The site of a proposed nuclear power plant [Ed.].

point, toward the end of the twentieth century, one does not really know who had more revolutionary success, strategically speaking. I will say this provocatively, since it is a matter of provoking discussion: one does not know whether it was the Third International or Gandhi. Admittedly, Gandhi did not attain an India based on handicrafts, but the Third International did not attain a socialist world either. So perhaps that's it, more or less; in any case, using the lesson of Gandhi should really serve, in the long run, to politically boost the alternative movements, the small, marginal – or not so marginal – groups that exist, making it possible to build a bridge between them and the bulk of the labour movement, which I consider, in any event, to be the main actor.

In my opinion, and to conclude, this entails a corollary for the left-wing militant in general, and the worker in particular, even more particularly the communist worker: start weaving, so to speak, have a loom at home; one cannot continue speaking out against pollution while polluting intensely. I suppose that as recently as fifteen years ago, such a statement from an individual with a left-wing, Marxist background would have been considered a sure sign that he had gone mad. In light of the results of an exclusively politicist, purely Leninist policy, I think it can be said today that it is possible to express something like that without necessarily being suspected of insanity. The question of credibility is starting to become very important, and succeeding in getting union organisations, for example, to develop alternative ways of living is, I think, not merely a way of morally nourishing groups of activists, but also something that is a corollary of a strategic line.

CHAPTER 12

Three Notes on the Clash of Cultures and Genocide

Clash of Cultures, Ethnocide, Genocide

> 'Thus it was', says Geronimo, 'in the beginning: the Apaches and their homes each created for the other by Usen himself. When they are taken from these homes they sicken and die. How long will it be until it is said, there are no Apaches?'[1]

Geronimo's words suggest a vision of the question of ethnocide and genocide widespread today: the former is certain, and the latter probable, because of the simple clash between cultures, without any ill will, so to speak, on the part of those who exercise domination. The theoreticist passion – a bad passion that wreaks Byzantine havoc in European social thought – has built upon this idea and, at the same time, has given it foundations, with the work of ethnologists and anthropologists. The best-known theoretical construct in this connection is perhaps Lévi-Strauss's thesis of 'cold' societies and 'hot' societies. This thesis guides an analysis abounding in fruitful suggestions and also probably in truths. Yet we must avoid construing it and using it in such way as to make us lose sight of other facts that are sometimes more important. Hot societies would be those erected on change, as it were: the societies with history, as are those of the Near and Middle East (with their Mediterranean extension) from the time of the Neolith. Cold societies would be those that do not undergo social change but live on the assumption of immutability. If a cold society clashes with a hot one, the ruin of the former is certain. And it is likely that cultural death (ethnocide) will be followed by physical death (genocide).

People tend to respond to this with evidence of rapid and beneficial adaptations of populations whose cultures have clashed with European culture, more specifically, with capitalist cultures in various stages of development. Ignoring opinions which strike me as intolerable and even infuriating – such as that which includes among those beneficial adaptations the depressing ethnocide

---

* Notes first published in 1975 as part of Sacristán's editorial commentary to his translation of *Geronimo: His Own Story* (Geronimo 1970). Republished as 'Tres notas sobre choque de culturas y genocidio', *mientras tanto*, 63: 77–87.

1 Geronimo 1970, p. 68.

 | DOI 10.1163/9789004280526_015

of the Hawaiians, prostituted in the tourism industry – it must be acknowledged that the North American Indians, and among them the Apaches, had already assimilated, however 'cold' their societies were, basic changes before the arrival of the Europeans (the introduction of agriculture as a secondary occupation, and even a primary one, among the Pueblos, Comanches, Kiowas, etc.). Furthermore, they rapidly assimilated productive forces or instruments of production taken from the culture of the invader with whom they clashed: who can imagine a Sioux without a horse, or Geronimo and Naiche without the small horses in the famous photograph by C.S. Fly (the Apaches even rode with stirrups)? The Utes and the Shoshones, the first North American Indians familiar with horses, did not receive the horse until 1680, a century and a half before Geronimo's birth, who seems to have come into the world with an Apache pony between his knees, although he had lost none of the qualities of the powerful walker characteristic of the Apaches. The fact is, however, that the Chiricahuas did not receive the horse until the beginning of the nineteenth century or, at the earliest, the end of the eighteenth, that is to say, during the later years of Geronimo's grandfather. In the culture inhabited by Geronimo – who as a boy hunted rabbits on horseback with a club, and as a warrior galloped with his body hidden behind the small horse's mane – this animal, labour power or *instrumentum semivocale*, was undeniably 'inborn' in the Apache; it was an enrichment of the Apache world from their clash with Euroamerican White culture. The same can be said for firearms, which are also, unmistakably, instruments of production for a hunting people. And the same can even be said for more complicated things, like medicine. When Cochise saw his father-in-law and chief, Red Sleeves, almost mortally wounded, he speedily took him to a good Mexican surgeon, instead of arranging for the laboured rites of the shamans in the camp. Yet it was not the case that Cochise had abandoned the shamanistic vision of medicine. The fact that he threatened the surgeon and the rest of the inhabitants of the town of Janos with the destruction of the area if Red Sleeves died proves that Cochise continued to think in accordance with those notions from his tradition. It seems reasonable to think that Cochise had perceived as a fact (perhaps without having yet integrated it into his mental universe) the greater efficacy of the White Man's surgery. Still, the mere fact of assimilating something need not necessarily be ethnocidal, for if it were, any innovation perceived as a work of nature would be so as well.

It is advisable, then, not to take the contrast between cold cultures and hot cultures (ahistorical cultures and historical cultures) too literally, or to presuppose that the unquestionable seriousness of the clashes between cultures inevitably entails ethnocide: there are probably no completely ahistorical cultures, nor is it likely that every change foreign to a culture is lethal for it (or for its individual members) in the sense of implying the loss of the consciousness of continuity.

For the European who does not want to be blinded by progressivism, it is even more advisable to free oneself from a temptation that is likewise a falsification: that of disregarding the topic of the clash of cultures, seeing in it nothing more than a decadentist, romantic, testimonial fashion. Numerous Indians, behind whose words no European class interest can be found, have expressed their feeling of death due to the clash of culture's consequences. The great Indian chiefs – Sitting Bull of the Sioux, Ten Bears of the Comanches, Satanta of the Poncas, Joseph of the Nez Perce – and Geronimo himself, despite the fact that he was not much given to meditation, have all expressed that feeling with words so beautiful that they bear within themselves the proof of their truthfulness. I hope that it will not be said that they practiced the testimonial neo-romanticism of the intellectuals of imperialist decadence, or that such neo-romanticism will be attributed to Philip II's admirable official, Governor Juan López de Velasco. In his *Geografía y descripción universal de las Indias* [*Geography and Universal Description of the Indies*], which starts in 1574, this Juan López, whom Anglo-Saxon historians call 'Velasco', perceives American questions quite a bit better than the US Administrations prior to Franklin D. Roosevelt. Among other things, he sees that although the conquest had reduced the Indian population of Mexico since 1500, owing to the excessive burdens borne by this population and some of their own customs (an allusion to cannibalism), there was nonetheless no need to fear for its extinction, since in 1574 its numbers were increasing. With respect to the present discussion, López de Velasco's *Geografía* is of interest from two points of view. On the one hand, it reveals directly and naively the seriousness of the cultural assault (rather than a 'clash of cultures'). Example:

> [A]nd all of the friars and religious who wanted to go to the Indies have been given everything necessary to reach them, at the expense of the Royal Treasury, and one has always undertaken, in order to be able to better teach the Indians, to confine them in towns and teach them the Castilian language in the schools, including children's schools and doctrinal seminaries that have been made and are being made every day on the King's orders to teach therein the children of the principal Indians, so that they will teach the others and because of this example the rest will be willing to come to the doctrine and good breeding.[2]

2 López de Velasco 1971. [Sacristán does not provide a page number for this reference, which I have translated from the Spanish (Ed.)].

On the other hand, however, Juan López knows – and indicates that many others already knew, in the sixteenth century – of the bad effects of transculturation, at least within the framework of, and as regards the questions allowed by, his own ideological limitation, his 'bronze bell'; the fact that, as with other laws in the Indies, the relevant regulations were often a worthless piece of paper does not undermine my claim. López de Velasco writes, on page 18, column a, of Jiménez de la Espada's edition of his text in volume 248 of the BAE:[3]

> From the start, removing the Indians from their lands to take them to Spain was particularly and generally prohibited, as it was to take them from warm lands and parts to cold ones and vice versa, for it has always been accepted that they receive from that a great deal of injury and harm to their health ...[4]

Barrett says the same thing in his note to Geronimo's texts discussed here.

As for the Apaches, Turner stresses the seriousness for them of that elementary physical element of transculturation, the change of lands; in this regard he mentions the Chiricahua rite, practiced almost immediately after the birth of a child, that consisted in placing the newborn in a tree or bush in the very place in which he or she had been born, in order to tie him to that precise bit of land. On the other hand, however, we must not forget that the Apaches had not been in Arizona any earlier than approximately 1300, and had not stayed there uninterruptedly. How, then, if their bond with the land was for them a question of life or death, without qualification, did they endure and even forget altogether the abandonment of the earlier stations of their extraordinarily long migration, without preserving so much as a trace of them in their sagas, as did, by contrast, the Aztecs?

Consummated or Frustrated Genocide?

As a conclusion to the note on the so-called clash of cultures, I stated my conviction that none of those encounters with serious ethnocidal consequences had been innocent, pure fate. I believe that the Latin conquistadores and colonisers of America – Castilians, Portuguese, Frenchmen – exterminated fewer people overall than the Anglos – not, of course, because of greater kindness,

3 Biblioteca de Autores Españoles [Library of Spanish Authors] [Ed.].

4 López de Velasco 1971. [Sacristán does not provide a page number for this reference, which I have translated from the Spanish (Ed.)].

but because of the type of socio-economic system that they brought, which had shaped, with its economic customs, their mindset as farmers, stockbreeders or, in general, actors in the primary sector, with many semi-feudal elements (Castilians, Portuguese) and pure merchants (some parts of all three groups, but above all the French in the north). If the Anglos were later able to displace them, and especially the French, with such ease, it was because they embodied a somewhat more developed capitalist system of production, which allowed for much denser colonial populations.

But the presence of an exterminating element can be found in both colonising cultures. Those who can most be spared this judgement – although none can be absolved altogether – are the French merchants, who sometimes even did things in good taste, as in admiring and idealising the most noble Indian tribes, who did not succumb, moreover, until the arrival of the Anglos' more destructive capitalism. The Nez Perce exemplify this case in a moving way.

As for our forefathers: they exterminated the gentle Caribbean Indians – no matter how much rhetoric the Pink Legend's defenders lavish upon this subject – and reduced the California Indians, and so many others, to a degradation comparable to the Americans' prostitution of the Hawaiians. Later, their archaistic (from the European point of view) mode of production permitted the exercise of less homicidal psychic impulses, and their colonisation proved compatible with the Indians' biological recovery. Regarding this phase, whose beginning could be dated symbolically in New Spain, with the reaction to the killing of Cuauhtemoc and the consolidation of the viceroyalty, it is interesting to consider the destructive effects not only of the intentional extermination, which are, of course, undeniable, but also those stemming from the clash of cultures. The urbanising concentration of populations practiced by the Spanish began, as is well known, with a host of juridical requirements, and continued in that vein until the seventeenth century. At the end of the sixteenth century (1599), Juan de Torquemada had even promised the Indians, in the name of the Crown, the preservation or restitution of their territories, although he stated conditions that turned his attempt into the true invention of the later US system of reservations, in terms of this system's few good aspects and many bad ones. At any rate, the Indians north of Mexico affected by this policy – among them, perhaps, the southern Apaches – took to the hills *en masse*, increasing the 'Chichimeca' (the nomadic and aggressive population).

We must also include as part of the culturally caused genocidal process the many Indian – among them Apache – deaths resulting from exile. I have not read anywhere of Apache survivors from among those who were taken to Yucatán. It is true that theirs was not a mass transfer and that the individuals who were thus transferred were able to blend in among the country's Mayas.

However, judging by what the Apaches had to endure in Florida, even that merging, if it did occur, could not have been very pleasant. As soon as they reached Florida's hot humidity, so different from the dryness of the Colorado plateau, about one hundred Apaches died. The doctors' diagnosis was tuberculosis. The United States government, under pressure from the Apaches' memorable friends, took pity on the children of the dead and had them enter the school for Indians in Carlisle, Pennsylvania, which was primarily for the Eastern and prairie Indians, although there was also a certain Comanche presence, which at least reminded the Apache children of something of their own: the old tribal wars. Yet not long after their arrival, fifty Apache children would be dead.

These culturally induced tragedies occurred against a consciously and willingly prepared genocidal background. It is not merely a question of massive killings that were more or less exceptions, such as the one perpetrated by the Tucson Ring White mafia against the Aravaipa Apaches, whose chief was Eskiminzin. These Apaches, long convinced – unlike the Chiricahuas – of the inevitability of having to submit to the Whites' power and way of life, and prepared to do so by the cultural legacy of the Pueblos, suffered in a matter of minutes 108 deaths, mainly of sleeping women and children, during a night-time assault on their Camp Grant reservation, then under the protection of the United States government (April 1871). However, it is not a question here of macabre anecdotes. Or perhaps it is also a question of these anecdotes, but only as extreme signs of a general policy of extermination, which is easy to hide under the heading of a 'clash of cultures'.

Of course, that policy referred to all of the Indians in the United States, not only the Apaches, and this is really the main difference between the fate they suffered and that which befell the Mesoamerican and South American Indians. It is also true that the subsequent development of big capitalism, which in its early stages required their almost total extermination, placed the few survivors, as compensation, in better conditions of struggle than those faced by those Indians – who were many – further to the south, whom the old epifeudal and mercantile culture could hardly aim at exterminating. A few examples will help to clarify this issue.

General William T. Sherman, whose memory the US army considers so glorious that it named a famous tank after him, was one of the first 'civilised' persons to understand the Indians' cultural requirements, and in 1862 (the year of an important uprising among the Sioux) Sherman wrote to his brother, a senator:

> We must act with vindictive earnestness against the Sioux, even to their extermination, men, women and children. Nothing else will reach the

> root of this case ... The more we can kill this year, the less will have to be killed the next war, for the more I see of these Indians the more convinced I am that all have to be killed or *maintained as a species of pauper*.[5]

The last sentence, which I have italicised, almost explicitly tells us why neither the French, nor the Portuguese, nor the Spanish could have formulated such a premeditated genocide: one needs the imagination of a subject from the Bronze Age or the Age of Capital to reach that understanding. Turner, to whom I owe this quotation, also includes another, from the Southern governor of Arizona, John R. Baylor. It has to do with instructions for the Commander of the Arizona Guards and is likewise from the year 1862:

> I learn from Lieutenant J.J. Jackson that Indians have been in your post for the purpose of making a treaty. The Congress of the Confederate States has passed a law declaring extermination to all hostile Indians. You will therefore use all means to persuade the Apaches or any tribe to come in for the purpose of making peace, and when you get them together kill all the grown Indians and take the children prisoners and sell them to defray the expense of killing the Indians. Buy whisky and such other goods as may be necessary for the Indians and I will order vouchers given to cover the amount expended. Leave nothing undone to insure success, and have a sufficient number of men around to allow no Indian to escape.[6]

On the other hand, among the tactics of the generals, as much in Sherman's case as in Sheridan's, was the conscientious extermination of the bison. This is evident in the military command's sour response to a group of Whites who regretted the ecological catastrophe.

So as not to ignore something that affected Geronimo himself, I should note that the extermination was aimed at him in a very personal way: President Cleveland had ordered that Geronimo be hanged as soon as he was captured. This was prevented by a group of White friends of the Apaches. However, the decisive fact for judging the importance of a resolutely genocidal intention, and avoiding its concealment beneath the complicated problem of the clash of cultures, is the US law from 3 March 1871, which declared that it was unnecessary to negotiate with the Indians in order to occupy their territory. That law was the end of the decency of the civilised states, the end of a fiction, which from Hernán Cortés until the American Civil War had allowed the Whites to

5 Cited in Turner 1970, p. 12, emphasis added.

6 Cited in Turner 1970, p. 29.

regard themselves as the juridical successors of the Amerindian sovereignties. The complement to that measure took some time to arrive: the Allotment Act of 1887. This law parcelled up the reservations according to the logic of capitalist economics, eliminating or seriously injuring the Indians' collectivism and granting them the famous equality of individual opportunity. That is, it proletarianised them all and allowed the White agrarian landowners and businesspeople to buy the territory that was called 'surplus', the reservation lands left over after an individual plot of land had been assigned to each Indian. This law was based almost exclusively on the assumption of a coming total genocide, the death of every Indian. Genocide, not ethnocide. It is true that as the great Indian wars had occurred between 1850 and 1870 (Victorio's and Geronimo's campaigns from the 1880s are actually heroic holdouts), the Indian population had fallen to a minimum in the period in which the civilised people promulgated their genocidal laws of 1871 and 1887.

However, half a century later, between 1920 and 1925, liberal US geographers and sociologists began to probe [*agitar*] this subject, showing that the Indians were not becoming extinct, but were in fact increasing in number. (The same phenomenon had occurred in the area of the Hispanic conquest after the end of the great wars, as Juan López de Velasco, Philip II's sensitive official, pointed out, with fewer calculating machines, in 1574.) In 1934, President Franklin D. Roosevelt established the Indian Reorganization Act, which annulled the Allotment Act of 1887, froze the parcelling up of the reservations, set up Indian self-government (tribal councils) on them, granted credits, and so on.

Roosevelt's law had good results, above all when it first went into effect, but it did not prevent the conferral of power, supported by Whites at the state and federal levels, on Indian chiefs who had been debased by the prevailing socioeconomic system. The conduct of the official Sioux councils at the time of the Wounded Knee incident a couple of years ago offers a good example of what those organs of self-government are in reality.

When we wish to take stock of the attempted genocide endured by the North American Indians, we can say that that attempt, including in the case of the Apaches, was thwarted. Yet at the same time we must remember those against whom the attempt was not thwarted.

Those who succeeded in surviving are not disappearing. They are not (as of the 1970s) even half of those who presumably existed at the time of the Europeans' arrival, but they are reproducing faster than the rest of the US population, including Blacks, the 'Buffalo-soldiers', as the Indians used to say.

Finally, the Indians of interest to us here are those who, within the United States, best preserve their languages, cultures, and even religions, under Christian names that barely disguise the old rites. And their example indicates that it is perhaps not always true that, as Geronimo said as an old man, we must not fight battles that we know are lost. It is doubtful that there would be an Apache consciousness today if Victorio's and Geronimo's bands had not braved the ordeal of a decade of admirable defeats a century ago.

A few figures about the Apaches: in 1970, there were a few, isolated, individual Lipan and Kiowa Apaches, 1,000 Jicarilla Apaches, 8,000 Western Apaches and 1,100 Chiricahua and Mescalero Apaches.

Returning to Arizona

We cannot rule out the possibility that the lofty pathos of Geronimo's final phrase is but a skilful rhetorical choice on Barrett's part. Yet the sober and energetic feeling strikes me as more characteristic of the two Chiricahuas, of Goyaalé and his interpreter, Asa.

That protest reveals a tenacity quite typical of Geronimo's mettle. Other prominent Indians bowed down in the face of what appeared to be irremediable: the Ponca Indian chief Standing Bear, prisoner in a Fort Omaha jail, said to General Crook, in the period in which the latter was beginning to open his eyes: 'I thought God intended us to live, but I was mistaken. God intends to give the country to the White people, and we are to die. It may be well; it may be well'.[7] Or else they succumbed to flights of mysticism, sedating themselves [*opiándose*] with visions of a hereafter transcendent to all else. Black Elk, one of the last Sioux visionaries, is one example of this understandable evasion:

> I looked about me and could see that what we then were doing was like a shadow cast upon the earth from yonder vision in the heavens, so bright it was and clear. I knew the real was yonder and the darkened dream of it was here.[8]

And narrating another mystical celebration that he oversaw:

> Because of my vision and the power they knew I had, I was asked to lead the dance next morning. We all stood in a straight line, facing the west, and I prayed:

7 Sacristán does not provide a reference for this quotation, but the passage can be found in Brown 1970, p. 359 [Ed.].

8 Black Elk and Neihardt 1972, pp. 129–30.

> 'Father, Great Spirit, behold me! The nation that I have is in despair. The new earth you promised you have shown me. Let my nation also behold it.
>
> After the prayer we stood with our right hands raised to the west, and we all began to weep, and right there, as they wept, some of them fainted before the dance began.
>
> As we were dancing I had the same queer feeling I had before, as though my feet were off the earth and swinging.[9]

The contrast between the two forms of self-defence and Geronimo's sober resolution is remarkable. The Chiricahua has neither visions nor fainting spells (although he listens to the visions of others with a polite scepticism), and he knows from his ancestors that Chiricahua good feeling is expressed in action. In both his narrative and his actions in Florida and Oklahoma, Geronimo tenaciously seeks an objective that he thinks attainable: the return of the Apaches to Arizona. Even if he himself may not return. He even appears to insinuate that this is a price that he is willing to pay. But he knew that this people had to return; he will die, he tells us, in the manner of a satisfied old man.

Now that the great warrior can no longer hear us, I will confess to the reader my impression that perhaps it was not worth it. Today, Arizona is, indeed, the most Indian state in the United States. It is home to 90,000 Indians belonging to 14 tribes – including the Apaches – spread over 19 reservations. Heading the list are the tough Navajos, 80,000 people, some 50,000 of which live on the reservations. Lower down are the Apaches and the Hopi Pueblos. There are also Papagos and Pimas. The civilised peoples who manipulated the poor Papagos, making them fearsome yet sad auxiliaries in the hunt for the Apaches, have paid them very poorly: sociologists tell us that the Arizona Papago (half of all Papago) make up the poorest community in North America, with a family income that does not amount to more than 6% of the family income received by Anglos. There are few Blacks in Arizona: 3 percent of the state's total population, which is 1,770,900. Finally, there are 450,000 inhabitants, a little more than one quarter of the total, whose last names are 'Castilian', who spontaneously refer to themselves as Mexican, and among whom the movement led by [César] Chávez will probably have a bright future.

Arizona has been a state since 1912. Shortly after the proclamation of statehood, Indians and mestizos, as well as quite a few Whites, were on the verge of doing something of interest to the entire world: Arizona's copper miners organised as part of one of the very few revolutionary unions to have emerged

---

9 Black Elk and Neihardt 1972, pp. 187–8.

from the American proletariat, the Industrial Workers of the World, which so impressed Lenin and Gramsci. However, in 1917 those 'agitators' were deported by the most dynamic sector of world capitalism, as they say, and without any regard, on this occasion, for ethnic considerations. Apart from that, the capitalism of the civilised peoples, Midas in reverse, has found a way of turning even the arid purity of the Colorado plateau into excrement: in Arizona's subsoil there is copper, petroleum, methane, and, if that were not enough, uranium. And these have not been the only misfortunes spoiling the return to Arizona. There have also been the typical acts of pettiness, absolutely negligible from the standpoint of the dynamic sector, which says that only the emotional, testimonial revolutionary finds them regrettable. For example, the prehistoric dwellings of a reddish earth that were found in north-east Arizona and made up the Chelly National Monument, formally property belonging to the Indians, were destroyed when some planes from the US air force broke the sound barrier while flying over them. Of course, it is true that the Federal Government compensated the Indians with 1.5 million dollars between 1956 and 1958 for the first damages of this sort.

CHAPTER 13

On the Subject of 'Eurocommunism'

I

The rather abrupt manner in which someone posed the question yesterday – 'Is Eurocommunism a strategy for socialism and are there others?' – gave rise to a discussion in the all-or-nothing style, confronted with which we must at least address a more analytical consideration, a study of 'dimensions', as Ernest Mandel has attempted to do in his recent articles on the subject.

The Reality and Realism of 'Eurocommunism'

'Eurocommunism' is eliciting a fair amount of communist debate. Some have gone so far as to say that it is the most important political event since World War Two, or since the Chinese Revolution, or since the end of the Cold War. The bourgeois press – inventor of the term 'Eurocommunism', which the Communist Parties involved rejected until the expeditious style and populist talent of Santiago Carrillo consecrated it – has given the topic publicity, but that is not the agent primarily responsible for its prevalence. 'Eurocommunism' is the great topic of reflection in the communist movement today because it embodies the main social reality of this movement outside the Soviet and Chinese spheres. (The Russians are guilty of a certain recklessness in contrasting the 'real' character of their 'socialism' with the movement inspired by the Italian, French or Spanish Communist Parties, for one can reply to them there is more social reality in 30 percent of an electorate [including no less than 50 percent of the proletariat], as in Italy, than in the Czech political police and the armour-plated occupation forces.) Outside the bloc under Russian hegemony and the Far East, the three main 'Eurocommunist' parties, if not the Japanese party as well, make up the greatest socio-political phenomenon to come out of the movement that arose as a reaction against Social Democracy's abandonment of proletarian internationalism – the 1914 nationalist vote for war credits.

---

* First published in 1977. Republished as 'A propósito del 'eurocomunismo', in *Intervenciones políticas. Panfletos y materiales III*, edited by Juan-Ramón Capella (Barcelona: Icaria Editorial, S.A., 1985).

 | DOI 10.1163/9789004280526_016

Three Correct Ideas in 'Eurocommunism'

The first of these ideas is a good perception of social facts and, above all, of the non-realisation of the revolutionary prospects that inspired the constitution of the Communist International in 1919. That perception, if it is not accompanied by a reaffirmation of the revolutionary goal, may be the starting point for a regression toward social democracy. Even in this case, however, the 'Eurocommunists' can maintain truthfulness and consistency. The 'Eurocommunist' leaders are generally not guilty of opportunism, but openly state the consequences of their analysis. The good perception of reality and the truthful expression of what one sees (independently of the fact that one infers a social-democratic perspective from what is seen) reinforce, in turn, the 'Eurocommunist' parties' insertion in social reality, above all that of the proletariat. For the workers are much more intelligent and critical, and are much better informed, than many radical groups, with their paternalist prophesying, seem to think. The workers compare the reality that they see and in which they live with the intensely idealised versions of this reality presented by some groups and with the plausible versions of it offered by social democrats from the 'Eurocommunist' or socialist parties. They add things up and see the result.

The second correct idea involves the practice of an effective self-criticism of one's own tradition. That allows 'Eurocommunism' to set in motion an authentic reflection, of interest not only to the sect's faithful, but also to many workers.

The third correct idea is the unprejudiced analysis of new developments in the social structure. Thanks perhaps to this liberation from the dogmatism (whether sincere or hypocritical) of the politicians in the East, that fresh analysis in turn permits a new search for alliances based on the structure of social classes and the different social strata as they exist in society today, and not in poor manuals.

II

'Eurocommunism' as a Retreat

However, above that analytical dimension (in which 'Eurocommunism', in apparent contradiction to its limited taste for theory, stands out in comparison with the rest of the communist movement), there is no totalising socialist dimension. The 'Eurocommunist' analysis is not part of a revolutionary dialectic. Or to put it in the words of one of yesterday's interventions, 'Eurocommunism' is not a strategy for socialism. It is precisely when presented as a socialist strategy that it loses even its analytical quality and becomes a deceptive ideology. As a socialist strategy, 'Eurocommunism' offers the insipid utopia of a ruling class willing to abdicate graciously and a rising class capable of changing the relations of production (*starting* with the property relations) without exercising coercion. To believe in such a utopia (if there is anyone who does believe in it) it is necessary to have lost the idea of what a consciously desired change in the mode of production means, as well as the idea of what it means to be a class in danger of expropriation by the class that it currently dominates and exploits.

To the extent that it can be taken seriously, 'Eurocommunism' is not a strategy for socialism. On the contrary, it is simply the real communist movement's latest retreat since its defeat in the years 1917–21. It is true that a retreat can be organised as preparation for an offensive, or in order to make it possible to one day prepare an offensive. Yet the first condition for this consists in knowing that it is a matter of a retreat. The worst thing about 'Eurocommunism' is its euphoric presentation as a 'road to socialism', for that presentation implies a will to disregard the state of retreat and, with that disregard, the abandonment of any serious, non-bourgeois reformist notion of socialism.

The Movement is Becoming Everything

In general, the position of the Communist parties in the capitalist countries in which they have a certain importance is Bernsteinian, to say it with a traditional concept: those parties limit or reduce themselves to promoting and inspiring the working-class movement in its daily life, including the struggle within the movement for the threads of political power as it exists in the bourgeois state; and they do not even pose the question of the movement's aims. This 'movementism' is typical of the 'Eurocommunist' parties, with varying degrees of emphasis; and it is also typical of the lesser communist parties, with more or less of a delay in the positions adopted. In this connection we may recall, as illustrative examples, that about eight years ago the minority parties of the extreme Left (and their flimsy circle of spellbound intellectuals) censured the PSUC's defence of the Catalan language ('the language of the bourgeoisie', as they said in Spanish, with a strong Catalan accent), before becoming prominent *Catalanistas*; and only four years ago they fought, using serious accusations, against the amnesty slogan then advocated almost exclusively (among the communists) by the PCE-PSUC. Here in Barcelona there is another spectacular example of the same thing, which is the Asamblea de Cataluña [Assembly of Catalonia]. When it was created, with the absolutely decisive effort and initiative of the PSUC, the minority communist parties thought it a reprehensible surrender of the working class's interests to the bourgeoisie. Shortly afterwards they had jumped on the bandwagon, and when it reached a dead end, they were caught by surprise, as they were busy trying to hitch up some sleeping cars so as to be able to travel alongside it for a long time.

The reduction of the communist parties to the movement within the existing social framework has a solid foundation in the fact that events have not confirmed the expectations of 1917–19 or the two main *ad hoc* explanations later invented to patch up the torn theory. Those two explanations are: that of the stages of the world revolution, starting with the consolidation of socialism in one country alone (the expectation that inspired the Stalinist tradition); and the idea that the decisive obstacle in opposition to the revolution was a subjective deficiency consisting in a lack of revolutionary leadership (an explication still maintained today in various Trotskyist milieus). The purely 'movementist', Bernsteinian politics of all the somewhat important Communist parties is always based on the failure of that expectation, whether it is openly acknowledged (as in the reformist consistency of the 'Eurocommunist' parties), or is concealed (as is the case in more opportunist groups), or lastly is ignored (as in the case of other small, ideologically more confused communist parties, which are at least still free of the bourgeois reformism of the first group and the opportunist insincerity of the second one).

III

The Needs and Features of a Communist Regeneration

The revisionism that Bernstein formulated in another juncture of European society (not without parallels to our own era) exhibits many things in common with the practice of the contemporary European Communist parties. To begin with, some quite similar class roots: the progressive shift of hegemony within the party to dominant petty-bourgeois groups of professionals (but not pure intellectuals or theorists, as in the extremist parties), with a decline in the workers' strength within the political leadership (despite being a majority within the organisation, in contrast to what happens in most of the minority communist parties), is as obvious in the 'Eurocommunist' parties as it was in turn-of-the-century Social Democracy. They also have in common a good, sensible perception of reality. Furthermore, and very much in keeping with the leadership's class roots, they share a positivist conception of reality as fundamentally unchangeable. Finally, they have in common an unbridled politicism in which the positivist judgement concerning an unchangeable reality is wedded to the vain boastfulness of the petty bourgeois, especially the intellectual devoid of passion for ideas.

The general orientation of a Marxist communism today must consist in the reaffirmation of the revolutionary aim (without which it would not be a communist orientation) and the attempt to know our situation with a scientific honesty (without which it would not be a Marxist orientation). The first thing needed to articulate that orientation – there is nothing wrong with repeating something when it is a matter of such importance – is a self-critical awareness of the failure of, or errors in, the predictions made in 1917–19 and even of the errors in the literal meaning [*literalidad*] of the Marxian perspective. It is necessary to know and acknowledge, with the freedom from vanity and dogmatisms required for thinking scientifically, that the 'material conditions', which in the Marxist schema were laid down, from the nineteenth century onward, as the presuppositions of the proletarian revolution, were satisfied long ago, and that in this regard we need not wait for anything, no 'stage' through which we would still have to pass for objective or material reasons. The 'material conditions' presupposed by the Marxist tradition have been attained with an abundance that Marx could never have imagined; the public limited company or 'capital by stock' which, according to Marx, 'mutates into communism', even seems antiquated, and yet, all the same, there has not been a social revolution. As a result of this, there no longer remains even a shadow of support for a mechanistic Marxism, which can certainly only be imputed to Marx in the moments in which he was entranced by some discovery or in which he too was nodding off, but which is, with no less certainty, an element of great importance in the movement's tradition and in the ideologism of various groups. Overcoming this mechanistic model, so out of place when there no longer remains any mechanism whose effects we need to await, is a necessary condition for scientifically reconstructing the revolutionary perspective, for truthfully distinguishing between knowledge and desire, between what there is and what the movement wants there to be.

Given the current development of the productive forces and the present structure of the relations of production, the idea that the movement is necessarily carried along by a current that falters at certain specific levels, like a river with a floodgate, is a scientific myth that must be replaced by the vision of a movement situated on a terrain about which it knows some things but is ignorant of a great deal; a movement that is rationally prepared for obstacles, making the maximum use of what it knows and never confusing this, naturalistically, with what it wants; and which thus knows *that there is only a point to the movement because it seeks a revolutionary goal, communism*. From the point of view of meaning, of the reason for being, the movement is nothing, the goal is everything. Antonio Gramsci (who is used so naively today) expressed something similar, saying that there is little use in setting up in our imagination detailed speculative constructs, like the utopian revolutionaries, and less still in becoming locked into the daily struggle for inescapable and important, yet insufficient, goals, in the style of the reformists. Rather, it is a matter of working for the realisation of an 'ethico-juridical principle', the principle of a liberated society. The positivist submission to our present society, at best leavened with the theory of stages and the gradualisms of a fanciful road of reforms, is as unscientific as the utopians' instructions for the method of frying eggs in the liberated society.

Practice and Ideology

Having reached this point, one might wonder if these reflections are not, as we say, a waste of energy. Since one acknowledges that the 'Eurocommunist' analysis of the state of the societies in question is quite accurate, and in particular it acknowledges that, in the context of the economic crisis, the correlation of political-military forces suggests a new appeal from the bourgeoisie to fascism (to bring about the 'social pact' once and for all and by force) more than any revolutionary possibility, we should not worry (it might be said) about the reformism, which at least achieves a real intervention in political life. Nor should we worry about the ideological blindness of other, minority communist parties, which at least maintain, albeit as sleepwalkers, the small flame of the ideal alongside the actual movement. That proposition could even be embellished, as a kind of consolation, with Marx's famous dictum, this time applied to ourselves: 'They don't know it, but they are doing it'.

That attitude cannot be adopted, however, because a reformist politics tends to produce a loss of revolutionary will in militants, and because ideological illusions tend, in the end, to produce scepticism or desperation among them. The result of the simultaneous, separate presence of reformism and ideologism will not be an integration of communist desire and knowledge into the actual labour movement, but a marked divergence of the one from the other, the definitive social-democratisation of some 'Eurocommunist' parties on the rise (at least electorally), the dogmatic entrenchment of some minor groups (probably already in relative decline), and, above all, the disillusioned neutralisation of a popular sector that will be ready to succumb to fascist demagogues, who may perhaps once again appear in anarchist guise, just as the Falange covered itself with the confederal black-and-red in the 1930s.

The tendency to take refuge in ideological fictions is quite intense, for ideology is security in the face of the uneasiness produced by the movement's current situation. The 'Eurocommunists' relieve this natural anxiety by ignoring the crisis and having high hopes for a smooth transition to the new society; the communists from the minority parties achieve the same thing by imagining, with an edifying consistency since 1919, that the revolution is about to break out. But they are enduring a great deal, even if they do not show it. The fact that yesterday there were some rather anxious and tense reactions could not have been due, as someone said, to the fact that a few of us reviewed things critically; that would be to grant some chance words more efficacy than they could possibly have. The worry became apparent because it was latent. Apart from that, a communist is not called upon to put our minds at ease, to lie to a blind and faithful people, in the manner of Dostoyevsky's Grand Inquisitor, at the expense of killing the resurrected Christ himself.

IV

Elements of a Contemporary Communist Politics

On the other hand, the rejection of 'Eurocommunism' as the ideology of a supposed road to socialism does not condemn one to passivity. The criticism of 'Eurocommunism' implicitly contains a politics. It is not, of course, a 'road', a 'strategy', nor does it pretend to be one, for the simple reason that it does not believe in strategies as commonly understood; it does not believe that there is any scientific value to the traditional, built-up predictions of what is going to happen and how it is going to happen. Those strategies are, to a great extent, ad hoc creations [*construcciones*], justifications for current practice. A rational communist politics need not produce those kinds of ideas [*construcciones*], less so today than ever, amid the movement's theoretical crisis and practical perplexity. What it needs to do is clearly and visibly situate the revolutionary principle behind its practice, situate its 'ideal', to say it with the most 'pretentious' ['*cursi*'], ethical, and pre-Marxist of all the words relevant here. What is scientific is knowing that an ideal is a goal, not a presupposed result falsely deduced from a pseudo-scientific chain of strategic predictions. What is scientific is to assure oneself of the *possibility* of an ideal, not the irrational determination to demonstrate its future existence. And what is revolutionary is to act at every moment, even in situations involving a mere defence of the most elementary things, of bread itself (as in the present economic crisis), with an *awareness of the goal* and of its radical otherness with respect to this society, rather than swaying back and forth in the illusion of a gradual transition that can only lead to the acceptance of this society.

Two Main Criteria

That political position has two criteria: one must not deceive oneself, and one must not sacrifice one's identity [*no desnaturalizarse*]. One must not deceive oneself with the reformist milkmaid's calculations, or with the leftist faith in the historical lottery. One must not sacrifice one's identity: neither dilute programmes nor deduce them from putative gradualist roads to socialism, but rather stick to platforms bound up with the daily struggle of social classes and in accordance with the correlation of forces at every moment, but on the basis of a programme that it is not worth calling 'maximum' because it is the only one: communism.

I have already said a bit about not deceiving oneself, within the confines of what can be said in an intervention such as this. As for not sacrificing one's identity, it is necessary to mention briefly two of the various consequences. The first is that the stated practice excludes all pacts with the bourgeoisie in the strict sense. This need not entail any cruelty: one can truly value the management skills of any capitalist who happens to have them, as well as his other outstanding qualities, without for this reason ceasing to aim at his expropriation. The second is that adherence to a platform of struggle governed by the communist 'ethico-juridical' principle must include the development of innovative activities in everyday life, from the indispensable reorganisation of the culture-nature relationship to experimentation with relationships and communities for living together. This indicates that there are other spheres of organisation for the revolutionary historical bloc, which are inaccessible to reformists and dogmatists with, as it were, 'purity of heart'.

The Need for Exploration

In general, the communist political position noted here needs, above all, to explore certain fields. Here is a brief list of the main ones: the accentuation of the destructiveness of the productive forces under capitalism, underscored by Marx in *The Communist Manifesto*, in the *Grundrisse*, in *Capital*, etc., but barely heeded in the history of the movement; the crisis of culture and civilisation in the advanced capitalist countries, which involves a vulnerability revealed yesterday in New York's second great blackout, and in power's natural tendency toward a despotic regression in order to confront that vulnerability of social life; the persistent problems of imperialism and the Third World; and, to conclude on one point, the spectacular degeneration of parliamentarism in the most advanced capitalist countries, likewise an omen (we can only hope that it is a false omen) of a new regression of those societies toward forms of tyranny.

CHAPTER 14

On Stalinism

It is clearly not possible, in the time that each of us is devoting to this theme, to attempt a very complete characterisation of a historical subject as complicated as Stalinism, for although Stalinism is often spoken of as if it were a topic that is easy to delimit, easy to define, for which one could provide precise or at least reasonably accurate dates, it seems, at least to me, that anyone who is truly interested in the topic knows, if he or she has dealt with it at all, that things are not like that, that a delimitation of the concept of Stalinism – what it is or was – is not easy, and that it is not easy to give dates either.

This was already brought out on the first day of this series. One of the people who was present intervened to remind us, for example, of despotic deeds, let us say 'Stalinist' deeds, or of those that are usually described as Stalinist, under Lenin's rule. And others could also be recalled – a member of the panel even reminded us of some others: the problems with Makhno's movement were brought up, if I am not mistaken, by Solé Barberà, and some people out there brought up, I believe, events such as Kronstadt, and to a certain extent the Tenth Congress of the Bolshevik party, that is, the prohibition of the organisation of factions and tendencies.

It is worth remarking that all of this – the three examples that emerged the other day, which I am repeating now – occurred in a fairly short span of months: all of those things took place from 1920 to the spring of 1921. But apart from that, it is not at all difficult to search further. Anyone who wants to look even further back than these first years of the Soviet government will come across, in the earlier generation of the Marxist classics, Engels's celebrated phrase, according to which there is nothing more authoritarian than a revolution. This is not only his phrase, but also something that is historically well documented in all of the revolutions that we know of.

It is true that when faced with the tangle of events that occurred under the direct rule of Lenin and the group of old Bolsheviks, and which reproduced that kind of historical synthesis which Engels's phrase (about every revolution being an exceedingly authoritarian event) is meant to represent, one can make the following argument: all the same, had Lenin and the old Bolsheviks

* Lecture delivered in 1978. First published as 'Sobre el stalinismo', in *Seis conferencias*, edited by Salvador López Arnal (Barcelona: Ediciones de Intervención Cultural/El Viejo Topo, 2005).

 | DOI 10.1163/9789004280526_017

remained in power, those phenomena would only have occurred during the revolutionary period; they would not have been eternalised, as they were under the government of Stalin and his team, practically up until our own time. And that is true. Still, yesterday's mention of all these deeds of a despotic, and in some cases even cruel, nature should at least teach us, before we label them 'Stalinism' (as with a certain common sense they can be so called), not to paint a naïve picture, counterposing, on the one hand, something perverse, which would be Stalinism, and, on the other, something very pure and innocent, which would be historical Leninism.

Having said this, one must in any case immediately add that there is no lack of highly visible differences between historical Leninism and historical Stalinism, between real Leninism (that which actually existed) and likewise real Stalinism. In order to limit myself in this brief review to things that we all more or less surely have in mind, I would group the most visible differences around the following:

To begin with, the amount of accumulated power in the Stalinist system. At the moment in which the Stalinist system can be regarded as having really taken shape, that is, at the end of the 1930s, shortly before the outbreak of World War II, the Stalinist system was, viewed from a social point of view, a highly state-controlled economy, which was at the same time indissolubly joined to a state apparatus that was highly centralised in its own right. And on top of that, this highly centralised state apparatus was in practice joined to the executive authorities of the sole political party. The concentration of power that arose from this, when the economy was functioning, was, of course, something far beyond what Lenin knew during his lifetime. In the Leninist era understood in a strict sense, such a measure of power had never been concentrated in the hands of the central authority.

This would be the first distinguishing feature among those that are most visible, those that are noticeable at first glance: the different degree of concentration of power.

The second distinguishing feature that I would like to underscore, without detracting from others that could be mentioned (what I am doing is abbreviating, so as to be able to bring together the largest possible number of details), is, I would say, this: although the Cheka was without doubt founded under Lenin, although there already were under Lenin, under classical Leninism, phenomena as painful as, for example, Kronstadt, and many others, the terror during Stalin's era was nevertheless different, in that its chief tendency was to be terror against the Bolshevik old guard, against the Party itself. In saying this, I do not mean to forget the millions of ordinary Soviet citizens who suffered that terror and who lived and died in the forced labour camps of the Stalinist era.

However, what I want to stress is that what was radically new about the Stalin period is that one can clearly see that all of that terror had the liquidation of the Bolshevik old guard as its most well-defined goal.

This is something that the people of the time saw quite clearly. People who fled that era's Communist parties in fright have left quite striking recollections and images of the new officials, a fearsome young guard 'with new leather harnesses', according to a phrase from one of that period's celebrated writers, whose main task in the heart of the Russian Communist Party had been the murder of old Bolsheviks, or the old Bolshevik leadership, including, naturally and quite notably, Trotsky.

This would be the second feature: repression to the point of terror, and which was brought to bear, moreover, against the Party itself and, notably, against the group of old Bolsheviks.

The third feature would be, in my opinion, Stalinism's support for Russian nationalism. At the same time as members of the Bolshevik old guard were dying under Stalinism, and in the midst of a campaign to discredit them, the regime, at the very same time, sought and obtained support from an element that had until that time seemed improbable in a Marxist party, namely, from patriotism, from the nationalism of the non-communist masses.

All of this is related to the final feature that I would offer, quite distinct from any of the forms of harshness or acts of violence from the period of Soviet power during Lenin's lifetime. This fourth feature follows somewhat from the preceding features: ideological cynicism, the complete lack of concern among the members of Stalin's governing circle regarding the things they said (I will elaborate on this a bit later). For this group, ideology and theory are at every moment a mere cover for practical necessities, as they displayed a contempt for theory that Lenin's cohorts had never felt. If the Leninist group had sinned in this connection, their sin was quite the opposite, since they had the habit – typical of intellectuals – of always focusing on the details of theory.

It is necessary to say, at any rate, that despite considering these distinguishing features, these properly Stalinesque features, as I have just summarised them (without thinking, let me repeat, that in doing so I have done anything exhaustive or definitive, but rather something that can fit into half an hour), new, I acknowledge, and believe that one must acknowledge, that these features have their roots and precedents in the previous period. Not merely czarist precedents, not merely Oriental precedents, as Lenin said, precedents which he himself had noted, before his death, during his own period of government. Lenin had noted the extent to which some of the behaviour of the new officials resembled the behaviour of the old officials, the czarist officials, the extent to which they were in large measure the same, and the extent to which those that were different also resembled the old behaviour.

But I am not referring to that alone. I am also referring to precedents for those Stalinist features that did not come from czarist Russia but were born under Lenin's government. For starters, and even though I earlier gave as a distinguishing feature of Stalinism the enormous concentration of power as compared with what had occurred during Lenin's time, we must nevertheless not forget that such a great concentration of power was already partly predetermined by the civil war and foreign intervention. A regime that is born of a civil war and foreign intervention will inevitably have a government in which the military aspect is predominant. And that military aspect, on the other hand, has always been predominant in every revolution. So, all of this meant that from the very beginning there was a concentration of power virtually unknown up to that time in the societies of the Russian empire. But even the tendency to ideological deformation – the last feature to which I referred, the ideological cynicism – or to deform the theory, had if not precedents in Lenin (I don't think there were precedents), then at least *roots* in the situation of Lenin. Why? Because what the Russian Bolsheviks, and subsequently all Communists in the Third International, had experienced as a socialist revolution was not at all what they had imagined and thought a socialist revolution would be until only a short time before.

It is true that in Marx himself, in some writings from the last period of his life, there was another possibility for understanding the socialist revolution; yet, oddly enough, these writings from the last period of his life did not become known until well into the 1920s. What I mean is that the Bolsheviks from the period of the Revolution did not know these writings by Marx, which consider another possibility for the transition to socialism. They did not know them. They lived, accordingly, in the awkward situation of calling 'socialist revolution' something that was, in terms of their intellectual preparation and set of concepts, *not* a socialist revolution.

Many people have said this and many already said it at the time, and it was noted not by a single tendency, but by members of every imaginable tendency. On the one hand, there was the social-democratic tendency, Kautsky and the German Social Democrats, who, on seeing that the conditions that they knew from the classic Marx, the Marx of *Capital*, did not exist in Russia, held that the revolution should never have taken place. That's on the one hand. Then on the other, there were the communists further to the left – for example, and most notably, Gramsci – who thought, indeed, that, as Gramsci himself wrote in a celebrated article, there had been a *revolution against Capital* (this is the title of the famous article by Gramsci), but that it did not matter, for they had a much more idealist training than Marx, and thought that by an act of will and culture everything could be fixed. And lastly, there was a third tendency, which also thought that the revolution was anomalous, or poorly understood, and that was the extreme Left of the Communist International, which was called the Council Communist left: Pannekoek, Korsch, authors like that, from the extreme Left, whom Lenin considered leftist. What they thought was that Lenin and the Russian Bolsheviks had made a bourgeois revolution and they needed to recognise it as such, as a bourgeois revolution, and therefore organise power and everything else from that point of view, though with a possibility of social change, but very much in the long run and deriving from the revolutionary nature of political power, which would surely give rise to quite new problems.

This difference between earlier theory and what occurred there, between what a socialist revolution was believed to be and what had actually happened in Russia, and between this and the theorisation of what had happened, would later yield, within Stalinism, what I have called 'ideological cynicism', that is, the open falsification of the theory and its utilisation to justify any practice, including – we are going to call things by their name, it being a matter of the Stalinist period – any murder.

Still, even if, regarding this point, *the root* of Stalin's vice lay there, in the earlier period, there is an important difference with respect to Lenin. Lenin knew very well that the Revolution he had led did not follow the traditional schema of Second International Marxism, of the Marxism proceeding from a direct interpretation of *Capital*. And as the majority of those present here remember very well, he was awaiting the intervention of a worldwide, or at least European (in the end, at least central European), revolutionary movement. When the revolution in the West did not occur, there was a moment, I believe, in which we must note in Lenin a kind of illusion that will later be characteristic of Stalinism: the illusion that can be summarised in the famous rhetorical phrase or figure of speech that 'communism is the soviets plus electrification'. Yet that illusion must not have lasted very long. As is well known, in the final period of his life, with many health problems, in that curious illness that left-wing psychoanalysts will have to analyse a bit – why did Lenin's final illness have, as one of its consequences, the impossibility of communication? Why did he sink into his illness in that way? I do not want to do anything more than pose the question; one cannot venture to say anything about this in just a few minutes – Lenin, as is well known, attempted a reconsideration of things. There are specialists – I am not a historian and cannot venture an opinion in this regard, I mention this only as information – who think that, indeed, Bukharin had many elements for the development of socialist thought that Lenin was himself considering using.

In any case, what we do not find in Lenin's last phase is the glorification of the present state of things, as if this were what had been desired and sought after. Rather, there was a long state of crisis, however insufficient it may have been. I am not going to go into detail with regard to whether or not Lenin's final self-criticism is sufficient. At any rate, the great difference, from my point of view, is that instead of having that final, problematic, self-critical consciousness of Lenin, Stalinism consists of *canonising as correct theory* what is merely the state of necessity, the state of necessity of hunger, of scarcity, of repression, etc.

Thus, in the attempt to present the dramatic situation of the old Russian empire as if it were the realisation of socialism, and later on even as communism, as we shall see, the apparatus of Stalinist propaganda drove the old concepts, the old ideas, to often grotesque extremes. On other occasions this was not the case; at other times they were more or less debatable hypotheses, which certainly had some element of truth. For example, the famous and central Stalinist thesis – which I have never believed was entirely false – according to which the class struggle intensifies as the building of socialism advances. It is not the case that I accept this blindly, but I think it has a certain justification, at least with regard to class struggle on a world scale. But at other times the building of the theory to justify practice – in these cases it was clear that it justified the practice of internal repression – almost becomes a joke, and if Stalin was not making the joke then his closest colleagues were playing the joke on him. For example, the idea of socialism in one country: one does not even understand what it means. It is absolutely incomprehensible, and it hardly seems possible that it lasted for years in Stalinist propaganda. Zinoviev joked to Stalin about communism in one street, in an era in which it was still not known that under Stalin you paid for those things with your life (as did Zinoviev, of course).

No less incredible was, for example, the idea of social fascism. I have brought with me a copy of Stalin's main statement on social fascism – that is, the hypothesis that the social democratic parties were fascist parties, were fascism – because read today it seems incredible, yet it was the official doctrine. The central passage, written by Stalin in the period of the Sixth Congress of the International, reads as follows:

> [I]t is not true that fascism is only the fighting organisation of the bourgeoisie. Fascism is not only a military-technical category. Fascism is the bourgeoisie's fighting organisation that relies on the active support of Social-Democracy ... They are not antipodes, they are twins. Fascism is an informal political bloc of these two chief organisations [Social Democracy and the bourgeoisie] ...[1]

1 Stalin 1953, p. 294.

If we bear in mind that the number of Social Democrats killed by Nazism, while probably not amounting to the 350,000 Communists killed by Germany under the Nazis, must have been close to 250,000, according to the most credible estimates, this statement sends shivers down one's spine. Apart from the fact that it also sends shivers down one's spine to think that Marxists have allowed the name of a party – 'Social Democracy' – and the name of a social class – 'bourgeoisie' – to appear on the same level of analysis, both of them being 'organisations'. This was truly an insult to the brains of that era's Marxists, but it is clear that they bore the insult.

Even the notion of socialism has remained distorted since that time. In the socialist tradition, a certain form of life was called 'socialism'. Beginning with Stalinism, and for many, many years, we have used – me too; I remember when I did so – 'socialism' to mean merely the obtaining of certain instruments that were part of what we believed socialism to be, for example, the state's takeover of the economy. In this period the very word 'socialism' was damaged in practical terms.

In sum, I would say that the major difference between all of the harsh acts that may have taken place in Lenin's time and the Stalinist system is this pragmatism, this utter violation of ideas and concepts, used to justify any practice, even the most macabre ones. That ideological pragmatism also explains, in my opinion, the difference of cruelty, the difference that exists between Lenin's political harshness and the murder of the entire Bolshevik old guard.

I do not want to finish without touching on a few other points, if only very briefly. After having said that what seems essential to me is that pragmatism as a distinguishing essence with respect to Leninism, I would like to spend five minutes on the roots of Stalinism and another five, or fewer, on the possible current state [*actualidad*] of Stalinism.

. . .[2] Stalin's team, I think it is quite true, I think it is fundamentally true, and Stalinism would certainly not have been possible in England.

This can be stated in a bit more detail. I deliberately chose the example of England. As surely most of those present here remember, the most serious attempt on the part of an old Bolshevik leader to understand what was happening in the old Russian empire was Preobrazhensky's thesis on original socialist accumulation, which said that the first task for socialism in power was to achieve an accumulation of the means of production like that achieved by the bourgeoisie in England in the seventeenth, eighteenth and nineteenth centuries. As is well known, this original accumulation in England caused the population – mainly the working-class population, of course – an amount of

2 A brief lapse in the recording [Ed.].

pain and suffering which, if experiences of suffering could be added up, would surely not be less than, and perhaps quite the contrary, the sum of suffering that occurred in the Soviet Union during that original socialist accumulation.

The trouble is that the original socialist accumulation, as Preobrazhensky called it, quite probably should not be viewed as socialist. Why would it be socialist? What it achieved was in large measure the same thing as original bourgeois accumulation had achieved, namely, an industrial civilisation. In this regard, I believe – I say this because I think it is good to risk stating one's own opinion – that the extreme Left in the 1920s, those whom Lenin criticised for being leftists, was right. I believe that when Pannekoek said that what was being done there *was the same thing* as what had been done in the English bourgeois revolution, he was right; it was an original accumulation of capital. Nevertheless, that original accumulation occurred in the Soviet Union not under the control of the old ruling class, but under the control of a new class, a new – however one wants to call it – group, a new association of people, the officials of the party and the state, about which the leftists of the 1920s were, I believe, wrong. That is, this new accumulation does not exactly produce a bourgeois accumulation of capital in the classic style studied by Marx. It is a new social group, that of the leadership of the party and the state, which controls that accumulation and directs it, as various contemporary sociologists have shown. This is a theme that is, as is surely known by everyone, currently the object of a great deal of research. (Precisely for lack of time I will not spend any time reviewing the precedents for the analysis in which some contemporary sociologists are currently engaged, whose origin is found in the extreme Left of the 1920s and whose second, extremely important, theoretical link is, as is well known, Trotsky.)

Lastly (I will not waste time on this, it is not worth it; if I did, we would far exceed the time set aside, the few minutes that I wanted to reserve for the current state of Stalinism), just as it is usually thought that Stalinism is a phenomenon well demarcated in time and something from the past, it is also usually said that there is no Stalinism today. I do not believe this, and would simply like to suggest a few directions for analysis, without delving into them, regarding contemporary Stalinism. One of these directions comes from a very capable French politician, sociologist and political scientist, Martinet, who had been a member of the Third International and who was one of the few to say very early on that those histories from the 1930s had to be a lie. Martinet has performed a sociological analysis of great interest: Stalinism, meaning the Stalinism of Stalin, that which existed in the Soviet Union, greatly resembles those regimes that are appearing today in the Third World. There is a certain industrialisation, a certain accumulation of capital, not controlled by the old ruling class, which was the colonial class, part of an empire (Algeria, for example, or, in the present, Somalia), but controlled by a new elite, a new vanguard, a new team of technicians and politicians who, without all of the Stalinist orthodoxy, are incorporating some elements from the Stalin tradition: industrialisation on the basis of a very authoritarian regime, with appeals to what they call, quite ideologically, 'scientific socialism'. The scientific socialism of Barre, or of Nasser, when Nasser was still alive, or of the Algerians, is as pretentiously ideological as was Stalin's, and resembles it quite a bit socially. The somewhat weak part of Martinet's analysis is perhaps the fact that although he regards all of this as contemporary Stalinism, the state's takeover of the economy in these states tends to be less intense than it was in the case of the Soviet state, while it is of course just as intense as in some of the popular democracies, at least in their initial phases.

I think we can also speak of the persistence of Stalinism in the West, in the very countries of the metropolis. It is present, on the one hand, in the delusional dogmatism of some people, delusional and scarcely capable of understanding reality; but it is likewise present, in my opinion, on the other side, in the pragmatism of many labour parties. To put it briefly and to save time, I find it to be as much a case of pragmatic pseudo-theory to say, in order to falsify the day's practice, that communism can be built in one country or that bread is going to cease being a commodity (ideas carried in the pockets of Soviet soldiers killed: a leaflet that said this during World War II was captured by the Germans and shown to the entire world), just as much pseudo-theoretical pragmatism to say that it is possible to establish communism in one country as it is to say that communism or socialism is possible without a violent, revolutionary clash with the current ruling class. The one thing strikes me as just as ideological as the other, just as pragmatic and, in a certain sense, just as Stalinist, in the sense, that is, of pseudo-theory to justify practice. In one case it may be a very violent practice, in the other it may be a parliamentary practice. It is hardly a revolutionary practice, incidentally, in either case. Stalin was always very careful to present himself as the centre; he never wanted to play on the left.

Yet I would not want to end on a note of little optimism either, for what is encouraging, in my opinion, is the fact that many of us, after long experience – without having forgotten the reality of the class consciousness of Stalinism: an ideological class consciousness, without question; a false consciousness, without question; involuntary self-deception, without question; but tremendous class consciousness – and after having gone through it all, can say these things today, which perhaps means that the real crisis of Stalinism, the somewhat definitive crisis of Stalinism, may be the beginning of a recovery of non-ideological revolutionary thought, which does not deceive itself with either delusional, pseudo-revolutionary illusions, as I said before, or with the illusions of the parliamentarist, reformist kind, which at this moment are the dominant ones in the West.

That class consciousness which was present in the past in the Stalinist working class – those who have neither been Stalinists nor been in Stalinist parties will have to take my word for this, but those who have been will know that it is true – resulted in reactions that were, admittedly, very primitive and, as I have acknowledged and stressed, ideologically false reactions, based on false consciousness, yet very authentic. They are, for example, the stuff of history: the references, the exclamations, the labour folklore which tells us that when confronted with an injustice, the oppressed man in some Mediterranean country, specifically in southern Italy, reacted with the phrase 'Just wait till the man with the big moustache gets here!' ['*¡Ya vendrá el bigotudo!*'], as an expression of his fury, his hatred, his class reaction in the face of an injustice endured. The extent to which Stalinism was, with false consciousness, the bearer of class consciousness is something known to all of us who had to explain to communist militants that it was true, that what bourgeois people had said for so long turned out in the end to be true, namely, that the Stalinist government had murdered the Bolshevik old guard. Those of us who had to bear and explain this news, and who have seen militants cry upon hearing it, when they had no choice but to believe it because we gave them the data and told them 'this comes from here, that took place there and the other thing happened like that', know very well that underneath that false consciousness there was an authentic class consciousness, class struggle. What we must guard against, besides the loss of real consciousness, which the old Stalinism lost, is the loss of even the illusory, but at least existing, class consciousness among the ideological residue – which is parliamentarist, reformist, a kind of pragmatism; extreme, right-wing Stalinism, so to speak – under which a large part of the labour movement now leads their lives.

CHAPTER 15

Marxist Parties and the Peace Movement

In issue no. 22 of *mientras tanto*, we published an article entitled 'Fundamentalism and the Peace Movements' ['El fundamentalismo y los movimientos por la paz']. The theme of that article – devoted to a multi-authored work in English edited by E.P. Thompson, copies of which are to be introduced into the countries of Central and Eastern Europe – was a discussion of what seemed to be the 'chief difficulty' in the dialogue between the peace movements in Western Europe and the movements for political freedoms in Central and Eastern Europe. The same article listed other important difficulties in that discussion with the East; for example, everyone's different appraisals of ancient and recent European history, the differences flowing from their own feelings about themselves from a political standpoint, the differences regarding their assessments of the risks facing the species today, etc.

Yet before addressing those questions, which have to do with the relationship between the peace movements and dissident movements in Central and Eastern Europe, I would like to briefly discuss some aspects of the relations between those peace movements and the traditional revolutionary organisations in the West. It is worth briefly stating which organisations or currents these are among us: first and foremost, we are talking about those situated to the left of the PCE and the PSUC, as well as some militants from these two parties, from Izquierda Socialista, from UGT and from CC.OO. (There seems to be nothing problematic about the CNT's relationship to the peace movement, not even in its most radical or 'Gandhian' forms.)

The doctrinal past of these organisations (which we called, with a naïve smugness, 'the theory') does not predispose them toward a radical fight for peace, or even toward anti-militarism. This is the first thing to note, and it is not worth dwelling on it with lots of examples and quotations, which will be familiar to the reader, who is perhaps bored with them. The fact is that, starting from Marx's phrase regarding the status of violence as the midwife of history, an idea was transferred, through a highly questionable extrapolation, to the institutional and specifically military level, beginning shortly after the October

* First published in 1985. Republished as 'Los partidos marxistas y el movimiento por la paz', in *Pacifismo, ecología y política alternativa*, edited by Juan-Ramón Capella (Barcelona: Icaria Editorial, S.A., 1987).

 | DOI 10.1163/9789004280526_018

Revolution and, above all, beginning with the consolidation of Stalinist bureaucratic despotism.

What triggered the process was, as is obvious, the military and economic siege (both internal and external) to which every true revolution is subjected, every revolution that is not a 'democratic transition' prepared and staged by the ruling classes, but rather that clearly aims at destroying or significantly diminishing the power of these classes. This automatic mechanism is so well known – from the Castilian uprising and the Valencian 'germanía' movement, passing through the German peasants and Anabaptists, the French Revolution, the Commune and the Russian Revolution, and up to the Mexican Revolution – that it is not worth spending more time on it.

The mediation between Marx's idea (which does not refer to institutional violence, nor does it go beyond the realm of a given society) and the new doctrinal warmongering of the Third and Fourth Internationals (the Second practiced the *old* capitalist warmongering from early on: from the time it voted in favour of war credits in 1914) became, once the Russian Civil War had been left behind, international policy. In this policy, the permanent 'national' army was re-established. The ideological version of this decision was defensive, and fairly sincere: in the Stalinist sphere it was a matter of 'the defence of the socialist fatherland', and in the Trotskyist sphere it was 'the defence of the first workers' state in history', however bureaucratic it was. The idea of 'class struggle on a world scale' fulfilled its function in the new militarism, not, of course, because it was false or did not refer to anything, but because of the way it took shape politically. For example, Werner Hoffmann, the Minister of Defence of the German Democratic Republic and former combatant in the International Brigades during the Spanish Civil War, went so far as to say that the atomic bomb is a weapon in the class struggle (presumably 'on a world scale'); and it will not be necessary to remind anyone of Mao Zedong's sinister ineptitude in presenting nuclear war as the prelude to socialism.

As was stated in the 'Letter from the Editors' that appeared in issue 22 of *mientras tanto*, communist parties have had an instrumental conception of wars as means to defend or reach socialism. They thereby reclaimed the traditional doctrine of Catholic Scholasticism, the doctrine of the 'just war'. The specifically Marxist way of doing this prolonged the fatalism that can be deduced from Hegel's philosophy, as it is incorporated and extended in Marx's *The Poverty of Philosophy*: the revolutionary just war was covered by the Hegelian-Marxist thesis that history always advances 'by means of its bad', or 'worst', side.

No less obvious than all of this is the fact that the radical Marxist organisations are energetically fighting, more and better than anyone else (at least in this country), for the cause of peace. In some cases their struggle is only obliquely or secondarily for peace, since they would perhaps not always be disposed to pursue it beyond the fight against the entry (or continuance) of Spain in NATO. But that is, for the moment, of little importance, for the opposition to NATO is the real, living manner in which an argument *against* appears today: if anyone in Spain today claimed to be – as do the not-even-Social Democrats of the current government – for peace and not against our presence in NATO, we would say that he or she is an abject coward, a simpleton or a hypocrite.

The situation of the radical Marxist parties resembles somewhat that of the Christian confessions on this score, above all that of the Catholic Church. Catholics who fight for peace also find themselves faced with the hurdle of the 'just war' doctrine, invented by their own forefathers, and within the Church there have also been, naturally enough, tensions similar to those that can be detected in the usual revolutionary camp.

As it is simply a truism (and should therefore not be read as an empty statement), perhaps it can be said that the appropriate way of improving this state of affairs consists in revising the doctrine so as to bring it into harmony with a practice that all of these movements consider more essential for them than some formulations from their doctrinal past. And they are right: radical Marxists, because the essential thing for them must be the desire for emancipation, which is completely incompatible with anything like a world war in today's circumstances; Christians for socialism (not merely those who are today members of CPS), because their reading of the Gospel's 'Thou shalt not kill' (and even other, more positive, more effusive maxims) presumably stands out more than 'I did not come to bring peace', so overused and abused by the warmongering pseudo-democrats of Central and Eastern Europe, blinded by their justifiable dislike of those who lord it over them.

It is very important, particularly in the confused ideological state of our age of 'disillusionment' and cynicism, that the radical Marxist organisations remain within the front for peace, without assuming a prominence that frightens away good fighters, but also without concealing the dignity of their past, with its struggles for the freedom of the oppressed, or their ability to link the struggle for peace to social emancipation, reciprocally grounding the one in the other. These organisations are called upon to maintain, through a Marxist shaping of opinion [*conceptuación*], the emancipatory perspective. Given the importance of their presence, the fundamentalism into which they occasionally lapse and their hesitations are much more fruitful and much less dangerous than the parallel phenomena [*manifestaciones*] among the fundamentalist dissidents of Central and Eastern Europe.

It is not the case that many of the demands made by those people in the Russian sphere of influence are devoid of truthfulness and importance. True, above all, is their claim that one cannot establish a lasting peace, more deeply rooted than the indispensable yet insecure 'no-war', except by achieving the reunification of Germany and political freedom for the peoples of Central and Eastern Europe. (As the voices that reach us are neither German, nor Polish, nor Baltic, but mainly Czech and Slovak, they fail to add some obvious requirements, relating to other nations, for a solid peace in Europe.)

But that alone – and this exhausts the doctrine of the fundamentalist dissidents from Central and Eastern Europe – is not enough (if we are going to discuss fundamentals), for that solution would simply take us back to the map of bellicose states of interwar Europe.

The perspective of the traditional Marxist movements is less dangerous, even when it is likewise guilty of fundamentalism, since it does not start from the premise of a premeditated provocation by the Soviet army, as do some dissidents from Central and Eastern Europe, avowed advocates of military action against the Soviet Union; and it is more fruitful because it does not content itself with a return to the *status quo ante*, which had such disastrous consequences. We should probably hope that those movements overcome the chasm and inconsistency that exists between their doctrine of war and their actual practice today, assimilating to a certain degree the antimilitarist and pacifist causes.

CHAPTER 16

The Marxist Tradition and New Problems

Over the last few years, I have grown accustomed to the fact that whenever I collaborate with someone, that person always reminds me – always with generosity and more or less elegance, and generally without wanting to do so – of my age, by referring to what happened twenty or thirty years ago. At any rate, if it is possible to believe that the interest in commemorating Marx is as intense as it seems to be here today, judging by the number of people here and noticing in particular those who are young people, one can rightly consider any length of time devoted to the efforts of publishing to have been time well spent.

Nevertheless, if I have chosen to consider the theme of the state of the Marxist tradition with regard to what I am going to call 'new problems', which I will clarify later, it is because, in my opinion – and I will say this at the very outset – the state of the Marxist tradition is not nearly as positive as it might seem – far from it – on this afternoon in this city. Rather, we should start from the quite remarkable and even astonishing fact that an economic, and even cultural and political, crisis of the magnitude of the one endured by the capitalist societies in recent years (since the beginning of the 1970s), far from leading to a new prestige for the basic ideas of the Marxist tradition, or socialist tradition in general, is proving instead to be the source [*agente*] of, or at least coeval with, a period in which Marxist ideas in particular and socialist ideas in general enjoy little repute in the capitalist countries.

Granting the relativity of all comparisons, we may say that the crisis of the 1930s, which was without question more serious than the present one, nonetheless did not have similar effects in regard to the erosion or degradation of the prestige of Marxist socialism and socialism generally. Without a doubt, the crisis of the 1930s caused a vigorous defensive reaction on the part of Europe's upper classes. All of the European fascisms and the New Deal, the new economic policy of the Administration in the United States, can be thought of as reactions to, and defensive developments caused by, the great crisis of the 1930s. However, if on the ideological level, on the level of political and social ideas, there were certainly intellectuals who adopted radical right-wing positions, especially in the Latin countries and also in Germany, the great majority

* Lecture given in 1983. First published as 'Tradición marxista y nuevos problemas', in *Seis conferencias*, edited by Salvador López Arnal (Barcelona: Ediciones de Intervención Cultural/ El Viejo Topo, 2005).

 | DOI 10.1163/9789004280526_019

nevertheless felt a push in the other direction. This was a time, that of the crisis of the 1930s, in which the intellectuals of the capitalist countries in general, and those of Western Europe in particular, found themselves drawn to solutions which, if not openly Marxist, were at least vaguely socialist.

By contrast, in the current crisis – surely the century's second most important one, after the crisis of the 1930s – it appears that the upper classes need not defend themselves, as it were, but rather seem to be on the attack, on the offensive, in the capitalist countries, without implementing policies to alleviate the system's problems, like the Keynesianism resulting from the new US economic policies in the 1930s; and they even abandon social or charitable measures that were a common tactical heritage of Europe's upper classes, practically since Bismarck's time, since the end of the nineteenth century. Even governments from a left-wing tradition, as might be the case with the current Spanish government, react during the crisis with a certain cavalier approach [*holgura*] toward the working classes, permitting themselves to reduce subsidies and aid, and thus refraining from using relief measures, which at other times had been the basis for achieving a minimum consensus. And as for the intellectuals, everyone is familiar with the more or less important shift to the right, even of those who were on the Left; and among the economists, who as intellectuals tend to be more sober than the rest (more sober than the philosophers or sociologists), less exposed to the fluctuations of fashion, it is also becoming fashionable to underestimate Marx's contribution, once one has duly acknowledged that he produced the only attempt at a general theory of the system. It is no longer fashionable to praise, as did Schumpeter or Leontief, the intellectual quality of the dynamic, totalising thought of Marx's system.

So, in the sphere of the intellectuals, which naturally has particular relevance when we are speaking about the validity of ideas, the gravitation of intellectual groups toward the right and, in any case, away from Marxism, even among those who had been rigid and rather simplistic Marxists at other times, is occurring on many levels. It sometimes takes a slightly grotesque form, namely, in the work of intellectuals who are not especially solid, as has occurred with the Parisian fad of the 'new philosophers', which I hope will be brief. However, on other occasions, which are not few in number, the phenomenon is more substantial and more serious, and is based either on a very radical pessimism, or else, on the contrary, on the emergence of new perspectives.

The changes stemming from pessimism, which is quite common in both Madrid and Barcelona among intellectuals coming out of the Marxist Left, take many forms. The most interesting form, for me, is that of those who, having at least quite a few years of ideological struggle behind them, often working in political organisations, decide one fine day that the world no longer offers any hope, that all that can be done is to prepare oneself to die well when the first rockets explode, and that therefore one should not devote oneself to sociological theory or more concrete problems. It is more worthwhile, instead, *merely* to read poetry, a bit of philosophy (the most speculative kind possible), and wait for the end. Out of basic discretion I will not give any of the names with which I could document this description, but I assure you that I have encountered many in recent months and I assume that most of you have also encountered one.

What interests us most today, however, is another type of withdrawal from the field of socialist thought in general, or Marxist thought in particular, which is the type that coincides with what I called the emergence of new perspectives. This is the case of the old militant from the Marxist Left whom we find divorced from traditional political activity and yet is, however, active in a feminist group, or a pacifist group, or an environmentalist group, to mention – if only by way of example: I know there are many more – the three new movements that strike me as most important, since they correspond to the three most substantial new problems. This is a new development of considerable importance. I do not mean to say that the other one is not (pessimism is also a fact of the greatest importance), but the second development matters more to me for the reflection that I want to offer you this evening, for it suggests that there are problems that have not been considered, or have been poorly considered, by traditional Marxism.

By 'traditional Marxism' I understand a fairly broad set of intellectual and practical motivations. I use the phrase 'Marxist tradition' or 'traditional Marxism' deliberately, with the aim of acknowledging the plurality of strands and inclinations in the Marxist past and to avoid epistemologically more ambitious expressions like 'Marxist theory' or 'Marxist system', which could, however, leave out some of the fabric's interesting threads.

Those problems, perhaps disregarded, or in any case insufficiently considered, by the Marxist tradition are on some occasions first perceived by intellectuals with a suitable training. On many other occasions, however, they are first perceived by the sensibility of sectors of the population who are perhaps not yet well trained intellectually, but who, on the other hand, have a mentality much less smothered [*recubiertos*] by education: specifically, sectors of the youth. In either case, it may happen, especially when actions become intellectual fashions, that the appearance of new problems occurs with great superficiality and publicity.

The tendency to speak about many things without having first studied them is found not only among ignoramuses, but also among intellectuals.

A extremely large part of the contemporary culture business, much larger than in other eras because of the power of the media, is thought that is insufficiently based on knowledge; and this is also often bound up, in the case of the intellectuals, with ambitions or a will to power or simple vanity, which leads them to place things that their colleagues have not said in the foreground. Still, having acknowledged all of these superficial and frivolous aspects of a large part of public intellectual life, there remains the main, basic fact that there is real novelty in the new movements, exemplified by the three that I have mentioned, because there is novelty in the problems addressed. And that novelty does not come into conflict solely, as on other occasions, with the mental and political conservatism that may express itself quite perversely and with considerable ill will, but also often with the Left, with the traditional thought of the Left.

As for the malice with which conservative thought responds to the new concerns, these last few days, with peace demonstrations throughout Europe, have furnished us with some notable examples. The right-wing German, Dutch and Danish press have followed the line of comparing this type of movement – which involves huge demonstrations of hundreds of thousands of people *unorganised* by any party, *insufficiently represented*, or not represented at all, in the parliaments – with, or assimilating it to (by means of a very wicked use of the word 'movement'), the first moments of the European fascisms, which were also more or less amorphous movements in their appearance, barely coordinated politically and with little or no parliamentary representation. This has been the case above all in [West] Germany, where, faced with the strength of the movement, one of the last resorts of the right-wing press and politicians has been to stamp these new movements – feminism, environmentalism and pacifism – with the labels 'apoliticism', 'confusion', and 'crypto-fascism'.

It seems to me that there is no reason to spend much time condemning this type of groundless, malign opinion. Moreover, what interests us is the other thing, what interests us is the clash, or at least disagreement, more or less frequent and more or less radical, between the new movements and the Left *as well*, and in particular with Marxist organisations and traditions. Let us consider this with regard to the three great movements already referred to, beginning with feminism.

While the Marxist tradition's past is far from being the best place as regards early expressions of feminist concerns, looking at the texts dispassionately it becomes clear that it was not the worst place either. Bebel, one of the first Social Democratic leaders, wrote a rather beautiful book on the woman question, and Engels himself had in his works, though in a dispersed form, at least two fundamental elements for the treatment of the woman question in our societies: first, an acknowledgement of their condition of oppression and humiliation, as he says in a text that we can perhaps go over; and second, an attempt to explain that situation.

As for recording that condition of humiliation or oppression, the following passage from a well-known popularisation, *The Origin of the Family, Private Property and the State*, may serve as an example of the fact that Engels saw this as the present state of women, not merely something from the past. In this passage, we read:

> This humiliated position of women, especially manifest among the Greeks of the Heroic and still more of the Classical Age, has become gradually embellished and dissembled and, in part, clothed in a milder form, but by no means abolished.[1]

There is, then, first the acknowledgement of a particular oppression or degradation, to use his words, of women throughout the past and in our present culture, followed by, as I said, an attempt at explanation. Engels's hypothesis is that the ties of kinship, lineage and sex are more dominant in a society the less labour has developed, and the scarcer and more primitive are its products.

Contemporary feminism would no doubt regard this explanation as inadequate; above all, it is not the explanation that it finds most interesting, for there is a tendency among the majority of the feminist movements – I confine myself to noting this, without passing judgement on it – to limit themselves to the specifically feminine aspect of the problem and to more or less ignore and neglect the broader, not specifically feminine, social background to the problem. Engels's reflection, according to which sexual oppression, like all forms of domination based on ties such as those of lineage, is inversely proportional to the development of the productivity of labour and the organisation of labour itself, is of course a reflection that situates the problem within a framework that is obviously not strictly limited to the feminine. In any case, however modern one is and however concerned one is about the strictly feminine aspects of the problem, it seems that a reflection of this sort also has considerable usefulness for any thought dealing with female emancipation.

Oddly enough, while Marx's ideas were in agreement with Engels's formulations, as they were concerning so many other things (in the majority of cases, though not in all), and especially as regards texts such as the one I have cited, which is from a period in which there was a very close collaboration between the two writers, in terms of sensibility Marx was nonetheless truly a man

1 Engels 1990, p. 165.

of, as it were, another era much more than Engels. Engels had a much more open-minded personal life than Marx in family matters and in his view of the position of women in his life. Let me note, in passing, that Marx's life was too focused on his fundamental work to allow him to develop his sensibility in every respect.

I would like to mention a couple of details from Marx's life that reveal a man whose sensibility in this realm is quite remote from ours. First of all, there is the matter of his son, Frederick. All indications are that this was his, and not Engels's, son, that it was his natural son, but that he believed, on account of social considerations that would strike any socialist today as very strange, that it was necessary to hide this fact and to make others believe that it was Engels's son. It is for this reason that he gave him the name Frederick, with Engels's consent. Also: When Marx was much older and one of his daughters had a son, Marx congratulated her for having a boy rather than a girl, telling her that 'for my own part I prefer the "manly" sex for children born at this turning point of history. They have before them the most revolutionary period man had ever to pass through'.[2] It is possible that this was simple realism, but I think that it is also a sensibility characteristic of another world. Oddly, but as in other areas and contrary to a common view of things, Engels is here the one who has at least a keener sensibility, if not thought, with regard to the problem.

At any rate, the movements that are heirs to the classics, the later Marxisms, are quite a bit better than the classics themselves when it comes to the woman question. To limit ourselves to our case, our own country, we can say that reclaiming the theme of the emancipation of women in Spain after the Civil War was an initiative not merely of Marxist cultural milieus, but precisely of Marxist parties. I do not think I am mistaken if, following the editors of the Autonomous University's sociological journal *Papers*, I point out that issue 12 of *Nous Horitzons*, the theoretical-cultural journal of the PSUC at the time, published in 1967 the first contribution – after the Civil War, that is; before the Civil War there had been, naturally, a great deal of development – to this problem: an article by Giulia Adinolfi, which was later reprinted in issue 9 of *Papers*, in 1978, when the journal presented a history of the feminist movement in Spain.

And not only this. Later too, the theme of feminism was promoted predominantly by some communist parties, by practically all of them, but in an especially notable way by some of them. For example, the Movimiento Comunista, in which there is a great deal of development of, and work on, this problem,

2 Marx 1992b, p. 89.

and which surely is unparalleled in Spain, at least in terms of the political material produced and the dissemination of ideas.

In general, we can say that of the three major new movements corresponding to new problems arising in the second half of the [twentieth] century, the woman question is that for which the Marxist tradition was best prepared, better prepared, as we shall see, than it was for the peace movement or environmentalism. If we consider this carefully, it was of course better prepared than conservative traditions and as well prepared as the best anarchist groups could be in this realm, in which, moreover, there was a certain indeterminateness when identifying which contributions were anarchist and which ones were Marxist. Think, for example, of Kollontai's contributions: one does not know very well whether she is doing Marxism or libertarianism in her texts.

So, then: Why do some contemporary feminist currents seem to need to define themselves in terms of resistance to the Marxist tradition? With regard to this problem, I believe that we can differentiate a couple of causes, one of which is more superficial and the other, deeper cause. The more superficial cause, it seems to me, is the perfectly comprehensible inclination to not quite limit oneself to, but at least focus on, the *specifically* feminine features of the problem, with an attention to these problems that we might call 'microscopic', whereas in the Marxist tradition one tends to err in the opposite direction. Once the fact of women's oppression had been formulated, one immediately proceeded, as in the text from Engels that we have seen, to insert it within a general social framework, without further concern for the details, except in exceptional cases, like that of Kollontai.

However, this cause strikes me as superficial; another cause strikes me as a deeper explanation. I think what has led to a certain gap, though not a complete separation, between the feminist movements and the main, central Marxist tradition is not so much the deficiencies of the Marxist tradition regarding the woman question as the beginning of a crisis in the overarching Marxist vision itself and the overarching hope that it represents for many people (and represented for even more people in the past). Perhaps, once this era of crisis is over, it will once again represent this for many more, but not at present.

In connection with the despair and pessimism that I referred to earlier, found above all in intellectual milieus but also among working-class strata and the people more generally, which takes the form of a certain passive consensus around what is currently the only thing on offer [*lo que hay*], I think that the insertion of the woman question, like any other, within the overarching Marxist perspective or overarching Marxist hope has lost strength in our day, not because of the particular treatment of the woman question but because of the general vision of change, of social renewal. There can be no doubt that we are living in a time, without knowing how long it is going to last, of a loss of hope in revolutionary social change among great masses of the population, and its replacement (fortunately I see that in this city some very noble social interests have been preserved, but this is less true in other places), to a greater or lesser degree, by a certain hope, which if not stupid is at least passive and obscure, that technology or economics will bring about social change. At the same time, there has been an emergence of particularisms, professional associations [*gremialismos*], sectorialisation of the interests of many parts of the population and, on an international level, nationalisms, as if the oppression of the powers that be particularised the oppressed, making them take refuge in smaller and smaller niches (their profession, their home or, to take another example, their cuisine), or exacerbating the feeling of social, racial or national peculiarity.

While that is not, to be sure, a complete explanation of the phenomenon (nor do I intend it to be), it seems to me that it gives us a clue as to why it is that despite the fact that the Marxist tradition is one of the best positioned on the whole, as it were, as regards the problem of the oppression of women, the feminist movements of the second half of the twentieth century (i.e. the second post-war period) have nonetheless on more than one occasion defined themselves precisely by means of a challenge to Marxism's overarching social outlook, shutting themselves up in a particularisation of the female problem.

Let us move on to consider briefly another of those major movements that correspond to major new problems, the peace movement. In this area, the heritage, the legacy left by the first classics – Marx, Engels, etc. – was an ambiguous legacy, a double legacy, so to speak. On the one hand, we find in the Marxist classics the conviction that internal violence within a state is inevitable, that is to say, we find a belief in the inevitability of civil war, to say it in a very generic manner, and also in the inevitability of war between states. Texts to this effect are dispersed throughout their works; it is not worth the trouble to provide documentation. We could present a whole series of quotations in connection with the fundamental idea that violence is the mother of great historical changes, if it were necessary to document the point, which it is not.

Alongside this idea, however, there are more doubtful texts, which can be situated in periods far enough removed from one another to make us think that it is not merely a question of evolution in Marx and Engels's thought, even though there was a large measure of such evolution, but rather of the coexistence of two lines or strands of thought. I have chosen a couple of interesting examples. For instance, in 1874 Marx believed that a general European war would be not only favourable for the revolution, but a necessary path to it. For example, in this passage from a letter to Sorge, Marx's main confidant in North America, he says:

> General European conditions are such as to increasingly wage a *general European war*. We shall have to pass through it before there can be any thought of decisive overt activity on the part of the European working class.[3]

That was in the year 1874. However, six years later, in 1880, a European war struck him as an obstacle to the revolution, although he continues to believe it can hardly be avoided. For example, in this passage from a letter to Danielson, his Russian translator:

> I hope there will be no general war in Europe. Though, ultimately, it could not check, but would rather intensify, the social, I mean thereby the *economical*, development, it would certainly produce a useless exhaustion of forces for some longer or shorter interval.[4]

Similar oscillations can be found in Engels. Engels was so convinced of the inevitability and necessity of an armed revolutionary action that he specialised in military topics and was the military specialist among the early group of classics. We still find in *Anti-Dühring* (strictly speaking, not in *Anti-Dühring* but in the preparatory materials that he chose not to use in *Anti-Dühring*) a long statement maintaining that mandatory military service is advantageous for the people because it teaches them how to use weapons. Nevertheless, a few years later, the development of the first repeating rifle, which was breech-loading and held several cartridges in its bullet case (its magazine), made him think that the age of people's insurrections, at least in their urban form, had come to an end, for that weapon made it impossible to stand up to an army, that weapon – the repeating Mauser with five cartridges, which is what he was familiar with – which nowadays must be found only in museums. Yet, while the texts do show a certain oscillation, with its corresponding ambiguity, there is no doubt that they sound more like something from another age than do those that refer to the woman question. Texts that present a weapon (which is now a museum piece) as news that changes everything are obviously texts and thoughts from another era.

On the other hand, if one traces the history of traditional movements that accepted violence and traditional non-violent movements, if, for example, one does a comparison of Leninism and Gandhism in terms of their results, I trust I will not be considered unduly pessimistic if I say that both have had the same

3 Letter to Friedrich Adolph Sorge, 4 August 1874; Marx 1991b, p. 30, original emphasis.

4 Letter to Nikolai Danielson, 12 September 1880; Marx 1992a, p. 32, original emphasis.

negative result, negative not in the sense that they were bad forms of thought in themselves, but in the sense of not having achieved their objectives. Many of us may think that Leninism has so far not attained what it sought, and that Gandhism too has not attained what it sought in India. So, if one must judge matters by their results, the situation truly does cause a certain perplexity, and the old conviction of realist politics, according to which only one of the two forms of politics could be effective (surely the violent one), while the other must necessarily prove sterile, is, it seems, untenable, at least in general terms, although it can no doubt be maintained in particular cases, which we will consider in a moment.

In the Marxist tradition, however, the fact that the abandonment of violence or a militaristic outlook has generally been accompanied by a reformist ideological outlook was of great importance. This cannot be said of the late Engels. While admitting that the new weapons of which he was aware made the battle of the barricades anachronistic, to use his phrase, it nonetheless cannot be said that the late Engels was a reformist. His vision of socio-political change continued to be a revolutionary vision; in many other cases, however, the abandonment of the idea of violence as the necessary mother of social change was indeed accompanied by the adoption of positions that were no longer revolutionary but simply reformist. Hence the highly problematic situation for the Marxist tradition today, in the movements struggling for peace, and in the revolutionary movements, in the movements for social change. It is not a matter of simple theoretical problems. Anyone who has a bit of experience with revolutionary groups and formations – as, for example, it is quite possible to have with Salvadoran or Nicaraguan groups – is aware of the thorniness of this problem for the Marxist tradition today.

The problem is so difficult that at times it gives rise to naïve declarations that leave one wondering whether to laugh or cry, as was the case with the placard – which some will remember from a recent demonstration – that said 'armed struggle for peace' [*'lluita armada per la pau'*], which truly sounds paradoxical, an unacceptable paradox, but a paradox that reflects a real situation. It is a paradox not of hypocrites or fools, but rather of people who really find themselves faced with a serious problem, not people who come up with strange phrases, but people who truly need to respond to a situation no less paradoxical than the phrase with which they react [*contesta*] to it.

It will not be necessary to list all of the aspects of this problem. All of you know what they are. For example, how could one think of disapproving of armed struggle in El Salvador or in many other places, if one bears in mind, at the same time, what has been called – I do not know if the expression is still used – structural violence in that country, or in those countries, and police violence, political violence, understanding by 'structural violence' the violence exercised by the system itself in its economic development, in daily life, and by 'police' or 'political' violence that which is consciously exercised by those who possess power? It is obvious that one cannot merely take into consideration one side of that violence. Yet, on the other hand, this does not eliminate the depth of the problem, for one knows, at the same time, that in any of those places the conflict could become the spark that ignites a much greater conflict, at the end of which neither the Salvadorans nor the Nicaraguans nor the Americans would have anything to fight for, that is to say, a worldwide conflict with the armaments that now exist.

Faced with the enormous complexity of the problem as seen from the Marxist tradition's perspective, the peace movement tends to react in a way that may seem rather simplistic, but which is also quite solid as a form of consciousness. That is to say: with the conviction that all of that complexity to which I am referring is the fruit or expression of an anachronistic politics, of a way of conceiving of political issues that no longer works with the new weapons and humanity's new conscience. Anachronistic not only because, on the most basic level, it does not reckon with the enormous efficacy of the current forces of destruction, but also because, on the main level, the social and political level (and not the material level of armaments), it does not sufficiently take into account, so the peace movement claims, the mediocre if not outright bad results of almost all of the century's great social upheavals.

It is common, at least among some sectors of society that are actually on the Left (as is obvious), to immediately express in this connection a great disappointment with the results of the Russian Revolution. But it is not just a question of the Russian Revolution. What about the Mexican Revolution? The century's great revolutions still seem to be struggling within a *chiaroscuro* condition, about which the least that can be said is that they only represent in a very mediocre way the objectives for which the revolutions were made. Hence the evolution, in many left-wing milieus and even, for example, among the Marxist Left, and among the last remnants of what was the movement of '68 in Germany or in the United States, toward positions not merely connected with the struggle for peace, but of outright pacifism in both national and international affairs. One of the leaders of the German movement of '68, Rabhel, recently published an entire pacifist manifesto in this regard.

In this situation, former Marxists evolve toward positions of a certain intimism in personal life and in their conception of social institutions, a bit under the influence of Illich, who is an anti-Marxist, not a Marxist, but in any case quite influential in Marxist milieus, and under the influence of Gorz, who in another time was or sought to be super-Marxist and is now not a Marxist at all. They hold positions that in the last analysis are based on an acceptance of the current state of affairs, if not, as in the case of Gorz, half militaristic: pacifist with regard to the established order, and militaristic with regard to the Soviet Union. The most recent Gorz, already a long way away from *La morale de l'histoire* and those things from the 1950s and 1960s, proposes in practice acceptance of the idea that the capitalist system can only be perfected in the sense of giving greater autonomy to the individual for the production of that which is superfluous, reducing the labour time for the production of what is necessary and avoiding the intervention of the state. But if the individual only produces what is superfluous and if the state does not have to produce anything, tell me who produces what is necessary: the multinational corporations, obviously. It is a clear acceptance of the current state of affairs, while at the same time Gorz is almost openly calling for a crusade against the Soviet Union, which is the final result of the intimism of Illich, who many people on the Left believe, oddly enough, to be a revolutionary.

Others, however, while accepting the need for new approaches, explore different routes, whether it be the authoritarian method, as in the case of Harich, an important communist philosopher from East Germany, who imagines a world government assigned to solve once and for all the problem of peace (among others), or by other more or less authoritarian means, or by developing a federalist line of thought.

At any rate, this problem for the peace movement, the innovations in the new technologies of destruction and the very partial character [*relatividad*] of the century's great revolutions, is, in my modest opinion, open country for the Marxist tradition, as it is for any other, apart, of course, from the lunatic attitudes of those who think that the most normal thing to do is to continue along a realist path of increasing weaponry and that since there have always been wars it will not be possible to prevent there being more of them. When these primitive, and nowadays absolutely suicidal, ideas are rejected, any minimally responsible view has to acknowledge that here we really do encounter a field of unresolved problems.

Let us devote a few minutes now to the last of the three major new problems and corresponding new movements to which I have referred, the environmental movement. It has become quite common to see in the Marxist classics authors who were completely unaware of this problem, to think that Marx knew nothing about it and that what he did say was actually counterproductive. This opinion seems to be the view of even very intelligent, very highly educated people. Among us, for example, Joan Martínez Alier, who is a very competent man, appears to be convinced of something that is, in my opinion, a mistake.

The basis of this erroneous opinion is the conception of needs in the Marxist classics up to Lafargue. From Marx through Lafargue, to say nothing of later vulgar, common Marxism, it was apparently thought that the development, the perfection, of humanity rests fundamentally on an increase in its needs. Lafargue, one of Marx's son-in-laws, coined the famous phrase according to which the worst of the workers' harms was the fact that they did not feel any needs. It is obvious that he was thinking not of the needs that nowadays come to mind in the industrialised countries, but those that we can perhaps see in other lands. He was referring to the lack of a need for hygiene, for adequate food, for electricity, for ventilation in housing. In any case, this idea that the progress of humanity is the progress of needs seems to suggest a destructive notion of the development of economic life and everyday life, since a constant increase in needs ought to require or imply or entail a constant increase in production, with the resulting environmental and anti-ecological effects.

The other reason for holding that there was no sound thinking in the Marxist tradition in regard to ecological problems was the thesis concerning the basic contradiction between the forces and relations of production as the motor of historical progress. Marx's formulation rests, to put it very briefly, on the idea that history advances, as he wrote in *The Poverty of Philosophy*, through its worse side, that is, by means of the clash stemming from humanity's capacities, its productive forces, which within certain relations of production (i.e. within certain property relations and regulations) cause great evils, thereby arousing a revolutionary consciousness in their victims. For example, great industrial progress, while representing a potential for emancipation, for covering needs, and so on, entailed, on the other hand, such horrible living conditions for the early European working class transplanted from the countryside that it was supposed to provoke a revolutionary consciousness among this class; the terrible state of the situation would lead to a revolution by means of which this situation could be overcome. This assumed, then, that progress rests in a fairly fundamental way on, among other things, a constant development of the productive forces and, consequently, of production, an idea which today is usually regarded as a very anti-ecological idea, and as a policy of unreal, unbridled development, for it ignores the limitations on the earth's natural resources, the planet's limitations. It is, moreover, undesirable, given that it would entail a rapid degradation of our life environment.

The truth is, however, that the classics' thought in this regard is somewhat more complicated. We can say that there are at least two big, more or less dense chapters in Marx's works that do not tally with this picture. One of them is his long treatment of the conditions of the quality of life of the working classes. It is very well known and I am not going to dwell on it. It contains his detailed denunciations concerning the adulteration of the food eaten by the workers, the unhealthy conditions of their lives and work, and so on. But there is also another, less well-known text – despite being in a readily accessible place: it is in Chapter 15, Section 10 of *Capital*, Volume I – that deals with agriculture under modern industry. Marx develops there an argument of the greatest interest for our topic. On the one hand, he acknowledges that on being introduced in agriculture, large-scale industry boosts or greatly increases the population's revolutionary capability because it destroys the most traditional, most conservative peasant culture, and in addition, turns the peasants into urban labourers, that is to say, people with revolutionary potential. On the other hand, however, thanks to the long, serious studies that he had made of agrochemistry (Marx had read one of the founders of biochemistry, Justus von Liebig, and quite a few other authors, such as Von Frass, who were important for understanding questions related to agricultural chemistry), Marx realises that by this point it is already easy to understand that the capitalist mode of exploiting agriculture, as he says, lays waste to not only the worker, but also the soil.

Naturally, that is the downside of things; there is also an upside, which is the boost to the prospects for revolution deriving from the changes in, or alteration of, the population caused by its passage from the country to the city. Yet Marx points out that in this particular case, that of agriculture, the downside is much more serious than in other cases, for, as he literally states in Chapter 15 of *Capital*, Volume I, 'it disturbs the circulation of matter between man and the soil… [I]t therefore violates the conditions necessary to lasting fertility of the soil'.[5]

There exists an analysis, which he did not incorporate into *Capital*, in which Marx studies agricultural cycles that are autonomous (that is, independent of industrial and commercial cycles). He based his work on calculations borrowed from Liebig and other agrochemists regarding the time that the soil needs, or needed, to recover its usable mineral richness in the agricultural conditions of the time, and he reaches the following conclusion concerning technified capitalist agriculture:

> [A]ll progress in capitalistic agriculture is a progress in the art, not only of robbing the labourer, but of robbing the soil; all progress in increasing the fertility of the soil for a given time, is a progress towards ruining the lasting sources of that fertility… Capitalist production, therefore, develops technology, and the combining together of various processes into a social whole, only by sapping the original sources of all wealth – the soil and the labourer.[6]

5 Marx 1996, pp. 506–7.

6 Marx 1996, pp. 507–8.

It is clear that each age reads the texts of the classics, whether Marx or Kant, in accordance with its fundamental interests; this is the only way to explain why this text, which is in Volume I of *Capital*, the most widely read volume of *Capital*, seems not to have been read very much, and thus the claim that Marx never dealt with these things could be justified. The problematic aspect of Marx's text consists in the fact that having produced this analysis, Marx holds that the process is *inevitable* under capitalism. Marx believes that capitalism will completely obliterate the natural relation between man and nature without anyone being able to prevent it; that is, he professes a completely pessimistic fatalism, to which we surely cannot adhere today. A long period of time has passed since the era in which Marx thought the revolution to be imminent, and the accumulated environmental damage is so great that it does not seem reasonable today, one hundred years later, to keep thinking that it is necessary to wait for capitalism to end before doing something to restore the relation between man and nature. But Marx thought just that. When, in the same Chapter 15 of *Capital*, Volume I, he describes what, from that point of view, the new society will be like, he says:

> [W]hile upsetting the naturally grown conditions for the maintenance of that circulation of matter ['between man and the soil'], *it* [capitalism] *imperiously calls for its restoration as a system, as a regulating law of social production, and under a form appropriate to the full development of the human race.*[7]

It must be said that this cluster of reflections from Chapter 15, Section 10 of *Capital*, Volume I, is incredibly anticipatory. It is very common to hear that some prediction or other from Marx has not come true, but one really cannot cite any other sociologist or economist from the 1860s who was capable of describing what we have just read, which are things that occurred after the Second World War. The moment in which, for example, *agribusiness*, the American agricultural business, realised that the agricultural techniques then being applied were highly dangerous and began to export them and to take corrective measures occurred in the 1970s, not in the 1870s. This was one hundred years later, but in countries like ours no one seems to have noticed this yet.

In a controversial discussion in Madrid last week, precisely during a commemoration of Marx, one of these intellectuals – formerly a left-wing Marxist, of a party very much on the extreme Left – presented a defence of the Green

7 Marx 1996, p. 507, emphasis added.

Revolution and the use of insecticides and fungicides in great quantities, with the argument that they are necessary to feed the population, as if the problem did not require a global, dialectical treatment but merely that specific response of producing all of this now, without thinking about the consequences. Yet surely anyone who looked at yesterday's newspapers knows that thousands of tons of fruit have been returned to us from Central America because of a toxic excess of insecticides. It was in yesterday's papers. And in their trade relations with countries that produce monoculture or crops for export, the Americans themselves constantly ensure that the final product that the US itself has sold to these countries never reaches the US. Mexico is the most notable case. Mexico uses huge quantities of fertilisers and insecticides manufactured in Europe, in Switzerland, and even insecticides prohibited in all of Europe, and above all in Switzerland. The Swiss continually sell them in Mexico and in Latin America, and the Americans do the same. Yet when Mexican apples from Chihuahua reach the United States, the first control that they must pass is to determine whether they have traces of toxic American products, and huge batches are rejected.

I think that it is neither an exaggeration nor foolish devotion to say that this situation was foreseen in Marx's texts from Chapter 15 that I have just summarised. This is one of the most notable points. Nonetheless, what separates him from our current situation, what requires us also to reconsider Marx's theses on the problem and to create a new socialist environmentalism, is the fatalist thesis. As I said before, it seems to me that no reasonable person can continue thinking today that the politico-ecological solution is that which Marx stated – wait for the inevitable ecological disaster that capitalism is going to produce – because too many years have passed and the damage is already too serious. There is no choice but to take action now, and in the manner that people are taking action.

In Marx's immediate legacy this set of problems was lost. As I said a moment ago, it is as if the texts to which I have referred, despite being in *Capital*, Volume I, had been in some hidden notebook that no one had ever been able to find, for they were never cited until the ecological question [*problemática*] emerged. It can be said, however, that during the post-World War II period the Marxist tradition was not so poor in connection with this problem, just as it was not so poor in the case of feminism. There was a fair amount of interest and, it must be said, among *all kinds of Marxisms*, as much in revolutionary Marxism as in the Marxism of a more reformist sort. For example, among the German reformists there is a very noteworthy author, Eppler, a Social Democratic member of parliament who was at the same time an estimable writer, and, within radical Marxism, within revolutionary Marxism, we would have to note above all – or among others: there is always a value judgement in this – Harich's contributions, which I cited earlier, and those of Bahro. There are translations of Harich, and of Bahro too. The main books of both men have been translated. But moreover, there is the clear and intense presence of Marxist groups and organisations within the environmental movement.

At the end of this overview I would like to note a common denominator of a reasonable and vital socialist response to the new problems, which may perhaps strike you as a bit too philosophical and barely scientific, yet it strikes me as quite deeply rooted in the Marxist tradition. All of these problems have a common denominator, which is the transformation of daily life and of the consciousness of daily life. A subject who is neither an oppressor of women, nor culturally violent, nor a destroyer of nature is – let us not deceive ourselves – an individual who must have undergone an important change. If you like (I say this to attract your attention, although it is a bit of a provocation), it has to be an individual who has experienced what in religious traditions was called *a conversion*.

This is a realm in which there is no choice but to express oneself in terms that may strike you as a bit utopian; yet one must have the determination not to blush on that account: so long as people continue to believe that owning a car is fundamental, people will be incapable of building a communist society, a non-oppressive society, a peaceful society, a society that does not tend to destroy nature. Why? Because it is a question of *essentially* non-communist goods, as Harich would say. Imagine one billion Chinese, every family, with its car; or the four billion inhabitants of the earth, each family, with its car. That is unsustainable. The earth can only bear this if many do not have a car.

Take the example of the car. I could obviously take many others; I could take the decisive example, the US consumption of energy per capita, which is the decisive fact, but let us take the example of the car. The automobile can only work on the earth, so to speak, if only a part of the privileged peoples own an automobile. If you fill Africa, Asia, America and Oceania with automobiles, it is obvious that the earth will not bear it; the earth will not bear the atmospheric change. And the same is true of any of the other examples one might want to give.

The necessary changes require, therefore, a conversion, a change in the individual. And I should note here, so as not to fuel the suspicion that I have moved far away from the Marxist tradition, that the fundamental idea that the transformation of the individual is the basis, the fulcrum, of revolution is stated in writing in Marx's works, starting with the *Grundrisse*. In the *Grundrisse*, Marx says that the essential thing about the new society is that it has materially transformed its members [*poseedor*] into new subjects. The more analytical, more scientific basis of that transformation is the idea that in a society in which it is not exchange value but rather use value which is predominant, needs cannot expand without limit: one might have an *unlimited* need for money, for example, or for exchange values in general (to be wealthy, for power), but one cannot have an *unlimited* need for objects to use, for use values.

So, the final reflection that I have allowed myself, in a realm that might seem utopian, is, whether utopian or not, in any case quite overtly present in the classic initiator of the Marxist tradition, that is, in Marx himself. I will finish on that note, and I thank you for listening.

PART 3

Interviews

∵

CHAPTER 17

'Gramsci is a classic, he is not a fad': Interview with the *Diario de Barcelona*

Wilful and passionate. *Antonio Gramsci's political and intellectual activity is well enough known, and is the focus of attention when it comes to doing his biography. What was Gramsci like apart from those activities, how would you characterise his personality?*

He was quite short, and hunchbacked because of an accident that he suffered in his childhood. During a transfer, while already a prisoner, he was introduced to an anarchist, who refused to accept that such a small man could be Gramsci.

As a young man he was wilful and passionate. Prison and physical suffering made him quite neurotic, as they would anyone in his circumstances, or perhaps a bit more than they would anyone else. At the end of his life, the suffering abated and gave way to melancholy, and he was once again capable of writing stories, for example, and, in general, of talking to children.

What were the main elements that went into Gramsci's political development?

First, the experience of social ills. Then that of the organised labour movement, in Sardinia and, of course, in Turin. Then the Russian Revolution and the defeat of the revolution in the West. And, only last of all, what he learned in reading the classics of the emancipatory tradition, especially the Marxist classics.

The revolution in the West. *From 1921, the moment in which, as a communist member of parliament and party leader, Gramsci dedicated himself completely to the struggle against Mussolini's fascism, until his death in 1937, after 11 years of imprisonment – this entire period is characterised by active theoretical reflection, which is expressed in the* Prison Notebooks *and in the* Letters, *written from the successive prisons through which he passed. Briefly, what are the ideas and contributions that come out of this theoretical reflection?*

* Interview with the *Diario de Barcelona*, first published in 1977. Republished as '"Gramsci es un clásico. No es una moda". Entrevista con *Diario de Barcelona*', in *De la Primavera de Praga al marxismo ecologista*, edited by Francisco Fernández Buey and Salvador López Arnal (Madrid: Los Libros de la Catarata, 2004).

 | DOI 10.1163/9789004280526_020

Well, I don't think that Gramsci was already sure in 1924 that the main and immediate enemy was fascism. I believe that at that time, although he had already grasped that the revolution was not at hand, he continued to think of fascism as something fleeting and not very different from other forms of capitalist domination. I don't think that Gramsci could have corrected that euphoric error of the Third International before his imprisonment. On the other hand, he had corrected it by 1928, when the Sixth Congress of the International exacerbated that error to a catastrophic degree. That is the moment, in my opinion, in which his greatest contribution materialises: the explanation for the difficulty of revolution in the West. Others, chiefly Trotsky and Lenin, had already seen this fact. But Gramsci places that fact at the centre of his thinking and discovers in it the vital complexity of the, so to speak, Western state, that is, of the capitalist state that exists on the basis of a truly capitalist foundation, and is rooted in a society that has no contradictions with that foundation, aside from those that form a part of that mode of production. Let's leave it at that: I think it is better to underscore that central point than to recite a list of Gramsci's merits without our being able to dwell on any of them.

What role did Gramsci play in the international communist movement?

Before his arrest, Gramsci did a number of things of international importance: his help was decisive in imposing the policies of the International's Executive on the Italian Communist Party; and, later, in confronting the growing Stalinist style (only briefly, just before his arrest, by demanding that the majority of the Russian executive not crush the defeated minority, namely Trotsky). I say that he opposed the Stalinist style because Gramsci did not oppose the content of Stalin's policies. He defended them in his prison writings, though it is true that he did this by idealising them.

Once in prison, Gramsci was the object of international activity on the part of the communist, and in general democratic, movement. Incidentally, Barcelona – and, more precisely, Radio Barcelona while under popular control during the [Spanish] Civil War – can be cited honourably in this connection.

Gramsci fad. *In the last two years, a great deal has been said and written, particularly outside Italy, about Antonio Gramsci's contemporary importance. Above all, we have witnessed a considerable increase of interest in his political thought. What factors, in your opinion, explain this great interest?*

I have seen this and it has surprised me. When, in 1958, I published the first exposition of Gramsci's thought that had been written here, the only people who paid any attention to it, as far as I was able to find out, were the communist prisoners in the Burgos prison. And it was in one of the books most widely available in Spanish libraries. By contrast, the series on Gramsci in the Faculty of Geography and History over these past two weeks had an audience worthy of the reading of a good poem, because of its size and vitality.

With regard to the causes, I believe that it is impossible to answer with just one explanation. Each one is who he is. The Italian communists have almost always borne Gramsci in mind, perhaps because having a classic author of such fecundity in one's most direct tradition is something which provides consistency, identity. In other cases, the adherence to Gramsci is adherence to his propositions, or to some of them. Finally, in still other cases, it is not so much adherence to individual propositions as to Gramsci's attitude and aims, without forgetting their personal side: in short, to what is usually called, rather unfortunately, 'the method'.

Don't you think that there exists, paradoxically, the danger of lapsing into a dogmaticisation of his theory, a dogmaticisation which he himself fought against with a truly refreshing political line?

Of course. And it would be a shame, since Gramsci is one of the authors who least deserves that. First of all, one can only call his thoughts 'theory' in a very vague, almost etymological sense, in the sense of a vision; and, in addition, because his entire work – the written part and the active part – his method, as we say, is openness, a receptivity [*disponibilidad*] to experience in accordance with one's aims. Gramsci was – an interesting paradox – a typical 'philosopher of praxis' and, at the same time, the Marxist classic most capable of contemplation. Contemplation of the external and internal world.

Late last year, photos of Antonio Gramsci with the caption 'Antonio Gramsci, the Lenin of the West' were circulating in France. This and many other sorts of advertising could be regarded as the culmination of the Gramsci 'fad'. To what extent can we say that the same thing has begun to happen in Spain?

I don't know to what extent, but I also have the same impression. And I think it's regrettable.

Gramsci and Eurocommunism. *Lately, people have been turning to Gramsci's thought in looking for the sources of what has come to be called Eurocommunism. Do you find this assumption valid?*

Well, here we go again, as Forges would say. First of all, the word 'Eurocommunism' doesn't go beyond the level of precision of advertising language, so it is impossible for me to use it. And, secondly, Gramsci is a classic, that is, an author who has the right never to be in fashion and to be always read. And by everyone. This issue has already arisen in connection with the previous questions, if only obliquely. No one has the right to put a classic into the petrol tank, as if it were the tiger in the commercial. Incidentally, one cannot reproach the Italian communists at all in this regard: they were the first to say that Gramsci is not their own private property.

That's the essential thing. But in any case, so that it doesn't seem that I am trying to cover anything up, I'll add this: in Gramsci's work there is, of course, a valuable attempt to ground emancipatory thought and practice in the reality of full-fledged capitalism, a capitalism with its own foundation. However, assuming that the word 'Eurocommunist' means something precise, and that this something is the endorsement of a parliamentary road to another society and the rejection of the concept of the dictatorship of the proletariat, it can be pointed out that Gramsci never believed that the overcoming of capitalist society could be achieved by non-revolutionary means, and especially not by parliamentary means: everything that he called a 'war of position' was, for him, preparation for an inevitable phase of attack (inevitable if there is to be a social revolution, which, on the other hand, has been perfectly avoidable up to now). Nor did he think that one could avoid the regime of coercive liquidation of bourgeois property, which the Marxist tradition calls 'dictatorship of the proletariat'. Which does not mean, of course, that he identified that regime with a given state's methods and practices of governing.

CHAPTER 18

Manuel Sacristán Speaks With *Dialéctica*

You have made inroads in many different fields: the translation of various classic authors (Marx, Engels, Gramsci, Lukács); in the field of logic, we are familiar with your book on symbolic logic; in literature, we know of your work on Heine and Goethe; and we know that most recently you have been working on the importance of ecology for politics and the social sciences. We would like to know about the evolution of your theoretical concerns and what most interests you today.

The evolution of my theoretical concerns doesn't exactly correspond to what I've had to do. Let's take, as an example, translation. It isn't very nice to say it, but the fact is that I've translated in order to be able to eat. Under Francoism, I was expelled from the university for many years, and even during the periods in which I worked at the university my academic status was economically quite mediocre. So, I translated, and did editorial work, to subsist. Yet if, after translating for a certain amount of time, you have made deadlines and met certain criteria for quality, you can take some initiatives; by this means I was able to put into practice a modest publication programme, although only after several years of translating everything that was put in front of me.

As translation is very poorly paid and unstable work in Spain, it turns out that almost no one does it on a professional basis. When editors find a person who truly does translation on a professional basis, they end up allowing him or her a certain latitude for individual initiative. From the moment that that occurred in my case, I was in fact able to follow a programme that consisted in disseminating socialist thought, mainly from the Marxist tradition. At the same time, I translate quite a bit of logical and epistemological literature, which corresponds to my primary area of work in philosophy.

(I never liked the epistemology predominant in the Marxist tradition; I always thought that the minority schools of Marxism were better in that area. For example, between Bogdanov and Lenin, Bogdanov was right. I mean in the area of epistemology, not in the area of politics, in which Lenin was surely more realistic.)

In the work that I myself have written and signed, or published anonymously or with pseudonyms in the illegal communist press, I could not do

* First published in 1983. Republished as 'Manuel Sacristán habla con *Dialéctica*', in *De la Primavera de Praga al marxismo ecologista*, edited by Francisco Fernández Buey and Salvador López Arnal (Madrid: Los Libros de la Catarata, 2004).

 | DOI 10.1163/9789004280526_021

much of what I wanted to do. For fifteen years I was a member of the Central Committee of the outlawed communist party, and for ten of those fifteen years, a member of the Executive Committee. And this was all in very unusual and delicate circumstances: I was 'legal' in Spain – my documentation was all in order and I was a university professor or, at other times, a translator who lived as such legally. On the other hand, I was involved in a great deal of illegal activity, and in situations of great responsibility. That required a very great expenditure of time and energy. A person who is living legally, openly, and is nevertheless active underground must spend many hours covering his or her tracks – far more so than if the person were wholly underground and lived in a Party safe house. So I led two lives, which produced a kind of schizophrenia. It was a major handicap for lasting intellectual work. And so I consciously chose, as a formula for writing, the short text, the article, the essay, the preface. That has its pros and cons. I don't regret having worked that way, because in the last analysis it was a solution that allowed me to intervene quite a bit, despite the difficulty of my situation, in theoretical and political debate in Spain, legally and illegally. The first texts by Marx and Engels published legally in Spain after the Civil War were texts that I translated and published. They are texts on Spain by both authors, *Revolución en España* (Barcelona: Ariel, 1960). I translated the texts and wrote the preface – a preface of fifteen or twenty pages. Something that could be written in one or two days was my literary formula for the type of life that I led. It seems to me that there was no other solution.

That was not the only limitation on what I've written over all these years. There is another limitation, which is their generally occasional character. The great majority of my writings, apart from those that are pure diversion (which are the pieces of literary criticism), were written for an urgent Party discussion or some political or theoretical discussion, whether legal or illegal, going on in the country. For example, one of the few things of mine that have been translated into other languages (in this case Italian), the essay 'Three Lessons on the University and the Division of Labour' ['Tres lecciones sobre la Universidad y la división del trabajo'], was written at the request of a student and as an intervention in a debate between the PSUC's student organisation and a tiny group, the 'Student Strike Committees' ['Comités de Huelga Estudiantiles'], which maintained the thesis that the immediate abolition of the university should have been the demand of communist students at the time (late 1969). The majority of my writings are occasional pieces in the most literal sense: writings by request and for a specific date.

Those have been the two main limitations on what I've written. They are very serious limitations. Let me repeat, however, that when I look over the life I have led, I think it was natural for me to have acted that way; and if I had to begin again, I would probably do things the same way. There doesn't seem to have been any other possibility. The only two times that I wrote at length I had to interrupt my activity as a militant. It was when I wrote my doctoral thesis and when I wrote the manual of logic. It was clear both times that it was impossible to write a long text and carry out conspiratorial work on a daily basis. And earn a living on top of that. I think that I see clearly the limitations of what I have written, which has always been done with urgency. Knowing my situation, I thought very carefully about the questions before sitting down to write, but I then wrote in one sitting because of the fear that I would not be able to finish what I had begun if interrupted.

All of that concerns the past, which I believe counts for more, at my age and with my poor health, than the future. Yet that doesn't mean that I don't have projects.

At the forefront, in the centre of the things that I am doing – and not just me but an entire collective – is the journal *mientras tanto*, with which we are trying, very modestly (since we have never sold more than 3,500 copies of an issue), to prepare the way for thinking, from a socialist point of view, about new problems of contemporary civilisation. Problems unforeseen – and perhaps unforeseeable – by the classic authors, and caused by the development of certain modern productive-destructive forces, particularly technological forces. Our efforts take two directions. As the journal's editorial committee, we work on those problems analytically and theoretically; as a collective, we try to get the most responsive sectors of the unions – mainly Comisiones Obreras – to concern themselves more with these new problems and to move closer to the groups representing an alternative culture: anti-nuclear committees, environmental organisations, feminist groups; in general, countercultural groups that are not necessarily irrationalist and anti-socialist.

I should say that in Spain there is practically no right-wing alternative thought. In Spain, the thought predominant in alternative groups, in contrast to what has been the case in Germany and France, is almost exclusively socialist in a broad sense, that is, Marxist or anarchist. The work that we intend to do is, therefore, not necessarily impossible. In any case, it's difficult, and not only because of ideological difficulties, but also because of the strength of the economic crisis in all of Europe. These two things taken together – the crisis reinforcing the influence of the bourgeois way of life on the working class – often make it very difficult on the Left to pose problems that are in themselves decisive for the future. I'll give an example. The previous German Social Democratic government tried to pass legislation, a few years before the fall of Chancellor Schmidt, to abolish the asbestos industry. It was a question of one of the most carcinogenic industrial processes that we know of, and the product isn't harmless for those who use it either, although the greatest threat is, of course, to the workers in this sector. Well, the labour union and the employers' association came together as allies in opposition to this measure. This is only one example, but I believe that it is a good illustration of the problem that I am referring to. Capitalist civilisation has led us to a situation – at least in the advanced capitalist countries – in which important sectors of the proletariat are capable of defending the production of their own cancer in exchange for being able to replace their car at the end of the season. We have to face those problems head on; they can't be covered up.

I must say that in Spain the situation doesn't seem to be quite as difficult regarding these questions. For example, in the two major unions, those of Communist and Social Democratic inspiration (Comisiones Obreras and UGT), there are sectors that are not only ecologically oriented, but opposed precisely to the nuclear electricity industry. They see very clearly that it is not true that the nuclear industry promises jobs beyond the construction phase of the plants; they know about the extremely high cost of a nuclear kilowatt hour (hidden in the enormous state subsidies in funding and infrastructure, from the research phase forward); and they very clearly perceive the military interest of the supposed 'atoms for peace'. So, the situation is quite a bit better than in France, where the union with a communist majority is foolishly pro-nuclear in every area, even the explicitly military area, and only the CFDT has a sector responsive to the new civilisational problems. (And it has experience in this: the CFDT is the main union active in the French plant for reprocessing radioactive waste in La Hague.) Nor does there seem to be a very strong awareness of these problems in the main German union, the DGB, although there is such awareness in sectors of the SPD, the German Social Democratic Party. This party even includes some of the most important authors in this sort of research on the socialist treatment of the new civilisational problems; among them I should emphasise Eppler.

The collective behind the journal *mientras tanto* is working analytically and politically, and within the limits of its modest means, in this area.

Would environmental proposals lead to a reformulation of the strategy followed by the communist parties?

I think that it's preferable to study the question on a level deeper than that of strategy, and logically prior to it. I believe that the problem of the conception of the role of the development of the forces of production in their tendential clash with the relations of production contains a series of questions that require reconsideration. So that we understand each other: I believe that the Marxian model of the role of the forces of production in social change is correct; I believe that known history substantiates the Marxian conception, which is coherent on a theoretical level and plausible on a historical, empirical level. So I don't think it's necessary to revise those theses. Nor do I intend to proceed as Croce did at the beginning of the century, producing a kind of stocktaking, according to which the Marxian model worked well until the twentieth century, but no longer works. No; that distinction between the past and present, besides being imprecise, strikes me as insufficiently established.

Another kind of distinction between past and present would be relatively justified: one that adopted Marx's work itself as a watershed, that is, one that focused on the potential gaining of awareness – specifically by the working class and therefore also by the human species – of the efficacy of those forces of production in social change. To the extent that gaining that awareness facilitates a certain power over those forces, we could say that the situation changes starting with Marx, at least intellectually. However, that does not, in my opinion, negate the validity of Marx's schema regarding these questions. No, the new development does not consist in the fact that we have discovered that the model is false. The model is adequate. The new development is the fact that we now have reasons to suspect that the social change at whose gates we stand is not necessarily going to be liberating merely because of the effect of the dynamics, which we are now considering, of a part of the Marxian model. We have no guarantee that the tension between the forces of production-destruction and the relations of production that exist today must give rise to emancipatory prospects. The very opposite could also occur. I once gave the following example to clarify what I mean in this regard. In conservative thought there are utopias, perspectives that construct an exceedingly oppressive, hierarchical and exploitative (because they oppress in order to exploit) future on the basis of giving free rein to the most problematic productive-destructive forces of advanced capitalism, in particular that revered panacea, the golden calf of all developmentalist optimism, which is the energy of nuclear fusion. Think, for example, of Adrian Berry's utopia, *The Next Ten Thousand Years*, which Alianza Editorial translated a while ago. I don't know if you were curious enough to read this monster. Adrian Berry's perspective is opposed to the Stockholm manifesto, *Only One Earth*. Berry argues that to say that there is a single earth for the human species is to uphold an obscurantist thesis contrary to the progress of science and technology, for there are actually many possible earths for humanity. Therefore, there is no need to curb the indiscriminate quantitative growth of the species, whether demographic growth or growth in production and energy consumption. And he indicates the route by which he thinks that in the next ten thousand years humanity will be liberated from all limitations on indefinite expansion in every direction. That route begins with an authoritarian unification of humanity. Berry assumes that this will occur by means of one or more nuclear wars. (One may assume, even though the author does not say as much, that the aim of those wars is to destroy the USSR and subjugate the non-White peoples.) Once humanity has been unified, we will undertake the colonisation of the moon, and the devastation caused on earth by the unifying wars will be compounded by that which is caused by the immense generation of energy necessary for the lunar enterprise. In addition, we will be allowing an indefinite growth of the human species. Once the moon has been colonised, we will break up, by means of nuclear explosions, the largest planet, and the one most appropriate for the aims pursued by Berry, Jupiter. Once Jupiter has been broken up, some of its parts will be good for colonisation, while other parts will serve as solar reflectors for the rest of the fragments and for the moon itself. After the conquest of Jupiter, we shall be able to go beyond the planetary system. By that time, the earth will presumably be devastated as a result of the billions of human beings and the operations that will have been necessary to carry out the Jupiter enterprise.

The first critical reflection that occurs to me is: If it is so easy to make Jupiter and the moon inhabitable, why not keep the earth inhabitable? Surely that would be even easier. Next, the political conditions of Berry's plan for conquest seem clear enough: an authoritarian regime and an extreme hierarchisation, controlled by those who direct the cosmic enterprise.

That is one example of the problematic situation that the efficacy of the developing productive-destructive forces pose for a socialist perspective today. It is obvious that the development of the productive-destructive forces that we are considering would clash with the relations of production, but it would not be in an emancipatory sense; rather it would be in the sense of demanding different, more tyrannical relations. Of course, this does not affect at all the theoretical value of Marx's propositions. But it does pose a new problem.

On what level, then, do we see the need to revise the predominant tradition in socialist thought? As I already said, not on the theoretical level. The tension between the forces of production and the relations of production continues to be something that can be realistically confirmed and that has considerable explanatory capacity with regard to known history, the present, and the possible future evolution of the present. In this connection, it is good to remember that, at the cost of a certain ambiguity, the Marxian schema is not deterministic. There have undoubtedly been versions of a deterministic tendency in the work of certain Marxist authors, like Bukharin, or rather anti-Marxists, like Loria. However, that is not the case in the main Marxist traditions. So, the plausibility of the Marxian schema, with its non-deterministic character, on the one hand, and the plainly ambiguous potential of the productive-destructive forces developing today, on the other, suggest that the level on which it is necessary to revise a certain progressivist optimism of eighteenth-century origin, present in the socialist traditions, is the level of political assessment. The problem is how to react politically when faced with the present tension between the developing productive-destructive forces and the existing relations of production. And I think the main part of an adequate solution consists in distancing oneself from a simplistic response based on an unshakeable faith in the emancipatory direction of the development of the productive-destructive forces. If we wanted to formulate this in a philosophical manner, we could suggest that it is a matter of breaking with the residue of Hegelianism, which urges us to have faith in the supposedly objective laws of historical development. To the contrary, we would have to understand that today a socialist programme does not require (and perhaps never required) primarily the development of the productive-destructive forces, but rather requires that we control them, and selectively develop them, or curb their development. And if we prefer to say the same thing in a more imaginative fashion, we could begin by noting the obvious inadequacy today, given its naïveté, of Lenin's famous phrase, according to which communism is the soviets plus electricity. It is not clear that the famous Dnieper dam has brought us much closer to communism. One might suspect, rather, that the rigid organisation of society for the production of these kinds of works has contributed considerably to the destruction of the soviets.

All of these considerations lead more or less directly, at least for me, to the conviction that the self-critical revision of socialist thought today must tend to reinforce the importance of the subjective revolutionary factor instead of objectivism, which is of Hegelian origin but was paradoxically proclaimed by the most anti-Hegelian philosophers, like Della Volpe or Althusser, in the 1960s. The bad thing is that precisely the presumptive revolutionary subject, whose function we need to underscore, finds itself in a very poor situation today in almost all of the advanced capitalist countries. Yet it seems to me that placing the emphasis on the subjective element is one consequence of my analysis that I cannot avoid.

A socialist politics with respect to the contemporary productive-destructive forces would have to be quite complex and proceed with what we might call 'dialectical moderation', selectively pushing ahead and pulling back, with socialist values fully present at every moment, so that it could calculate precisely the ultimate 'socialist costs' of every development. That politics would have to stay as far away as possible from simplistic yet apparently radical programmes, such as the progressivist simple-mindedness of unchecked development and the romantic simple-mindedness of obstruction, pure and simple. The first programme does not offer any socialist security, but does offer a very high probability of suicide. The second one is, for starters, impracticable. Let me illustrate this in terms of the most fundamental of all the contemporary, objective productive-destructive-forces, namely science.

Science, in the contemporary sense, is socialised knowledge, with a more or less immediate technological influence. Its intrinsic danger as extremely efficacious knowledge derives from this latter fact: the excellence of physics as knowledge, for example, is the basis of nuclear and chemical weapons. The romantic reaction to that fact, which consists in trying to undo what has been done, and, in practical politics, in blocking research, is, I think, to begin with, unviable, besides being undesirable. History shows quite well that all attempts to block research in the eras about which we have knowledge have totally failed: from Galileo to, unfortunately, the proposal for a moratorium on genetic engineering presented by Crick and other Nobel laureates about ten years ago. On the other hand, that policy is not desirable either, for what characterises contemporary techno-science (like all knowledge in fact) is not its alleged goodness or evil, but its constitutive practical ambiguity. For example, the same genetic engineering for which they requested a moratorium in light of the risks involved in manipulating certain viruses and the nightmare, still a long way off, of political interventions in the human genetic makeup, is one of the main hopes in the fight against cancer.

From the political-moral point of view, science is ambiguous, so to speak, if we don't want to use the word 'neutral', regrettably demonised in certain milieus on the Left (in which people barely remember which author proposed that the word 'swine' [*canalla*] be used for those who practice science with any interest other than one that is purely scientific, namely Karl Marx, and not some positivist). From a political-moral point of view, the products of science are ambiguous and bear within themselves a risk that is probably proportional to their epistemological quality. It is not true that nuclear physics practiced by socialist scientists is less dangerous than that practiced by capitalist scientists. It may turn out that the applications are better in a socialist society, but that derive not from the structure of the knowledge of nuclear physics itself, but rather from the socialist society.

I would like to point out briefly that none of what I have said in this connection has any affinity with apparently parallel developments, appearing today or thirty years ago, which criticise the Marxian conception that we are discussing. I am referring to Kostas Axelos and Jürgen Habermas. I don't agree either with the insertion of Marx's thought into the Heideggerian conception of the fate of metaphysics – the essence of Axelos's critical vision – or with Habermas's strange, to my mind, speculation, which, besides accepting the thesis, which I consider impracticable, of a blocking of the development of the productive-destructive forces, separates the realm of work from the realm of communication, with the traditional philosopher's capacity for ignoring the most glaring facts: there is no work without communication, and perhaps the most characteristic communication of the human species, structured language, was born precisely in work, as Marx suggested, by the way, in *The German Ideology*. My claim has to do with a political conceptualisation and not the history of metaphysics (which I consider arbitrary and unverifiable) or philosophical anthropology (a kind of speculation which I think is almost as irresponsible as the other kind). It's in the political realm that we need to eradicate the elements of eighteenth-century progressivism and Hegelian objectivism present in Marx's legacy and, through Marx, in numerous Marxists.

Here we come up against the limits of Marxian thought.

I don't think Marx's last word on all of the questions that we're discussing is entirely clear. Despite his aim, which he always had, of producing a finished work in the literary sense (which is one of the reasons why he left many unpublished manuscripts), Marx died without completing his ideas, without attaining peace with himself. This must have had to do with the fact that the last part of his life coincided with an important transition in scientific knowledge. The year of Marx's death, 1883, was the year in which Dilthey's *Introduction to the Human Sciences* appeared and, above all, the year of the publication of Mach's *History of Mechanics* and the two essays by Podolinsky in *Die Neue Zeit* on thermodynamics and the law of value; they included concepts that Marx was not able to consider, but address problems that Marx himself perceived more or less clearly and which, in my opinion, gave pause to the late Marx. In the letters of the late Marx you can find statements that must have been surprising for many 'Marxists'. We're now used to several of them, for example, Marx's attitude toward the Russian village community. Today we know that Marx wrote to Vera Zasulich that the Russian village community could be a road to socialism and that it was not true that the road through capitalism was the only one possible, as the Russian Marxists thought. Nor are we surprised by Marx's statement, in that very same letter, according to which he had studied the development of certain peoples, namely, those of Western Europe. But let's not forget that when Riazanov found that letter by Marx (among Plekhanov's or Axelrod's papers, if I'm not mistaken), he didn't think that it was authentic, and he only published it after he had found the draft in Marx's handwriting. Riazanov was really very competent. No less surprising for the Marxist *vulgate* are some of the late Marx's considerations and reflections to which I am inclined to attach some importance, for example, melancholy considerations rejecting the introduction of the railroad into the Rhine's tributary valleys.

People will say that these are statements in letters, that they cannot be compared with *Capital*. Of course they cannot be compared with *Capital*, but they are also significant. There is an abyss between the Marx who wanted the US to invade Mexico once and for all in order to incorporate it into world capitalism, and the Marx who would have preferred that the railroad stop in the major Rhenish cities and not continue to make inroads into the peasant countryside. (What would he have thought of the Nazi highways?) There is a distance here that is not theoretical – that is, it does not refer to the *explanation* of what is real – but political, as it refers to the *building* of the new reality. I admit that such reflections from the late Marx – the letter to Vera Zasulich or the letter to Engels on the railroads – have opened up for me the possibility of thinking that there is no contradiction between maintaining the Marxian model with regard to the effect of the development of the productive-destructive forces and their clash with the relations of production, and a socialist political conception that does not place its trust blindly and indiscriminately in the development of the productive-destructive forces, but rather conceives the function of socialist management – to say nothing of communal management – as the administration of those forces, and not as a simple removal of the fetters that the current relations of production impose upon them. I think that once it has been formulated in those terms, it turns out to be obviously consistent with the idea of a socialist society, with a regulated society.

You have mentioned that many of Marx's theses are not only objective in a scientific sense, but also to a great extent remain valid today. But what are the Marxian ideas that definitely belong to the nineteenth century and are therefore outdated?

In my view, it is mainly a matter of questions that have to do with cultural sensibility. The philosophical and political elements of Marx's thought are to be found in the realm of values (on a mental level) and class struggle (on the level of reality). Content of this sort is not invalidated in a logical sense; it is neither 'demonstrable' nor 'refutable'.

On a strictly scientific level, it is possible to review Marxian propositions that more or less lend themselves to doubt or invite rejection, either as a result of criticism of their internal consistency or because of their inadequate empirical foundation. And it is also possible to find Marxian propositions that are of little relevance for the analysis of the contemporary world, without it being possible to consider them false on those grounds; rather, they would be like counterfactual conditionals. Those are all types of natural outdatedness in non-formal scientific contexts, that is to say, in all real science.

However, it seems to me that the elements of Marx's thought that are least fruitful for socialist thinking today are those that have to do with the cultural sensibility of a man from the second half of the nineteenth century, who in many respects did not go beyond the cultural norms of his era. I am thinking of several things, from certain aspects of his idea of personal behaviour to elements of his political expectations and including his perception of socio-historical events. I'll give an example of what I mean. In the personal realm, for example, the fact that the person who was in all probability his biological son – and, to top it off, his son with Helene Demuth, the family servant – received the name Frederick, in order to make people believe that he was Engels's son. This incident reveals a sensibility in regard to family life that has very little to do with a desirable contemporary socialist sensibility. On a political level, I think of the optimism with which Marx in the 1860s and 1870s ignored (probably because of the acrimony of the struggles within the IWA) the anarchists' most pessimistic suggestions concerning questions of power. And on a socio-historical level, the example that I am most interested in is the practical assessment of the development of the productive-destructive forces, a question that we have already dealt with at some length.

I think those cultural limitations are the elements of Marx's thought that most bear the stamp of his era and are most outdated.

To what extent is there in Marx's thought a basis for an explanatory theory of politics in the contemporary sense?

I think that Marx's idea of explanation is mainly historical. Marx thought that the knowledge most worthy of the name is historical knowledge. I believe, therefore, that the most Marxian way of answering the question would be to see if Marx's system or model facilitates an explanation of the genesis of what the State is today. On the other hand, if what we mean by 'explanation' is what is today current in the philosophy of science (which is of predominantly analytical influence), it is difficult to claim that there is in Marx's work an explanation of that sort. I'm not saying that one cannot forge a Marxist explanation in a nearly analytical sense. But I don't think that it would be the most Marxian explanation.

To continue with the idea of outdatedness, in one current of contemporary Marxist thought the Marxian way of understanding the dialectic seems to be regarded as contradicting the scientific core of his major works. Is the dialectic outdated in this sense?

I don't have a historical answer to that question. I mean that I'm not sure what Marx thought the dialectic was in the end. You'll recall that when Engels began to gather Marx's papers after Marx's death, he wrote to Bebel to say that the main part of those manuscripts was a treatise on dialectic. That shows, first of all, that Engels had not looked at those papers very carefully when he wrote to Bebel, and secondly, that Marx's close friends thought that what Marx was writing in his final years was on dialectic (so that Loria's spitefulness, in assuring that Volumes II and III of *Capital* did not exist, perhaps reflected the belief of many other people). The question of what the late Marx thought dialectic meant is of great interest to me, and I enjoy studying this question very much. However, I don't have any solid results yet. My own opinion on the dialectic, which I believe is inspired by Marx's scientific work, can be expressed in one negative thesis and one positive thesis.

The negative thesis says that the dialectic is not logic. We have to reject the Hegelian confusion between logic and experience. The Hegelian dialectic is bad logic (because it requires that logic yield real content) and bad experience (because it forces experience to submit to a logical schema from within, so to speak). It brings together the worst of both worlds – the formal and the empirical. Incidentally, the infallibilism with which a certain tradition has viewed the important question of the development of the forces of production, which we discussed earlier, comes precisely from that spurious Hegelian mix of the logical and the empirical, the rational and the real. The dialectic is not logic, and when it is presented as logic, when someone tries to demonstrate something on the basis of, for example, the 'law of the negation of the negation', it's either embarrassing or laughable, starting with Engels. His example of the grain of barley, according to which the ear of the cereal can be explained as the 'negation of the negation' of the seed, is the prototype of bad Hegelian, obscurantist thinking, since we begin to know when we forget such pseudo-explanations and pseudo-methods of that sort and fathom the grain of barley with chemistry.

This does not mean that I scorn such an obscure idea of dialectic, or its vague and extremely trivial 'laws'. In my opinion, those ideas belong to a fruitful and important class of mental creations, which it would be bad to lose. It consists of the vague, quasi-poetic thought with which philosophers have described, in their circumlocutions, everyday, pre-scientific experience. Some of those concepts are poetically felicitous; others less so. 'Negation of the negation' is less so, but it belongs to the same family of other formulations which are more felicitous, like the phrase from Aristotelian epistemology, according to which the soul is 'in a way all existing things', which claims to 'explain' why the spirit knows reality. Or the ideas of potentiality and actuality, of matter and form. They are concepts that secure and exalt common everyday experience. We all know that if a body changes its state, it is because it could change, on account of its 'potentiality'. The fecundity of those vague philosophical phrases – apart from their beauty, when they can claim beauty – is that they can suggest, by articulating common knowledge, questions and inquiries. (Galileo 'measured' atmospheric pressure for the first time in an attempt to specify the reach of another one of those notions, the 'horror of a vacuum'.)

Therefore, I do not scorn the 'laws of the dialectic' as philosophical propositions with a greater or lesser capacity for articulating common, everyday knowledge. I do think, however, that passing that off as logic or scientific method has been a disaster.

Yet Marx himself believed that his conception and method were the dialectic…

Here we run up against words. When we use words like 'method', 'demonstration', 'definition', and so on, today, at the end of the twentieth century, we are referring to instruments that have been refined to a great extent, and formalised or made quite precise. When a philosopher from the nineteenth century (like Marx) says 'method', he is thinking of 'a general way of thinking', an intellectual style. When we say 'method', we are thinking of, for example, the method of the adjustment by least squares or, in the material realm, the method of the lead chamber process to obtain sulphuric acid, or (again on a formal level) Quine and Gentzen's method of natural deduction. In short, we are thinking of artefacts that have been made so precise that their operations can be described as a standardised succession of steps, such that any competent professional can repeat them in the same order and with the same result. That is not 'method' for a philosopher from the nineteenth century, who only knew, with that degree of formalisation, the mathematical operations that he had mastered and who was, on the contrary, accustomed to using the word 'method' in connection with the general operation of Kant's, Hegel's or Aristotle's thought. Therefore, asking what Marx understood by 'dialectic' requires that we undertake a study of this sort of subject: the general operation of his thought, its intellectual style. If, instead of doing this, we look for precise rules, we will run into the scientific silliness of quantity and quality, the negation of the negation, the major discovery that everything moves, etc.

My positive thesis is that 'dialectic' does mean something, contrary to what has been claimed so often by the analytical philosophers, for example, Popper or Bunge. 'Dialectic' is a certain intellectual labour, which, on the one hand, is present in science, and yet, on the other, goes far beyond it, in the dual sense that it operates in ordinary, pre-scientific knowledge and in another type of knowledge, methodologically beyond scientific knowledge. That type of intellectual labour has existed as a (rather obscure) programme in European philosophy of knowledge since German historicism; it finds its speculative realisation in Hegel and seeks an empirically plausible realisation in Marx.

The dialectical style consists mainly in aiming at a goal for knowledge which had been formally excluded by philosophy of science since Aristotle, on the basis of the principle, explicit in some eras and tacit in others, that 'there is no science of particular things', of the concrete. On the contrary, both Hegel and Marx, each in his own fashion, have a research programme that seeks knowledge of something particular or concrete. In the case of Marx, it is existing capitalist society. I do not mean by this, of course, that in *Capital* there are no powerfully abstract elements, nor am I denying that the concept of 'mode of production' is an abstraction, nor am I denying that what is theoretically constructed is an abstract artefact. However, despite that, what is created in *Capital* – and even more so in Marx's work taken as a whole – has a level of concreteness foreign to the traditional ideal of science, so effective in the natural sciences. *Capital* is not reducible to the formulation of categories, like 'mode of production', 'socio-economic formation', etc., but is also an attempt at an integral understanding of a specific historical phenomenon (hence the importance of the historical expositions in what was the only book wholly written by Marx), as the author himself wrote to Vera Zasulich.

I think Marx tried to carry out that dialectical programme, though quite unknowingly. In the Epilogue to the second edition of *Capital*, when he comments on the criticism that he had received, Marx states that he had proceeded, first of all, as any other scientist would, that is, establishing the facts and their necessary connections; and he admits that we may, if we like, read *Capital* as one piece (as we would say) of ordinary empirical research. But Marx did something more: once he had all the data ordered and connected – and that is all that we could ask of a scientific theory in the usual sense – he sought to reconstitute, in a way that he himself once described as an artistic totalisation, the concrete whole that he was studying. I believe that this is the reason – which quite consciously comes to the surface in Marx's correspondence – why on a certain occasion he rejected the idea of publishing the book in instalments, arguing that his writings, whether good or bad, always aimed at comprising an artistic whole.

It seems to me that this is the key to the dialectical programme (whether or not Marx thought it out): the search for a type of knowledge that uses the products of 'normal' science in a way that integrates them 'artistically' into a concrete totality that evokes the real (historical), concrete phenomenon that one is studying. The articulation of the relationship between science and dialectic consists in the possible integration of the scientific results within a description that is dialectical. However, once this has been achieved, the dialectical point of view intervenes on the inside of the scientific work in a narrow sense, orienting the perception of relevant facts or aspects for the purpose of a future totalising articulation.

So then, in Marx there is a 'normal' scientific core and a philosophical, cultural – perhaps political – conception, which constitutes the dialectic?

What is dialectical appears on the purely contemplative level. If we wanted to use the word 'science' in a broad sense, as the tradition did and not as it is commonly used today, we could say that the dialectic, the totalising, concretising vision, is also science. However, if, for the sake of the correct understanding among people, we prefer to use the word 'science' in the predominant sense today, then we must say that the dialectical concretising is more a philosophical objective than a scientific one, closer to a view of the cosmos than to a formalisable theory.

It is also possible to think of the dialectic, as I already hinted at before, as a somewhat imprecise tradition that begins to equip itself with the means for attaining exactness – and not merely philosophical goals – with the appearance of certain contemporary techniques, for example, set theory. Perhaps this doesn't exhaust everything that the philosophical idea of dialectic has come to mean since Plato, but it does capture well one aspect of it. For example, when we call a model of interactions 'dialectical', it is clear that we are thinking of something that can be perfectly captured by systems theory, including the characteristics that are typical of the Hegelian and Marxian dialectic, namely the capturing of change. It is obvious that systems theory does that in a much clearer way than Hegel. Nonetheless, I believe that that does not exhaust the realm of 'the dialectical', at least as Marx practices it, because in his work I see an intent to concretise that goes beyond what he might achieve by means of systemic analysis: a historically precise concretion that fully individualises the object.

The most recent efforts to explain Marx as a 'normal' social scientist have been those of Della Volpe and Althusser, yet in our view they have resulted in antinomies. According to what we are hearing, you are looking for a new solution to the problem.

That's what I'm aiming for. I respect Althusser's efforts – more *Pour Marx* than the sleepwalking obscureness of *Lire le Capital* – and especially the efforts of Della Volpe, who was working during a very inauspicious time. To clarify the different stages in the formation of Marx's thought – a programme that Gramsci was the first to formulate, in jail, without being able to even consider its execution – and to identify the legacy of Hegel as burdened with obscurity and anti-scientificity, despite its fruitfulness in other respects, was a programme worthy of applause. However, I think in both cases the programme was vitiated by those authors' weaknesses. One of these weaknesses was their separation from everything that the twentieth century had contributed in terms of philosophy of science. Della Volpe and Althusser found themselves in the unpleasant situation of having to reinvent the analysis of science developed in the twentieth century. In addition, since they succumb, to a large degree, to the prejudice that holds that the existing philosophy of science cannot be valid because it is bourgeois philosophy, they rediscover Mediterraneans but call them by a different name. They rediscover the analysis of theory and experience, but they can't call them that because that is bourgeois philosophy and, to cap it all, Lenin wrote his worst book against Mach and empirio-criticism. And it's clear that Mach is an unavoidable link between Kant and twentieth-century philosophy of science. That is their first weakness. The second is their apologetic bias.

I think that one finds the rational route for interpreting Marx's work if, to begin with, one abandons the apologetic urge and studies Marx against the backdrop of his time, which can be done knowing that there is, first, an aspect of Marx's work as timeless as the New Testament or Garcilaso's poetry, which is his work as a philosopher of socialism, as a formulator or elucidator of socialist values. And secondly, if one breaks away from the remnants of what we might call Zhdanovism or Lysenkoism, and stops confusing the question of the origin of a cultural product – in this case, contemporary philosophy of science – with the question of its validity. Not in order to believe that philosophy of science is going to be valid *en bloc*, an absurd proposition if we bear in mind that in contemporary philosophy of science there are several schools alive and kicking and incompatible in many things: the most neo-positivist tradition, represented today by Carnap's disciples; the more purely analytical and anti-positivist tradition of the Popperians; the structuralist view originating in Sneed's work; the influence of Kuhn and Feyerabend … It is not a matter of viewing the philosophy of science *en bloc* as a true or false doctrine, but as an area of research which is not at all superfluous and which we must develop, since it is an obscurantist prejudice to hold that because it arose in this phase of capitalist culture it cannot have any validity whatsoever.

If those two prejudices – the apologetic prejudice and that which has to do with the analysis of theories and experience – are overcome, one is no longer a hostage to the dilemma between glorifying Marx's supposedly purely scientific literal meaning and an impassioned rejection of his work when one discovers that not all of it – far from it – fulfils the formal requirements of science today.

Yet there is also another problem: all of those authors in the philosophy of science draw frequently, if not exclusively, on the natural sciences, and there is always something that is at odds with the social sciences.

It's true; the majority of twentieth-century philosophers of science are people who come from the natural sciences or mathematics or logic. It is also true that the majority of them are conservative, and some of them have a bit of trauma, like Popper, who must still remember the young communist he once was. However, there is something more important, which is the polysemy of the word 'science'. 'Science' has meant many things, even in recent times. In our era, its usual usage has been highly influenced by physics and also, more recently, by biology. One consequence of this is that when the majority of philosophers of science speak of the social sciences they only refer to a very modest stretch of social knowledge, namely the most formalised or formalisable, a few things from economics and econometrics, psychometrics and sociometrics, linguistics and not much else. This problem does not have any easy solution – far from it. On the other hand, however, I believe that there is room for methodologically simple recommendations: the social scientist should not worry much about the fact that in his or her field there are no consistent bodies of analytical-philosophical subtleties such as those that exist for the natural sciences. The social scientist should cheerfully embark upon his or her work, without any great philosophical-methodological worries, because if there is no good philosophy of the social sciences, it is probably because there are no social sciences that are very good. More than 700 years ago, Hugh of St. Victor began his *Dialectic* by pointing out to his readers that people spoke before there were grammars, and reasoned before there were any treatises on logic. Presumably there will have to be solid social science before there is good philosophical analysis of it.

You have said that there is in Marx a philosophical dimension that is predominantly political, but are there other dimensions that are also philosophical?

Without question. There is an entire metaphysics, in the contemporary sense of the term, that is to say, a series of philosophemes that go beyond the reach of Marx's positive scientific conception, which, in this field, is indebted to Hegel, Feuerbach, and the philosophy of the eighteenth century, besides other, less obvious influences, such as that of Leibniz. All of that forms part of Marx's culture, and is surely among the least enduring parts of his thought.

A final question about the current development of Marxism in Europe, and one that touches on the well-known theme of the crisis of Marxism. In a conversation with the editors of Dialéctica, *Perry Anderson said, in connection with this subject, that from the theoretical point of view there had been, in recent years, a great deal of development, and so from that point of view there was no crisis, but for those aspects concerning political practice there was a crisis. In the last few years we have seen a regression of Marxism in Europe. What are the fundamental causes of this phenomenon?*

There are two arguments in favour of Anderson's opinion. First, the fact that he notes the theoretical development of Marxism. The other is the fact that a theory is not indissolubly bound to a practice. Stalinism spread the very opposite idea – the idea that a theory dictates a practice, and only one practice (and vice versa) – quite widely. That is a mistake: any theory can, in principle, yield countless practices (although naturally not all conceivable practices). With the same elementary mechanics, we have two techniques for achieving one purpose (namely, raising a weight): the lever and the crane. They are different techniques, but they have the same theory underpinning them.

So, Anderson's opinion is well reasoned: the theory has been developed to a great degree, and it is not unambiguously responsible for the practice. Yet, the thesis nonetheless leaves me unsatisfied – and even more so precisely when I think about Anderson's country: British Marxism strikes me as one of the most learned, penetrating, and intelligent in the world, but the British Marxist movement strikes me as one of the weakest in the world. It is not especially conclusive to say, 'Marxist theory has been developed quite well, the trouble is that Marxist practice has collapsed', because while practice does not uniquely dictate theory or vice versa, it is still the case, as I said earlier, that the Marxist tradition is not a pure theoretical tradition. It's a political tradition, a conscious, organised intervention in the class struggle, on the basis of a scientific foundation in the narrow sense and an even broader foundation of a philosophical nature. Of course, there have been and are academics who have worked on Marxist problems without any political concerns, but that is not the essential part of the Marxist tradition, but is rather a marginal phenomenon (and one which hardly occurs in Europe, although it is, I think, of some importance in Mexico). So, the practical crisis of Marxism, the ebbing of practice, strikes me as a fact of great importance for the complex historical phenomenon that is Marxism. Perhaps we could preserve the truth of Anderson's assessment by speaking of the defeat of Marxism in Europe (and where has this not occurred?)

I'm not capable of listing the causes of this state of defeat because I have neither enough empirical material nor the appropriate research techniques. We philosophers are encyclopaedic ignoramuses, ignoramuses required to think about everything. Nonetheless, like any citizen whose eyes are open, I can see some of those causes. I believe that the most important cause is the USSR's disrepute among large sectors of the European working classes and the extinction of the remnants of the revolutionary aspirations that still existed within Social Democracy after World War II. One would also have to point to the important draining of Socialists and Communists that took place in Europe. We often talk about the six million Jews exterminated by the Nazis, but very seldom about the Socialist and Communist cadres murdered in Central Europe. Their number is estimated at 600,000 in Germany alone: an entire generation. That matters, as does, in the case of Spain, the death or exile of almost all of the Socialist and Communist cadres during and after the Civil War.

Only after noting that would I consider the mistakes and defects of the communist parties, the main people keeping up, at least in the form of an aspiration, a Marxist tradition. There have been, without a doubt, many mistakes and defects. But without trying to generalise and limiting myself to the Spanish experience, and despite the fact that my disagreements with the PCE were ultimately so great that I had to leave the Party, I think that that Party's state of extreme defeat is better explained by the retreat of the working class in the face of the crisis than by its debits in the balance of history. I would even go so far as to say – in examining the errors it made – that the most serious of all the PCE's mistakes was not any of the ones that led me to leave the Party, but that strange passion for neurotic, hopeless self-criticism, as a result of which it seemed to be the only social force without, so to speak, a right to its own original sin, or that the Communist Party was the only force whose original sin was forever unforgivable. I think that the Party's foolishness in the self-critical assessment of its own past – it was blinded by values that are either plainly or ambiguously bourgeois (from the exalted parliamentary democracy to hobnobbing with the upper class in the lounges of the Hotel Palace) – has contributed a great deal to fracturing the political identity of the labour vanguard in Spain. This sector endured quite well some elements of self-criticism that were serious, but it started to lose its bearings to the extent that the process of self-criticism began to become something that instead resembled an explosion of self-destructive exhibitionism.

I don't think that we can generalise from the Spanish experience. In Europe there are still Communist parties that are extremely averse to a self-critical examination of their long history – the Portuguese Party, for example, and, to a lesser degree, the French Party. In any event, let me repeat that despite my deep disagreement with the PCE's policies, to say nothing of those of the PCF, I believe that the causes of their crises go far beyond the mistakes and defects of the leadership in these Parties, and reflect a state of defeat among the working classes. I think that we need to start from this realisation in order to continue the struggle clear-sightedly.

CHAPTER 19

Interview with *Naturaleza*

Why, as a Marxist, are you interested in ecological questions? Why form a green party?

There are several Marxisms. And not merely in the most strictly scientific (economic and sociological) respects, in which change over time is normal (since there is no real science – that is, science that is not purely formal, like logic or mathematics – which is not in permanent revision), but also in the philosophical, evaluative and political respects. Well, one feature common to all Marxisms is the criticism of this society and the attempt to rationally identify the elements and agents of a possible just and emancipated society. Within those two contexts – the criticism and the programme, so to speak – the concern with the environment inevitably arises today.

As for the formation of green parties, I don't think that one can state a categorical thesis for all cases. I don't even think it is correct to adopt a position of principle for the German case. And the German case is the clearest one: there is no left-wing party of any importance there which promotes revolutionary thought and includes ecological questions, whereas there are, on the other hand, traditionalist circles of right-wing origin that converge with groups from the radical Left, or the remnants of such groups, within the environmental movement. It's a situation that seems to demand the formation of a green party. Apart from this, political practice seems to be ratifying the formation of this party: in the recent elections for the Federal Diet [*Bundestag*], the Greens obtained 7 percent of the votes cast, practically the same amount as the Liberal Party which forms part of the government, while the radical left group that had obtained the most votes from the end of the World War II up to now – the German Peace Union [*Deutsche Friedensunion*] – barely ever exceeded one percent on the federal level. Nonetheless, I don't think that the need to form a green party is beyond dispute even in Germany.

Do you think that environmentalism can operate in isolation from social struggle, for example, in a green party?

The main reason to doubt the advisability of forming a green party is precisely that environmentalism cannot operate, as is obvious, in isolation from

* First published in 1983. Republished as 'Entrevista con *Naturaleza*', in *De la Primavera de Praga al marxismo ecologista*, edited by Francisco Fernández Buey and Salvador López Arnal (Madrid: Los Libros de la Catarata, 2004).

 | DOI 10.1163/9789004280526_022

social struggle. Even a minimal environmentalism clashes with vested interests, as soon as it goes beyond mere landscape conservation, and even then.

What has prompted some people in several European countries to believe that it is necessary to organise an environmental party is the fact that the most traditionalist sectors of the radical Left continue to think of social struggle – in part because of contamination by capitalist progressivism, in part because of ignorance, and in part because of mental laziness – as unaffected by the civilisational problems to which environmentalism is a response. It is necessary to consider, at one and the same time, two aspects of the situation in which we find ourselves: on the one hand, the future of the human species – which is the main question for any revolutionary thought – fundamentally depends on the way in which the problems that I have just mentioned are resolved; on the other, an ecological practice immediately clashes with the present mode of production. It seems that the uniting of those two aspects ought to easily resolve the question, showing revolutionary groups that they must be environmentalists and environmentalists that they must be socially revolutionary. Yet it doesn't always happen this way, because of the weight of each group's traditions. And it is right to acknowledge that the psychological difficulties are often serious. The new problems that have given rise to the environmental movements often require quite traumatising revisions of certain traditional points of view on the Left. For example, the ideal of a simple and universal democratisation of the goods present in daily life, if one understands 'democratisation' as unrestricted enjoyment. One relevant case is the traditional enjoyment by aristocrats and the wealthy of the best coastal spots of a densely populated country, such as the coasts of the Spanish, French and Italian Mediterranean. From the moment in which access to Catalonia's Costa Brava was democratised, for example, what had been a paradisiacal pleasure became a stupid stay in a noisy cement landscape. The modest people who today can afford a week of vacation in Tossa de Mar are not enjoying the same thing as the few rich people who had a house there fifty years ago enjoyed (and that's why the rich go to other places, of which there are fewer and fewer). Traditional leftists only focus on the fact that – to use this example – there are still many people who cannot spend a vacation on the Costa Brava. The pure greens focus only on the fact that it is no longer worth getting those vacations. It is a question of two manifestly one-sided ways of thinking, which will not succeed in solving the problems.

Having accepted this, whether or not the formation of a green party is advisable, or whether, on the contrary, it is more appropriate to make environmental propaganda the work of inter-party groups and movements that attempt to influence the labour parties, is something that needs to be decided on a case-by-case basis, without positions of principle that cannot be modified.

How do you view the environmental movement in Europe and the United States, and how do you view it in the Third World?

The environmental movement everywhere comes up against obstacles rooted deeply in people's psychic makeup, firmly moulded by two hundred years of bourgeois progressivist ideology. One must not think that the only obstacle is the urgency of unmet basic needs in the Third World. First of all, there are also pockets of considerable poverty in the industrialised countries. Secondly, the deep-rootedness of bourgeois progressivist values constitutes, in the industrialised countries, as important an obstacle to an ecological consciousness as the lack of food in central Africa might be. I have spoken of the depressing example of the asbestos industry in the German Federal Republic many times, but it is so instructive that I don't mind repeating it. At the end of the 1970s, the Schmidt government prepared a bill that envisaged the abolition of the asbestos industry in four years. One of the most carcinogenic industries there is. The bill was withdrawn due to the joint pressure of the employers and the asbestos *workers*, who were fearful of losing their jobs and apparently resolute in preferring lung cancer to a tough period, which of course would not have been one of physical hunger, but only one of a transitory reduction in their standard of living, that is to say, what the bourgeois mentality calls 'standard of living'. (The bill envisaged gradual job substitution and funding for research and development of substitutes for asbestos).

In the industrialised world, the primary political task of the environmental movement is to make the labour Left see that, on account of environmental problems, some of their short-term interests come into conflict with their medium- and long-term interests, as is illustrated very well by the example of the asbestos industry that I have just repeated. And this task of analysing the opposition between short-term and long-term interests, with the resulting effect on the consciousness of the revolutionary class, is a classic task of revolutionary Marxism. I think that it is necessary in the so-called Third World to make people see that a large part of the misfortunes, even the failure to satisfy basic needs, is due not to so-called backwardness but to the irruption of capitalist ways of producing and consuming that have destroyed the old economic fabric and its functionality, without offering another equilibrium. In this area as well there is a horrible example to cite, which is the spreading of transnational corporations' powdered milk – especially Nestlé's – in Black Africa, which has resulted in an important reduction in the mothers' lactation capacity and an increase in the infectious gastrointestinal illnesses among children, because of the preparation of this milk with non-aseptic water, which is commonly drunk in those places. Or the more complicated example of the Green Revolution, for which Mexico was a guinea pig. These days it seems clear that the energy yield of that industrialised agriculture, with its large inputs of synthetic fertilisers and pesticides, is lower than that of the most modest *chinampa* [floating garden] or that of an old maize field, to say nothing of the toxic effect, built up in the food chain, of numerous insecticides, herbicides and fungicides, or the troubling long-term effect of the standardisation of seeds, of the loss of genetic variety. Yet on a psychological level as well, the harm, which will last a long time, has already been done. It will be extremely difficult to convince people of that truth: the Nahuatl *chinampas* are preferable to agribusiness from almost every point of view, and, above all, from the most important one – avoidance of serious risks for our species in the future.

In short, though with different problems, the environmental mission faces the difficulty that every revolutionary undertaking faces, which is the same in Sweden as in the Congo.

How much does the environmental struggle in the First World help the struggle in the Third World?

I think that for now, and for quite some time, there will be no direct assistance. I believe that the best assistance in this realm is indirect: it involves the peoples of the Third World seeing – as Gandhi did, even though his heirs have disregarded his vision – that the capitalist mode of production (including, of course, its basic technical aspects, uncritically inherited by the Eastern European regimes) produces rather sinister products, along with others that are, without question, worth preserving.

How do you view the First World countries' concern with the nuclear problem?

The first and most serious ecological problem confronting the species, above all in Europe, is the nuclear-military problem. Nonetheless, the ecological-political awareness of that problem is quite inconsistent, even within the European Left. In France, for example, the situation is disastrous: socialists and communists, as well as figures on the anti-communist Left, like André Gorz, are victims of the nationalist sickness and have supported the nuclear military policy (the autonomous French *force de frappe*) of all French governments, from De Gaulle and Pompidou on the Right to the Socialist-Communist government of Mitterand. In Germany, England, the Scandinavian countries, Italy and Spain the situation is clearer. In these countries there is no pro-nuclear Left in the military sphere and there is a large anti-nuclear Left in the civilian sphere, whereas the entire Right, from moderate to fascist, is pro-nuclear in both spheres. (The environmental groups of German conservatives are the only important exception.) In Spain, the anti-nuclear movements are largely responsible for the fact that in the two big unions representing the majority of the workers, Comisiones Obreras and the Unión General de Trabajadores, as well as in the anarchist union, Confederación Nacional del Trabajo, there are important anti-nuclear sectors of workers, who know that the real cost of the nuclear kilowatt-hour is much higher than what the electricity businesses say (on account of the enormous state subsidies in infrastructure and in funding research and development); that the jobs created by that industry are scarce and temporary; that it is doubtful whether the normal, light water reactors will pay for themselves within the twenty to thirty years of life that they are estimated to have; and that the military interest in obtaining material for the Bomb plays a decisive role in states' nuclear energy programmes.

Would you claim that there is an antagonism between technology and environmentalism?

There is no antagonism between technology (in the sense of techniques with a theoretical-scientific basis) and environmentalism, but rather between technologies that destroy the conditions of life of our species and technologies that are favourable to it over the long run. I believe that one must pose things in these terms, not with a poor mystique of nature. We must not forget, after all, that it may be the case that we are able to live thanks to the fact that in a distant past certain organisms that breathed in an atmosphere loaded with carbon dioxide polluted their environment with oxygen. It is not a question of ignorantly adoring a supposedly pure and immutable nature, good in itself, but of preventing it from becoming unliveable for our species. It is quite difficult as things are already. Nor must we forget that a radical change in technology is also a change in the mode of production and, therefore, in consumption, which is to say, a revolution; and that for the first time in known history it is necessary to cause that revolutionary technological change consciously and intentionally.

Do you believe that science popularisation has been an important factor in the boom in environmentalism?

It certainly has been, without question. For most of us who are trying to promote an ecological politics without being biologists – but rather are economists, or engineers, or philosophers, or architects, etc. – good biological popularisations have done us a great service by facilitating the first steps toward interpretations of ecology. The same thing could be said about the people who did not have enough mathematical training to take an interest in ecological models.

How did the idea of founding the ecological communist journal mientras tanto *arise?*

It arose from the desire to contribute to the reception and working out, within the Spanish Left, of the new civilisational problems that we have been mentioning. The journal's collective comes, almost in its entirety, from the Communist Party, from the Communist Youth and from other smaller communist parties, but the scope of its collaborators and readership today extends to several kinds of environmentalist milieus: anarchist, feminist and, in general, countercultural milieus.

What is your opinion of André Gorz?

André Gorz – perhaps better known by his journalistic signature of Michel Bosquet in *Le Nouvel Observateur* – had many achievements in ecological politics over the years, but his recent evolution has left me concerned and perplexed, above all because of its open call for the violent overthrow of the Soviet regime, something which in the current world situation could only be brought about by means of a world war led by the United States government and nourished by Yankee big capital. Gorz has gone so far as to admit this, and has reproached the German liberals *of Der Spiegel* for placing the avoidance of nuclear catastrophe above the liberalisation of the Soviet regime. According to Gorz, that instinct for preservation is due to the fact that the Germans do not love freedom. His position strikes me as insultingly unfair to the Left and to the German liberals and, moreover, absurd and suicidal. Worse still: suicide for millions of Europeans whose opinion Gorz has not requested. On the other hand, his latest political formulations strike me as leading to an acceptance of world domination by the great transnational corporations. Indeed, if one limits, as he asks, the power of the state but grants basic communities economic responsibility solely for the sphere of 'the production of the superfluous', as Gorz says, and this without any revolution but rather by the decision of the powers that be, as we read in his *Ecology as Politics* utopia (reprinted in *Farewell to the Working Class*), then I cannot see how we can prevent big transnational capital from totally controlling 'the production of what is necessary'. And I believe that this sad ending to Gorz's supposedly libertarian thought is due in large part to his acceptance of Ivan Illich's ambiguous privatism.

And what is your opinion of Rudolf Bahro, who abandoned a communist party and helped to found a green party?

Rudolf Bahro's intellectual career is very interesting. If one reads *The Alternative in Eastern Europe*, the book he wrote in prison in the German Democratic Republic (where he had been responsible for training officials in the communist party, the SED) carefully, it will be obvious that when he began to write it, he did not have any idea of environmentalism, and was even subject in part to the bourgeois ideology of industrial efficiency. However, in the course of his purely formal-political and economic critique of the systems of Eastern Europe, Bahro came up against environmental problems, almost certainly because of the influence of the true pioneer in these studies among Communists, the likewise East German Wolfgang Harich. Once in exile in the West, Bahro first attempted – rather naively – a unification of the West German Left, and later sought its integration into the environmental movement. After numerous failures, he realised that both projects required a period of maturation and contributed to the creation of The Greens [*Die Grünen*]. I already mentioned earlier the reasons for which Germany seems to be the European country in which the existence of an environmental party is most justified.

CHAPTER 20

Interview with *Mundo Obrero*

From your position as a philosopher and scientist, how do you view Spanish society in late 1984? What do you think of the most recent changes?

It's very difficult to answer such a radical, comprehensive question. Obviously, I cannot give a sociological analysis just like that, in merely answering a question, quite apart from the fact that that is not my function either. What one can do, I think, is point to the main features of the situation from one's own point of view.

For a person with my background and my convictions, there can be no doubt about it: the main feature of the situation is the collapse of the Left. This is the situation's decisive feature. I must say, although it may seem smug, that I saw it coming. I had been a member of the PSUC's Central Committee since 1956 and a member of its Executive Committee for more than ten years, as well as being a member of the PCE's Central Committee. In the summer of 1970, there was a very important plenary meeting that I will never forget, because it was the moment when I decided that I could not continue working there. I said quite clearly then that we were heading toward a collapse, that if we continued like that we would fade away. As for the PCE, a policy like the one it represented could have only one real political outcome, if it was going to be the policy (I didn't agree with it, but it was the only one that would have been a real policy): merger with the PSOE. And this, years later, was what Santiago Carrillo would say in an interview with Oriana Fallaci.

That was not an idea that appealed to me. I was not in it for that, of course, but in any event that would have been a policy. What has actually been done is nothing, neither that nor the opposite of that, nor anything else that could be sustained as a policy.

Viewed very subjectively, and very much from the position that I occupied as a Communist militant, the most painful part of this whole development was the complete collapse of the PCE on the basis of a lack of policy, something *which could already be seen in the 1960s*. People who were not especially smart

* First published, in an abridged form, in 1985. This was Sacristán's last interview. Republished as 'Entrevista con *Mundo Obrero*', in *De la Primavera de Praga al marxismo ecologista*, edited by Francisco Fernández Buey and Salvador López Arnal (Madrid: Los Libros de la Catarata, 2004).

 | DOI 10.1163/9789004280526_023

had already said so. I am not especially smart as a politician, but I had already realised this in 1970, and I said so. I really don't say this out of arrogance; I say it as a way of letting off steam, because this was very painful and, in addition, it was the fundamental damage. The PCE's collapse is this country's greatest misfortune. There is nothing to compare it with; that is the source of it all, the source of the collapse of the entire Left.

I forgot to mention another aspect of the situation, which is the PSOE's treachery. But anyone who is surprised by the PSOE's treachery has never read any history. That is what a Social Democratic party is made for – to prevent the triumph of the workers; that's what the Socialist Party is made for. Not from the very beginning by any means, not when it was the Second International, but certainly ever since there has been a Third International. So, since the PSOE's backsliding had to be taken for granted, was a given, the PCE's collapse must be seen as the decisive cause of the Left's collapse.

There were also less momentous things, but which were likewise very important. In following that strange policy, which was in fact a lack of policy, the PCE's and PSUC's leadership ended up doing astonishing things. For example, the Centre de Treball i Documentació [Work and Documentation Centre] (CTD) in Barcelona has preserved some documents from the era of working underground, and among them you can see a report from a member of the leadership in Paris which is a monument to political foolishness. In the letter, he announces the good news that they are axing the PSUC's organising within education – I was still in the Party at the time – because, it seems, we were proving too revolutionary or too leftist for him, and for that reason he thought that liquidating the movement was perfect. That letter is in the CTD, you can read it; this is not a legend. So, it went as far as acts of madness like that, which are a sign of a complete lack of political intelligence, a lack of thought, a lack of authenticity.

As a matter of fact, things of that sort had occurred much earlier. I remember that in 1958 we began to prepare, in the committee of intellectuals of the PSUC in the interior,[1] something that we called the 'First Congress of Catalan Culture', which had been thought out very seriously, as something very important, with commissions working in different areas: language, geography, history, science. Then, the person who at that time served as our link to the Executive in Paris thought that what should come out of all this was a piece of paper with lots of signatures, instead of a real congress, which is what we wanted. On that occasion, we in the interior won out and there was a congress; we did something quite serious because it the first time under Francoism that

1 That is, within Francoist Spain [Ed.].

nearly three hundred intellectuals had been mobilised as an opposition. Yet the leadership was of the opinion that what we needed to do was gather a few signatures, display them, and that would be the end of it. In short, there were many crazy actions like these.

In any case, these crazy actions were secondary. The main thing, in my opinion, was the lack of a consistent policy, and perhaps also important – it is very painful to say so – was the lack of personal nobility, which is revealed in actions like the ones I have just mentioned. You have to have very little capacity as a leader, which did not prevent them from having great capacity as militants, who fiercely and heroically endured interrogations. In enduring clashes with the enemy most were of a very high calibre, yet in thinking about things quality was clearly lacking. But let me say again, the essential thing was the nonexistent policy.

Starting from the fact of the PCE's collapse we could begin to draw concentric circles over Spanish society as a whole (I apologise for speaking this way, like an old man, but the fact is that I am an old man; I must speak about my recollection, I don't have any other choice). The first wave, so to speak, would record the fact that we overestimated the education of the working class during our period underground. That seems clear. We had reasons for deceiving ourselves, for believing this. For example, in 1964 or 1965, the then leaders of the Italian Communist Party, those who would later go on to found *Il Manifesto*, were here. Rosana Rossanda, for example. We showed these people very little of what we had organised, extremely little, and the little that they saw was, they said, more than they had achieved in Italy under Mussolini. So, we had reasons for believing that we were going to be a very important force. This belief was mistaken. It later became apparent that the Spanish population was actually much more ideologically dominated by forty years of dictatorship than we had thought. That seems clear. But we didn't see it; we just didn't see it.

We need to add to this that the Party leadership's work with the intellectuals was a disaster. It is impossible to invent a better procedure for ending up without any intellectuals than the one that the leadership came up with. One must bear in mind the incredible fact that in 1966, 1967 and 1968, the PSUC's core of intellectuals – to restrict myself to Catalonia, which is what I know best – was still the strongest. We almost had hegemony. A communist intellectual was slipped into every publication, in every place there was at least one if not several; and it went from there to a complete lack of intellectuals. Taken together, these two things make for a fairly bleak outlook.

Taking a step further outward from what was the history of the Party, I must say that there is not an important communist presence in the new social movements either. These movements are something very important... and, unfortunately, quite confused. The lack of political thinking is obvious. Right now, within a few days, the Green Party is going to be founded and there is already a split before it has even been created; and many environmental groups are convinced that this party should not have been created yet, that the founding of the party is premature and the product of opportunisms. I'm not saying that that is true; I'm not sure. But I am sure that more than half of the environmental movement thinks that. Consequently, this birth is in all likelihood really a miscarriage.

So what I mean to say is that I see a very bleak outlook, in terms of the prospects for renewal at this moment. The PCE hardly exists, the working class seems to be quite far removed from an active class consciousness, and the alternative movements are ill hatched. So, the truth is that there are not many reasons for being optimistic.

That's from a political point of view. From a more sociological point of view – I am not especially competent here, since it is not my field, but in any case ... – the consequences of a total subordination of Spanish economic life to that of the US are already visible. And that will surely have quite serious consequences, whose full scope we haven't seen yet.

How do you view the PSOE's evolution in recent years, up to the moment of taking power and, after that, in the last two years of its government?

Well, the truth is that I myself am not at all surprised. And I am not at all surprised because of general historical considerations. They have always done the same thing. From the time they assassinated Rosa Luxemburg (or from the time they defended the assassination, so that no one says later on that I'm making a false accusation), from the time they covered up the assassination of Rosa Luxemburg up to the present they have always done the same thing. That's the case in general terms. But more specifically, the fact is that those of us who were in the anti-Francoist movement know very well who the prominent figures in today's PSOE really are. For example, when we managed to destroy the SEU and Franco invented something called the Asociaciones Profesionales de Estudiantes (APE) [Professional Student Associations] in order to prevent the Sindicato Democrático [Democratic Union] that we were creating from coming into being, some individuals who are important in the PSOE today voted for Franco's APE. In other words, it is not just a matter of European history or the usual history. We knew these people and, since we knew them, what has happened has not surprised us.

The group to which I now belong, which puts out a journal, *mientras tanto*, consists almost entirely of former Communists, of people from the PSUC, and the fact is that what the PSOE is doing is not a surprise for any of them. If other communists are surprised, it is because they didn't really know what the PSOE was. I don't mean, of course, the tons of – well, not quite tons, but many – honest militants in the PSOE. I don't mean that, but rather the Social Democratic spirit and the actual Social Democratic leadership. So I'm not surprised at all. They absorbed the international impetus *to prevent* the Communist Party from moving forward. That was their only aim during the Transition. And, unfortunately, they achieved it.

What particularities do we find today within the political and social behaviour of Catalan society as compared with Spanish society? Could you say something about what Catalan nationalism represents with respect to Spain?

To be honest, I think that the Iberian nationalisms are very much alive, all three of them. Paradoxically, the one that is probably least alive is Spanish nationalism (this is why I didn't say four), and in the following sense: in the case of the Spanish nationality, the nationalists are right-wing, including many people in the PSOE, but truly right-wing. By contrast, in the other three nationalisms, nationalism is not exclusively right-wing – for obvious reasons: because of centuries of political or physical oppression – but there is in fact also left-wing nationalism, as one Catalan political group's very name indicates; and I think that the vitality of the peninsula's three non-Spanish nationalisms is such that – although this may sound utopian – the situation will *never* become any clearer so long as there is no genuine exercise of the right to self-determination. So long as that does not occur, there will never be clarity here, neither here [in Catalonia] nor in the Basque Country nor in Galicia. Only if we meet that apparently utopian requirement of complete, radical self-determination, with the right to separate and form another state, and then see what the peoples say when presented with such a clear, unequivocal choice – only that would allow us to one day re-establish a good, clean situation, whether it be that of a federal state or that of four states. But in any case, with clarity.

It seems to me that no matter how much you think about it, no matter how many political and juridical techniques we use in trying to organise something different from that, it will never come out satisfactorily. That will always be a justification for the greatest evil afflicting Spain, which is the army: this is the country's fundamental problem.

Today there is apathy [desmotivación]...

Or – sorry – perhaps instead of 'army' we should say *political army*, like the one we have.

Not a professional army.

No, a political army, like the one we have.

There exists among people today, among the various social groups, an individual apathy [desmotivación].

I'm afraid that's right, if I have to judge things by my modest, direct experience at the university, and in this Department [of Economics]. In reality, my experience has not been continuous, because I began as a professor in 1953; and they eliminated me in 1965. In a brief period of democratic administration, when Estapé was rector in 1972, they rehired me. I was laid off again at the end of 1973 because there was a change of rector and the new one was a very fascist type; I didn't return until the death of Franco. Which is to say, there were gaps in my experience. But if, despite this, I can offer an opinion about these 30 plus years of the University of Barcelona, I would say that I have never seen a time of greater political lethargy, not even during the whole of Francoism, or what I have seen of Francoism in the university since the 1950s. We face great political lethargy. Here I teach fourth- and fifth-year courses in the Economics Department – which is a department in the social sciences, a department directly linked to socio-political problems – and, nonetheless, I don't think that there are, among all of the students with whom I am working this year, more than seven or eight who take an interest in Catalan or Spanish politics. The situation is *worse than ever.*

Was there, during the period of the Transition, from the death of Franco until 1980, more activity?

Yes, there was a great deal of activity; there was quite a bit of enthusiasm. For example, and this is something that is particularly painful for me, in those years there was an important development of the educational section of Comisiones Obreras within departments. We had assemblies and meetings in order to form the union and then, once it had been formed, we could get, without much of an effort at mobilisation, 300 people in the main lecture theatre. That's quite remarkable. Nowadays, on the other hand, there is no union life at all at the university.

In addition, the political parties have abandoned political activity in the university.

That too. I don't know why. You can't really accuse them of having abandoned this activity, but we can say, at the very least, that they don't achieve much of anything. There are some members of parties: a few communist youth here, some socialist youth there, a minimal representation of what were the most radical communist parties (the MC, the LCR, maybe someone from the

POSI), but that's it, one or two; it doesn't go beyond that, and they're not in a position to do anything.

But it is not just the parties. Here's a disastrous example: last week, or a week and a half ago, student assemblies were organised here to discuss the statutes for students in the Department. From all of the students who come in the afternoon, who couldn't number less than 3,000, 30 appeared at the assembly. From all of the afternoon students, from the first year to the fifth! It's true that the afternoon students are people who work, in the morning or until mid-afternoon; there are many employees of insurance companies, of banks and savings and loans. But at other times, those who attended an assembly to vote on statutes would not have been merely 30 out of 3,000.

I don't have the figures for what happened in the morning. Perhaps it was better in the morning, but I haven't had the chance to find out.

Does the university in general, and the universities in Barcelona in particular, have much real importance in Spanish society today?

Until now the universities in Barcelona have had very little. There have been efforts to make it have more, but Barcelona is a city full of life of another sort, not university life but commercial and industrial life. It has always been a city with important centres of extra-university culture, even in the cultural dimension (painters, musicians, even writers in the Catalan language who had nothing to do with the university), though perhaps less so now. That has meant that Barcelona's universities have had even less importance in Barcelona than Madrid's universities have had in Madrid, to say nothing of the importance of the University of Salamanca in Salamanca or the University of Valladolid in Valladolid. It has less importance.

Still, there are quite a few efforts to establish greater links to society, not so much on the part of the University of Barcelona, but by the Polytechnic University, because some of the Polytechnic's departments have a very direct social application [*inserción*]: industrial engineering, architecture, computer science, chemistry and physics; even biological sciences have a direct application in industry. Others, however (mathematics or philosophy, for example), much less so. And the latter, philosophy, is not applied on the level of a department but rather individually, and in a way that is perhaps not especially healthy.

What are your plans for work?

I am currently studying the relationship between the methodology of the social sciences and the methodology of the natural sciences, as well as its relationship to mathematical logic and to the formal sciences. Also, the topic of the dialectic. Then, much later on, when I have finished with these topics, I have some other things.

Apart from this, I always participate, time and again, in the debates on the pacifist movement, in which I am quite interested. An article on this is going to appear in the next issue of our journal. It consists of some notes in which I intervene in the debate on questions of war and peace between Thompson, who has a programme for European nuclear disarmament, and [Jan] Sabata, a Czech professor and dissident.

One subject that I still haven't abandoned, although one day or another I'll have to abandon it, since you can't always be doing this, is what we might call 'Marxist philology', the review of Marx's thought. I have already published four or five pieces in the journal involving a rereading of Marx. The classics are always worth rereading.

From your point of view, what is the hope, the alternative – not merely political, but also on the level of ideas – for Spanish society today?

I don't know, since I think the situation is very bleak, just as I described it earlier, very bleak. From my point of view, which is a social left point of view, I don't think we can recover in the short term – far from it. I don't think it's possible. I don't think that the communist parties – the PC or the MC, LCR or the rest of the left parties – can recover, nor do I think that the alternative movements have caught on yet; and unionism, which is something very important, doesn't seem to be making any progress either. The membership numbers for CC.OO. and UGT are more or less frozen where they were. The same holds for CNT; numbers are low for all three groups. They are very low for the CNT, and the numbers for CC.OO. and UGT are low for a country like this.

To be honest, we simply have to endure, we have to endure. I don't see any other option for the near future. Let's say 'endure', and also make as much left-wing propaganda – communist propaganda, that is – as possible. It's a disgrace, outrageous, that in the midst of a capitalist economic crisis like few others, a crisis of immense brutality, the propaganda turns out to be capitalist; the ideological hegemony turns out to be capitalist in the midst of a disaster like the one we're living through. Millions and millions of people out of work is compatible with the euphoric hegemony of capitalist ideology. It's infuriating, but that's the way it is.

Further Reading

1959, 'Prólogo a *Revolución en España* de K. Marx y F. Engels' ['Preface to Marx and Engels's *Revolution in Spain*']
1967, 'La formación del marxismo de Gramsci' ['The Development of Gramsci's Marxism']
1968, 'Cuatro notas a los documentos de abril del Partido Comunista de Checoslovaquia' ['Four Notes on the Communist Party of Czechoslovakia's April Documents']
1968, 'Por qué leer a Labriola' ['Why Read Labriola?']
1968, 'Sobre el uso de las nociones de razón e irracionalismo por G. Lukács' ['On G. Lukács' Use of the Notions of Reason and Irrationalism']
1969, *El orden y el tiempo: introducción a la obra de Antonio Gramsci* [*'Order and Time: An Introduction to the Work of Antonio Gramsci'*]
1969, 'Checoslovaquia y la construcción del socialismo' (entrevista con *Cuadernos para el Diálogo*) ['Czechoslovakia and the Building of Socialism' (interview with *Cuadernos para el Diálogo*)]
1970, 'El filosofar de Lenin' ['Lenin's Philosophising']
1970, 'Lenin y la filosofía' ['Lenin and Philosophy']
1970, 'Russell y el socialismo' ['Russell and Socialism']
1971, 'Agnes Heller' ['Agnes Heller']
1971, 'Sobre el "marxismo ortodoxo" de György Lukács' ['On George Lukács's "Orthodox Marxism" ']
1972, 'Sobre el comunismo de Bujarin' ['On Bukharin's Communism']
1973, 'De la dialéctica' ['On the Dialectic']
1973, 'Karl Marx' ['Karl Marx']
1977, 'Sobre economía y dialéctica' ['On Economics and the Dialectic']

* The following list comprises significant texts, including interviews and lectures, of special relevance to the main topics covered by the present anthology: Marx and Marxism; political ecology; communist politics; and the New Social Movements. It is by no means a complete list of Sacristán's works relating to these topics. The texts are listed in chronological order, and in most cases according to the original publication date. The only exceptions are posthumously published lectures, one posthumously published interview, and a piece that appeared in English not long after its original publication in Spanish. The dates given for the posthumously published lectures and interview correspond to the year in which they took place; the date given for the work available in English translation is the date of its publication in English. Complete bibliographical details for all of these works can be found under 'References'.

1978, 'En la edición castellana del libro de Wolgang Harich *¿Comunismo sin crecimiento?*' ['On the Occasion of the Spanish Edition of Wolfgang Harich's *Kommunismus ohne Wachstum?*']

1979, 'Carta de la Redacción del N.º 1 de *mientras tanto*' ['Letter from the Editors in *mientras tanto* no. 1']

1979, 'Una conversación con Manuel Sacristán' ['A Conversation with Manuel Sacristán']

1979, 'Reflexión sobre una política socialista de la ciencia' ['A Reflection on a Socialist Science Policy']

1980, '¿Por qué faltan economistas en el movimiento ecologista?' ['Why are Economists Lacking in the Environmental Movement?']

1981, 'Las centrales nucleares y el desarrollo capitalista' ['Nuclear Power Stations and Capitalist Development']

1982, 'A propósito del peligro de guerra' ['Concerning the Threat of War']

1982, 'Trompetas y tambores' ['Bugles and Drums']

1982, 'Realismo fantasmagórico' ['Phantasmagoric Realism']

1983, 'Manuel Sacristán. Un marxista que se acerca al anarquismo' ['Manuel Sacristán: A Marxist Who Leans Toward Anarchism' (interview)]

1983, 'La salvación del alma y la lógica' ['Logic and the Salvation of the Soul']

1983, 'La situación del movimiento obrero y de los partidos de izquierda en la Europa occidental' ['The State of the Labour Movement and Left-Wing Parties in Western Europe']

1984, 'La OTAN hacia dentro' ['NATO On the Inside']

1985, 'El undécimo cuarderno de Gramsci en la cárcel' ['Gramsci's Eleventh Prison Notebook']

1985, 'Sobre Lukács' ['On Lukács']

1986, 'Changing the Nature of Politics' ['El fundamentalismo y los movimientos por la paz']

References

Aristotle 1984, 'On the Soul', translated by J.A. Smith, in *The Complete Works of Aristotle*, edited by Jonathan Barnes, Princeton: Princeton University Press.

Axelos, Kostas 1976, *Alienation, Praxis, and Technē in the Thought of Karl Marx*, translated by Ronald Bruzina, Austin: University of Texas Press.

Black Elk, Nicholas and John G. Neihardt 1972, *Black Elk Speaks: Being the Life Story of a Holy Man of the Oglala Sioux*, New York: Pocket Books.

Blaug, Mark 1968, 'Technical Change and Marxian Economics', in *Marx and Modern Economics*, edited by David Horowitz, New York and London: Monthly Review Press.

Bolchini, Piero 1980, 'Foreword', in Karl Marx, *Capitale e tecnología: manoscritti 1861–1863*, edited by Piero Bolchini, translated by Laura Comune Compagnone, Silvana Marzagalli and Piero Boratto, Rome: Editori Riuniti.

Botey, Jaume 1997, 'Aproximación a la figura de Manuel Sacristán y su experiencia en la formación de personas adultas', in *Homenaje a Manuel Sacristán: Escritos Sindicales y de Política Educativa*, edited by Salvador López Arnal, Barcelona: EUB.

Braithwaite, R.B. 1994 [1955], *Theory of Games as a Tool for the Moral Philosopher* and *An Empiricist's View of the Nature of Religious Belief*, Bristol: Thoemmes Press.

Brown, Dee 1970, *Bury My Heart at Wounded Knee: An Indian History of the American West*, New York: Holt, Rinehart & Winston.

Capella, Juan-Ramón, 1987, 'Aproximación a la bibliografía de Manuel Sacristán', *mientras tanto*, 30–31: 193–223.

——— 1995, 'Bibliografía de Manuel Sacristán Luzón: addenda', *mientras tanto*, 63: 155–9.

——— 2004, *La práctica de Manuel Sacristán: una biografía política*, Madrid: Trotta.

——— 2007, 'Manuel Sacristán: esbozo de una biografía política', in *El legado de un maestro*, edited by Salvador López Arnal and Iñaki Vázquez Álvarez, Madrid: Fundación de Investigaciones Marxistas/Ediciones de Intervención Cultural.

Cervantes, Miguel de 1998 [1605; 1615], *Don Quixote de La Mancha*, translated by Samuel Putnam, New York: The Modern Library.

Cohen, G.A. 1995, *Self-Ownership, Freedom, and Equality*, Cambridge: Cambridge University Press.

——— 2000, *If You're an Egalitarian, How Come You're So Rich?* Cambridge, MA: Harvard University Press.

Colectivo Editor 1987, 'Presentación', *mientas tanto*, 30–31: 3.

Dobb, Maurice 1968, 'Economic Thought IV: Socialist Thought', in *International Encyclopedia of the Social Sciences*, Volume 4, edited by David L. Sills, New York: Macmillan.

Domènech, Toni 1987, 'Sobre Manuel Sacristán (apunte personal sobre el hombre, el filósofo y el político)', *mientras tanto*, 30–31: 91–9.

Endemann, Wolfgang 1974, 'Foreword', in Karl Marx, *Mathematische Manuskripte*, edited by Wolfgang Endemann, Kronberg im Taunus: Scriptor Verlag.

Engels, Frederick 1987a [1913; written 1866], 'Engels to Marx, 2 October 1866', in *Marx and Engels Collected Works*, Volume 42, New York: International Publishers.

——— 1987b [1913; written 1866], 'Engels to Marx, 5 October 1866', in *Marx and Engels Collected Works*, Volume 42, New York: International Publishers.

——— 1987c [1878], 'Anti-Dühring', in *Marx and Engels Collected Works*, Volume 25, New York: International Publishers.

——— 1990 [1884], 'The Origin of the Family, Private Property and the State, in the Light of the Researches by Lewis H. Morgan', in *Marx and Engels Collected Works*, Volume 26, New York: International Publishers.

——— 1996 [1883], 'Preface to the Third German Edition', in Karl Marx, *Capital: A Critique of Political Economy*, Volume 1, in *Marx and Engels Collected Works*, Volume 35, New York: International Publishers.

Fernández Buey, Francisco 1995, 'El marxismo crítico de Manuel Sacristán', *mientras tanto*, 63: 131–54.

——— 1996, 'Francisco Fernández Buey': Interview with Salvador López Arnal and Pere de la Fuente, in *Acerca de Manuel Sacristán*, edited by López Arnal, Salvador and Pere de la Fuente, Barcelona: Ediciones Destino.

——— 1997, 'Cultura obrera y valores alternativos en la obra de Manuel Sacristán', in *Homenaje a Manuel Sacristán: escritos sindicales y de política educativa*, edited by Salvador López Arnal, Barcelona: EUB.

——— 2003, 'Sobre la evolución política de Manuel Sacristán', *Papeles de la FIM*, 21: 31–41.

——— 2005a, 'Tiza blanca en pizarra negra: entrevista a Fernández Buey': Interview with Salvador López Arnal, *El Viejo Topo*, 209–210: 52–4.

——— 2005b, 'Prólogo', in Manuel Sacristán, *Seis conferencias*, edited by Salvador López Arnal, Barcelona: Ediciones de Intervención Cultural/El Viejo Topo.

Fernández Buey, Francisco and Salvador López Arnal 2004, 'Introducción', in Manuel Sacristán, *De la Primavera de Praga al marxismo ecologista*, edited by Francisco Fernández Buey and Salvador López Arnal, Madrid: Los Libros de la Catarata.

Folch, Xavier 2000, 'Una conversación con Xavier Folch': Interview with Salvador López Arnal, *El Viejo Topo*, 140: 31–43.

Garaudy, Roger 1960, *Perspectives de l'homme*, Paris: PUF.

Geronimo 1970 [1906], *Geronimo: His Own Story*, edited by S.M. Barrett, New York: Ballantine Books.

Gorz, André 1982, *Farewell to the Working Class: An Essay on Post-Industrial Socialism*, translated by Mike Sonenscher, Boston: South End Press.

Gramsci, Antonio 1970, *Antología*, translated and edited by Manuel Sacristán, Mexico City: Siglo XXI.

Grau Biosca, Elena 2006, 'Giulia Adinolfi, un pensamiento vivo', in *Del pensar, del vivir, del hacer: escritos sobre* INTEGRAL SACRISTÁN, edited by Joan Benach, Xavier Juncosa and Salvador López Arnal, Barcelona: Ediciones de Intervención Cultural/El Viejo Topo.

Hegel, Georg Wilhelm Friedrich 1977 [1807], *Phenomenology of Spirit*, translated by A.V. Miller, Oxford: Clarendon Press.

Heine, Heinrich 1891 [1837], *Florentine Nights* in *Florentine Nights, The Memoirs of Herr von Schnabelewopski, The Rabbi of Bacharach and Shakespeare's Maidens and Women*, translated by Charles Godfrey Leland, New York: John W. Lovell Company.

Hollander, Samuel 2008, *The Economics of Karl Marx: Analysis and Application*, Cambridge: Cambridge University Press.

Insitut für Marxismus-Leninismus beim ZK der SED 1975, 'Foreword', in *Marx-Engels Werke*, Volume 20, Berlin: Dietz Verlag.

Integral Sacristán 2006, produced and directed by Xavier Juncosa, El Viejo Topo, 4 DVDS.

Kägi, Paul 1965, *Genesis des historischen Materialismus. Karl Marx und die Dynamik der Gesellschaft*, Vienna: Europa-Verlag.

Kosík, Karel 1976, *Dialectics of the Concrete*, translated by Karel Kovanda, Dordrecht: D. Reidel Publishing Company.

Lafargue, Paul n.d., 'Reminiscences of Marx', in *Reminiscences of Marx and Engels*, Moscow: Foreign Languages Publishing House.

Lenin, Vladimir I. 1966 [1920], 'KOMMUNISMUS: Journal of the Communist International', in *Collected Works*, Volume 31, Moscow: Progress Publishers.

Llorente, Renzo 2004, 'Review of Salvador López Arnal (ed.), Manuel Sacristán, *Escritos sobre* EL CAPITAL *(y textos afines)*', *Studies in Marxism* 10: 120–2.

López Arnal, Salvador 1997, 'Desde un punto de vista no estrictamente lógico', in *Homenaje a Manuel Sacristán: escritos sindicales y de política educativa*, edited by Salvador López Arnal, Barcelona: EUB.

——— 2004a, 'A modo de presentación: "Rigor, largueza y diversidad de un pensador"', in Manuel Sacristán, *Escritos sobre* EL CAPITAL *(y textos afines)*, edited by Salvador López Arnal, Barcelona: Fundación de Investigaciones Marxistas/Ediciones de Intervención Cultural/El Viejo Topo.

——— 2004b, 'Notas', in Manuel Sacristán, *Escritos sobre* EL CAPITAL *(y textos afines)*, edited by Salvador López Arnal, Barcelona: Fundación de Investigaciones Marxistas/Ediciones de Intervención Cultural/El Viejo Topo.

——— 2010, *La destrucción de una esperanza: Manuel Sacristán y la Primavera de Praga*, Madrid: Akal.

——— 2011, *Entre clásicos: Manuel Sacristán y la obra político-filosófica de György Lukács*, Torrejón de Ardoz (Spain): La Oveja Roja.

López Arnal, Salvador and Joan Benach 1999, 'Aproximación a las nociones de dialéctica en Manuel Sacristán', in *30 años después: acerca del opúsculo de Manuel Sacristán Luzón "Sobre el lugar de la filosofía en los estudios superiores"*, edited by Salvador López Arnal, Pere de la Fuente Cullel et al., Barcelona: EUB.

López Arnal, Salvador, Francisco Manchado Alcudia and Pilar Sanz González 1999, 'La labor socrático-traductora de Manuel Sacristán', in *30 años después: acerca del opúsculo de Manuel Sacristán Luzón "Sobre el lugar de la filosofía en los estudios superiores"*, edited by Salvador López Arnal, Pere de la Fuente Cullel et al., Barcelona: EUB.

López de Velasco, Juan 1971 [1894; written 1571–4], *Geografía y descripción universal de las Indias*, edited by Marcos Jiménez de la Espada, Madrid: Atlas.

Manzanera Salavert, Miguel 1993, *Teoría y práctica. La trayectoria intelectual de Manuel Sacristán Luzón*, unpublished doctoral dissertation, available at http://www.sodepaz.org/images/libros/teoriaypractica_msacristan.pdf.

——— 1995, 'Relación de los textos de Manuel Sacristán en los archivos documentales', *mientras tanto*, 63: 77–87.

Marcuse, Herbert 1972, *Counterrevolution and Revolt*, Boston: Beacon Press.

Martín Rubio, Christian 2005, 'Mientras la esperanza espera. Materiales en torno a la oposición a la cátedra de lógica de la Universidad de Valencia en 1962', in *Donde no habita el olvido*, edited by Salvador López Arnal *et al.*, Barcelona: Montesinos.

Marx, Karl 1962 [1867], 'Das Kapital: Kritik der politischen Ökonomie', in *Karl Marx/ Friedrich Engels Werke*, Volume 23, Berlin: Dietz Verlag.

——— 1974 [written roughly 1873–83], *Mathematische Manuskripte*, edited by Wolfgang Endemann, Kronberg im Taunus: Scriptor Verlag.

——— 1975a [1902; written 1840–1], 'Difference Between the Democritean and Epicurean Philosophy of Nature' in *Marx and Engels Collected Works*, Volume 1, New York: International Publishers.

——— 1975b [1842], 'The Philosophical Manifesto of the Historical School of Law', in *Marx and Engels Collected Works*, Volume 1, New York: International Publishers.

——— 1975c [1927; written 1843], 'Contribution to the Critique of Hegel's *PHILOSOPHY OF LAW*', in *Marx and Engels Collected Works*, Volume 3, New York: International Publishers.

——— 1975d [1932; written 1844], 'Economic and Philosophic Manuscripts of 1844', in *Marx and Engels Collected Works*, Volume 3, New York: International Publishers.

——— 1975e [1844], 'Critical Marginal Notes on the Article "The King of Prussia and Social Reform. By a Prussian"', in *Marx and Engels Collected Works*, Volume 3, New York: International Publishers.

——— 1975f [1844], 'Letters from the Deutsch-Französische Jahrbücher', in *Marx and Engels Collected Works*, Volume 3, New York: International Publishers.

——— 1975g [written roughly 1873–83], *Manoscritti matematici*, translated and edited by Francesco Mararrese and Augusto Ponzio, Bari: Edizioni Dedalo Libri.

——— 1976 [1847], 'The Poverty of Philosophy', in *Marx and Engels Collected Works*, Volume 6, New York: International Publishers.

——— 1977 [1867], *Capital: A Critique of Political Economy*, Volume 1, translated by Ben Fowkes. New York: Vintage Books.

——— 1980a [1854], ['The Rumours About Mazzini's Arrest. – The Austrian Compulsory Loan. – Spain. – The Situation in Wallachia'], in *Marx and Engels Collected Works*, Volume 13, New York: International Publishers.

——— 1980b [1854], ['The Spanish Revolution. – Greece and Turkey'], in *Marx and Engels Collected Works*, Volume 13, New York: International Publishers.

——— 1980c [1854], 'Espartero', in *Marx and Engels Collected Works*, Volume 13, New York: International Publishers.

——— 1980d [1854], 'Revolutionary Spain', in *Marx and Engels Collected Works*, Volume 13, New York: International Publishers.

——— 1980e [1854], ['Revolution In Spain. – Bomarsund'], in *Marx and Engels Collected Works*, Volume 13, New York: International Publishers.

——— 1980f [1854], ['The Details of the Insurrection at Madrid. – The Austro-Prussian Summons. – The New Austrian Loan. – Wallachia'], in *Marx and Engels Collected Works*, Volume 13, New York: International Publishers.

——— 1980g [1958; written 1854], ['Unpublished Extract From a Series of Articles "Revolutionary Spain" '], in *Marx and Engels Collected Works*, Volume 13, New York: International Publishers.

——— 1980h [written 1861–3], *Capitale e tecnología: manoscritti 1861–1863*, edited by Piero Bolchini, translated by Laura Comune Compagnone, Silvana Marzagalli and Piero Boratto, Rome: Editori Riuniti.

——— 1981 [written 1843–5], 'Exzerpte', in Karl Marx and Friedrich Engels, *Exzerpte und Notizen 1843 bis Januar 1845*, in *Marx/Engels Gesamtausgabe*, Part 4, Section 2, Berlin: Dietz Verlag.

——— 1982a [1851], 'Marx to Roland Daniels, second half of May 1851', in *Marx and Engels Collected Works*, Volume 38, New York: International Publishers.

——— 1982b [1880; written 1846], 'Marx to Pavel Vasilyevich Annenkov, 28 December 1846', in *Marx and Engels Collected Works*, Volume 38, New York: International Publishers.

——— 1983a [1913; written 1854], 'Marx to Engels, 3 May 1854', in *Marx and Engels Collected Works*, Volume 39, New York: International Publishers.

——— 1983b [1913; written 1858], 'Marx to Engels, 16 January 1858', in *Marx and Engels Collected Works*, Volume 40, New York: International Publishers.

——— 1983c [1913; written 1858], 'Marx to Engels, 1 February 1858', in *Marx and Engels Collected Works*, Volume 40, New York: International Publishers.

——— 1983d [1922; written 1858], 'Marx to Ferdinand Lassalle, 22 February 1858', in *Marx and Engels Collected Works*, Volume 40, New York: International Publishers.

——— 1983e [1922; written 1858], 'Marx to Ferdinand Lassalle, 11 March 1858', in *Marx and Engels Collected Works*, Volume 40, New York: International Publishers.

——— 1983f [1913; written 1858], 'Marx to Engels, 2 April 1858', in *Marx and Engels Collected Works*, Volume 40, New York: International Publishers.

——— 1983g [1922; written 1858], 'Marx to Ferdinand Lassalle, 12 November, 1858', in *Marx and Engels Collected Works*, Volume 40, New York: International Publishers.

——— 1983h [1922; written 1859], 'Marx to Ferdinand Lassalle, 19 April 1859', in *Marx and Engels Collected Works*, Volume 40, New York: International Publishers.

——— 1985a [1913; written 1860], 'Marx to Engels, 19 December 1860', in *Marx and Engels Collected Works*, Volume 41, New York: International Publishers.

——— 1985b [1913; written 1862], 'Marx to Engels, 2 August 1862', in *Marx and Engels Collected Works*, Volume 41, New York: International Publishers.

——— 1985c [1913; written 1862], 'Marx to Engels, 9 August 1862', in *Marx and Engels Collected Works*, Volume 41, New York: International Publishers.

——— 1985d [1922; written 1861], 'Marx to Ferdinand Lassalle, 16 January, 1861', in *Marx and Engels Collected Works*, Volume 41, New York: International Publishers.

——— 1986a [1856], '[Revolution in Spain]', in *Marx and Engels Collected Works*, Volume 15, New York: International Publishers.

——— 1986b [1902–3; written 1857], 'Introduction', (*Economic Manuscripts of 1857–1858*), in *Marx and Engels Collected Works*, Volume 28, New York: International Publishers.

——— 1986c [1939; written 1857–8], 'Outlines of the Critique of Political Economy (Rough Draft of 1857–1858)', in *Marx and Engels Collected Works*, Volume 28, New York: International Publishers.

——— 1987a [1939; written 1857–8], 'Outlines of the Critique of Political Economy (Rough Draft of 1857–1858)', in *Marx and Engels Collected Works*, Volume 29, New York: International Publishers.

——— 1987b [1859], 'A Contribution to the Critique of Political Economy. Part One', in *Marx and Engels Collected Works*, Volume 29, New York: International Publishers.

——— 1987c [1956; written 1865], 'Confession', in *Marx and Engels Collected Works*, Volume 42, New York: International Publishers.

——— 1987d [1913; written 1865], 'Marx to Engels, 31 July 1865', in *Marx and Engels Collected Works*, Volume 42, New York: International Publishers.

——— 1987e [1913; written 1865], 'Marx to Engels, 19 August 1865', in *Marx and Engels Collected Works*, Volume 42, New York: International Publishers.

——— 1987f [1913; written 1865], 'Marx to Engels, 22 August 1865', in *Marx and Engels Collected Works*, Volume 42, New York: International Publishers.

——— 1987g [1913; written 1866], 'Marx to Engels, 10 February 1866', in *Marx and Engels Collected Works*, Volume 42, New York: International Publishers.

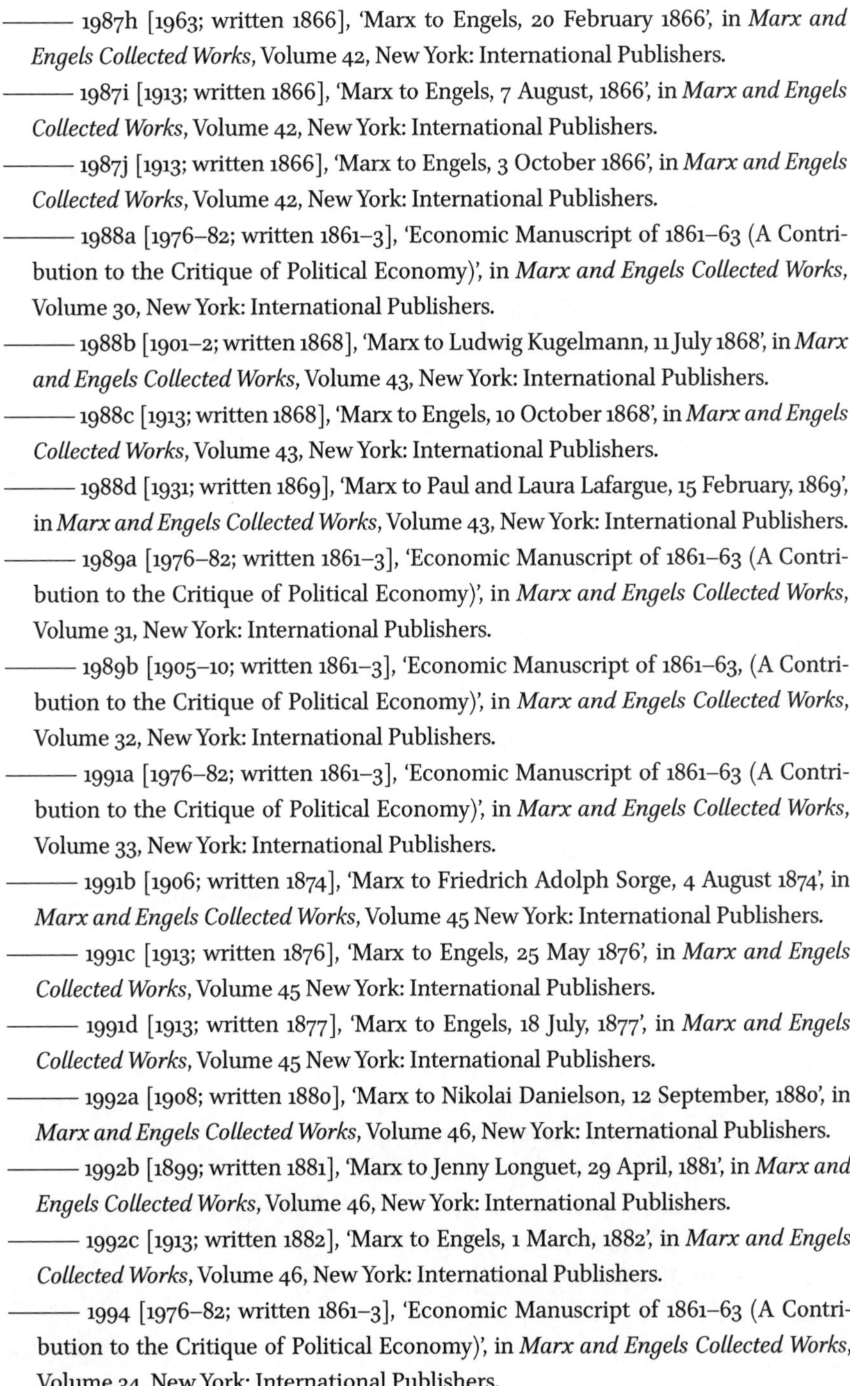

——— 1987h [1963; written 1866], 'Marx to Engels, 20 February 1866', in *Marx and Engels Collected Works*, Volume 42, New York: International Publishers.

——— 1987i [1913; written 1866], 'Marx to Engels, 7 August, 1866', in *Marx and Engels Collected Works*, Volume 42, New York: International Publishers.

——— 1987j [1913; written 1866], 'Marx to Engels, 3 October 1866', in *Marx and Engels Collected Works*, Volume 42, New York: International Publishers.

——— 1988a [1976–82; written 1861–3], 'Economic Manuscript of 1861–63 (A Contribution to the Critique of Political Economy)', in *Marx and Engels Collected Works*, Volume 30, New York: International Publishers.

——— 1988b [1901–2; written 1868], 'Marx to Ludwig Kugelmann, 11 July 1868', in *Marx and Engels Collected Works*, Volume 43, New York: International Publishers.

——— 1988c [1913; written 1868], 'Marx to Engels, 10 October 1868', in *Marx and Engels Collected Works*, Volume 43, New York: International Publishers.

——— 1988d [1931; written 1869], 'Marx to Paul and Laura Lafargue, 15 February, 1869', in *Marx and Engels Collected Works*, Volume 43, New York: International Publishers.

——— 1989a [1976–82; written 1861–3], 'Economic Manuscript of 1861–63 (A Contribution to the Critique of Political Economy)', in *Marx and Engels Collected Works*, Volume 31, New York: International Publishers.

——— 1989b [1905–10; written 1861–3], 'Economic Manuscript of 1861–63, (A Contribution to the Critique of Political Economy)', in *Marx and Engels Collected Works*, Volume 32, New York: International Publishers.

——— 1991a [1976–82; written 1861–3], 'Economic Manuscript of 1861–63 (A Contribution to the Critique of Political Economy)', in *Marx and Engels Collected Works*, Volume 33, New York: International Publishers.

——— 1991b [1906; written 1874], 'Marx to Friedrich Adolph Sorge, 4 August 1874', in *Marx and Engels Collected Works*, Volume 45 New York: International Publishers.

——— 1991c [1913; written 1876], 'Marx to Engels, 25 May 1876', in *Marx and Engels Collected Works*, Volume 45 New York: International Publishers.

——— 1991d [1913; written 1877], 'Marx to Engels, 18 July, 1877', in *Marx and Engels Collected Works*, Volume 45 New York: International Publishers.

——— 1992a [1908; written 1880], 'Marx to Nikolai Danielson, 12 September, 1880', in *Marx and Engels Collected Works*, Volume 46, New York: International Publishers.

——— 1992b [1899; written 1881], 'Marx to Jenny Longuet, 29 April, 1881', in *Marx and Engels Collected Works*, Volume 46, New York: International Publishers.

——— 1992c [1913; written 1882], 'Marx to Engels, 1 March, 1882', in *Marx and Engels Collected Works*, Volume 46, New York: International Publishers.

——— 1994 [1976–82; written 1861–3], 'Economic Manuscript of 1861–63 (A Contribution to the Critique of Political Economy)', in *Marx and Engels Collected Works*, Volume 34, New York: International Publishers.

——— 1996 [1867], 'Capital: A Critique of Political Economy, Volume 1', in *Marx and Engels Collected Works*, Volume 35, New York: International Publishers.

——— 1997 [1885], 'Capital: A Critique of Political Economy, Volume 2', in *Marx and Engels Collected Works*, Volume 36, New York: International Publishers.

——— 1998 [1894], 'Capital: A Critique of Political Economy, Volume 3', in *Marx and Engels Collected Works*, Volume 37, New York: International Publishers.

Marx, Karl and Frederick Engels 1959 [1854–73], *Revolución en España*, translated by Manuel Sacristán, Barcelona: Ediciones Ariel.

——— 1975 [1845], 'The Holy Family or Critique of Critical Criticism', in *Marx and Engels Collected Works*, Volume 4, New York: International Publishers.

——— 1976a [1932; written 1845–6], 'The German Ideology', in *Marx and Engels Collected Works*, Volume 5, New York: International Publishers.

——— 1976b [1848], 'Manifesto of the Communist Party', in *Marx and Engels Collected Works*, Volume 6, New York: International Publishers.

Marx-Aveling, Eleanor n.d., 'Karl Marx', in *Reminiscences of Marx and Engels*, Moscow: Foreign Languages Publishing House.

Medina, Esteban 1982, 'Teorías y orientaciones de la sociología de la ciencia', *Revista Española de Investigaciones Sociológicas*, 20: 7–58.

Meek, Ronald L. 1967, *Economics and Ideology and Other Essays*, London: Chapman and Hall.

Mehring, Franz 1980 [1913], 'Geschichte der deutschen Sozial-demokratie, Part I', in Gesammelte *Schriften*, Volume 1, edited by Thomas Höhle, Hans Koch and Josef Schleifstein, Berlin: Dietz Verlag.

Merton, Robert K. 1968 [1949], *Social Theory and Social Structure*, Glencoe: The Free Press.

——— 1973, *The Sociology of Science: Theoretical and Empirical Investigations*, edited by Norman W. Storer, Chicago: University Of Chicago Press.

——— 2002 [1938], *Science, Technology & Society in Seventeenth-Century England*, New York: Howard Fertig.

Mills, Charles Wright 1962, *The Marxists*, New York: Dell Publishing Co., Inc.

Monereo, Manuel 2007, 'Iba en serio', in *El legado de un maestro*, edited by Salvador López Arnal and Iñaki Vázquez Álvarez, Madrid: Fundación de Investigaciones Marxistas/Ediciones de Intervención Cultural.

Morishima, Michio 1973, *Marx's Economics: A Dual Theory of Value and Growth*, Cambridge: Cambridge University Press.

Nora, Simon and Alain Minc 1980, *The Computerization of Society*, Cambridge, MA: The MIT Press.

Ovejero Lucas, Félix 2007, 'Manuel Sacristán: un marxista socrático', in *El legado de un maestro*, edited by Salvador López Arnal and Iñaki Vázquez Álvarez, Madrid: Fundación de Investigaciones Marxistas/Ediciones de Intervención Cultural.

Pala, Giaime 2007, 'El intelectual y el partido. Notas sobre la trayectoria política de Manuel Sacristán en el PSUC', in *El legado de un maestro*, edited by Salvador López Arnal and Iñaki Vázquez Álvarez, Madrid: Fundación de Investigaciones Marxistas/ Ediciones de Intervención Cultural.

Ríos, Víctor 2007, 'El compromiso de Manuel Sacristán', in *El legado de un maestro*, edited by Salvador López Arnal and Iñaki Vázquez Álvarez, Madrid: Fundación de Investigaciones Marxistas/Ediciones de Intervención Cultural.

Robinson, Joan 1965, *Collected Economic Papers*, Volume 3, Oxford: Blackwell.

Rosenberg, Nathan 1976, 'Marx as a Student of Technology', *Monthly Review*, 28, 3: 56–77.

Sacristán, Manuel 1963, 'La veracidad de Goethe', in Johann Wolfgang von Goethe, *Obras*, translated by José María Valverde and Margarita Fontseré de Petit, Barcelona: Editorial Vergara.

——— 1983a [1959], 'Prólogo a *Revolución en España* de K. Marx y F. Engels', in *Sobre Marx y marxismo. Panfletos y materiales I*, edited by Juan-Ramón Capella, Barcelona: Icaria Editorial.

——— 1983b [1967], 'La formación del marxismo de Gramsci', in *Sobre Marx y marxismo. Panfletos y materiales I*, edited by Juan-Ramón Capella, Barcelona: Icaria Editorial.

——— 1983c [1968], 'Por qué leer a Labriola', in *Sobre Marx y marxismo. Panfletos y materiales I*, edited by Juan-Ramón Capella, Barcelona: Icaria Editorial.

——— 1983d [1968], 'Sobre el uso de las nociones de razón e irracionalismo por G. Lukács', in *Sobre Marx y marxismo. Panfletos y materiales I*, edited by Juan-Ramón Capella, Barcelona: Icaria Editorial.

——— 1983e [1970], 'El filosofar de Lenin', in *Sobre Marx y marxismo. Panfletos y materiales I*, edited by Juan-Ramón Capella, Barcelona: Icaria Editorial.

——— 1983f [1970], 'Russell y el socialismo', in *Sobre Marx y marxismo. Panfletos y materiales I*, edited by Juan-Ramón Capella, Barcelona: Icaria Editorial.

——— 1983g [1970], 'Lenin y la filosofía', in *Sobre Marx y marxismo. Panfletos y materiales I*, edited by Juan-Ramón Capella, Barcelona: Icaria Editorial.

——— 1983h [1971], 'Agnes Heller', in *Sobre Marx y marxismo. Panfletos y materiales I*, edited by Juan-Ramón Capella, Barcelona: Icaria Editorial.

——— 1983i [1971], 'Sobre el "marxismo ortodoxo" de György Lukács', in *Sobre Marx y marxismo. Panfletos y materiales I*, edited by Juan-Ramón Capella, Barcelona: Icaria Editorial.

——— 1983j [1972], 'Sobre el comunismo de Bujárin', in *Sobre Marx y marxismo. Panfletos y materiales I*, edited by Juan-Ramón Capella, Barcelona: Icaria Editorial.

——— 1983k [1973], 'Karl Marx', in *Sobre Marx y marxismo. Panfletos y materiales I*, edited by Juan-Ramón Capella, Barcelona: Icaria Editorial.

——— 1983l, 'Nota Previa', in *Sobre Marx y marxismo. Panfletos y materiales I*, edited by Juan-Ramón Capella, Barcelona: Icaria Editorial.

——— 1984a [1961], 'La filosofía desde la terminación de la Segunda Guerra Mundial hasta 1958', in *Papeles de filosofía. Panfletos y materiales II*, Barcelona: Icaria Editorial.

——— 1984b [1968], 'Corrientes principales del pensamiento filosófico', in *Papeles de filosofía. Panfletos y materiales II*, Barcelona: Icaria Editorial.

——— 1985a [1968], 'Cuatro notas a los documentos de abril del Partido Comunista de Checoslovaquia', in *Intervenciones políticas. Panfletos y materiales III*, edited by Juan-Ramón Capella, Barcelona: Icaria Editorial.

——— 1985b [1976], 'Nota a la *Pequeña antología* de Ulrike Marie Meinhof', in *Intervenciones políticas. Panfletos y materiales III*, edited by Juan-Ramón Capella, Barcelona: Icaria Editorial.

——— 1985c [1978], 'En la edición castellana del libro de Wolgang Harich *¿Comunismo sin crecimiento?*', in *Intervenciones políticas. Panfletos y materiales III*, edited by Juan-Ramón Capella, Barcelona: Icaria Editorial.

——— 1985d, 'Nota previa al volumen', in *Intervenciones políticas. Panfletos y materiales III*, edited by Juan-Ramón Capella, Barcelona: Icaria Editorial.

——— 1986, 'Changing the Nature of Politics', *Journal of European Nuclear Disarmament*, 19: 21–2. [Translation of Sacristán 1985, 'El fundamentalismo y los movimientos por la paz', in *Pacifismo, ecología y política alternativa*, edited by Juan-Ramón Capella, Barcelona: Icaria Editorial].

——— 1987a [1979], 'Carta de la Redacción del N.º 1 de *mientras tanto*', in *Pacifismo, ecología y política alternativa*, edited by Juan-Ramón Capella, Barcelona: Icaria Editorial.

——— 1987b [1980], '¿Por qué faltan economistas en el movimiento ecologista?', in *Pacifismo, ecología y política alternativa*, edited by Juan-Ramón Capella, Barcelona: Icaria Editorial.

——— 1987c [1982], 'A propósito del peligro de guerra', in *Pacifismo, ecología y política alternativa*, edited by Juan-Ramón Capella, Barcelona: Icaria Editorial.

——— 1987d [1982], 'Trompetas y tambores', in *Pacifismo, ecología y política alternativa*, edited by Juan-Ramón Capella, Barcelona: Icaria Editorial.

——— 1987e [1982], 'Realismo fantasmagórico', in *Pacifismo, ecología y política alternativa*, edited by Juan-Ramón Capella, Barcelona: Icaria Editorial.

——— 1987f [1983], 'La salvación del alma y la lógica', in *Pacifismo, ecología y política alternativa*, edited by Juan-Ramón Capella, Barcelona: Icaria Editorial.

——— 1987g [1984], 'La OTAN hacia dentro', in *Pacifismo, ecología y política alternativa*, edited by Juan-Ramón Capella, Barcelona: Icaria Editorial.

——— 1987h [1985], 'El undécimo cuaderno de Gramsci en la cárcel', in *Pacifismo, ecología y política alternativa*, edited by Juan-Ramón Capella, Barcelona: Icaria Editorial.

——— 1995 [1959], *Las ideas gnoseológicas de Heidegger*, Barcelona: Crítica.

——— 1996a [1983], 'Entrevista con *UnomásUno*': Interview with Javier Molina, in *Acerca de Manuel Sacristán*, edited by López Arnal, Salvador and Pere de la Fuente, Barcelona: Ediciones Destino.

——— 1996b [conducted in 1983], '¡¡Una broma de entrevista!!': Interview with *Argumentos*, in *Acerca de Manuel Sacristán*, edited by López Arnal, Salvador and Pere de la Fuente, Barcelona: Ediciones Destino.

——— 1998 [written 1969], *El orden y el tiempo: introducción a la obra de Antonio Gramsci*, edited by Albert Domingo Curto, Madrid: Editorial Trotta.

——— 2003, *M.A.R.X.: Máximas, aforismos y reflexiones con algunas variables libres*, edited by Salvador López Arnal, Barcelona: Fundación de Investigaciones Marxistas/Ediciones de Intervención Cultural/El Viejo Topo.

——— 2004a [1969], 'Checoslovaquia y la construcción del socialismo': Interview with *Cuadernos para el Diálogo*, in *De la Primavera de Praga al marxismo ecologista*, edited by Francisco Fernández Buey and Salvador López Arnal, Madrid: Los Libros de la Catarata.

——— 2004b [1983], 'Manuel Sacristán. Un marxista que se acerca al anarquismo': Interview with Joaquim Ibarz, in *De la Primavera de Praga al marxismo ecologista*, edited by Francisco Fernández Buey and Salvador López Arnal, Madrid: Los Libros de la Catarata.

——— 2004c [1995; conducted in 1979], 'Una conversación con Manuel Sacristán': Interview with Jordi Guiu and Antoni Munné, in *De la Primavera de Praga al marxismo ecologista*, edited by Francisco Fernández Buey and Salvador López Arnal, Madrid: Los Libros de la Catarata.

——— 2004d, 'Coloquio: "El trabajo científico de Marx y su noción de ciencia"', in *Escritos sobre* EL CAPITAL *(y textos afines)*, edited by Salvador López Arnal, Barcelona: Fundación de Investigaciones Marxistas/Ediciones de Intervención Cultural/El Viejo Topo.

——— 2004e, 'Sobre economía y dialéctica', in *Escritos sobre* EL CAPITAL *(y textos afines)*, edited by Salvador López Arnal, Barcelona: Fundación de Investigaciones Marxistas/Ediciones de Intervención Cultural/El Viejo Topo.

——— 2005a, 'Sobre Lukács', in *Seis conferencias*, edited by Salvador López Arnal, Barcelona: Ediciones de Intervención Cultural/El Viejo Topo.

——— 2005b, 'Coloquio [following 'Sobre el estalinismo']', in *Seis conferencias*, edited by Salvador López Arnal, Barcelona: Ediciones de Intervención Cultural/El Viejo Topo.

——— 2005c 'Reflexión sobre una política socialista de la ciencia', in *Seis conferencias*, edited by Salvador López Arnal, Barcelona: Ediciones de Intervención Cultural/El Viejo Topo.

——— 2005d, 'Las centrales nucleares y el desarrollo capitalista', in *Seis conferencias*, edited by Salvador López Arnal, Barcelona: Ediciones de Intervención Cultural/El Viejo Topo.

——— 2005e, 'La situación del movimiento obrero y de los partidos de izquierda en la Europa occidental', in *Seis conferencias*, edited by Salvador López Arnal, Barcelona: Ediciones de Intervención Cultural/El Viejo Topo.

——— 2005f, 'Fragmentos del coloquio de la conferencia "¿Por qué faltan economistas en el movimiento ecologista?" ', in *Homenaje conmemorativo a Manuel Sacristán Luzón (1925–1985)*, número especial de [special issue of] *El Viejo Topo*, Barcelona: El Viejo Topo.

——— 2005g, 'Sobre el 23-F', in *Homenaje conmemorativo a Manuel Sacristán Luzón (1925–1985)*, número especial de [special issue of] *El Viejo Topo*, Barcelona: El Viejo Topo.

——— 2005h, 'A Félix Novales', in *Homenaje conmemorativo a Manuel Sacristán Luzón (1925–1985)*, número especial de [special issue of] *El Viejo Topo*, Barcelona: El Viejo Topo.

——— 2005i, 'A Eloy Fernández Clemente', in *Homenaje conmemorativo a Manuel Sacristán Luzón (1925–1985)*, número especial de [special issue of] *El Viejo Topo*, Barcelona: El Viejo Topo.

——— 2005j, 'Coloquio [following 'Tradición marxista y nuevos problemas']', in *Seis conferencias*, edited by Salvador López Arnal, Barcelona: Ediciones de Intervención Cultural/El Viejo Topo.

——— 2009a [1960], 'Jesuitas y dialéctica', in *Sobre dialéctica*, edited by Salvador López Arnal, Barcelona: Ediciones de Intervención Cultural/El Viejo Topo

——— 2009b [1973], 'De la dialéctica', in *Sobre dialéctica*, edited by Salvador López Arnal, Barcelona: Ediciones de Intervención Cultural/El Viejo Topo.

——— 2009c, 'En torno al marxismo de Lucio Colletti', in *Sobre dialéctica*, edited by Salvador López Arnal, Barcelona: Ediciones de Intervención Cultural/El Viejo Topo.

——— 2009d, *Pacifismo, ecologismo y política alternativa*, Madrid: Icaria Editorial/ Diario Público.

——— 2013, *Sobre Gerónimo*, edited by Salvador López Arnal, Barcelona: Ediciones de Intervención Cultural/El Viejo Topo.

Sagalés, Llorenç 2002, 'Una conversación con Llorenç Sagalés sobre Manuel Sacristán': Interview with Salvador López Arnal, *Papeles de la FIM*, 19: 79–97.

Sahlins, Marshall 1968, 'La première société d'abondance', *Les Temps Modernes*, 268: 641–80.

Sempere, Joaquim 1987, 'Manuel Sacristán: una semblanza personal, intelectual y política', *mientras tanto*, 30–31: 5–31.

——— 1996, 'Joaquim Sempere': Interview with Salvador López Arnal and Pere de la Fuente, in *Acerca de Manuel Sacristán*, edited by López Arnal, Salvador and Pere de la Fuente, Barcelona: Ediciones Destino.

——— 2006, 'Manuel Sacristán: militante comunista contra el franquismo', in *Del pensar, del vivir, del hacer: escritos sobre* INTEGRAL SACRISTÁN, edited by Joan Benach, Xavier Juncosa and Salvador López Arnal, Barcelona: Ediciones de Intervención Cultural/El Viejo Topo.

Stalin, Joseph 1953 [1924], 'Concerning the International Situation', in *Works*, Volume 6, Moscow: Foreign Languages Publishing House.

Tello, Enric 2007, 'Manuel Sacristán (1925–1985): ¿El primer marxista ecológico post-estalinista?', in *El legado de un maestro*, edited by Salvador López Arnal and Iñaki Vázquez Álvarez, Madrid: Fundación de Investigaciones Marxistas/Ediciones de Intervención Cultural.

Turner, Frederick W. 1970, 'Introduction', in Geronimo, *Geronimo: His Own Story*, edited by S.M. Barrett, New York: Ballantine Books.

Vega Reñón, Luis 2005, 'El lugar de Sacristán en los estudios de lógica en España', in *Donde no habita el olvido*, edited by Salvador López Arnal *et al.*, Barcelona: Montesinos.

Wright, Erik Olin, Andrew Levine and Elliot Sober 1992, *Reconstructing Marxism: Essays on Explanation and the Theory of History*, London and New York: Verso.

Zelený, Jindřich 1968, *Die Wissenschaftslogik bei Marx und Das Kapital*, Frankfurt: Europäische Verlagsanstalt.

Index